# A Light to the Mountains
# Morehead State University
## 1887-1997

# *A Light to the Mountains*
# Morehead State University
## 1887-1997

# Donald F. Flatt

Jesse Stuart Foundation
Ashland, Kentucky
1997

*A Light To The Mountains:*
*Morehead State University, 1887-1997*
Copyright © by The Jesse Stuart Foundation

## FIRST EDITION

Library of Congress Cataloging-in-Publication Data

Flatt, Donald F., 1937-
    A light to the mountains : Morehead State University, 1887-1997 /
by Donald F. Flatt.
        p.    cm.
    ISBN 0-945084-60-9
    1. Morehead State University--History.    I. Title.
LD3541.M89F53   1997
378 . 769 ' 57--dc21    --dc21
[378 . 769 ' 57]                                          97-15542
                                                              CIP

*Published By:*
The Jesse Stuart Foundation
P.O. Box 391  Ashland, KY 41114
(606) 329-5232
1997

*For*
*Carolyn*
*The "Light of My Life" for Over 40 Years*

*and*
*More than 40,000 Other MSU Alumni*

## Chronology

1887-1922    Morehead Normal School

1922-26      Morhead State Normal School

1926-30      Morehead State Normal School and Teachers College

1930-48      Morehead State Teachers College

1948-66      Morehead State College

1966-        Morehead State University


## Presidents

1923-29      Frank C. Button
1929-35      John Howard Payne
1935-40      Harvey A. Babb
1940-46      William H. Vaughan
1946-51      William Jesse Baird
1951-54      Charles R. Spain
1954-77      Adron Doran
1977-84      Morris L. Norfleet
1984-86      Herb. F. Reinhard, Jr.
1986-87      A. D. Albright
1987-92      C. Nelson Grote
1992-        Ronald G. Eaglin

# Preface

"Let things settle down for now, and one day historians will delve into what actually happened," wrote Mrs. Frank C. Button upon the death of her husband, the first president of Morehead State University, whom she felt did not receive appropriate recognition for his role in locating a state school at Morehead. Sixty years later, her words appear prophetic, for after seven years of research, I am pleased to share my account of what has happened at MSU since 1887.

Four themes stand out in the University's history: First, politics dictated the selection of Morehead as the site for a state school in 1922 and has frequently dominated the institution ever since. Second, Morehead State has repeatedly featured either a powerful Board of Regents or a strong president as its leader. By the mid-1990s, MSU had matured sufficiently to make room for both a forceful president and a powerful board functioning concurrently. Third, students have continually been provided high quality education even during times of negative publicity prompted by political turmoil. Fourth, its mission has caused the institution to serve as a "light to the mountains" since its beginning as a church school.

Every graduate of Morehead State has a personal version of the school's history. Since enrolling in 1957, I have seen the institution from almost every angle - as student, teacher, administrator, and researcher. The University has been more of an experience to me than a place! While such intimacy affords certain advantages, it also poses a number of problems for a historian. Close acquaintance with most of the presidents since the Fifties along with loyalty to the institution made objectivity extremely difficult at times. But this work represents a professional attempt to tell the story of Morehead State as objectively as possible, even while a large number of the participants in the narrative are still living.

In an attempt to appeal to the average reader, I have eliminated footnotes and settled for a bibliography. Furthermore, anecdotes have been liberally sprinkled throughout the book. This historical work is based upon archival documents and extensive interviews. The MSU Foundation, Inc., and the MSU Alumni Association, Inc., made it possible for me to conduct interviews throughout the nation, tracking down former participants in "the story" from coast to coast. Authors of institutional histories could not experience stronger support and less administrative interference in carrying out such a project. The University permitted me to teach half-time during two years of intensive research and writing, and the MSU Foundation provided office space, two research assistants, and constant encouragement especially when I was tempted to shelve the project.

Something of this magnitude is never the work of one person alone. Hence, I wish to express special gratitude as a slight compensation to those individuals without whose assistance this book could never have been completed:

President and Mrs. Ronald G. Eaglin's strong emphasis on heritage and institutional pride enabled me to transform a seven-year dream into reality. The understanding and support of John Philley, executive vice president for academic affairs, and Lemuel Berry, dean of the Caudill College of Humanities, along with the cooperation of Ron Mitchelson, chairman of the department of geography, government, and history, facilitated the completion of the book during the celebration of MSU's 75th birthday as a state institution of higher learning.

Joint sponsorship by the MSU Foundation and the MSU Alumni Association turned my hobby into a book. Invaluable assistance was given by Keith Kappes, vice president for university advancement, who has the most extensive knowledge of what has happened at MSU over the past three decades of anyone I know; his value to various administrations cannot be overstated. Linda Simpson, administrative assistant to Kappes, and Shirley Parker, accountant with the Office of Alumni Relations and Development, helped in countless ways. Bill Redwine, director of alumni relations and development, provided significant records and clues in my efforts to locate those to be interviewed.

Jerome Crouch, whose trained eye as a former editor of the University Press of Kentucky has made many writers feel better about their skills than they did before submitting to his guidance, succeeded in that respect with me as well. His vast experience placed a premium on conciseness; his instincts about the art of writing immediately illustrated his mastery of the trade; and his quiet yet assertive demeanor made it easier to accept valuable suggestions on various aspects of the book.

John Kleber, chairman of my 19-person Advisory Board, prodded me to make the important transition from enjoying the luxury of researching to initiating the actual writing of the book. His broad experiences provided a context for putting every crisis into proper perspective. Members of the Advisory Board generously shared their time, energy, insights, and personal institutional knowledge, thereby assuring balance and preventing needless pitfalls.

Nolan Fowler, a former Morehead State University professor, was my mentor at Morehead State in the Fifties, and he inspired me to become a history professor. He shared his broad knowledge of institutional and Kentucky history and his editing expertise in correcting this manuscript throughout the entire venture. His reputation for dispensing "red ink" on papers is as well deserved and beneficial today as it was when I was an undergraduate student. Without his unselfish devotion to my success from the Fifties to the present, this chapter of my life would never have unfolded.

The extraordinary guidance of James Gifford, executive director of the Jesse Stuart Foundation, on every aspect of the book's production is deeply appreciated. And JSF staff members Yvonne Melvin, Brett Nance, and Bridget Tolliver used their professional skills to strengthen the manuscript and prepare it for final publication. Rocky Zornes contributed extensively to the image of the book through his cover art and graphic design.

Research assistants Cindy Utley Franklin and Joey Roberts located significant documentary materials in the MSU Archives and other places on campus. Laura Caudill played a major role in the book's production and continues to take significant steps to insure the marketing of the finished product. Michelle Johnson Roberts efficiently handled those last-minute errands which are necessary in preparing a book for the press, and Tim Holbrook's photographic skills added to its quality.

Larry Besant, director of the Camden-Carroll Library, permitted use of the Breckinridge Room in the library as my office for three semesters of research. The cooperation and unfailing courtesy of the library staff were appreciated. Clara Keyes, who is in charge of the MSU Archives, and her efficient assistants, Alma Fairchild and Teresa Johnson, diligently responded to all requests thus making my work easier and more pleasant.

The services of eight proofreaders were invaluable, including those of Laura Caudill, Carolyn Flatt, Nolan Fowler, Keith Kappes, John Kleber, Sue Luckey, Charles Pelfrey, and James Wells.

I am grateful to Morehead State University for providing a sabbatical for one semester in the early phase of the project and to the MSU Research Committee and the Kentucky Oral History Commission for issuing grants to help finance the research.

Our supportive children, David Doran Flatt and Nancy Melissa Spivy, along with nine exuberant grandchildren, will finally learn that I am neither wedded permanently to the MSU Archives nor to a computer. And my wife Carolyn, who has an eye for quickly detecting poor writing and a heart of compassionate instincts which often provides more appropriate ways to express the negative, can now return to the pursuit of some of her own dreams.

Although I have received bountiful aid from many individuals, I alone accept personal responsibility for the book's accuracy, contents, and interpretations. It was hard to complete this labor of love; various obstacles during the past year, including major surgery, delayed publication of the book and denied me time to index this first edition. However, I plan to prepare an index for the second printing.

My deepest gratitude is reserved for Adron and Mignon Doran who opened doors of opportunity for me, deeply influencing every aspect of my life as they were taking their "footsteps across the commonwealth."

Finally, in honor of my thousands of students during a 35-year career, I have designated that any and all profits from the sale of this book be used to further improve our "light to the mountains."

Donald F. Flatt

*"Still it may happen that the light of the scholar's study will shine longer and brighter."*
*— Charles A. Beard.*

# *Introduction*

"$\mathcal{A}$d Astra Per Aspera" To the stars through adversity. The people of Kansas have aptly chosen those words as their state motto. They might just as well describe the history of Morehead State University, a school born from nineteenth century conflicts, nurtured in twentieth centrury adversity, and poised for greater achievements in the twenty-first century. Now, seventy-five years after it became a state institution, it is time to note how Morehead State University overcame adversity to become a place of enlightenment and source of pride in the mountains of eastern Kentucky. For the first time, a comprehensive history offers an insightful view of the past. The task was difficult since few written documents existed. What did exist was supplemented by oral history, and to this author Dr. Don Flatt brought the benefit of more than thirty-five years of campus association. His work provides a vivid memory of the institution, which expands our understanding of the present and guides us into the new millennium.

Nestled on the western slope of the Appalachian mountains, Morehead State University is a unique educational institution with an interesting beginning. While the streets of Morehead still resonated with the sound of gunfire from a classic feud, plans were afoot to establish a Christian school. The combination of religion and education was touted as a way to mitigate the violence and uplift the locals. This popular idea had been carried by missionaries around the world, and now it would be tried at home. Its success is evident a century and a decade later in the now peaceful streets of the town with the university located at one end and St. Claire Medical Center at the other. In the area lying between the two institutions, a modern morality play was acted out, one in which good triumphed over evil.

The drama that is Morehead State University has been shaped by its stage and the many players who acted out their roles. The stage is wide and across it passes succeeding generations of administrators, faculty, students, and staff caught up in cross-currents that produced unique adversities that, at times, earned it bad reviews. It is fortunate that two early performers were Phebe Button and her son Frank, who left the prairies of Illinois to assume leadership of the Morehead Christian Normal School. In carrying out the school's purposes, they planted a missionary spirit that can be seen today in the university's personal concern for the well-being of the whole student. Frank Button established precedents followed by all presidents. Each in his own way exerted an inordinate influence and was the center of attention. Reflecting an individual leadership style characteristic of eastern Kentucky, all left an indelible mark. Each man faced adversities, some personal and others inherent in the complex structure of higher education. All experienced a parsimonious state legislature that reflected a public unwilling to adequately support higher education. Yet all were politically astute and found the wherewithal to build a modern facility. Working along side each president was a spouse with her own social goals. Some were more visible, yet all added a personal dimension that enhanced the well being of students and faculty.

In 1881 the Chesapeake & Ohio Railroad was completed through northeastern Kentucky. Over its tracks and along the Midland Trail, later US 60, came militia to stem the feud and later faculty members to assume the challenge of educating Appalachia's youth. The adversities of the faculty were many, but none more serious than egregiously low salaries. With growth and better transportation, the faculty's size, diversity, and role changed resulting in an inevitable erosion of the sense of family, to be replaced by a greater sense of professionalism. Today the faculty is encouraged to look beyond the surrounding hills for a wider recognition that can come only through increased scholarship. Hence the initial emphasis on teaching was broadened to include research and service. For its part the faculty demanded and received a larger role in campus governance. Through it all, the missionary spirit remains the one constant. Complementing the faculty is an increasingly professional support staff, little seen and under appreciated. Still Morehead State University could not function without it.

Nor could it exist without its students. Early in the century a remarkable Rowan County woman, Cora Wilson Stewart, proved the modern adage, "If you build it, they will come." It was her idea to begin moonlight schools in order to increase adult literacy. The image of people, walking out of the hollows after a day of hard work, guided by the light of the full moon, to be taught reading and writing, is enduring. Today, improved transportation precludes the need to walk, but the thirst for knowledge continues.

Morehead State University has done an excellent job of motivating students and parents to seek the American dream that lies in following the footprints of their predecessors. Most students come from eastern Kentucky, and most remain there after graduation. The region's culture of poverty inspires parents to help their children become upwardly mobile in order to become a valuable component of the larger American society. To help the process, in 1923 the school assumed the task of training teachers. Until the implementation of recent educational reforms, through no fault of their own, the students who came from and the teachers who remained in the region were part of a broader educational system denied adequate financial support. Penury took its toll, the results were dedicated but underpaid teachers and students who were denied the benefits of a rigorous curriculum. Yet from these adversities came the same indomitable mountain spirit to overcome obstacles which Stewart recognized that first moonlit night when many hundreds rather than the anticipated few appeared at the school house doors. African American students suffered the additional adversity of racial prejudice. Beginning in the 1950s Morehead State University often led the way in accepting minority students. Their success reflects well upon the original missionary spirit. All those who succeeded truly possess the qualities of Thomas Jefferson's ideal student—desire and ability. In retrospect, these pages show that Morehead State University need not suffer the slings and arrows of daunted criticism by those ignorant of just how hard its students had to struggle for the American dream of upward mobility.

It is impossible to estimate the contributions of these students to the political, economic, and cultural life of the region and beyond. Most of the graduates surpass their parents in our competitive, capitalistic society. Together they constitute a vibrant alumni group. It is understandable why they manifest a sense of loyalty to alma mater. Because the small town offered few diversions, students were thrown into a myriad of campus activities. When combined with the need to live on campus, the result was a concomitant closeness that deepened student friendships and increased their sense of affection for a nurturing environment. Doubtless the material presented here will jog many pleasant memories.

As pivotal as the campus was to student life, to some degree those memories must encompass the town, county, and region. The symbiosis of town and gown has not always been easy. Modern day feuds provided their own unique adversities, yet both recognized the inexorable need for each other. A significant change came in 1963 when the St. Claire Hospital was built, and Morehead State University was no longer the only game in town. The hospital's evolution into a large regional medical center stimulated the community's growth and brought in new people with different perspectives. They no longer arrived over the C&O, whose tracks were removed for a bypass, but over the interstate highway. Around the interchange of this new east-west link, businesses sprang up as Main Street merchants, who so long met student needs, closed their doors. Beyond the arteries of commerce lie the magnificent natural beauty of the county, its hillsides restored after decades of deforestation. The ideal setting of a valley surrounded by ancient knobs, is taken for granted and its potential remains untapped. The Daniel Boone National Forest offers a wide variety of flora and fauna, flowing creeks, and miles of hiking trails all within easy distance of the campus. The irony is that those who follow in the twenty-first century will rediscover what their nineteenth century predecessors knew, namely that treasure lies in the environment, in this classroom of nature tucked away from urban problems.

The University will doubtless face more adversities in the years ahead. New challenges include enrollment, regional prosperity, federal and state funding, and accountability. The curriculum must continually be reviewed to offer the enduring legacy of a liberal education combined with the practical needs of an increasingly technological world. While meeting those challenges, the campus will remain the central gathering place for intellectual and social growth, but more instruction will be taken by distance learning into the hollows from which students once walked to find learning. What these pages do predict is that Morehead State University is up to meeting the new challenges, for it has grown strong in adversity. It has never forgotten the Buttons' challenge to bring light to the mountains, although it now may be a light from the flickering images on a computer monitor or television screen. Yet it shines no less brightly.

John E. Kleber

Dr. John E. Kleber is professor emeritus of Morehead State University and editor of the *Kentucky Encyclopedia*.

*An aerial view of the MSU campus as it looked in 1996.*

# Chapter 1

# Formative Years, 1887-1922

In the year 1997 Morehead State University celebrated three-quarters of a century as a state institution. The University is located in Morehead, a city of some 12,000 and the county seat of Rowan County. Its campus, situated in the foothills of the Cumberland Plateau, comprises 945 acres, including a golf course and a farm. The 500-acre main campus spreads in a semicircle at the base of the hills to the north of the city. Graced by Eagle Lake, the physical plant, encompassing more than fifty major structures, is valued at over $110 million. The enrollment stands at close to 8,500 with a staff/faculty numbering 1,000. Its annual budget amounts to about $67 million. The University is divided into four colleges that offer courses in nearly 130 fields. Its academic facilities include Camden-Carroll Library with 415,000 volumes and 294,000 microform titles. Extended campus centers are located in Ashland, Prestonsburg, and West Liberty. The University operates under the direction of an 11-member Board of Regents, consisting of eight citizens appointed by the governor, with three other seats held by elected faculty, staff, and student representatives.

An educational institution sporting the above figures is substantial. It is a source of pride at all levels—city/county, Eastern Kentucky, the state, and the whole South. But it was not once so—far from it! One could even say that no member of the higher education fraternity in the state has experienced such a checkered past as has Morehead. The school is like Joseph's coat of many colors, in light of the many institutional changes in its career, and it has suffered "great tribulation," considering the many vicissitudes of fortune it has endured.

As a state school the institution has borne five titles: Morehead State Normal School (1922-26), Morehead State Normal School and Teachers College (1926-30), Morehead State Teachers College (1930-48), Morehead State College (1948-66), and Morehead State University (1966-Present). But the state school chartered in 1922 enjoyed (and suffered) a prior existence of 35 years as Morehead Normal School, under the auspices of the Kentucky Christian Missionary Society (later the Christian Women's Board of Missions). This normal school, which opened in 1887, had its origins in the infamous Martin-Tolliver feud of 1884-87. Hence, it isn't too much to say that had there been no feud, there would be no Morehead State University! This work is an attempt to chronicle the steps—often faltering, frequently zigzagging, and sometimes even retrogressing—whereby from tentative beginnings grew the respected university of today. In nearly 110 years, the sweep of history has carried Morehead State University and its honorable predecessor, Morehead Normal School, from the flickering lamp of Mrs. Phebe Button in a rented room to the high-tech world of a radio telescope which reaches from a campus hillside literally to the stars.

## Rowan—A Lawless County

By the end of the nineteenth century, Rowan County as well as most of Eastern Kentucky was lagging behind the rest of the nation in social and economic development and was not far advanced from rowdy days of the frontier. Nothing illustrated its frontier traits better than the Martin-Tolliver feud, also known as the Rowan County War, which resulted in twenty murders and assassinations, along with sixteen wounded, in a county with a total population of only 4,420 in 1880. Lawlessness reached an unprecedented scale as businesses were destroyed, houses were burned, and families were fright-

*The Gault House (located where the old Battson Drug building stands) on Main Street served as headquarters for the Tolliver faction.*

ened away. Men roamed the streets of Morehead and the byways of Rowan County ready to enforce their will with rifles and pistols.

The feud that laid waste to Rowan County and the town of Morehead, like many that broke out in Eastern Kentucky, may well have had its roots in the violence and animosities bred in the region during the Civil War. The county was divided by a bitter enmity between adherents of the Democratic and Republican parties who were almost equally matched in numbers. Overt hostilities began on election day, August 4, 1884. But the spark that set in train the bloody events to follow occurred the week before in an apparently innocent misunderstanding over a hotel room. William Trumbo, a prominent businessman, and his wife Lucy were attending a dance in Morehead. During the evening Lucy retired and by mistake fell asleep in a room rented by H. G. Price, a well-to-do timber dealer. On returning to his room and finding Mrs. Trumbo asleep in his bed, Price allegedly made indecent advances, which sent the woman screaming to her husband. Trumbo finally quieted his wife by promising to settle with Price later.

The voting on August 4 was accompanied by the customary drinking and fighting. With the saloons open as usual, votes were bought by a blending of whiskey and money, and of course there were many who required no such prompting to indulge themselves or to argue the progress of the elections and their outcome. That night Trumbo encountered Price in a saloon and demanded an apology for his conduct the week before. Claiming innocence, Price refused whereupon Trumbo struck him. Then Floyd Tolliver, a Democrat and a friend of Price, knocked down John Martin, a Republican and a relative of Trumbo. Martin drew a pistol, and in the ensuing fracas he was wounded and a bystander, Solomon Bradley, was killed. Unable or unwilling to decide, a grand jury subsequently indicted both Tolliver and Martin for Bradley's death and set their trial for December.

But neither Floyd Tolliver nor John Martin lived to be tried. Some weeks later the two encountered one another in the Gault House saloon where, amid drinking, a heated argument developed over the election day fight and Tolliver, trying to draw his pistol, was fatally shot by Martin. Dying, Tolliver reportedly reminded his friends of their promise to kill Martin. Martin was jailed, first in Morehead and then in Winchester, some 45 miles distant, where it was thought he would be safer. Back in Morehead, Craig Tolliver, who had assumed leadership of that faction, plotted revenge. Forging a court order for Martin's return, he dispatched five of his men

*The main battle was fought on Railroad Street outside the American Hotel and Saloon and the Exchange Saloon near the Depot.*

posing as officers to bring the prisoner back to Morehead. Sensing that something was amiss, Martin pled, unavailingly, with the Winchester jailers to confirm the bogus order before releasing him. With Martin in custody, his captors boarded the afternoon train for Morehead. As night was falling, the train reached the town of Farmers, and here Craig Tolliver with a group of other masked men halted and boarded the train and gunned down the hapless Martin, but he managed to survive the rest of the journey to Morehead and to make his way to the Powers Hotel where he died the next morning.

With these two deaths the lines were drawn in Rowan County between the Tolliver and Martin factions and their supporters—the Bowlings, Days, and Youngs for the Tollivers and the Humphreys, Logans, and Powerses for the Martins—and the stage was set for three years of killing, intimidation, and lawlessness in the county. Led by the ruthless and cunning Craig, the Tolliver faction consolidated its power and gained political control of the county and of the lucrative liquor trade. Members of the gang watched the roads in and out of Morehead, men were ambushed, gun battles frequently erupted on the streets, and citizens of the town were often afraid to venture out of their homes. The corrupt state of local government is shown by the fact that Craig Tolliver was successively elected town marshal of Morehead and then county judge with a total of only fifty votes.

Efforts by the state to restore order to Rowan proved ineffectual. Twice in 1885 militia were dispatched to Morehead, but the effects of such intervention proved temporary as the local citizenry were either too apathetic or too frightened to wrest control of a corrupt government that would not prosecute the hoodlums roaming the streets. In the end, it seemed as though the state government in Frankfort simply washed its hands of the whole troublesome affair.

But finally Craig Tolliver, early in 1887, overreached himself in an effort to quell Boone Logan, a local attorney and an open opponent of the Tolliver regime. Evidently seeking to get at Logan indirectly, Tolliver had a relative of John Logan, along with four others, indicted on a trumped-up charge of attempted murder and sent them off to jail in Lexington. Then to prevent Logan's sons from testifying in their father's defense, members of the gang went to the Logan home, again with arrest warrants on bogus charges, where they persuaded the two sons to surrender peaceably, then killed them and trampled their bodies in the mud. The flagrance and brutality of the killings at last seemed to arouse the revulsion of the area's citizenry.

Boone Logan, outraged by this attack on his

*William Temple Withers, ex-Confederate general, pledged $500 annually to send someone to Morehead to preach and to found a school.*

relatives, sought aid in Frankfort, but Governor J. Proctor Knott refused to do anything, telling Logan in effect that Rowan County would have to clean up its own mess. Rebuffed by Frankfort, Logan secured a quantity of arms and ammunition and covertly began organizing resistance to Tolliver and his gang. Then before daybreak on June 22, 1887, Boone Logan and 113 vigilantes from Rowan and surrounding counties quietly encircled Morehead and closed in on American House, the scene of ensuing battle. Before they could serve warrants on the Tollivers, shots rang out from the hotel, initiating a two-hour battle that saw Craig Tolliver and most of his gang killed. The deaths of Tolliver and other gang members effectively ended the Rowan County War, the bloodiest internecine conflict in Kentucky's history.

## Cleaning Up the Mess

The town lay in virtual ruin, its businesses destroyed and its economy in shambles. One individual testified that his family had been too scared to wander outside their home after dark for over two years. Somehow, Morehead managed to lick its wounds and survive. Logan and others created a Law and Order League, which acted as a police force until state troops arrived in August to insure a semblance of order during the trials of those accused of murder. Those on trial included Zachary T. Young and his son, Alcanon W. (Allie), who later became an influential member of both the General Assembly and the Board of Regents of Morehead State. Neither was convicted. General Sam E. Hill, who was sent to Morehead to report on affairs, became so disgusted with the place that he advised the governor to do away with Rowan County and divide it among surrounding counties.

The situation in Morehead was the focus of national attention. A story on the front page of the June 23, 1887, issue of *The New York Times* described the previous day's two-hour battle on the streets of Morehead as "the best piece of work that has been done in Kentucky within a half century." An editorial in the same issue challenged the citizens of Kentucky to take action and commented: "They must be aware that a community in which a band of assassins can control the politics and

*Phebe Button gave up her place at the Kentucky Female Orphan Academy in Midway to assist her son, Frank C., in founding the Morehead Normal School.*

7

the society of a whole county is no more entitled to be called civilized."

The future of Rowan County was decided in Frankfort in the spring of 1888. Since the feud had reduced the community to near anarchy, the General Assembly complied with recommendations to oust the county's public officials and appoint new ones in their place. The outraged General Assembly only narrowly defeated a motion to abolish the county.

Finally realizing that lawlessness had almost wiped out the county, its citizens endeavored to change both reality and image. The leaders of Morehead decided on a combination of religion and education as the way out of the darkness produced by violence. Local religious groups endeavored to prevent such behavior from happening again by creating a different social order. The Baptist Church controlled its members by disfellowshipping those charged with such things as licentiousness, drunkenness, engaging in the sale of liquor, and manifesting indifference toward church attendance. The best solution to overall community improvement, Baptists decided, lay in conducting evangelistic revivals. So, in late August 1887 George O. Barnes, noted evangelist, arrived in Morehead for a revival. The Christian Church, however, followed an alternative route by establishing a normal school.

## The Founding of Morehead Normal School, 1887

Entering the campus of Morehead State University today, one catches a glimpse of a towering obelisk announcing the year 1887 as the date when the school was founded. This inscription emphasizes the significant role of the old Morehead Normal School in laying the groundwork for the present state institution.

The Christian Church had dreamed for years about starting a school in Morehead. As early as the 1870s, it was contemplating the establishment of a congregation there, along with a school, for doing missionary work in the mountains. The dream gathered new force after the Martin-Tolliver feud demonstrated the tremendous need for more education to help create serenity out of turmoil. The Christian Church's decision to build a school was in keeping with the thrust of the Social Gospel, a popular movement in American religion during the latter part of the nineteenth century. To Christianity's traditional concern for lost souls, the Social Gospel added a commitment to reforming society on this earth as well. Thus, the Christian Church's mission plan, involving building both a church and a school, combined its traditional interest in evangelism with its growing commitment to the Social Gospel. As Presbyterians were starting schools at Jackson and Pikeville in the 1880s, the Christian Church moved to create schools at Hazel Green and Morehead. Morehead Normal School became one of more than twenty-five private normal schools built in Kentucky between 1870 and 1905.

Northeastern Kentucky certainly needed a normal school, not just another elementary school poorly staffed and financed. The pattern generally followed in Kentucky was for governors to propose educational reforms, the General Assembly to refuse adequate funding, and the local school boards to be afraid to request additional support from their constituency. Since board members were more concerned with holding down the amount spent on teachers' salaries than improving the quality of what was taught, local school systems generally got what they paid for—very little. Most public schools in Kentucky were in session only five months and met in one-or two-room schoolhouses, with hardly any provision for books or classroom supplies. W. T. Parker, Rowan County superintendent of education in 1886-87, described its schools' deplorable conditions: "The schools of this county seem to be progressing slowly. It is difficult to arouse an interest in their duty. There is no improvement in the teachers. School houses are very bad, some of them are not fit for a summer school, much less a winter school."

As an influential religious group in Kentucky, the Christian

Church was in a good position to extend its missionary work to Morehead and thereby improve the teaching profession in Eastern Kentucky. Meeting in Maysville in August 1887, the Disciples' state convention authorized the founding of a school at Morehead. Important people fell in line with the convention's decision. William Temple Withers, an ex-Confederate general, prominent lawyer, and successful breeder of standardbred horses at his beautiful Fairlawn plantation on the outskirts of Lexington, pledged a large annual contribution to send someone to Morehead to start a school and to preach the gospel in a region which needed "not less law, but more gospel." As an elder of the Main Street Christian Church in Lexington, he suggested that the church's State Board operate the school. Withers contributed $500 during each of the last two years of his life, and his estate matched this amount for an additional year. Sentiment at the convention was strong on behalf of Morehead. In his baccalaureate address at the Normal School in 1902, the well-known Christian Church minister, Charles S. Loos, reminisced about Morehead's selection fifteen years earlier. He referred to this decision as manifesting an "enlightened and heroic Christian purpose" in erecting "a pharos of intellectual and spiritual light, that should send

*The house on the right served as a residence and a school for the Buttons. It stood on the back of the lot where the Adron Doran University Center is now located. Across Second Street was the building which once served as Allie Young's law office.*

its illuminating and awakening rays of knowledge, and of hope through the valleys, and over the mountains beyond it."

Although many doubted that anyone would be willing to go to Morehead under the circumstances, Mrs. Phebe (the family used the Biblical spelling without an "o") E. Button, and her son Frank answered the call. Phebe had left her native Illinois in the 1870s to teach at the Kentucky Female Orphan Academy at Midway, a Christian Church school in which Withers served on the board of trustees. By special dispensation, Midway permitted Mrs. Button's teenage son to attend the two-year college for girls—the only exception ever made at Midway until the 1980s. After graduation, the nineteen-year-old Button entered the College of the Bible in Lexington where he received a theological degree in 1887. Later he earned an M.A. degree from Bethany College in West Virginia. In September 1887 the Christian Church employed Frank C. Button to establish a school in Morehead while serving as minister of the local church. His mother, who asked to accompany him, was an experienced teacher and administrator, but she was looked upon as a frail, elderly widow. She had lost her husband and a little daughter and had herself suffered a major fall which made walking a chore. While many feared she would have little tolerance for the hard life in the mountains of Eastern Kentucky, her several tragedies strengthened her to cope successfully with whatever came her way.

Since Withers was financing most of Button's early work at Morehead, he often made contact with him. Shortly before Button's departure he wrote, "You and your mother can make your arrangements to go to Morehead as soon as you can conveniently do so—the sooner the better. I would like to have a conference with you before you start." Withers then assured him, "I will advance one hundred dollars on your salary, to enable you to move and get located in Morehead."

Conditions were still unstable when the Buttons arrived at Morehead in the fall of 1887. In the memoirs of her father, Ida W.

Harrison, daughter of General Withers, described Button's experiences during his first day in town. Button went "to see a man whose name had been given to him, and while they were talking, firing began on the street, and they had to take refuge behind an old stone chimney, until the fusillade was over." In 1906 Withers Hall was dedicated to this gentleman as a memorial, but his daughter added, "The true memorial is the changed ideals in the hearts of the hundreds of boys and girls trained there, and the part they have played in making a new and better day in Eastern Kentucky."

Morehead Normal School had a very modest beginning on October 3, 1887. The Buttons opened their school in two small, poorly ventilated rooms on the first floor of a two-story rickety dwelling; their living quarters were on the upper floor. This original school building faced Second Street on the back part of the lot where the Adron Doran University Center now stands. The normal school now had a home.

## What Was A Normal School?

Just what was a normal school? Today, Morehead State University has Normal Hall, a three-story home for married students. But the term is so strange to students that it is often the subject of joking remarks.

During the final three decades of the nineteenth century, the term normal school was already in vogue as the name for teacher-training institutions. It was commonly held that a teacher needed very little subject matter above the level being taught. In keeping with this common belief, the average school teacher in Kentucky had only a seventh-grade education until late in the nineteenth century. The Commonwealth of Kentucky lagged behind much of the rest of the nation in establishing public normal schools. When the General Assembly created Kentucky's public school system in 1838, it failed to make any provisions for training teachers. After written

*Hargis Hall, constructed in 1889, on land contributed by Thomas F. Hargis, another former Confederate officer, was the first classroom building. It was located near the present Allie Young Hall.*

examinations were substituted in 1870, a teaching certificate became increasingly difficult to obtain without having the equivalent of a grammar school education.

Kentucky paid little serious attention to the founding of public normal schools until 1880. Therefore, private normal schools quickly sprang into being to assist in meeting certification requirements. Sixteen private normal schools were already active in 1880 when the General and Mechanical College, later known as the University of Kentucky was started. In 1886, a State Normal School for Colored Persons was founded and later evolved into Kentucky State University, located at Frankfort.

Normal schools usually consisted of a combination of elementary and high school levels. While the quality of their work seldom

*Graduating class of 1909 at Morehead Normal School. (Left to right) Viola Jacobs, Mary Eaton, Vesta Kendall, Goldie Horton (Johnson), and Ada Taylor.*

exceeded that of the high school level—and was often far below it— the presence of normal schools indicated that qualifications other than good moral character and poverty were necessary to successful school teaching and helped make it possible to start looking upon teaching as a profession.

## Morehead and the Christian Missionary Society, 1887-1900

Morehead Normal School started out under discouraging conditions. Before leaving Midway, Phebe Button wrote a friend back in Illinois, "We will be so isolated that we will miss all the nice papers and periodicals that we have enjoyed, and I hope to enlist all of our friends in helping us by sometimes sending us papers of any kind."

She also wrote to her local newspaper there, "We start without school buildings or anything else, except our few books and what few household things we have." She then explained the nature of the new institution by stating it would serve as an elementary school as well as a place in which to train teachers.

Enrollment that first year was forever changing. The first student, an orphan named Annie Page, shyly appeared on the first morning of class in a little cottage where the Adron Doran University Center now stands. That afternoon Ethel Bertie Hamm also enrolled. Two others joined her on the second day and others followed, a trickle of humanity at first which grew into a steady stream. Twenty-two students were attending by the end of November. Although the Buttons already had more pupils than they could care for, enrollment jumped to fifty-two by February 1888. Ten other youngsters had to be turned away because of a lack of space. Between the middle of February and the last of March 1888 eleven students dropped out due to the opening of a new public school. The first school year finished with thirty-two pupils; enrollment hovered around that same number the following year.

Button subsequently wrote an article about the beginning of the school for a national publication of the Christian Church. A man in California read about Annie Page and wrote the Morehead principal to obtain additional information about her parents. It turned out that she was the man's niece, and he sent money for her to come to California. There she was well-educated and later was married.

Morehead Normal School intended to provide the kind of educational opportunities to Eastern Kentucky which were enjoyed by other parts of the state. Its founders looked upon three things as of utmost importance: training public school teachers, preparing for vocations, and bringing a liberal arts education to the people of the region at reasonable cost.

In order to carry out its mission, the institution needed a schoolhouse. Withers' liberality paved the way for the school during its first three years, including a $100 gift to be used in constructing a classroom building. At this point, the generosity of a second former Confederate officer and patron of the Christian Church, the Honorable Thomas F. Hargis, provided four acres of land for the campus, as well as $500 for a classroom building, to maintain a school intended "for the exclusive use and control of the Christian Church." This land was located on the west end of today's campus, in the vicinity of the present Camden-Carroll Library and Allie Young Hall. Hargis, a former Kentucky chief justice of the Court of Appeals living in Louisville but reared in Morehead, attached this conditional clause to the deed: "It must be used by second party for an academy and school of learning or it will be reverted back to the first party." By the summer of 1889, the two-room multi-purpose building had been completed. The removal of a partition permitted the use of one large room for church services and Sunday School. This sizable contribution for the benefit of both church and school must have brought a sense of cleansing to the soul of Judge Hargis. His race for circuit judge featured charges and counter-charges in the acrimonious campaign of 1874; his loss to his Republican opponent began a decade of political antagonism and unrest which provided the background for the Martin-Tolliver feud in 1884.

But the young school had to endure one major problem after another. Now that its need for a classroom building had been met, Morehead Normal School had to cope with a problem in leadership. Just as the Buttons' close relationship had brought them to Morehead, Phebe's illness led to Frank's resignation in 1892 to care for his mother. Although she died that same year, Button did not return as principal until 1896. Ralph Julian succeeded him as principal of the school and as minister of the local Christian Church for four years.

Morehead Normal School's increase in enrollment to around 200 clearly demonstrated the need for a dormitory. A generous $1,500 gift by Button's uncle, Robert Hodson, of Oquawka, Illinois,

*Cora Wilson Stewart attended and later taught at Morehead Normal School. While serving as superintendent of Rowan County schools in 1911, she organized the "Moonlight Schools", the forerunner of adult education in the U.S. and the world.*

led to the construction of the first boarding hall in 1894. Described as the "finest in Eastern Kentucky," Hodson Hall, a memorial to Mrs. Phebe Button and her niece, Hattie Hodson, was a three-story frame building with twenty-two apartments. A catalogue describes the rooms as "furnished with dresser, washstand, table, bed with springs, a good carpet on the floor, and nearly all are now papered." Room and board were $2 per week at a time when tuition was only $5 for a ten-week period. Hodson Hall was segregated into a section for women and another for men. Thus, Morehead started out with a coed residence hall, a most uncommon practice for the 1890s. Hodson Hall later became a girls' dormitory, after a separate men's residence was constructed.

Few records exist today dealing with such topics as curriculum, faculty, and students between 1887 and 1900. But a Morehead Normal School catalogue for the 1897-98 academic year furnishes an indication of the nature of the school during part of this time. There were four terms—beginning on August 29, November 7, January 23, and April 3—with commencement held on June 9. As president of the Kentucky Christian Missionary Society, J.W. McGarvey of Lexington was listed as president of the board of trustees. In addition to being principal, Frank C. Button taught English literature, Latin, Greek, and Sacred History. Cora Wilson (Stewart), who became well known early in the twentieth century as a fighter against illiteracy, was mentioned as an elocution and primary teacher. The school allowed a five percent discount if the $5 tuition for a ten-week term was paid in advance. Students had access to the principal's library, along with a school library consisting of some 1,000 books. Although Rowan had once been noted for its lawlessness, the catalogue describes it as "now one of the most law-abiding counties in Eastern Kentucky." "Easy of access by rail and stage," the town of Morehead had grown to about 1,000.

Morehead Normal School became interested in accreditation in the late 1890s. The school filed articles of incorporation with the state in the spring of 1898, requesting power to confer high school diplomas. Although its first request was denied, the school was finally chartered on May 6, 1899, thereby representing the first official connection between the institution and the state.

## Christian Women's Board of Missions Takes Over, 1900-1922

Management of the school changed hands in 1900. At a meeting in Indianapolis, J. W. McGarvey, influential church leader on the state level in Kentucky, raised the possibility of transferring the school from the Kentucky Christian Missionary Society to the Christian Women's Board of Missions. Rather than being dissatisfied with the school's past record or future potential, the missionary society simply wanted to focus on evangelistic work and to withdraw from educational work. At a time when most private normal schools failed to survive, the Kentucky Christian Missionary Society, in spite of limited financial resources, had successfully operated this school for thirteen years and had fulfilled the founders' mission to elevate the region's moral standards. During its first thirteen years the institution had trained more than 300 teachers. On July 31, 1900, the missionary society deeded the Morehead Normal School property to the Christian Women's Board of Missions.

One of the first steps of the new owners was to organize an advisory board which served to promote worthwhile projects as well as maintain rapport between the school and the town of Morehead. Rowan County School Superintendent Cora Wilson Stewart and Allie Young, a prominent young lawyer, served as early members of the advisory board. Since Morehead Normal School never became self-supporting, the Christian Women's Board of Missions sought funds through contributions from individuals and churches as well as from state and local auxiliaries. Tuition and gifts from the town of Morehead accounted for only one-sixth of the total cost of operating the school.

Progress from 1900 to 1922 demonstrated the wisdom of transferring the school's oversight to the Christian Women's Board of Missions. "Under this new and competent management," Button later asserted, "the buildings have been repaired and enlarged, the number of teachers has been increased, the courses of study have been strengthened, and a new epoch in its history has begun." A record enrollment of 284 was set in 1901; students included boarders representing sixteen counties and three states. The school endeavored to instill every future teacher with enthusiasm for work and with high ideals. In addition to being drilled each day in religion, they were given special instruction in reading, music, parliamentary law, physiology, physical culture, and Bible study. Button was thrilled to report at the turn of the century that "there are no saloons in Rowan County."

Commencement exercises in 1901 featured the delivery of student papers which represented "creditable efforts of serious thought, tinged with wit and fringed with smiles." Five women and two men graduated in the auditorium of the local courthouse. With Mrs. Ida W. Harrison, daughter of General Withers, delivering the commencement address, school publicist R. B. Neal claimed that the "argument for the co-education of the sexes" was clearly demonstrated. It was remarkable that from the school's conception women played a major role. At a time when such was not the norm, Button seemed to feel perfectly comfortable in serving as principal under the direction of the oversight of the Christian Women's Board of Missions.

By 1905 enrollment had grown to 363, representing twenty-one counties and five states. In looking back over the school's first eighteen years, Button stated that a total of 1,500 students, including 500 who had trained to be teachers, had attended Morehead Normal School. He estimated that these young teachers had subsequently gone out to instruct at least 100,000 pupils. During commencement he told students, "Whereas we have always begged you to 'Stay,' we now ask you to 'Go out' so as to make a difference in Eastern Kentucky."

Button was deeply impressed that one young man who graduated in 1904 had walked all the way from the Great Smoky Mountains of Tennessee to attend school at Morehead. The circulation of such stories inspired parents to send their children in larger numbers. Morehead Normal School experienced its largest enrollment—584—in the academic year of 1907-08. And the campus continued to grow. Its buildings included Hodson Hall, which was by then being used exclusively as a residence for girls; Withers Hall, a dormitory for young men; Hargis Hall, a classroom building; and Burgess Hall, a yellow-brick structure serving as the administration building and library, with offices, music room, YMCA room, and a third-floor chapel which surprisingly had a seating capacity of 500.

Tuition remained exceptionally low. If one took a general set of courses, the tuition was only one dollar per month; if one majored in bookkeeping, the cost increased to seven dollars, and the tuition for one majoring in stenography was $7.58. Living expenses were also low, as two dollars per week covered room and board, fuel, light, and washing of bed and table linen. In fact, money was not always required. Cornelius P. Caudill, later president of Peoples Bank in Morehead, related that Button once accepted a wagon load of potatoes to pay for his expenses and those of his four brothers.

Morehead Normal School experimented for ten years with a voluntary work project to provide jobs for students. Girls received a nickel an hour for housework, and boys the same rate for keeping buildings and grounds in good order. The school also began operating a broom factory, a 120-acre farm to raise broom corn, a printing business, and a furniture factory to give employment to students. But within a short time, the farm, broom factory, and printing plant were sold, although enrollment had increased during that period. The record is not clear as to why the school abruptly eliminated its labor program; at the time there were over 75 names on a waiting list for openings in the setup.

*In 1972, this rural school was moved from Little Brushy eight miles north of Morehead, to its present location beside the Breckinridge School building as part of the University's Golden Anniversary. It was one of several Rowan County schools used as a "Moonlight School".*

Students of Morehead Normal School were children of farmers, country preachers, rural school teachers, small town merchants, and lawyers. Their parents' definition of education often included the mere learning of the three R's. Various home situations, such as major family illnesses or being needed for work on the farm, prevented a majority of the students from completing their educational plans. While many students attended during the twenty-two years the school was operated by the Christian Women's Board of Missions, only 128 graduated. The year 1910 had the largest number of graduates to that date—sixteen, but the school averaged only five graduates per year between 1910 and 1922.

The institution continued to make a determined effort to change the image of the town of Morehead. A publication of the Normal School in 1908 went to extremes by making the community sound utopian:

*Harlan Hatcher graduated from Morehead Normal School in 1918. He later served as an English professor and academic vice president of Ohio State before becoming President of the University of Michigan from 1951 to 1967.*

Nestling in a beautiful basin, formed by the valleys of the Triplett and Dry Fork conjoining, surrounded by emerald mountains, lies the little town of Morehead. Serene and peaceful are the beautiful views of the valley, from surrounding heights. No scene could be more peaceful, more restful than the valley in which Morehead is located. Nothing more charming than the sunshine as it chases the shadows across the face of the mountains which surround it. Here can be heard the sweet notes of the Kentucky Cardinal. Here can be heard the dulcet strains of the mocking bird, and his worthy rival, the brown thrasher. The morning carol and the evening vespers of the birds—the music of the waters— true, pure, sweet, holy, is solace to the tired soul and strength to the weary body.

In spite of this idealistic description, a number of serious concerns arose at the beginning of the 1910-11 school year. Rowan County built its first public high school that year, as well as two new elementary schools. There was obviously less need for the Morehead Normal School in both elementary and secondary education. The academy, or high school, enrollment dropped to twenty-seven by 1910, in anticipation of the opening of the new school. In 1911 Button moved from Morehead to Versailles to serve as supervisor of rural schools in Kentucky under the sponsorship of the Rockefeller Foundation.

At this time, one of the school's graduates and teachers initiated a movement which would bring her international renown. Cora Wilson Stewart, whose devotion to her Alma Mater never faltered, began a program in the fall of 1911 to enable every illiterate person in Rowan County to read and write; 25 percent of its adult population was illiterate. She was enthusiastically assisted by the unpaid services of fifty other teachers, most of whom were also Morehead

Normal School graduates. These "Moonlight Schools," as they came to be known, had almost fairy-tale success during the three subsequent autumns. After being elected superintendent of Rowan County schools in 1901 and re-elected eight years later, Stewart became the first woman president of the Kentucky Education Association in 1911. That same year she launched an experimental adult education program to combat illiteracy in Rowan County. The Moonlight School met at nights because the majority of its students were employed during the day. Armed with both the unanimous support of faculty who performed this important community service without pay and with special reading books that Stewart developed for adult learners, the program enjoyed spectacular success. Although teachers expected 150 students the first year, 1,200 persons, ranging in age from 18 to 86, attended. The second year 1,600 enrolled. At the end of the third year, by Stewart's count, illiteracy in Rowan County had dwindled from 1,152 to 23. In 1914, the U.S. Commissioner of Education recommended to Congress that the Moonlight Schools become a model for the instruction of the 5.5 million across the nation who could not read. In the late 1920s President Herbert Hoover appointed Stewart to chair the Executive Committee of the National Advisory Committee on Illiteracy. She also presided over the illiteracy section of the World Conference on Education.

A second outstanding example of what Morehead Normal School meant to young people was Harlan H. Hatcher, one of the most ambitious and successful graduates ever produced by the institution. Harlan, whose father was a teacher, was born in Ironton, Ohio, but his family moved to Ashland, Kentucky. He came to Morehead on the advice of his father and completed his secondary training in 1918 in time to serve in the military during the latter stages of World War I. After he returned from the war, he took only eight years to earn his B. A., M. A., and Ph. D. degrees at Ohio State. Hatcher was professor of English, dean of the College of Arts and

Humanities, and academic vice president at Ohio State from 1928 to 1951. He then finished his distinguished career as president of the University of Michigan from 1951 to 1967. During that era, Michigan more than doubled its enrollment and took its place as one of the major research institutions of America. Hatcher, recipient of 35 honorary doctorates, has published twenty books and is currently working on his memoirs. When invited back to Morehead in 1995 to receive an honorary doctorate, Hatcher, then 97 years old, declined with regret, noting that the commencement date conflicted with a speaking engagement.

Another Hatcher was principal of Morehead Normal School during World War I. J. Wesley Hatcher, not related to Harlan, left Toledo, Ohio, where he was a popular Christian Church minister and moved to Eastern Kentucky to preach for the West Liberty Christian Church. During his tenure there he accepted an invitation to minister at Morehead and to serve as principal of the Morehead Normal School from 1913 to 1919. Enrollment reached 357 during his second year with ten faculty members in addition to the principal. Hatcher started a model rural school in a little cottage on campus to demonstrate to students what a mountain school ought to be, with its evening school for adults. For J. Wesley Hatcher, as with other principals before him, the chief concern of the school was to prepare young people to establish Christian homes and to become leaders in Bible school and church, in addition to preparing them to be teachers. But Hatcher was also pleased with the popularity of two courses not connected with religion: a class in physical culture, which met each morning at 5:30 for an hour's drill, and a special lyceum course, which introduced students to the world outside the mountains.

World War I obviously made its presence felt at Morehead Normal School. Principal Hatcher stated that after the declaration of war against Germany, a "spirit of anxiety and gloom affected us. Many of our boys have enlisted and others are expecting conscription, but we are trying to keep hope and faith and face the situation presented by our national crisis in the spirit of true patriotism." He had collected the names of 48 Morehead students serving in the armed forces, but "doubtless there are many others." Despite losses in the student body, in 1917-18 a dozen students received eighth-grade certificates and four individuals were granted high school diplomas, including Ruth Anglin, who later married Warren C. Lappin.

But the school was even more seriously affected when hit by measles in 1917 and by influenza the following year. The influenza epidemic, which killed over twenty million people throughout the world, shut down the school for three months in the fall of 1918. Morehead Normal School changed principals in the fall of 1919. Hatcher left after six years to pursue additional graduate work in order to improve his career opportunities. But the school was optimistic with the arrival of W.O. Lappin as its new principal. The Lappin clan, living in Illinois, contributed many leaders to the Christian Church during the first half of the twentieth century. After the close of the war enrollments rose, and crowded conditions forced the housing of four boys in each room at Withers Hall and filled the girls' dormitory.

Students of Morehead Normal School came from a remote but beautiful region. Area roads were so crude that "it took nearly all day" to make the trip from Morehead to Flemingsburg. On a trip through Eastern Kentucky, Woodrow Wilson once wrote:

> No one who has ridden, as I have, through the silent lengths of that great region, can fail to have his imagination touched by what he has seen, the almost limitless forests lying there untouched upon the long slopes of the towering hills, as if they had been there keeping their counsel and holding their secrets ever since the Creation; and here and there in the little clearings the houses of a secluded people, as reticent as the hills above them, slow to speak, their eyes watchful, holding back the secrets of their quiet life.

Morehead Normal School maintained strict rules and regulations governing social and private lives of students. All mail, incoming and outgoing, was censored; girls could not correspond with people living in town and were required to have a chaperon when they left campus for any reason. Wearing jewelry was frowned upon as "out of harmony with school life." School authorities made it clear that the use of tobacco and intoxicating drinks, possession of concealed weapons, and profane and indecent language were forbidden. The 1917-18 catalogue made it clear that "those who do not desire the regulated life thus provided for are advised to go elsewhere" since we are "not prepared to act as guardian of the idle, listless, or lawless."

Difficult times were just around the corner. As the Christian Church became more urbanized, the Christian Women's Board of Missions decreased financial assistance to schools which it operated in rural areas and increased support of Bible Chairs in large universities and in its own colleges such as Butler, located in Indianapolis. Lappin reported the school's enrollment as only ninety-three, the smallest number in many years, in the first term of 1921-22. Forced to discontinue its first six grades of elementary school, Morehead Normal School was overstaffed with its ten faculty members in addition to Principal Lappin. And only three students—Christine Ellenor Gearhart, Mary Edward Riley, and Frances Hildreth Maggard, much later a member of the English Department at Morehead State—received high school diplomas in the final commencement exercises on Friday, May 19, 1922, in Burgess Hall. The church-related school had now seemingly fulfilled its purpose of improving social and educational conditions. Because of low enrollment and the production of so few graduates, Morehead Normal School chose not to open its doors in the 1922-23 academic year. At the same time, talk began to circulate that Morehead might become the site of a public teacher-training institution to be located in Eastern Kentucky.

An aura of sadness filled the air as the faculty of the old Normal School held its final meetings. The school's ninety-three students included sixty in high school, nineteen in the eighth grade, and fourteen in the seventh grade. The beautiful penmanship of Inez Faith Humphrey, secretary for the faculty meetings, states that the first six grades had been eliminated. The next-to-last faculty meeting concerned the possibility of transferring the property of Morehead Normal School to the state so that it might become the campus of a new public institution. Principal Lappin used the last faculty meeting to read the bill concerning the creation of two new state normal schools.

When everyone sang the last verse of the school's "Alma Mater" at the final commencement exercise in 1922, the words reflected not only the usual sadness of departing students but the somber last farewell to an institution that was fast fading away:

Normal, dear Normal,
Bless us now that we must part;
Remember, Alma Mater,
Keep us in thy heart.

*State Rep. J.T. Jennings of Bath County publicly opposed fellow Republican and Gov. Edwin P. Morrow who lobbied personally to locate the new state normal school in Paintsville. However, Jennings never received recognition from the Democratic leadership for his support of Morehead as the site.*

# Chapter 2

# Morehead Goes Public

$\mathcal{T}$he twentieth century brought a major change in the training of teachers in Kentucky with greater involvement of state government. In 1906 the state created two public normal schools—Eastern at Richmond and Western at Bowling Green. By 1920 a marked improvement in teacher training had taken place; however, the number of graduates did not meet the demand.

Neither Governor Edwin P. Morrow nor the Kentucky legislature was satisfied with the state's lack of progress in education. Appearing before the General Assembly in 1920, Morrow painted a dismal picture of Kentucky's public education system: "The deplorable condition of our rural schools compels your immediate attention....Schools are taught in archaic buildings—buildings without proper equipment, and often without suitable playgrounds. Rural teachers are so poorly paid that many counties have been unable to procure the required number of teachers for their schools....Salaries paid to the teachers in rural schools range from $35 to $70 per month or from $210 to $420 per year. The inevitable consequence of failure to pay a living wage has been to drive from the profession its best material, and fewer young men and women are choosing teaching as a profession." The governor further warned that "immediate relief must be furnished, or the doors of these schools, poor as they are, will be closed to the children of the state and the general cause of rural education seriously hampered and retarded." Morrow, therefore, proposed the appointment of a survey commission of trained, educational experts to ascertain the causes and to suggest means of

*Judge (and Senator) Allie W. Young used his influence in getting a state institution located in Morehead as well as in securing funds for its early development.*

remedying Kentucky's educational situation.

Accepting the governor's challenge, the General Assembly authorized him to appoint an Educational Survey Commission and appropriated $10,000 for its task. The commission approached the General Education Board of New York City, which helped secure the services of a staff of four experts to make the study and provided an additional subsidy of $15,000 for the staff. Their fifteen-month investigation took them into sixty-six counties and included making a special study of educational conditions in thirty-three school districts and one-half of Kentucky's cities. To achieve the goal of better trained teachers, the commission advocated a three-pronged approach: Establish a sound certification system, raise teachers' salaries, and provide additional teacher-training facilities.

The two state normal schools could not turn out enough public school teachers even to replace those leaving the profession. The Kentucky Educational Commission believed the commonwealth needed five additional normal schools, a manifestly impossible goal.

A realistic alternative would be the establishment of at least one, and preferably two, state normal schools—one in the Big Sandy Valley of Eastern Kentucky and another east of the Tennessee River in Western Kentucky.

Things began happening quickly at this point. The commission submitted its report to Governor Morrow in November 1921. After he urged the legislature to heed its recommendations, the General Assembly required less than two months to enact a measure calling for the establishment of two additional normal schools. On March 8, 1922, Morrow signed the bill, which served as the first charter for these two schools. Since Morrow was a Republican, the Democratic General Assembly was unwilling to allow him to name the eight members of the State Normal School Commission, who would choose the locations of the two schools. Instead, an amendment stipulated five members should be appointed by the Speaker of the House, James H. Thompson, a Democrat from Bourbon County, and the other three, by Lieutenant-Governor S. Thruston Ballard, a Louisville Republican. Thompson selected Thomas A. Combs, a former state senator; Sherman Goodpaster, a former state treasurer and currently secretary of the Kentucky Jockey Club; Edward C. O'Rear, a former chief justice of the Court of Appeals and the only Republican appointed by the Speaker; W. S. Wallen, a state legislator from Prestonsburg; and Earl W. Senff, county judge in Montgomery County. Ballard chose Arthur Peter, a former county judge; Alex G. Barrett, a Louisville attorney; and J. L. Harman, president of Bowling Green Business University. The Commission, as constituted, was made up of four Democrats, three Republicans, and one independent.

## A Struggle for Location

All interested communities in the two areas specified by the Commission in Eastern and Western Kentucky were invited to submit bids on locating the two normal schools. Each bid must include the provision of adequate land for a college campus, along with money or buildings, equal to $100,000. The state would appropriate $30,000 annually out of its general funds to be used in the maintenance and operation of each school. Several communities vied for these two normal schools, partly because of the huge monetary outlay, for that time, which the institutions would receive from the state for their annual support. Ten Western Kentucky towns submitted bids, but only Ashland, Louisa, Morehead, Paintsville, and West Liberty, in the East, mounted campaigns for the site. Morehead, for instance, promised to donate the buildings and campus of the old Morehead Normal School, which Louisville architects Joseph and Joseph had appraised at more than $140,000. As early as November 22, 1921, three months before the General Assembly authorized the founding of the two schools, the town of Morehead initiated efforts to acquire the property from the Christian Women's Board of Missions. Local legend attributes Judge Allie W. Young's political connections with anticipating the legislature and thereby assisting Morehead to gain a head start in obtaining the institution. Paintsville, however, offered the even more valuable property of John C. C. Mayo. The commission found itself virtually unable to reach a decision on the Eastern Kentucky site. Members of the commission eliminated Ashland, Louisa, and West Liberty by the end of the twelfth ballot. A definite pattern developed in the four subsequent ballots, completed by November 18, 1922, as the same four members voted consistently for Morehead while the other four sided with Paintsville. Apparently deadlocked, the commission adjourned until November 25, 1922.

W. S. Wallen, a Prestonsburg attorney, became a controversial figure when on the following Saturday, November 25, he changed his vote from Paintsville to Morehead, thereby giving the nod to the latter. Speaker of the House Thompson's five appointees, including chairman O'Rear, a Republican, thus formed a winning coalition in favor of Morehead and Murray, while Lieutenant-Governor Ballard's appointees made up the losing coalition for Paintsville and Mayfield. Accordingly, it came as no great surprise when Morehead State later named its first new men's dormitory after Thompson. Although his vote was the determining factor for Morehead, Wallen not only failed to get a building named for him, but subsequently, a forlorn figure and unpopular in his region, he left Eastern Kentucky and moved to the Southwest.

Why did Wallen change his vote? He gave two reasons: Something had to be done to break the deadlock, and he "saw the light" during a trip to Morehead between the two meetings. Contemplating the beauty of the hillside campus and the valley below, he claimed a feeling rushed over him that God intended for the new school to be located on that very spot. While Wallen denied any outside influence, the next day's Louisville *Courier-Journal* believed the voice Wallen heard was that of Allie Young rather than God. Not only were Wallen and Young Democratic politicians, but they had also worked together as attorneys for an Eastern Kentucky coal company. For whatever the reason, Wallen's vote landed the college at Morehead, the only one of the five towns not located in the Big Sandy Valley, the region the school was designed to serve!

Not everyone was pleased with the commission's political decision. Several leading citizens from the Big Sandy Valley met the following day in Ashland to protest. And Governor Morrow said he would call a special session of the legislature to repeal the State Normal School Act of 1922. Several suits were filed in Franklin Circuit Court to challenge the validity of the Normal School Act, the commission's authority to establish the schools, and its right to name Murray's State's president, as the commission had already done.

On May 15, 1923, the Kentucky Court of Appeals, however, upheld the constitutionality of the Normal School Act as well as the commission's right to determine the locations for the two schools. The Court did rule that the commission lacked the power to name the President of Murray. Its mission accomplished, the commission turned over its work to the State Board of Education and bowed out of the picture.

Proceeding with plans to open the college at Morehead, the State Board appointed Frank C. Button as the school's first president primarily because he had already served as principal of Morehead Normal School. Not everyone was convinced that founding the church-related institution, which included only secondary and elementary school students, qualified Button for leadership of a college. Dean Warren C. Lappin once shared that his father, Warren O. Lappin, felt that he himself deserved to be the first president of Morehead State Normal School since he was the last principal of the old Normal School when it closed in the spring of 1922. After all, Button had been gone from Morehead Normal School since 1911.

Button was not the major force in locating the state institution at Morehead; he played an important role, however, in the school's first four decades—down to 1929. While serving twelve years as rural school supervisor with the State Department of Education, Button had associated with the same personnel who later surveyed Kentucky's rural schools in 1920 and decided upon the need for additional state normal schools. Because of his long affiliation with the Morehead Normal School, he was also in position to help negotiate the sale of its buildings and grounds. Hattie Button later claimed her husband "began in his quiet way to plan to have the Church Board sell the Christian Women's Board of Missions' school to the state." As a well-known minister of the Christian Church in Eastern Kentucky, he had formed many connections with Morehead's constituency which translated into parents' wishes to have their youth educated under his tutelage. While some were not totally pleased that Morehead was no longer a Christian school, they took consolation in the state school's selection of Button as president. For several years, they were unable to detect any drastic change between the church-related Morehead Normal School and the teacher-training institution operated by the state.

*Frank C. Button, who along with his mother Phebe, started Morehead Normal School in 1887. Button was the institution's leader for twenty-seven years.*

Allie Young's role in locating the school at Morehead is clear in spite of the contents of a letter written by Button's widow five years after her husband's death in 1933. She claimed her husband once requested Allie Young to return from New Orleans to Frankfort that he might lend his influence on behalf of locating the state normal school at Morehead but that he refused to come because of his doubt that such a request would ever be granted. By way of contrast, she says attorneys Elijah Hogge and James Clay, Sr., along with former state senator Sam M. Bradley, accepted a similar invitation, out of courtesy and appreciation to Button, although they, too, were not convinced the institution would ever wind up in Morehead. It was her husband, rather, who "had the vision to start the ball to rolling" that brought the school to Morehead, she asserted. She adamantly claimed that Button, not Young, was the real founder of Morehead State Normal School.

In all fairness to Button, this quiet Christian gentleman wielded insufficient clout with Frankfort's political leaders to pull off such a coup. Rather, it was Allie Young who was mainly instrumental in assuring that Morehead State University—not Paintsville State University—would be serving the people of Eastern Kentucky.

Paintsville actually had better credentials and more convincing arguments. But a political decision was made on behalf of Morehead—and politics was Young's turf, not Button's. Except for the political power of Allie Young in influencing Speaker of the House Thompson and his five members of the State Normal School Commission and the fact that a normal school had operated in Morehead for thirty-five years, PSU might well exist today. A once common expression around Morehead was "Moslems worship Allah; Moreheadians, and especially the college faculty and administration, worship Allie!"

Morehead State and Murray State, born in politics, have remained mired in the same throughout much of their seventy-five years as state institutions. The amazing redeeming feature has often been the ability of their faculties to keep uppermost in mind the institutions' primary reason for existence—the education of students—even while political battles were raging on every front.

## Morehead State Normal School, 1923-1926

Morehead officially changed its name to Morehead State Normal School at the beginning of the fall semester of 1923. That day, September 23, 1923, witnessed a carnival atmosphere as early that morning, crowds started arriving in Morehead by car, train, wagon, buggy, horseback, and on foot—from every section of Eastern Kentucky. By 10 a.m. more than 5,000 people were present, a huge gathering when one considers the ways of travel and Eastern Kentucky roads in the early 1920s! The deluge of people that sunny day included several former students from the old Morehead Normal School. At lunchtime the crowd consumed beeves and sheep roasted in open pits and great kettles of burgoo. Aside from feeding such a multitude of people, the biggest problem that day was preventing horses from being hitched on campus.

Morehead attorney James Clay served as master of ceremonies. After President Button extended the welcome address, McHenry

Rhoads, Democratic nominee for State Superintendent of Public Instruction, spoke on "Teachers Training." Further presentations were given by Judge M. M. Redwine of Sandy Hook; Professor W. L. Jayne, Republican nominee for State Superintendent; Judge Edward C. O'Rear, chairman of the State Normal School Commission; Charles D. Lewis, dean of the faculty at Morehead State Normal School; and Mrs. Cora Wilson Stewart

Ted Crosthwait, who later attended Morehead State and became superintendent of Rowan County schools, reminisced about Opening Day, when J. T. Jennings, his grandfather, had taken him there. Both Jennings, a "rock-ribbed Republican" representative and Allen H. Parks, a Democratic state senator, were members of the General Assembly from Morehead's area in the early Twenties when legislation was passed authorizing building two additional normal schools. Regardless of political party affiliation, both legislators strongly supported the Morehead location. Jennings favored Morehead while fellow-Republican Governor Morrow preferred Paintsville. In legislative debate, Jennings argued that Morehead should be selected because of already having "buildings in place, a faculty, and really strong community support." While Crosthwait cherishes the memory of the barbecue roast, he still wonders why "my grandfather's name was never mentioned that day" by those in charge of the program.

Button later described the enormous difficulties of that first year. "The buildings were inadequate. There was no water supply. There was no sewer system, and the streets were shoe top deep in mud." Button attributed part of the success that year to the "active and efficient" involvement of the Board of Regents. But the town itself squared off against these stark realities by bonding itself to the limit in order to finance a water system that would adequately take care of the college's needs. These difficulties were overcome through good town-gown relationships, as city fathers cooperated with school authorities. The faculty, however, felt it necessary at one point to pass a resolution asking the president to confer with members of the Town Board "concerning our lights, informing them that we feel that they are under obligation to supply the school with lights, that they might make good their promise to the State Board when they asked that the school be located here." And President Button soon learned that the state budget was sometimes as woefully lacking as that of the church. When it was reported to him that a kitchen range in the cafeteria was in a dangerous condition and might cause a fire, he said, "We'd better have it repaired or get a new one. It used to be the Lord who was taking care of us; now it's the state of Kentucky."

Charles Lewis, member of the State Department of Education in Frankfort, was given the choice of first deanship of either Murray or Morehead. A native of Eastern Kentucky, Lewis selected Morehead and moved there to organize the school's original curriculum and to hire its first faculty. Since the new dean had no middle

*"Miss Anna" Carter served as secretary to every President from Frank C. Button to Adron Doran, 1923 to 1963. She is shown at work as President Payne's secretary in the 1930's.*

name and believing he needed one, he selected "Dickens" because he enjoyed reading the works of Charles Dickens. Thus, Dean Charles Dickens Lewis hired a faculty of eight. In addition to keeping Inez Faith Humphrey from the Morehead Normal School as head of the Department of English, he brought in Dan M. Holbrook to head the Department of Mathematics; C.O. Peratt to head Science and Agriculture; Evelyn Royalty to head the Department of Expression; and Emma Shader (Sample) as director of Music. Obviously, the "head" was the only member of each department; Morehead State made up in titles what it lacked in salaries! The present buildings for married students in Lakewood Terrace, located just below the dam which created Eagle Lake, were named in the 1960s for this original faculty. Willie Mae Watson was Morehead's original "dean" of women; this term was used for decades as a title for any dormitory director. Anna Carter served as President Button's secretary. Ruby Vansant joined the faculty at the beginning of the second semester in 1924; Warren C. Lappin, principal of the Morehead High School, found time that spring to coach baseball at Morehead State.

The Normal School continued its mission to serve as "a light unto these hills." John M. Ridgway, student in the Twenties, suggests the transition from a church-related school to a state college in 1923 "did not end the spiritual tradition." The ever gentle, kind, and patient gentleman who served as President exercised a tremendous influence on the mountain people, who continued to bestow on him the affectionate title of "Brother Button," whether they were members of his church or not. Button was about 5'7" in stature with stately bearing and deep interest in people. One trait of this refined gentleman was that he never made disparaging remarks about others. While he tended not to be "a glad handing person," Button's gentleness came through in every statement he made. The "very devout" Inez Faith Humphrey, the only carryover from the Morehead Normal School faculty, continued to gather some of her "more responsive students around her each week for prayer meetings." And

Dan Holbrook enlivened his mathematics classes by frequently sprinkling in such Biblical quotations as "Your sins will find you out" and "Wisdom is the principal thing, but with all thy getting, get understanding."

With a faculty of eight and a student body of three college students and 70 students on the secondary level, Dean Lewis set about to attract additional students. Morehead State Normal School often used as a sales pitch that young people should stay at home and receive their college education. Two cousins from Elliott County, Eileen Gullett and Effie Rice, had attended Eastern State Normal School during the fall semester of 1923. In January, 1924, they were returning to Richmond for the second semester, traveling by mule-drawn wagon from Sandy Hook to Redwine, a distance of twenty miles, where they boarded a train for Morehead. Faced with a four-hour delay in Morehead before catching a train for Richmond, they accepted an invitation from Roscoe and America Atkins, a couple they had met on the train, to relax and wait at their home in Morehead. To pass the time, the four walked to nearby Morehead State Normal School campus. As they approached Burgess Hall, the group ran into Dean Lewis, wearing bib overalls and clearing horse weeds in preparation for the opening of spring semester three days later. Lewis, along with members of his faculty, suggested that the girls give up their plans to return to Eastern and enroll at Morehead instead. His offer of scholarships persuaded them to spend the night with the Atkins couple while making their final decision. Since they had no way to talk the matter over with their parents back in Sandy Hook, the girls stayed awake most of the night struggling with their dilemma. Thus they overslept the next morning, missed the train to Richmond and then concluded that their decision had been made for them. On Monday morning, they registered for classes at Morehead State and later graduated from there.

Allie Young's contributions to the institution are many. At the first meeting of the Board of Regents on April 15, 1924, Button announced that the institution had insufficient funds to finish the school year. Young responded he would provide an interest-free loan of $10,000 to run the school the rest of the year. Button also attributed Morehead's early building program to the efforts of Allie Young, who as a state senator secured appropriations of $1,220,000 during the four legislative sessions from 1924 to 1930. Even Mrs. Button, while denying that Allie Young played a major role in locating the school at Morehead, admitted that he performed an important service in obtaining money for the new school.

At the first meeting of the Board of Regents, that body decided to secure the services of the firm, Olmsted Brothers of Boston, to survey the grounds and draw up an architectural and landscaping plan for the campus. In carrying out their suggestions, Morehead State began creating a collection of Tudor-Gothic buildings that many still regard as the most beautiful part of the campus. The old Administration Building, now renovated into a very different Rader Hall, was completed in 1926. It housed administrative and faculty offices, classrooms, the library, post office, and bookstore. Allie Young Hall, a women's dormitory, was completed later that same year. In 1928 both Thompson Hall, a men's dormitory, and Fields Hall, a women's dormitory named for the wife of Governor William J. Fields of Olive Hill, were finished. Appointed to Morehead State's original Board of Regents, Mrs. Fields was the first woman to serve as a regent. All these buildings plus the power plant were constructed at a total cost of less than a million dollars!

But there were clouds on the horizon. The Efficiency Commission Report in early 1924 predicted failure for Morehead and Murray and condemned their location in small towns. Commission members feared that in such small places the schools could never train an adequate number of teachers each year. The commission recommended relocating some existing normal schools or establishing new ones and placing all four normal schools under one state board. The next General Assembly, however, totally ignored the first suggestion, while taking the opposite position on the second. Rather than creating any kind of central board, it moved the control of Morehead and Murray out of the hands of the State Board of Education and placed them under their own four-member boards, appointed by the governor, with the state Superintendent of Public Instruction serving as an ex-officio member and chairman of each board, in keeping with the manner in which Eastern and Western were already being administered.

## Morehead State Normal School and Teachers College, 1926-1930

In 1926 the General Assembly granted Morehead State the right to confer four-year college degrees and changed the school's name to Morehead State Normal School and Teachers College. The transition from state normal schools to state teachers colleges was made by most similar institutions across the nation between 1900 and 1926; hence, Morehead was one of the last schools to make this change. Having been started primarily to train elementary teachers, Morehead State could now begin the training of secondary teachers at a time when high school enrollment in the United States was booming; between 1910 and 1920 enrollment in American secondary schools more than doubled. The Kentucky legislature expressed further support of Morehead and Murray, not only by changing them into teachers colleges but also by providing appropriations to enable them to expand their campuses and faculties.

The Morehead faculty noted with great pride the success of Allie Young in continuing to channel money to the Morehead campus. A faculty meeting in 1927 passed a resolution "recognizing the great services rendered in the establishment, organization, and building of the said school by Judge Allie Young, and believing that his services will be needed in the next legislature and that he can do more for the institution than any other man who might represent our district." Hence, the faculty requested he become a candidate for re-election to the state Senate and called upon "all friends of the school to support him in this candidacy."

Morehead State students, however, were becoming alarmed that perhaps Allie Young was exerting too much control over their campus. Early in 1927, students carried a signed petition to President Button and the Board of Regents, asking them "to consider our wishes and rights" on such claims that students were being charged excessively for "the upkeep of the institution," cafeteria prices must be adjusted downward, registration fees should be removed from the general fund and placed in student activities "to make life more bearable in the institution," and the president's hands were being tied "by some force unknown to us," a possible reference to Allie Young. Students also requested that scholarships be based on "student needs" rather than "athletic ability," money be distributed equally in

"providing opportunities for girls and boys," and a school doctor be provided. During chapel the following week Button reported that Professor W. L. Jayne had driven him to Louisville over the weekend (the first

*Henry C. Haggan, member of the original faculty of Morehead State, and dormitory director during the early days of the institution.*

43

president never owned an automobile) for a meeting with Allie Young. Prefacing his report with "I am authoroized to say," Button informed the students which of their demands had been approved.

Morehead State retained many features from its days as a church-related institution. For example, daily chapel was still considered very important. The order of the 10 a.m. daily chapel included the following activities: a song by choir and congregation; announcements; Scripture reading and prayer; and the feature of the day, whether a speech or musical program.

Throughout the Twenties, Morehead State was concerned about becoming accredited. In December 1927, Button and Dean J. L. Chambers reported to the faculty on their experiences at a conference of the Southern Association of Colleges and Secondary Schools, in Jacksonville, Florida. Although they had intended to ask for accreditation, when they discovered that sixteen other teachers colleges were also applying for membership, they decided not to make an application for membership but to ask for an inspection the next year. In the meantime, success was achieved on the state scene. At a faculty meeting in January 1928, an announcement was made that Morehead State had been admitted to full membership in the Kentucky College Association and Dean Chambers was appointed as one of its directors. That spring's commencement program carried a statement from Frank L. McVey, president of the University of Kentucky, that Morehead's graduates would be admitted to advanced study at the University.

Morehead State's admission to membership in the Kentucky College Association encouraged the Button administration to continue its efforts towards accreditation by the Southern Association as well as by the American Association of Teachers Colleges. Early in 1929, President Button requested the assistance of Paul P. Boyd, dean of the College of Arts and Sciences, and Registrar Ezra L. Gillis, both of the University of Kentucky, to gather expert advice on necessary changes to insure accreditation by the Southern Association. After visiting Morehead State, Boyd and Gillis submitted their suggestions, along with a recommendation for a general survey of the college. In January 1929, the Board of Regents commissioned Frank L. McVey, president of the University of Kentucky, along with Charles H. Judd and George Allen Works of the University of Chicago, to review the situation of the college and recommend needed changes. Their findings could then be used in preparation for a December 1929 meeting in Lexington, when Morehead's bid for full membership in the Southern Association would be taken under consideration. Little did Button realize he would be demoted during this process! The faculty learned in the fall of 1929 that the Board of Regents had granted permission for making formal application for entrance into the Southern Association and to expend whatever money might be necessary to bring the school up to the standards of the Association. In November 1929, Joseph E. Avent of the College of Education at the University of Tennessee arrived on the Morehead State campus to inspect the school in connection with its application for accreditation in the Association.

### The McVey Report

Two significant reports have been requested in the history of Morehead State—the McVey Report in 1929 and the Albright Report in the 1980s. In neither case did the institution's president survive long enough to carry out their findings!

The McVey Report concluded that Morehead State had reached a turning point by the end of the 1920s but had not displayed the growth that might be expected. The Morehead Board of Regents met in March 1929 at Maxwell House, McVey's residence on the campus of the University of Kentucky, to review the report. During this session they proposed Button's resignation, the dismissal of ten faculty members, and the granting of leaves of absence to six other teachers who had not even made such a request! Regent Allie Young made the motion concerning Button's resignation and the changes affect-

*This admissions poster for the 1925-26 school year at Morehead State Normal School advertised the school's free tuition and $17 monthly room and board rates. The bottom photo shows the campus when MSU became a state institution in 1922. From left are Withers Hall, men's dormitory; Burgess Hall, library, chapel and offices; Hargis Hall, classroom building; and Hodson Hall, women's dormitory.*

ing about one-half the faculty. The board minutes, however, listed no reasons for firing these teachers. Button, who did not recommend their dismissals, knew nothing about the matter until it was brought up at the board meeting.

Neither did the faculty know anything until they received notices of dismissal, signed by Judge Senff, secretary of the board. They were simply informed their "services would not be needed" after September 1, 1929. No reasons were given. Upon the expiration of their "leaves of absence," the six other faculty members would not be rehired since they had not requested the leaves. Judge Senff explained: "The action of the Board in relieving certain teachers and granting leaves of absence to others for further preparation was done to increase the standard of efficiency."

The president claimed he was forced out. The relationship be-

tween Button and Allie Young had been strained for some time because of questions about school management. Among other things,
Young had been galled when Button asked for the resignation of his
son, Taylor, who had been hired twice as college business manager in
spite of Button's wishes to the contrary. Button's resignation became
effective on July 24, 1929, at which time he was made chaplain of
the college and assistant field representative for a year before being
named President Emeritus. While some expected the seventy-five
page McVey Report to cast light on these unusual events, it was not
made public. Judge Senff refused to make the report available without the consent of the Board of Regents.

The McVey Report expressed major concern over the small
number of volumes in the library. Morehead State's library opened
in 1923 with a collection of 4,360 books donated by the Christian
Church and the old Morehead Normal School; it had a book budget
of $500. Until 1929, the library was located in Burgess Hall, which
stood on the site of the present Camden-Carroll Library. At the
time of the report the college library contained between 4,000 and
5,000 volumes, considerably below the minimum of 8,000, then recommended by the Southern Association. Especially noted were the
inadequacies of reference materials and periodicals, particularly
standard scientific journals. Housed in one room of Burgess Hall, the
library needed a separate building of its own. The committee also
recommended the selection of a qualified librarian whose training
and salary would rank with that of a department head. By early fall
of 1929 the library had 8,000 books and was expecting 12,000, perhaps unrealistically, by the time the Southern Association met in
December.

The McVey Report blamed Morehead State for employing too
many poorly trained teachers. One is forced to question whether the
report was simply a device used to dismiss certain unwanted faculty
members in spite of their having more than met the necessary educational requirements. For example, Professor S. M. McGuire held a

master's degree from the University of Kentucky and was "eminently qualified" for his position as principal of the high school or normal department. Bettie Robinson, English teacher, held a B.A. from Georgetown College and an M.A., along with a supervisor's certificate, from Columbia University. To enhance her competency in teaching English, she had spent the previous summer in England and Scotland. Lola Traylor, teacher of modern languages, was a University of Kentucky graduate, who held a master's degree from Columbia University. (Rather than recommending her dismissal, the committee had suggested a small amount of further preparation might enable her to become head of the foreign language department.) The rest of the sixteen dismissed faculty members either had degrees or diplomas in special departments such as music and speech. Thus the Board of Regents in several cases may have used the committee report to get rid of whomever they wished. Obviously the Board was not carrying out the recommendations of the committee, which had declined to specify which teachers and other personnel should be dismissed. Instead, the report focused on four major areas of weakness relating to the administration and organization of the college: failure to arrive at a clear delineation of responsibilities for the president and the Board of Regents; an excessive number of administrative officers; inability to obtain competent administrative staff members; and failure to put together an annual budget, including expected income along with expenditures.

The McVey Report devoted the most space to the first area. The school's problem in the 1920s derived from the failure of the president to provide leadership. The report spelled out in considerable detail the duties and functions of a president, who should in the first place have a doctorate degree and administrative experience on the college level. Morehead's difficulties were traced to "a loose organization; absence of a definite understanding of duties; and the fact that the purpose of the school has not been thoroughly worked out." The report clearly implicated Button, who had already been on the job six years, and would have called for Button's resignation had he not already expressed his intentions of stepping down.

At the same time, the McVey Report severely reprimanded the Board of Regents for overstepping its boundaries by taking over responsibilities rightfully belonging to the president. The document concluded that a dominant personality on the Board of Regents—Allie Young—never permitted the president the necessary freedom to manage the school. The committee faulted the board's authoritarian manner of dismissing the faculty without involving the president. The same principle applied to promotions and changes in salary. Moreover a certain looseness of organization encouraged faculty and staff to ignore the president's authority and deal directly with board members. The Board of Regents found it easy to overstep its areas of responsibility because of Button's gentle, easy-going inactivity while making unrealistic efforts to please everyone. His weakness as chief executive was demonstrated, for example, by his admission to a 1925 board meeting that he had been unable to get a report on the financial condition of the school from his treasurer and had then implored the regents to request such a report!

The committee concluded this portion of the report by recommending a reorganization of the Board of Regents, making it, among other things, more representative of the school's mountain and Big Sandy Valley constituency.

A second problem area was an excessive number of administrators. The college's enrollment was insufficient to justify the employment of three major full-time administrators—president, dean, and registrar. The committee recommended doing away with the position of dean and having his professional duties carried out either by the President or the registrar.

The third charge—incompetent administrative staff members—was based primarily upon two serious incidents. Sam Bradley, college treasurer, was allegedly involved in a "misapplication of funds," as he could not account for $200,000, a loss that might have deeply affected the future of the college had not the Board of Regents arranged with Aetna Casualty and Surety Company to protect college funds. Bradley was promptly dismissed. The second incident involved the dean of the faculty, J. M. Chambers, who had recommended students for graduation and teaching certificates who had not fulfilled the necessary requirements, and who, the Board of Regents discovered, had been taking money from book companies in return for displaying their books on campus.

After Chambers' dismissal, the board on Button's recommendation, chose William H. Vaughan as his replacement. A committee, composed of Dean Vaughan, W. L. Jayne, and Warren C. Lappin, was then appointed to investigate the former dean's actions. Their findings were presented to the next board meeting. In addition to the previous charges against Chambers, the members learned that his wife had been paid by the American Book Company to exhibit its books at Morehead State. The committee also turned up evidence that Dean Chambers had allowed as many as fifty individuals to receive high school diplomas without sufficient credits. Furthermore, certain individuals had been receiving academic credits while employees of the institution, which was then against board policy.

The fourth problem area concerned the college's operation without a budget. Although the Board of Regents had approved the establishment of a budget system as early as its second meeting, in May 1924, Button had done nothing in this regard. With a Yale Ph.D. in economics, McVey was baffled that Morehead State had no estimates of the year's cost of operation or revenues. Failure to put together an annual budget exacerbated the college's financial problems. In spite of receiving liberal appropriations from the state, the college had lacked sufficient funds upon different occasions to pay current operating expenses. The committee recommended establishment of a budget, along with a bookkeeping system coordinated with the budget.

The McVey Report included other more specific recommendations: More emphasis should be placed upon secondary education. A rural demonstration school should be established to furnish a model for prospective teachers. Morehead State should not be attempting to produce agriculture teachers and therefore did not need to keep its farm. The English department should incorporate classes in public speaking. Physical education classes should be offered for women as well as men. Correspondence courses should be dropped immediately and all extension courses taught exclusively by college faculty. The college should organize a separate department of buildings and grounds, headed by "a trained engineer from an engineering college," who had experience in building as well as in plant management. And College Boulevard, which abruptly ended just beyond the Breckinridge Training School, should be extended.

Morehead State included a high school as well as a college. The McVey Report defined the institution's greatest weakness in teaching as a failure to make a proper distinction between the two levels. The committee found evidence that a high school level of instruction frequently prevailed in college courses. "Naming an institution a college does not make it one," it stated. Morehead State can become a college "only when it has students of maturity and a faculty that by training is prepared to maintain the standards of work" characteristic of a good college. The report expressed doubts that Morehead's faculty, with some exceptions, was equal to the task of teaching on the college level.

Morehead's educational program throughout the 1920s consisted of two divisions—the normal school and the college. A student was required to complete eight years of elementary schooling before enrolling in the normal school. A course in rural school management was considered important for each teacher since the majority of rural elementary schools in Kentucky were either one or two-room schools. The Normal School also offered a methods course allowing students to prepare their own lesson plans as well as to observe teachers conducting their classes. Another course was designed to permit students to do practice teaching in the elementary grades. The McVey Report, however, indicated that inadequate facilities made it virtually impossible for a student to do practice teaching. In an attempt to upgrade academic standards, the Board of Regents passed a resolution in December 1926 requiring department heads to have either a master's or a doctorate degree and all of the faculty to have a bachelor's degree by the fall of 1930, with provisions for leaves of absence to facilitate reaching such goals.

In May 1927 Morehead State produced its first graduates—twenty-seven were given life certificates, ninety-one graduated from the normal school and three received the bachelor's degree, including S. M. Hunt, Morehead; C. D. Mayse, Sandy Hook; and Russell

*The Morehead Normal School basketball team in 1900 is shown in hats, suits, and ties, while standing on an outside court near the present Camden-Carroll Library.*

Williamson, Inez. Morehead granted 573 provisional elementary certificates between 1927 and 1930 to 404 women and 169 men. The school year of 1929-30 was the first to see more students enrolled in college than in high school. Summer school throughout the 1920s had almost the same number of high school students as college. The school's enrollment, excluding summer school, jumped from less than a hundred students in 1923 to 788 in 1929. The student body continued to be provincial from 1923 to 1926, with more than 90 percent coming from Rowan County and counties located within a thirty-three mile radius. With 235 students, Rowan County had the largest enrollment at Morehead State; the next largest counties were: Carter, 114; Elliott, 90; Bath, 78; and Morgan, 71. Morehead State enrolled only two out-of-state students—from West Virginia—during that period.

Each student was required to have a major, consisting of twenty-four to thirty-four semester hours and two minors—one of eighteen hours and the other of at least twelve hours. Thirteen bachelor's degrees were awarded from 1927 to 1929. A vestige of Morehead's former religious affiliation included a required course in ethical education in order to inculcate moral values and right conduct in future teachers.

As early as the 1920s, Morehead leaders understood the need for a training school. Before Breckinridge was built, the training school was housed in the basement of Burgess Hall. By 1928 plans for a separate training school were being drawn up. The McVey Report the following year recommended that Morehead administrators give consideration to developing only one school that would serve the needs of everyone in the entire community, at a different site from the one on the campus then being considered. The school should also be financed jointly with the local community. Morehead State rejected these recommendations and bore all the cost in erecting a training school in 1931 on the original campus site. But the college accepted the committee's suggestion that the head of the training school and his faculty should be members of the education department of the college.

## Student Life in the Twenties

When the school was taken over by the state in 1923, there were only four buildings. The entire campus was located between what is today Rader Hall and Button Auditorium from east to west and between the Camden-Carroll Library and University Boulevard from north to south. Burgess Hall (completed in 1902 and named for Mrs. A. O. Burgess, national president of the Christian Women's Board of Missions) was a multi-purpose building which served as administration building, auditorium, library, bookstore, and president's home. The latter consisted of two rooms and a bath; the sitting room, however, doubled as a bookstore. Hargis Hall contained six large lecture rooms. Hodson Hall, girls' dormitory, was a three-story frame building with only one bathroom. As enrollment increased, it was necessary to post a schedule for each girl to bathe. A small outhouse was available near the rear of the residence hall for overcrowding. Withers Hall, boys' dorm, was a two-story building with two baths. Professor Henry Haggan served as its director. The Haggan apartment included four rooms and a bath, which left only one bath for the boys. "I don't know whether there were fewer boys or whether boys tend to bathe less frequently than girls, but it never became necessary to post a bath schedule," Haggan asserted.

Electricity was limited on campus to seven hours per day. At 4:00 each afternoon a whistle blew for the lights to be turned on, and they went off soon after the train passed through Morehead around 11 p.m. Passengers getting off the train on Railroad Street hurried to the hotel, the campus, or to their homes before the lights went out. One or two kerosene lamps had to be issued to each dormitory room because sometimes the current went off unexpectedly.

All students were required to be in their rooms by 7:30 each evening. Rooms were inspected every morning—often by the president's wife. The entire campus had only three telephones, a far cry from the 2,700 of today, including 1,800 in the residence halls. Five days a week, students assembled in front of Burgess Hall and marched into chapel in two lines. Since Haggan had considerable marching experience in World War I, it fell his lot to be in charge of the chapel lineup. Medical facilities were limited to one room in Withers Hall and one room in Hodson Hall which were set aside for students who became ill. However, there was no nurse. On one occasion a well-meaning citizen begged for the privilege of nursing a sick student back to health. She assured Haggan, "I know just what to do for him, because my husband died of the very same thing!" A well behind Withers Hall supplied the campus with water which was pumped to three horse troughs in the attic of Burgess Hall. These troughs then supplied water to all the campus buildings.

Morehead was not a "suitcase college" then since transportation to campus was a problem for many students. Those without cars or too far from the railroad either walked or rode on horses, mules, or jolt wagons. Sometimes, a student and his father would each ride horseback to campus; then the father rode back home, leading his child's horse. With these means of travel, young people opted to remain on campus until the end of the semester in lieu of taking the long walk home. Many roads were impassable during the winter months. The only paved road in Rowan County in 1923 extended from Brady Curve at the west end of town to the Licking River. Students coming to Morehead from counties to the west had to pay 25 cents to cross a toll bridge over the Licking River. The bridge owner, however, gave free toll to students carrying a pass from Dean Lewis.

Roads were likewise a problem inside Morehead. Emma Shader (Sample), the only living member of the original faculty of Morehead State Normal School, remembers getting her slippers stuck many times in the mud on Main Street. To prevent being splattered in wet weather, homes and other buildings on Main Street were four or five feet above the street, which explains why today one must walk up several steps to enter such structures as the old Battson Drug Store building on the corner of Main Street and University Boulevard. Georgia Ramey Barker, a student in the late Twenties, suggested that "hardly anyone had cars but the cars we did have would get stuck up in the quagmire." During extremely wet weather, one local gentleman repeatedly used his mules to drag cars out of the deep, muddy ruts in front of the court house. Crosthwait describes Morehead as a "country town" which set aside the first Monday of each month as Court Day when "crowds came to town and passed around the gossip of the day. There were many hound dogs" on hand as well. Horses in large numbers were tied up to hitching posts around the courthouse.

*George D. Downing coached every sport and served as athletic director at Morehead State from 1924 to 1935. The institution's former athletic dormitory was named in his honor. When such dorms later were banned by the NCAA, Downing Hall became an administrative building.*

The lives of students at Morehead State, often called "that little school in the hills" during the Twenties, were regulated to a degree that would be incomprehensible in the 1990s. Since the administration was looked upon as acting in the place of parents (in *loco parentis*), the college came up with a number of rules of conduct between males and females. A meeting in 1923 decided that between 7:50 a.m. and 4 p.m., "boys and girls were not to converse with one another," but spend all their time either in the classroom or in studying. The faculty made rules a little less severe in 1924-25. At the first faculty meeting of that year a stipulation was made that stated young men could take young ladies to "shows" on Saturday nights and call on them on Saturday evenings from 7:30 to 10. Young women could go to town on Wednesdays and Saturdays "without permission." During summer school of 1927 the Discipline Committee suspended two girls for the rest of the term, "on account of automobile riding at night." Shortly before, an announcement had been made in chapel that "all persons violating the rule about going out at night from Allie Young Hall would be automatically suspended from school."

Throughout the Roaring Twenties, faculty and Discipline Committee meetings were constantly dealing with problems related to drinking. One of the very first meetings of that Committee during the institution's first year as a state school was concerned with disorderly conduct at the men's dormitory the previous Saturday night, when four students had been drinking. But since two of them had already "gone home on the early morning train," the committee suspended one student for the remainder of the semester, while the other was confined to the campus for two weeks. In March 1926 a young man appeared before the Discipline Committee and confessed that he, along with others, had been drinking the previous night but revealed to the school authorities the identity of a Morehead barber who went to get the whiskey for them. The students were placed on probation.

Smoking was also a great concern. A 1924 decision asserted that boys were not allowed to smoke on campus—it was considered unnecessary to mention the girls. Smoking in buildings and on walks during the mid-twenties was absolutely prohibited; this rule applied to everybody, faculty as well as students. During summer school 1927, the Morehead State faculty passed a rule against smoking on campus or in buildings, except on the Boulevard and in the boys' dormitory.

But a number of activities outside the classroom were encouraged among the students. There were religiously-oriented organizations, such as the YMCA and YWCA, and three literary societies—Button Literary Society, James Lane Allen Literary Society, and a Drama Club. The institution published its first newspaper, the *More-Head Light,* in 1927. The masthead of the first issue contained six question marks for its name. William J. Sample, editor-in-chief, offered a prize of $5 for the best suggestion. Mrs. Picket M. Snedegar, a sophomore, won the prize with her suggestion of the *More-Head Light.* An appointed committee selected the *Trail Blazer* as the paper's new name two years later. Censorship of the press had already become an issue in the 1920s. Since objections were raised over several jokes in the paper, an administrative directive was issued, stating that its "copy should be brought to the President's office for O.K. before being sent to the press." The first college yearbook or annual, the *Raconteur,* was published in 1927. Morehead State had a chorus, band, and orchestra during the decade. A debating society was organized in 1924. And a major unique feature of the school's extracurricular activities included county clubs, thereby encouraging mutual association of students from their home areas.

Documentation on athletics is scant before 1930. Sporadic references are made to basketball in Morehead Normal School. Indications are that baseball was the major sporting event on campus before the 1920s. At any rate, old timers claim the local team was the best to be found in the mountain region during those years. After the school came under the jurisdiction of the commonwealth, baseball was the first organized sport with a coach to appear on campus. George D. Downing, a 1920 graduate of the University of Kentucky, was employed in 1924 as Morehead State's head coach of all sports and director of the physical education department. Downing had earned varsity letters at UK in baseball, football, and track.

During the fall semester of 1926, J. M. Clayton, a Morehead businessman, sponsored a contest to select a nickname for the athletic teams. Eunice "Peaches" Ellis (Cecil) won the $10 first prize with "Bald Eagles," which eventually was shortened to "Eagles" for the sake of convenience.

Morehead State played intercollegiate football and baseball from the time it became a state-supported school, but its basketball program was not added until 1928, the year the college became a member of the West Virginia Athletic Conference since there was no similar conference in Kentucky. The school's best season in football during the Twenties featured Coach George D. Downing's team in 1928, with seven victories and two losses; only Xavier and Marshall defeated the Eagles. Morehead defeated Eastern by a score of 18-0 that season and smothered Alderson-Broaddus and Sue Bennett by a combined score of 101-0. The "M" Club sponsored Morehead State's first Homecoming Day as the Eagles defeated Rio Grande College by a wide margin of 26-0. In basketball, Coach Downing's team of 1929 won nine games while losing only three. In May 1924 the faculty passed a resolution of preference for a woman coach for girls' basketball teams and other athletic teams in schools and colleges. Furthermore, it went on record for the appointment of a woman to membership on all local athletic boards and councils as well as on the State Athletic Association in Kentucky.

## Ending the "Roaring Twenties"

Since Button would serve no longer as President after September 1, 1929, a committee consisting of Governor Flem D. Sampson,

Allie W. Young, and Earl W. Senff was appointed to find his successor. On August 1, 1929, they recommended John Howard Payne, Superintendent of Schools in Maysville, for the position and the Board unanimously adopted their recommendation. Payne took over as Morehead's second President in the fall semester of 1929. In spite of the McVey Report's conclusion that the college was administratively overstaffed for its enrollment, the new president decided to retain Vaughan as dean of the faculty rather than divide his duties between himself and the registrar.

At the opening of the fall semester in 1929 Button introduced the new president to the Morehead State faculty then quietly stepped aside. His twenty-seven years at the Morehead helm helped bring a smooth transition from the frontier atmosphere of the 1880s to that of a peaceful community taking pride in its educational institution. He started the transition from a successful church-related normal school to a state institution of higher learning. Holding the record for longevity among the school's leaders, he built up a reservoir of good will and loyal following among the institution's constituencies that future leaders would need when they endeavored to bring about necessary changes. With the powerful assistance of Allie Young, he began one of the institution's two greatest eras of campus-building, at a time when financial resources were most difficult to secure. His kindness and gentility of spirit brought him and the college a great deal of affection from the people of Eastern Kentucky.

A decided air of expectancy was evident in 1929 since the college was now led by Payne, a professional educator. The McVey Report had predicted that with proper leadership the institution would take significant strides forward. Even the stock market crash that fall and the onslaught of the Great Depression failed to dampen the enthusiasm generally associated with beginning a new era.

# *Chapter 3*

# Morehead State Teachers College: Years of Turmoil, 1930-1948

$\mathcal{I}$n the 1930s and the war years, Morehead State Teachers College finally evolved from a denomination-oriented normal school to a state institution of higher learning. During these eighteen years, the college faced three great trials: the Great Depression, World War II, and the loss of accreditation by two national associations, all resulting from circumstances out of its control. To complicate matters, the institution had to face these troubled times in the midst of instability associated with frequently changing presidents. Morehead State inaugurated four leaders — John Howard Payne, Harvey A. Babb, William H. Vaughan, and William Jesse Baird— during this period. In addition, Dean Warren C. Lappin served the first of two stints as acting president.

## John Howard Payne:  A Tragic Figure, 1929-1935

The year 1930 saw the college inaugurating a new president and  receiving its third name in eight years.  Yet, Morehead State entered the new decade with major cause for concern.  The McVey Report had indicated the need for major changes before the institution could be accredited.  President Button, along with one-half the faculty, had just been deposed.  The school still retained some qualities of a church-related institution.  And it had yet to resolve the roles of its president and a dominating Board of Regents.

Morehead State also had to deal with such questions as the continuing argument over its location and the justification for a state college in the region.  Would the Great Depression's effects upon

Eastern Kentucky allow enough money for the region's youth to finance a college education? How would this economic catastrophe affect Morehead State's building and educational programs, its faculty, and its students? The new president had to cope with these questions while his predecessor, with reason enough to be upset over how the institution treated him, remained on the staff and looked over his shoulder. Thus, when John Howard Payne was inaugurated in the spring of 1930, he faced challenges that would daunt any man.

Everything about Payne, however, inspired confidence. Many Moreheadians thought that he "looked and sounded like a president." When Ted Crosthwait was a student, he saw Payne as a "big man with ruddy complexion, fairly heavy build, loud voice, an orator who loved to quote poetry, made gracious speeches and was very impressive on the platform." However, he was "a little bit aloof with the townspeople." Another student, Jeane Pritchard Keel, says the president "always struck me as being erect and correct in everthing he said and did." Lucille Caudill Little recalls that this "tall, handsome, in-

*John Howard Payne, Morehead State's second president, 1929-35. Although one of the two major builders of the "crescent moon" original campus, no facility was named in his honor.*

telligent" leader was forced to engage in "the game of politics yet didn't like to play the game." And Ralph Hudson, art teacher, characterized Payne as "a silver tongued orator."

The new president's educational background contrasted greatly with the ministerial training of his predecessor. After graduating from the University of Kentucky, he received a master's degree from Columbia University, whose college of education ranked near the top in its field. As a platform orator and extemporaneous debater, he had few equals. Already in great demand as a public speaker within the state, the president soon gained attention in national circles, as evidenced by an invitation to address the annual convention of the National Education Association in Los Angeles in 1931. The president, with roots firmly embedded in Eastern Kentucky, was asked to speak on "What A Teachers College Can Do for Rural Education." The people of Morehead exhibited great pride both in the newly-completed President's Home and in its first occupant.

Payne's inauguration in the spring of 1930 featured an impressive array of educators in the newly-constructed College Auditorium. With state Superintendent of Public Instruction W. C. Bell presiding, the program included Rainey T. Wells, President of Murray State, speaking for the state's colleges, and Maldon B. Adams, President of Georgetown College, representing private institutions. The keynote speaker, Robert Maynard Hutchins, President of the University of Chicago who later became one of America's most widely-respected educators, addressed an audience of 1,300 on "The Trend of Education." His father, William J. Hutchins, President of Berea College, gave the invocation for the inaugural ceremony.

In his inaugural address, Payne set standards which would be difficult for future presidents to match. Recognizing the importance of the institution's church-related background, he stated, "We want the spiritual note to be sounded in all of our teaching" since "religion is fundamental in the life of any people." At the same time he pledged his commitment to academic freedom and the search for truth. Aware of the role which politics had played, he expressed hope that the state's institutions might be spared the wasting effects of politics. Finally, Payne promised that Morehead State would combine good teaching with a quality of research commensurate with its purpose and needs.

An editorial in the *Louisville Courier-Journal* the next day commended Payne's dedication to research and challenged all state colleges in Kentucky to create rivalries in research activities comparable to those in athletics. Viewing research as a distinctive function of even a teacher-training institution, the editorial concluded: "It is the stamp of a first-class teacher, this ability to quicken intelligent curiosity." Payne followed up his inaugural's emphasis on faculty research with a front page statement in the *Trail Blazer*, challenging students themselves to pursue learning. The president invited every student to fall in love with learning since "she will bring you honor, distinction, power, and happiness as long as you both do live."

Rhetoric itself proved insufficient to change long-time practices. Within two months after the heralded and much-praised inauguration, heavy-handed politics was again the rule when Flem D. Sampson, Republican governor, changed the composition of the Board of Regents by replacing two of Allie Young's Democratic friends with two Republicans. Young, however, continued to dominate the Board.

But Morehead State immediately achieved success on a most important front. While chances for national accreditation were remote during the previous decade, recognition came quickly in the 1930s. Having been accepted as a member of the Kentucky Association of Colleges and Universities as early as 1928, Morehead State received accreditation from the Southern Association of Colleges and Schools in December 1930. Campus reaction was predictably jubilant, with the *Trail Blazer* reaching a crescendo of ecstasy with a front-page overstatement, "Morehead can now take its seat among the mighty. Its credits bear the same distinction as the credits of Vanderbilt, Tulane, Georgia Tech, or the University of North Carolina." Soon afterwards, Payne announced that the institution had applied for admission into the American Association of Teachers Colleges—an application that was accepted the following year.

Still, Morehead State found it difficult to meet certain minimum standards of the Southern Association. For example, in responding to the school's first triennial report in 1934, the Southern Association pointed out four deficiencies: Educational expenditures per student were too low; its ratio of students to faculty was unusually high, a situation made worse by involving faculty in conducting correspondence courses and extension work in addition to handling on-campus schedules; the library was sub par both in expenditures for books and in its use as shown by circulation figures; and few students were pursuing other degrees after graduation. In spite of these shortcomings, the institution managed to correct deficiencies sufficiently to avoid probationary status.

The Southern Association's visitation committee was most impressed throughout the 1930s with the school's physical plant. Following the blueprint of college Gothic-Tudor architecture laid out in 1923 by Olmsted Brothers, Button and Payne produced one of the two greatest building eras in the school's history at a time when materials and labor were cheap and money was scarce. From 1926 to 1935, the campus blossomed with new buildings dotting the hillside overlooking the town: President's Home, Senff Natatorium, Auditorium-Gymnasium, Fields Hall, Johnson Camden Library, Allie Young Hall, Administration Building, Thompson Hall, Breckinridge Training School, and Jayne Memorial Stadium. In 1933 the Board of Regents received word that a loan for building a new waterworks system and a new heating plant had been approved by the Federal Emergency Relief Administration. This project was also financed through a grant from the Public Works Administration as well as the sale of state bonds. The new heating plant, located between the south fork of Triplett Creek and the Chesapeake & Ohio railroad tracks, was completed in 1937. And shortly before the Payne administration ended, the Public Works Administration approved $460,000 for a four-story science building and a second dormitory for men. Thus, Franklin D. Roosevelt's New Deal assured that the building of the campus would continue in spite of the Great Depression and insufficient state support for the institution.

Morehead State never followed a plan in the naming of its buildings. Consequently, they were named for a hodgepodge of individuals: state politicians and their wives, a college president, other administrators, and faculty members. Senff Natatorium was chosen to honor Judge Earl Senff, a member of the Board of Regents and its secretary for eight years, who previously had served on the committee that chose Morehead as a college site. In 1935 the Board of Regents contemplated naming the Auditorium-Gymnasium after the school's first president, but this decision was delayed for several board meetings and finally dropped. Charles R. Spain, Morehead State's sixth president revived the proposal in 1953, and the board voted unanimously to honor the school's co-founder in this manner. Fields Hall honored Mrs. Dora Fields, wife of the governor. Fields, governor from 1924 to 1928, provided impetus for the legislature's authorization of a $25 million bond issue to upgrade the normal schools at Morehead and Murray. The library was named for U.S. Senator Johnson N. Camden, Jr., of Versailles. Why? He had been appointed—not elected—to serve as a Senator for less than a year (1914-15). Perhaps Young bestowed this honor in payment for an old political debt. The name of Judge Allie Young was given to the first girls' dormitory. The Administration Building, constructed in 1926, was renamed Rader Hall in 1965, a year after the sudden death of Clifford R. Rader, who had been head of the division of social sciences. Thompson Hall was named in honor of James H. Thompson, Speaker of the House in 1922 whose five appointees to the Selection Committee all voted for Morehead to be the location for the college.

*After Burgess Hall was torn down in 1929, groundbreaking began for the Johnson Camden Library, later Camden-Carroll Library. Note the mule-powered excavators.*

Breckinridge Training School honored Robert Jefferson Breckinridge, sixth Superintendent of Public Instruction, who was often referred to as the "father of the Kentucky public school system." Since Dean William Vaughan's dissertation was titled "Robert Jefferson Breckinridge as an Educational Administrator," perhaps he had a hand in naming the training school. Jayne Memorial Stadium was a tribute to Professor William LeGrande Jayne, head of the college's extension department who died in 1930. East Men's Hall, completed in 1938, was called Mays Hall in the 1960s, for Jess T. Mays, who taught industrial arts at Morehead State for three decades. The Science Building, finished in 1937, was designated Lappin Hall in 1958, in appreciation of Warren C. Lappin, who had been a member of the old Morehead Normal School faculty and subsequently joined Morehead State Normal School as baseball coach in 1924. The

President's Home remains the only one of the original buildings never to have been named after some individual.

Morehead State's building program was remarkable, given the Great Depression's impact on the foundation of the nation's system of higher education. Budgets and professors' salaries were slashed, and sixteen colleges in America were discontinued in 1932 alone. Students found it difficult to pay their bills and were often undernourished and ill-clothed.

Payne and his Board of Regents were frequently pressed by financial problems during the Great Depression. In December 1931 Payne discussed the institution's financial situation with the faculty and requested that all departments be as conservative as possible. In January 1932 the board expressed alarm over Morehead State's finances. Board members decided to conduct a sale of used chairs, water heaters, and gasoline engines to obtain additional funds for operating the school. They planned to discontinue summer school in 1933 but changed their minds in a later meeting. Such actions were necessitated by the fact that the General Assembly reduced its appropriation for operating expenses from $281,351 in 1930 to $175,360 in 1933. While federal money was easier to obtain during the decade, state appropriations were only $193,000 by 1939. But Morehead State's enrollment remained steady during the latter half of the 1930s.

The hard times of the depression provided an excuse for reviving the question as to whether or not Morehead and Murray should have been established as state colleges. A bill was introduced in the 1932 legislature to close both schools and convert them into mental hospitals to serve as additional facilities for the existing insane asylums. A letter to the editor of the *Courier-Journal* argued that both colleges had been established solely for political reasons, and since neither college was necessary, the state could save $3,000,000 by closing them. The *Lexington Herald,* praising the legislature for introducing such a bill, argued that closing Morehead and Murray would divert generous sums of money to rural schools and under-paid rural teachers. The editorial resurrected the contention that, even if a state school were needed in Eastern Kentucky, it should have been located at Paintsville.

All of public education in Kentucky suffered for several decades because of a provision in the state constitution of 1891 that no public official in the state, except the governor, could be paid more than $5,000 a year. This included college presidents and faculty. Faculty members, already paid too little, suffered further during the depression. In the early 1930s faculty salaries ranged from $1,000 to $3,375, annually. Payne was soon able, however, to bring the institution's salary schedule up to the standards of the Southern Association. Great pride was taken in the fact that no full professor was making less than $3,000 for nine months. These already low salaries had to be cut when the Board of Regents in June 1932 slashed the income of all employees making over $100 per month by ten percent. Teachers, however, sometimes received additional compensation for extra jobs. Such was the case with two teachers—professor of education Ernest V. Hollis and mathematics professor James G. Black—who earned $150 a year each by operating the film projector for the college. But unlike some other institutions, teachers at Morehead State experienced no "payless paydays" in the early 1930s and were always compensated on time.

Students also suffered. The Appalachian region from which most of them came was one of the hardest hit sections of the United States. There were times when students literally could not afford to eat. Footballer John Fitch recalls that students were "depression kids; we didn't have money. When you asked a girl out for a date, you made sure it was dutch treat!" Since the college cafeteria was operating at a loss because of a decrease in student patronage, the board decided in 1931 that each dormitory student must purchase seven meal tickets, costing $5 apiece, for each nine-week period. This requirement was ineffectual since many students had insufficient

*This aerial view of Morehead State's campus was taken by Ralph Hudson, art instructor, in 1934. While Hudson was taking the picture, A. Y. Lloyd, history and political science instructor, secured him by clinging to his belt. The pilot used a cow pasture just outside Morehead as a landing field.*

funds to comply with it. Other indications of the students' financial difficulties were increases in the number of bad checks and in theft on campus. The board ordered the administration in September 1932 to collect on all the bad checks and not to accept any further checks from students. The extent of student financial problems influenced the faculty to go on record in January 1933 with the declaration that "public education should be free in Kentucky" and that "no tuition fees should be charged to students residing in Kentucky." Unable to go that far, the Board of Regents in June 1934 agreed with Payne's recommendation to establish a local group known as the

Morehead Foundation, whose purpose would be to provide loans for students. (This organization was not permanent and has no relationship to the current MSU Foundation, Inc.)

Morehead State's enrollment did not decline during the Great Depression! While American colleges as a whole suffered a ten percent decrease in enrollment from 1932 to 1934, Morehead State enjoyed an increase. A steady flow of students from the mountains of Eastern Kentucky increased the college's enrollment from some 300 students in 1929 to 840 in the spring semester of 1935. Nearly every room in the three dormitories and most available rooms in town were filled. Two factors explained this growth in enrollment: Many young people chose to attend college because they were unable to find work in Eastern Kentucky's depressed job market, and government student aid through such programs as the National Youth Administration and the Federal Emergency Relief Administration made schooling possible in spite of difficult times. Improvement in Eastern Kentucky's roads also made Morehead State more accessible and better able to serve the region. For example, a new highway built in the early 1930s connected Morehead with Flemingsburg, thereby shortening the distance from Morehead to Maysville by 65 miles. Previously the route to Maysville extended through Mt. Sterling. With typical excessive excitement, a *Trail Blazer* reporter asserted, "This new road to Flemingsburg means as much to Morehead as the building of the Union Pacific-Central Pacific did to the nation." A second new highway improved Morehead's connection with Elliott, Morgan, and other mountain counties.

And when the students arrived, they found a school rapidly changing from a denomination-oriented normal college into a state institution of higher learning. President Payne and Dean William H. Vaughan made an effective team in achieving many of the necessary changes earlier described in the McVey Report. Morehead State discontinued its normal school in 1931-32. The college's twelve departments expanded to sixteen, with the addition of speech, commerce, library science, and industrial arts. Course offerings increased from 165 in 1928-29 to 180 in 1936-37.

The continuing trend toward specialization helped explain the expansion of the college's curriculum. During the decade, biology, for example, added seven courses—ecology, embryology, dendrology, genetics, bacteriology, plant physiology, and histology. Expansion of the curriculum was also influenced by John Dewey's philosophy of education as a means of promoting the development of the whole person. Hence, the college curriculum provided students with the opportunity to develop healthy bodies, social responsibility, artistic appreciation, and utilitarian skills through such courses as art and music appreciation, sports for all seasons, typing, first aid, home nursing, and child care and development.

The curriculum also expanded as new teachers were added who desired to develop courses in their own specialties. This factor became increasingly important as Morehead State encouraged its faculty members to further their graduate training. Morehead State started granting leaves of absence to teachers who had been part of the faculty for at least seven years and who agreed to return for at least a year of service after their leave expired. The college used this technique to get more in line with constant demands by accrediting associations for additional faculty members with doctorates.

Most of Morehead State's curricular changes were prompted by the Council on Public Higher Education, created by the legislature in 1934 to oversee the public institutions of higher education, and by a new teacher certification law, which was also passed in the same year. The council standardized teacher education programs and thereby eliminated much confusion in teacher preparation. The certification law ended the common practices of issuing elementary certificates based upon less than two years of college courses and high school certificates based upon less than four years of college except in emergency situations. By 1940, 40 percent of those certified by Morehead State had either master's or bachelor's degrees.

Approximately 97 percent of the 576 receiving bachelor's degrees from 1934 to 1939 embarked on teaching careers.

The Payne-Vaughan team introduced a more professional approach to the operation of the college. For example, such a large number of students asked teachers to change grades in 1929-30 that Morehead State's Executive Committee ruled that any teacher wishing to change a grade must appear before the committee and present the reason, after which the committee would decide whether the change would be allowed. Vaughan also started the practice of submitting the names of those who were either graduating or receiving teacher certification for faculty approval.

In 1934 two of Morehead's faculty made the news. Henry Clay Haggan, professor of agriculture and his ten-year-old daughter, Mary, were kidnapped by an escaped prisoner from Joliet, Illinois, who jumped in the back seat of their car as they stopped at the red light in front of the old post office in Morehead. When they stopped for gas several miles out in the country, Haggan informed the kidnapper that he had no money. The intruder then furnished him with a ten-dollar bill to pay for the gas. As Haggan started to hand him the change, he told the professor to keep it since he would probably need the money to get home. The kidnapper put the Haggans out and sped away in the stolen automobile. In an hour and fifteen minutes, though, Maysville officers had arrested the culprit as he was about to cross the Ohio River.

In that same year Arthur Lloyd, professor of history, was reprimanded when accused of engaging in improper political activities. Judge Daniel Boone Caudill, Morehead attorney and newly-appointed member of the Board of Regents, requested an investigation to decide if Lloyd had led a campaign to persuade college students to vote illegally in Morehead for his (Caudill's) opponent in the race for circuit judge rather than encouraging them to return home to cast their ballots. Although Lloyd had recently returned from Vanderbilt with a Ph.D., his promotion to head the history department was delayed, pending the outcome of this investigation. While Lloyd did not lose his job, he was ordered not to participate in further political activities of this nature, after which he was made head of the department.

The local newspaper was a strong supporter of President Payne and Morehead State. In August 1934 the *Rowan County News* asserted that Payne had "shown the way." Assessing Payne's five-year presidency, an editorial stated, "We have seen a plant more than doubled," while Morehead State had advanced to being "a big fish" in the state's educational advancement. Payne never passed up an opportunity to express his pride in Morehead State's association with the mountain region. In an article written for the *Courier-Journal* in 1932, he boasted, "We are the only state institution located in the mountains" and thus think of ourselves as being a "mountain college." Although he was pleased that the institution's graduates occasionally taught in urban settings, the president regarded the school's primary mission as serving the needs of Kentucky's rural schools.

Payne's last year at Morehead State was marked by irony. His public leadership received its highest marks ever, while his private life, including family and health problems, drove him out of the presidency. His fellow educators in 1934-35 honored him with election to the presidency of the Eastern Kentucky Education Association, the Kentucky Education Association, and the Kentucky Association of Colleges and Universities. During the summer of 1935, Payne became one of only six recipients of the prestigious Carl Schurz Memorial Foundation fellowships which allowed him to spend twelve weeks in Germany and Austria, studying methods of language instruction in European colleges and universities. Accompanying him were presidents of colleges from New Jersey, New York, Virginia, and Wisconsin.

These accomplishments were mixed with elements of failure. Neither Payne's training as an educator nor his experiences as a public school superintendent had adequately prepared him to cope with the power structure at Morehead State. Allie Young continued to interject himself into the running of the school. Payne's unsuccessful attempts to deal with this reality may have contributed to an intestinal disorder, which necessitated major surgery in the fall of 1934. Two weeks after surgery, the president left his hospital bed in Richmond to attend the Morehead-Eastern football game being played there. Against his doctor's instruction, Payne left Richmond for Ashland, where he presided over the annual meeting of the Eastern Kentucky Education Association. After pushing himself to the breaking point, the exhausted Payne returned to his hospital room in Richmond.

Things grew progressively worse for President Payne in the spring of 1935. His wife suffered a nervous breakdown. The state's major newspapers published editorials in September 1935 attacking one of his sons. As these family problems began to take a toll on him, the president allegedly increased his dependence on alcohol and prescription drugs. Dean Vaughan, who presided over faculty meetings during the

*Harvey A. Babb, Morehead State's third president, 1935-40.*

summer of 1935 while Payne was in Europe, found it necessary to continue that role early in the fall semester of 1935-36 while the president grappled with his personal and family problems. Finally, the Board of Regents decided it had no alternative to dismissing Payne and removing him from office as of September 30, 1935. A few weeks later, the former president was confined to Eastern State Hospital in Lexington after a Rowan County grand jury's hearing judged him insane, based upon the testimony of two Morehead physicians, Dr. Everett D. Blair and Dr. G. C. Nickell, who attested that the former president was subject "to moods of violence" which may have been made worse by "the use of drugs." After a brief hospitalization, Payne recovered and lived another twenty years. In 1951, three years before his death, Payne was present at the inauguration of Morehead's sixth president, Charles R. Spain, in the College Auditorium, and was recognized by the master of ceremonies.

The Payne years were a time of great transition for the college. Morehead State experienced the passing of an era with the death of Frank C. Button in 1933 and Allie Young two years later. Forced out of the presidency in 1929, Button maintained a relationship with the school that he had led for 27 years. Button died at St. Joseph's Hospital in Lexington in April 1933 at the age of 69. He was buried in Lee Cemetery at the foot of the hillside where he had helped to build Morehead State and within the city limits of a town he had served in many capacities, including that of mayor.

Young's funeral was conducted in the College Auditorium on the campus of Morehead State. Judge Senff eulogized his close friend, praising his success as a lawyer with clients such as the Chesapeake and Ohio Railway and the Consolidated Coal Company. His broad political experience included a close relationship with William Goebel, who was assassinated in 1900 shortly after the election. Later, Allie Young spent ten years as circuit judge, followed by a dozen years as state senator. Looking back over Young's varied career, President Payne stated, "Education has never had a greater friend than Judge Young," a statement especially true of the relation-ship between Allie Young and Morehead State.  He not only had been the most dominant force in bringing the state school to Morehead but had served as a major spokesman for bringing money to Morehead State, enabling Button and Payne to emerge as the builders of the original campus.  Shortly after Young's death in 1935, nine-year-old daughter Jane unveiled her father's portrait in College Auditorium beside that of Button.  She recently stated that Button and Young belonged together because "it took those two elements to get that college here."  The two portraits remain on display in their original locations today.

## Harvey A. Babb:  Administrator in Turmoil, 1935-40

With Payne's sudden dismissal, Morehead State had to find a new president during the fall semester of 1935-36.  The Board of Re-gents again chose as president a public school superintendent when it named Harvey A. Babb, who had been a Mount Sterling superin-tendent for sixteen years; he assumed office on November 1, 1935.  Babb received his bachelor's and master's degrees from the Univer-sity of Kentucky, where he starred as a football player in the pre-World War I era.

First Lady Elizabeth Babb loved to entertain.  Edna Babb Dar-ling relates a "family tale" that when her mother was asked to decide upon one occasion what kind of prison trusty she wished to use as her cook, she said she didn't want "a forger because the merchants might be upset that such a person might pass bad checks, and she didn't want a thief because taxpayers might worry about property being stolen."  Finally, Mrs. Babb, who ordinarily was "so proper and shocked at the least misbehavior," brightened up and said, "Well, I've thought and thought about it—just send me some poor lady who has done nothing but murder her husband; it's understandable, and cer-tainly we won't have to worry about her doing it again."

Edna's favorite experience growing up in the President's Home was the day poet Carl Sandburg spoke in chapel and later "had lunch with us in our dining room." She described the writer as "a precious man" who was "so down to earth." Sandburg had "gotten up early to get on the train, and his wife had fixed his lunch to take with him. He was a low-keyed, wonderful man who enjoyed the scenery of the countryside" on his journey to Morehead that morning.

The inauguration of Morehead's third president took place in the College Auditorium on May 5, 1936. Harry W. Peters, newly-elected State Superintendent of Public Instruction, presided. As keynote speaker, Frank L. McVey, author of the report which had helped Morehead State turn things around earlier in the decade, declared, "Today is a day of consecration, placing upon all here and everywhere in this state the oath of the real missionary to serve, to learn, to work, and to understand with sympathy and devotion." In his inaugural message, President Babb asserted, "If today from the valley below, you turn your eyes to the mountaintops which shelter the stately buildings and terrace slopes that adorn the college campus, you will doubtless recall the deep interest, the untiring loyalty, and the sincere devotion of the late Senator Allie W. Young to this institution. This college . . . became a child of his imagination, and it stands today as a noble tribute to his memory." An afternoon pageant on the history of the college was presented in front of Johnson Camden Library, with Lucille Caudill, speech and drama instructor, serving as the narrator. The script, featuring several musical numbers and dances, had been written by Caudill and three other instructors: Lucille's sister Louise, who taught physical education; Ernestine Troemel, home economics instructor, and Neville Fincel, economics teacher.

The inauguration was an indication of things to come. Albert B. "Happy" Chandler, newly-elected Democratic governor, was scheduled to speak; however, he cancelled at the last minute, claiming pressing business in the state's capital. Little did Morehead State

*Louise Caudill, left, physical education instructor and swimming coach, and Lucille Caudill, speech and drama instructor, taught at Morehead State in the mid-1930's. Their father, Daniel Boone Caudill, was a member of the Board of Regents.*

expect at that point that its new president, a Republican, would be kept at arm's length throughout the Chandler administration. A cool relationship with the governor spawned some of the conflicts which eventually helped to bring Babb's downfall. The president immediately found Frankfort's doors hard to open as he pursued financial support and other favors on behalf of Morehead State.

The Babb years, however, witnessed some major construction projects. Local residents were pleased when they drove through the campus and observed the completion of the Science Building in 1937 and East Men's Hall the following year; these buildings were financed with federal money which had already been received. Babb then obtained funds from the Public Works Administration in 1938 to pave the road from Breckinridge Training School back to U.S. 60. A flash flood in 1939 killed twenty-six people in Morehead; that tragedy later helped the college obtain money from the Public Works Administration to construct a dam on nearby Evans Branch, thereby achieving two objectives: (a) securing better flood protection in the Morehead region, and (b) providing a bigger, more reliable, and an independent source of water for the college.

President Babb spent most of his five-year presidency reacting to events rather than setting the agenda. Confronted with budget cuts during most of his administration, he was forced to make hard decisions that alienated many and pleased few. With his background as a college football player, Babb decided that building a winning football program would be the best and quickest route to much needed publicity for the college. He reduced support for other activities, including art and dramatic productions, saying they were not as visible in the operation of a college as football.

This decision produced one of his first clashes with faculty and students. In chapel one morning, the young drama instructor, Lucille Caudill, rose from her seat to challenge the president on his priorities. She pointed out that her four major dramatic productions had done more for student morale, at less cost, than football ever could. Caudill was taken by surprise when several other faculty and students supported her challenge. Being uninterested in leading a political crusade, Lucille and her sister Louise spent the following weekend in Lexington to escape the developing turmoil on campus.

This was the first in a series of confrontations which Babb had to face. In 1938 the General Assembly requested a joint investigation of the Babb administration by a legislative committee and the attorney general. As a result of the investigations, the committee accused the Babb administration of a number of illegal activities. At its next meeting, however, the Board of Regents gave Babb a vote of confidence, based upon its decision that a number of these charges were unfounded and politically motivated. But attacks on Babb by newspapers and legislative leaders prompted the board to remove the president's right to appoint faculty members and to turn this authority over to department heads. In 1939 the situation worsened when the *Rowan County News* leveled a volley of accusations against the president in a series of editorials entitled "How long must the people of Eastern Kentucky endure this evil?" Claiming that "graft and corruption" were rampant on campus, Jack Wilson, the paper's editor, demanded Babb's removal from the presidency.

Immediately after these editorials appeared, Wilson charged Babb's two sons, along with a friend, with assault and battery. The editor testified in court that they hurled a heavy rock through his window at night and called him vile names and attacked him physically, inflicting numerous cuts and bruises on his face and body. But Babb defended his sons after they pled guilty and paid their fines; he argued they were simply reacting as any sons would in the face of bitter attacks upon their father. Babb maintained that the editorials' falsehoods were inspired by Wilson's loss of a printing contract with the college. Rejecting this contention, the editor volunteered to appear before the Board of Regents to prove his charges of alleged mismanagement on the part of the president.

As might be expected, Babb received much criticism over this incident. The *Lexington Herald* editorialized in February 1939 that "neither expletives nor fists" can determine what is right or wrong at Morehead State and advised that both practices should be discontinued. Morehead State was "a great institution, serving a splendid purpose," as shown by its large enrollment and effective service to the youth of Eastern Kentucky. But the day of "either beating editors or brow-beating public officials" had passed, and public matters must be considered reasonably.

Babb approached the end of his four-year contract in 1939 amid speculation that it might not be renewed. Yet, after a four-hour meeting in February the Board of Regents extended his contract from November 1, 1939, to July 1, 1940. While the extension was for only eight months, Babb confidently asserted that he had been vindicated, although the board included reservations on hiring and dismissal practices.

The situation quickly got out of hand after the February 1939 decision to extend Babb's contract. During the spring semester, Babb dismissed a number of people for apparently political reasons. Among those fired were Clarence Nickell, dean of men and a former state senator who had directed Governor Chandler's program through the previous legislative session; George D. Downing, director of physical education and former successful head football and basketball coach; and Taylor Young, storeroom clerk and son of board member Mrs. Allie Young. Babb also rejected A.Y. Lloyd's request to return to teaching after serving as a member of the Chandler administration.

Learning that contracts of three popular faculty and staff members had not been renewed, students padlocked classrooms and marched down College Boulevard to the President's Home. When Babb came outside and promised to meet with them the next morning, most students returned to class. But matters went from bad to worse the next day. After the general convocation had assembled, Babb's first action was to dismiss it. James Stuart, a student and brother of Kentucky author Jesse Stuart, immediately countermanded the president's dismissal and informed the assemblage that he and five others had been designated to meet with Governor Chandler in Frankfort to present their views of the situation at

Morehead. Besides Stuart, this committee of six included Paul Thompson from Louisa, William M. Whitaker from Blackey, Herbert Triplett from Inez, Herschel "Jug" Conley from Oil Springs, and Adam Ritchie from Best. After Stuart's challenge, a lengthy, acrimonious exchange ensued between Babb and dean of men Clarence Nickell, with charges and countercharges ranging from corruption to political machinations to personal slights. The assembly ended on a note of defiance when Nickell refused Babb's request that he try to allay the crisis, saying "I did not create this situation, and I will do nothing to halt it."

The day after the aborted convocation a cavalcade of some 300 students, faculty, and staff, led by James Stuart, descended on Frankfort. Here, Paul Thompson protested before a crowded House chamber against Babb's coercion of the Morehead campus and his dismissal of faculty. Representatives of the group later met with Governor Chandler; afterwards, Thompson and Nickell expressed confidence in the governor's support of their cause. Chandler, in turn, promised to confer with the Board of Regents and with State Superintendent of Education Harry W. Peters in an effort to resolve the dissension afflicting Morehead State.

Such negative publicity for the college rendered Babb's position virtually untenable. Board members who had stood behind him earlier could no longer be counted on for support. In addition, Morehead State was reprimanded and placed on the Southern Association's questionable list because faculty salaries were too low and library holdings were inadequate. With these combinations against him, Babb's five-year troubled presidency came to an ignominious end in 1940.

## William H. Vaughan: Wartime Leader, 1940-1946

In May 1940 the Board of Regents elected William H. Vaughan, academic dean since 1928, to the presidency. On the day Vaughan was chosen, the members designated Babb to convey their decision

83

*William H. Vaughan,
Morehead State's fourth
president, 1940-46.*

to him and escort him to their meeting room, where they congratulated him in Babb's presence. Such embarrassment apparently deeply affected the outgoing leader, thereby straining his future relationship with Vaughan.

After Babb's contract with Morehead State was not renewed, he returned to Montgomery County and was named principal of Camargo High School. During the administration of Simeon S. Willis (1943-47), Kentucky's first Republican governor in twelve years, Babb was appointed director of the State Unemployment Compensation Commission. Critics alleged that he used his influence in Frankfort to undermine his successor at Morehead State.

Vaughan was the third former school superintendent to accept the presidency of Morehead State. A native and farm boy from Lawrence County, he received his bachelor's degree at Georgetown College and his master's and doctoral degrees from George Peabody College in Nashville. Vaughan enjoyed the distinction of being Morehead State's first president to hold an earned doctorate — a doctor of philosophy degree in education. He also studied one summer at the University of Chicago. After serving as a high school English teacher, principal, and city superintendent of schools in Louisa, he was employed as Morehead's academic dean.

Vaughan was a pleasant man who was not vindictive and tended to see the best in people, even when it might have been to his advantage to recognize the worst. Although he was not abrasive, the president ran the college with a firm hand. Medium-to-short in stature, broad-shouldered and stocky, this conscientious, hard-working individual was described as "bookish but boyish despite his bifocals." His dark brown hair was receding and he was balding on top. He enjoyed hiking and taking care of the rose garden at the President's Home. He rented a plot of ground at Salt Lick, ten miles away, and cultivated a "victory" garden during World War II. Vaughan was a devoutly religious man, orthodox in his Baptist views, and did not smoke or drink. He was a first-rate Bible student and often taught a Sunday School class.

Vaughan started his administration with a decision that made him popular with the faculty. Rather than having an inauguration, he staged a special occasion for saluting those faculty members who had been at Morehead State since its beginning as a public normal school. These teachers included Inez Faith Humphrey, Henry Clay Haggan, and Charles O. Peratt. This celebration took place at Homecoming in November 1940 which featured a football game against Transylvania.

Regarded more as scholars than administrators, Vaughan and Warren C. Lappin, his academic dean, created an environment which stressed academic improvement. For example, Chiles Van Antwerp, director of the Training School, was named chairperson of a committee charged with the responsibility of solving the problem of student absenteeism. The faculty accepted the committee's recommendation of a stricter policy, which stated that students would not receive credit in a course if their total absences exceeded 20 percent of the number of class meetings. All departments were required to follow this rule on absences. The Vaughan administration also directed the college to become more heavily involved in the professional development of its faculty. In 1941 Gabriel C. Banks, longtime English professor with an M.A. from Yale, served as chairperson of the Committee on Faculty Professional Standards and Ethics, which drew up twelve recommendations that were accepted by the faculty. Among this committee's recommendations were sabbaticals for study or periodic examination of courses for pertinence and currency, outside activities such as public service, research, and creative writing, and a statement on academic freedom and tenure drawn up by the Association of American Colleges.

In the early 1940s Morehead State added a graduate program to its curriculum. The School Code of 1934 provided for certain types of teaching certificates based upon the completion of a five-year curriculum. The University of Kentucky was the only state-supported graduate school from 1936 to 1941. Vaughan announced on September 24, 1940, that the Council on Higher Education had authorized the four teachers colleges to offer a master of arts in education degree in the summer of 1941. Morehead State implemented its master's degree program in the 1941-42 academic year; initially, only ten graduate courses in education were taught.

Between 1940 and 1948, Morehead State awarded a total of 565 degrees, including nine at the master's level. The institution's first master's degree was awarded to Francisco Manuel Inserni at the 1942 summer commencement. A majority of the degrees continued to be granted in the summer. Approximately 94 percent of the school's graduates accepted teaching positions in the academic year following graduation.

Kentucky experienced great difficulty in keeping certified teachers during World War II. Whereas only 500 emergency teaching permits had been issued from 1938 to 1941, the number jumped to 2,673 in the 1942-43 academic year and almost doubled that number two years later. Only a fourth of those who left the classroom went into the armed forces; many were lured by the higher wages of war-related industries, especially since the Kentucky legislature failed to provide salary increments equal to the rising cost of living. These basic factors, linked with lowering the draft age to eighteen, resulted in a sharp decline in the number of students who were training to become teachers. Among Kentucky's five teacher-training institutions, student teachers declined from 1,384 in 1939-40 to 378 five years later. Morehead State experienced an even greater decline in student-teacher enrollment, from 223 in 1939-40 to 50 by 1944-45. As might be expected, Morehead State's total enrollment decreased sharply during the war. Enrollment dropped from 767 in the fall term of 1940-41 to 260 in the fall of 1942-43; the spring semester's student body included only nine males! The number of students fell to 166 during the fall semester of 1944-45. Summer enrollment, however, fared well throughout most of the war, probably because of the large number of teachers with emergency permits who used summer vacations either to work on teaching certificates or to take refresher courses.

These low enrollments put the survival of the college at stake during World War II. Since the war caused college enrollment to plummet across the nation, the War Manpower Commission and the Navy Advisory Council on Education, along with other government agencies, decided to make use of college facilities to prepare the nation's youth for essential civilian activities, war industries, and military service. Early in the war, Vaughan arranged for a two-year, million-dollar contract with the federal government to train sailors on campus to be electrical technicians aboard fighting vessels. Morehead State became the first Kentucky college and one of the first in the nation to be selected for the Navy College Training Program. A committee, including academic dean Warren C. Lappin and W. H. (Honie) Rice, superintendent of buildings and grounds, journeyed to Detroit to inspect a school which served as the pattern for Morehead State's development of its naval program.

Because of its location, no one would ever have associated

Morehead State with the Navy. Situated in the hills of Northeastern Kentucky, far from a body of water "big enough to float a boat," Morehead State "joined the Navy" in June 1942. Governor Keen Johnson, U.S. naval officers, and other dignitaries participated in festivities celebrating this event. "We in Kentucky are happy as we make available the facilities of this fine institution as a training center for the nation's great Navy," Johnson asserted. Aware of periodic suggestions that Morehead State was not needed, the governor pointed out that the institution's primary role as a teachers college remained the same and that its educational advantages to the region would not be affected by sharing its facilities with the Navy.

The naval contract extended from the summer of 1942 to the summer of 1944. Money from the federal government those two years paid for instruction and dormitory facilities to accommodate up to 600 men at a time. The Navy supplied the salaries of four Morehead State teachers who transferred from regular teaching duties to assist more than twenty instructors brought by the Navy to Morehead.

Morehead State had to make several changes in its physical plant to handle its commitment to the Navy. A tool-making laboratory was constructed in the basement of Thompson Hall. The cafeteria, which normally served 700-900 meals a day had to expand to 2,500 meals daily. The problem became more acute with the added strain produced by governmental rationing of food products. Johnson Camden Library was enlarged, especially in the area of its holdings in science and mathematics. The college was forced to increase its maintenance crew. Most classrooms in the new Science Building were turned over to the Navy. Trainees were granted use of the College Auditorium-Gymnasium, Senff Natatorium, and Jayne Memorial Stadium, where the "Bluejackets," as the naval personnel were called, daily executed their maneuvers on the drill field. Although a controversy during the previous decade forced the college to quit showing movies because of competition with the town's the-

*This picture of the U.S. Navy Electrical School faculty, 1942-44, was taken on the front steps of the Science Building, later named Lappin Hall. First from left in the front row is J. G. Black, industrial arts. Fourth is Linus A. Fair, mathematics. Fifth is Warren C. Lappin, dean of MSC, and eighth is William Wineland, physics. The second row, from left, Henry Carey, anthropology, first; and Marvin E. George, music, third. Fourth in the third row is Thomas Young, art. Eighth in the last row is Paul C. Overstreet, physics.*

ater, the practice of showing motion pictures on campus was re-sumed for the exclusive use of the Navy. East Men's Hall and Thompson Hall were turned into barracks with double-deck bunks for use by naval personnel. Allie Young Hall, a women's dormitory, was converted into a men's residence hall to house regular students forced out of other residence halls.

The Navy Training School taught more than 3,000 second class seamen as 600 sailors were on campus at a time. The first class of 150 young men began on June 1, 1942; an additional 150 arrived on the first of each month until a total of 600 was reached by September 1. After completing four months of concentrated training, primarily in science and mathematics, on October 1, the original 150 pulled out to make room for another class. Once the program was fully in operation, a class of 150 completed training each month and was replaced by a new group of the same number. Those who completed this training received the rank of electrician's mate, third class.

Thus, two kinds of education—one for war and the other for peace—operated smoothly side by side. On a campus with only 260 civilian students, a military atmosphere prevailed when 600 Bluejackets marched in formation to chow and to class. By the fall of 1942, the town of Morehead had grown accustomed to being a "seaport" and watching trainees march through its streets at 5:30 a.m. The presence of sailors added excitement to coed social life; in fact, a few young ladies married Bluejackets.

Having a military program affected the institution as well as those receiving the training. On July 8, 1943, Vaughan told the board, "We have learned some things about teaching and education we didn't know." For example, the Navy instructors' use of a "matter-of-fact" speaking and reading knowledge of foreign languages influenced the manner in which these courses were taught to regular students. The use of Morehead State's campus to train personnel for a global war aroused greater interest in world affairs on the part of students and faculty. Social studies was greatly affected by the addition of courses on International Relations, Asia, Australia, and the Far East.

Morehead—both the town and the college—made a lasting impression on some of the naval personnel. When nineteen-year-old Al Silano arrived by train from New Jersey on Thanksgiving evening, 1943, he was overwhelmed that "a whole group of people was waiting for us" and provided turkey sandwiches, coffee, and soda pop. Salano was amazed during those four months that he often received invitations to private homes after church to feast on "Kentucky chicken suppers." However, nothing had prepared him for the seriousness with which Morehead fans took their basketball: It was "the only place I had ever been where I had walked out of a basketball game and had seen people crying."

Silano was impressed with his Morehead academic experience. In spite of being told by his high school counselor to forget college, he startled himself by making good grades in the science and math classes which were required in his electrical engineering program. He was especially impressed by such professors as Paul Overstreet who was "a gem—all my life I could hear his voice." To this day, he gives a remarkable imitation of Overstreet's high-pitched voice. "I learned more about electric circuits from that man in four weeks than I ever learned before or afterwards." After his Morehead encounter with higher education, he earned a Ph.D. in physics at Rutgers University, taught many years at the University of Arkansas, and was credited with six patents from the U.S. government. Silano praises Morehead State because "I got the lust for learning here. I have always tried to emulate the teachers I had here."

Faculty members who remained at Morehead State made several contributions to the war effort. For example, most faculty and staff members, regardless of salary, purchased war bonds with at least 10 percent of their salaries. Professor Haggan acted as field representative of the American Red Cross. And since the rationing of beef and pork created a demand for chickens, he offered his department's services for producing baby chicks. As of July 8, 1943, he had hatched and brooded a total of 17,000 chickens, free of charge to farmers and poultrymen in six counties. Farmers supplied the eggs and the feed; Haggan hatched and brooded them. His operation was located in the Science Building and ultimately provided some 75,000 pounds of poultry for the six counties involved.

The war also took its toll on the Morehead State faculty. The institution lost thirteen teachers between 1941 and 1946. Four resigned to enter the armed forces; four resigned to accept positions with higher salaries; two received sabbatical leaves for further study at half pay; one was fired; one pursued defense studies at the University of Michigan; and the other reached compulsory retirement age. After eighteen years of service, Bettie Robinson became the first Morehead State teacher to retire. The Board of Regents established a policy of leaving positions open to be reclaimed by teachers who entered the armed forces.

Morehead State experienced difficulty meeting operational expenses throughout the war years. The General Assembly increased its annual appropriations for operating expenses from $193,000 in 1939 to a mere $234,000 in 1945. No appropriations were made for buildings and grounds from 1932 until 1948. As a re-

*The "Bluejackets" or naval trainees marched down University Boulevard toward Main Street as early as 5:30 in the morning. Hundreds of sailors were trained here to be shipboard electricians.*

sult, the school's physical plant had begun to deteriorate when the war began. No capital outlay funds were made available to any of Kentucky's colleges in the first half of the 1940s due to the war. Morehead State's added income from the Navy Training Program made a vast difference to an institution in dire straits. Thus, Vaughan informed the board at the close of the 1942-43 fiscal year, "This has been the most successful year financially that the college has had since about 1933 or 1934."

The institution had to adjust to a postwar economy and an influx of students in 1945. Shortly after the Navy Training Program ended in the summer of 1944, Congress passed the GI Bill of Rights, which resulted in a great enrollment increase in American colleges. Many high school graduates, with the draft no longer hanging over them, attended college after the war. Close to one-half of Morehead State's students in 1945-46 were veterans under the GI Bill. Ivan E. Ball, a Morehead junior from Crockett, was the first veteran to receive educational benefits under the GI Bill in any Kentucky college. Receiving a medical discharge in November 1943, he served as Prestonsburg High School's basketball coach that winter before returning the following year to Morehead State, where he had been a student before the war. Large numbers of veterans followed his example.

The GI Bill brought an older student body which included large numbers of married students. Thus, lack of appropriate housing soon became a major problem. "When I first came," John Collis, a veteran, recalls, "the married students without children lived in Allie Young Hall, and the married students with children lived in Men's Hall. Dot and I lived in one room in Allie Young Hall." The dormitory had a room set aside "as a kitchen and eating area—we had one refrigerator for six families, and it was a little hard to maintain that cubicle in that little section of the refrigerator that was ours." After graduating in 1949, Collis served the institution for nearly forty years as head of the bookstore before retiring in 1988.

As has been true with other generations, students in the Forties lived with what they had. "We wore our dungarees or old clothes we'd had in the Navy," Collis states. A paperback cost from 25 to 50 cents; hardbacks, $2 to $2.50. "My wife and I could go to the movie and get a hamburger and share a big Pepsi for a dollar." Chapel was still held every Thursday morning. "I can see Catherine Bach and Virginia Hudgins going up the rows now," Collis says, "and if you weren't going to be there and you couldn't prevail on someone else, like a commuting student who didn't have to have an assigned seat, to sit in your seat, you were in bad shape because Dean Lappin would reduce your academic credits."

The college was much more conservative then. Collis and two other students decided to start a veterans' newspaper. The day after the second issue, which included an editorial critical of the administration, came out, "we were called into the president's office." President William Jesse Baird told these veterans, "Have a seat, boys. Are you the fellows who are publishing the veterans' newspaper?" After they hesitantly confessed, the president told them, "I just called you in to let you know that you just went out of publication." Silence prevailed as the three glanced first at one another and then at the president. Baird finally broke the silence by asking, "Did you all have anything you wanted to say?" When they answered, "I guess not," he kindly stated, "Well, thanks a lot for coming in, we'll see you."

On another occasion, Dean Lappin called Collis into his office and told him, "The president wants me to check with some of you veterans to see what can be done about the drinking that is going on at some of the dances." Collis replied, "These guys have fought three or four years in a war, and they've established a way of life that they are not going to change. If they want to drink, they are going to drink." To which Lappin replied, "That's what I've told the president."

The war helped Morehead State lose some of its provincialism. Subsequently, a greater distribution of students came from among

Kentucky's 120 counties and a substantial increase in the number of out-of-state students occurred. From 1923 to 1929, over 90 percent of Morehead State's student body came from Rowan County and counties within a thirty-three mile radius; only two students were from out-of-state. Between 1930 and 1948, less than 78 percent of the students hailed from Rowan and surrounding counties, while a total of 638 students attended from outside Kentucky. Of Morehead State's 16,245 students during this era, Rowan's 2,306 students led the way, followed by Carter's 1,867, Greenup's 1,071, Morgan's 933, and Boyd's 929. West Virginia contributed the most out-of-state students—174—Ohio was a close second with 167. And Morehead State enrolled its first student from outside the "48 states"—Francisco Manuel Inserni, from Puerto Rico.

An aura of anticipation prevailed after Morehead State survived the Great Depression and World War II. In spite of the war and the lingering effects of the Depression, Vaughan had put together an impressive record, including a great reduction in the college's financial obligations. Revenue bonds, floated during the previous decade to assist in the construction of three additional buildings, with an aggregate value of $436,000, had been reduced by $158,000 at the end of the war. The 1946 budget provided Morehead State with an appropriation of $306,000, a $72,000 increase over the previous biennium. And from a low of 166 students in the fall of 1944, enrollment soared to 614 by the fall of 1946.

While the institution geared up for growth, the faculty exerted a major effort to improve the quality of instruction. A Committee on the Improvement of Instruction raised the point of encouraging independent thinking among the students and challenged the faculty to rate their own effectiveness as teachers. The Committee went on to suggest, among other things, the adoption of a system of faculty ranking and faculty salaries, based largely on a study being made by the American Association of Teachers Colleges.

Thus, by the mid-1940s, the Morehead State faculty was contemplating a merit plan based on evaluation. As a part of it, a system of "auditing," whereby faculty members would attend and evaluate each other's classes, was being seriously considered. Later, however, they adopted history professor Nolan Fowler's motion to eliminate the section dealing with teachers' auditing each other's classes. There is no indication that this merit plan was implemented.

On June 18, 1946, a report of the Committee on Faculty Ranking and Salaries was adopted. This faculty plan spelled out the following package including four faculty ranks:

I. Instructor:
   A. Master's degree, or its equivalent.
   B. Superior promise as a teacher of future worth to the college.
   C. Salary: $2500 to $3300, including summer teaching.

II. Assistant Professor:
   A. One and a half years of graduate study (including master's degree or its equivalent).
   B. Three years of teaching experience in one's field with marked success.
   C. Evidence of increasing worth to the college.
   D. Salary: $3000 to $3800.

III. Associate Professor:
   A. Two years of graduate study.
   B. Five years of teaching experience.
   C. Superior work as evidenced by professional attitudes, extra-curricular participation in the work of the college, and participation in community life.
   D. Salary: $3500 to $4300.

IV. Professor:
   A. Doctor's degree, or its equivalent.
   B. Eight years of teaching experience.
   C. Or two years of graduate study and twelve years of

teaching experience and major contributions to the advancement of the field.

D.    Superior worth to the college.

E.    Salary: $4000 to $4800.

This was the first system of faculty ranking tied with a salary scale to be adopted by Morehead State.

Vaughan's saving the college from extinction in the early 1940s and placing it on a more professional footing provided no guarantee that the Board of Regents would renew his contract in 1946. He realized he faced the major task of preventing the institution from becoming embroiled in the kind of political strife it had endured for two decades. He did not anticipate, however, that the governor would be the instigator of the new turmoil.

In the gubernatorial campaign of 1943, Simeon S.Willis, an Ashland Republican, deplored the fact that the presidents of Eastern, Morehead, Murray, and Western were all Democrats. He pledged, if elected, to replace two of them with Republicans. Admitting that Murray and Western's regions were predominantly Democratic, Willis concluded that changes would have to occur at Morehead and Eastern. The *Courier-Journal* predicted on May 7, 1946, that the Democratic presidents at Morehead and Eastern would be replaced with Republicans by the end of Willis' term in December 1947. His first opportunity for such a change came at Morehead State.

Manipulating membership on Boards of Regents gave governors a deciding voice in the selection of college presidents. A governor could dismiss any board member "at his discretion and without necessary cause," with the exception of the Superintendent of Public Instruction, an elected official, who served as an ex officio member and chairman of each board.

As Vaughan's contract was about to expire in 1946, Willis took the necessary steps to insure that Morehead State would have a new president. Republicans had become impatient during his three years in office because Willis had refused to make wholesale dismissals of

97

Democrats. They were pressuring the governor to carry out his campaign promise. Shortly after taking office, Willis had appointed Roy Cornette, superintendent of Rowan County schools and chairman of Rowan County Republicans, to Morehead State's Board of Regents. As the date neared for deciding on the renewal of Vaughan's contract, Willis appointed Dr. James M. Rose, an Olive Hill Republican, to replace Donald H. Putnam of Ashland, a long-time supporter of the president, whose term had expired. At the same time, however, the governor made no effort to replace Mrs. Allie Young, a Democrat whose term had also expired, because Willis felt he could sway her in return for permitting her to stay on the board.

Afraid of what might happen at Morehead State, an official with the American Association of Teachers Colleges requested the Southern Association to do something about Vaughan's plight. Rufus C. Harris, chairman of the Commission on Institutions of Higher Education, replied that his organization could not enter the dispute since nothing had happened as yet. Ironically, the Harris letter was dated May 21, 1946, the same day Vaughan was fired.

In the late spring of 1946, *Rowan County News* editor, W. E. (Snooks) Crutcher, in a guest article appearing in the *Lexington Herald,* raised the possibility of another change in Morehead's presidency. As political storm clouds hovered over an institution which had ousted three presidents in twenty years, Crutcher wrote that most observers thought Vaughan would be rejected by a vote of 3-2 in spite of the fact that not one charge had been brought against him. Crutcher was strongly opposed to such a change. Believing that anything might happen if Vaughan were ousted, the local editor listed six arguments generally made by Vaughan supporters. First, failure to renew Vaughan's contract would go against the views of a majority of the Morehead State constituency, including students, faculty, administrative staff, alumni, Morehead townspeople, and Eastern Kentucky newspapers. Second, forcing the president out without leveling any charges against him would likely prompt an investigation by the Southern Association, with the possibility that the college would be discredited. Third, failure to renew Vaughan's contract would continue to make Morehead State a political football, as Democrats would likely oust the next president once they reclaimed the Governor's Mansion. Fourth, Vaughan would become the fourth president in twenty-four years whose contract was not renewed; by way of contrast, Western's Henry Hardin Cherry was completing a 31-year stint as president of that state institution in 1937. Fifth, Vaughan's removal would invite unfavorable statewide publicity. Finally, Vaughan was a popular Eastern Kentuckian, who commanded the respect of the citizenry from which Morehead State drew most of its students. His supporters hoped that the president's popularity and record, coupled with Willis' friendship with members of Mrs. Vaughan's family in Ashland, would make it difficult for the governor to tamper with his contract.

*Beginning in 1919, Warren C. Lappin served Morehead State as baseball coach, history and political science instructor, director of Breckinridge Training School, academic dean, vice president, and interim president on two occasions. He also served two years as principal of Morehead High School.*

After the board had been in session two hours, on May 21, 1946, it requested Vaughan to make a brief appearance. Returning to his office, he strolled over to a window and, as he gazed across the campus into the valley below, someone overheard him saying, "They want me to go out peacefully. They don't want me to ask for the investigation. But it is my duty to bring this thing to a showdown. If I back down now, they will fire the next president like they are firing me. I have got to go through with it to get this college on a firm foundation, once and for all." As one who had been a close observer of the circumstances surrounding the ouster of all three presidents under whom he had served, President Vaughan understood how close Morehead State had come to being investigated a decade earlier. Armed with first-hand knowledge, he was sure it was not a matter of if—but when—an investigation would occur.

Yet, nothing could deter either the board or the governor. After a three-hour session, the board announced its 3-2 decision not to renew Vaughan's contract. While board minutes failed to record how each member voted, it was generally understood that Cornette, Rose, and Young voted against the president. William Keifer, Ashland Democrat, was widely regarded as an outspoken supporter of Vaughan. Superintendent John Fred Williams, a Republican member of the cabinet, would ordinarily have been expected to support the governor's wishes, but he was already positioning himself to oppose Willis' candidate for governor the following year.

There were two reasons for Vaughan's dismissal, both of which related to politics. First, his removal enabled Willis to take the first step in keeping his promise to appoint two Republican presidents to head Kentucky colleges. Several Republicans who had never gotten over Babb's ouster in 1940 by a Democratic administration were determined for Vaughan to receive the same fate. Circumstances played into their hands as a rumor spread that the president had permitted use of college facilities for a "political sanctum" for Democrats to attack Willis when he was a gubernatorial candidate in

1943. Critics of Vaughan reminded everyone that Tom R. Underwood, editor of the *Lexington Herald,* had used the Jefferson Day Banquet on April 13, 1943, in Morehead State's cafeteria to make an after dinner speech containing charges against Willis. Both political parties had staged such dinners on campus for years because the college cafeteria was the only place in the entire region with seating capacity to accommodate large crowds. The Morehead State Board of Regents granted unanimous approval for the use of the cafeteria, and President Vaughan did not attend the banquet.

Allan M. Trout, reporter for the *Courier-Journal,* lists the gubernatorial election of 1947 as a second reason for Vaughan's dismissal. Willis had already decided to support Commissioner of Highways J. Stephen Watkins in the next gubernatorial election; it seemed obvious that Watkins' opponent would be John Fred Williams. Since Watkins would run on the administration's record, Willis found it necessary to keep his promise about breaking the Democratic monopoly on the college presidencies. Having decided to oppose the administration's favorite, Williams planned to run on a record of attempting to remove politics from Kentucky's system of higher education, and Willis no longer consulted his Superintendent of Public Instruction for advice on appointments to Boards of Regents. Given this political environment, no one was surprised that Willis and Williams lined up on opposite sides in the Morehead State controversy.

The decision to replace Vaughan had little to do with his performance and everything to do with politics. Yet, when a student delegation approached Willis to protest the president's firing, the governor assured them that politics had gone out when Vaughan left office. Asserting there were no politicians among any of his appointees to the Morehead State Board of Regents, Willis contended that he could not say that about Williams, who had been at odds with him ever since the 1946 legislative battle over the salaries of public school teachers.

Vaughan's greatest weakness was perhaps his naive under-standing and interpretation of the political process. Fred M. Vinson, his cousin who later served as Harry S Truman's Secretary of the Treasury and still later Chief Justice of the United States, felt that Vaughan was not political enough for his own good. Upon leaving Morehead State, Vaughan accepted an administrative appointment with George Peabody College, in Nashville, where he served until his retirement in 1962. At that time, he took a position with the Methodist Board of Education, from which he retired at the age of 69. Already in poor health, he died three years later, in 1972, of congestive heart failure.

With no applicants under serious consideration for the presidency, the Board of Regents asked Warren C. Lappin to serve as acting president from July 1, 1946, until a new president could be hired. Lappin was a graduate of Transylvania, holding a master's degree from the University of Chicago as well as a doctorate in education from Indiana University. His father, Warren O. Lappin, had been principal of the old Morehead Normal School when it closed in 1922, and Warren C. was a member of its faculty. By the mid-1940's, he had served as baseball coach, professor, director of Breckinridge Training School, and academic dean of the college.

## William Jesse Baird: Fighter for Recognition, 1946-1951

A search committee, consisting of board members Roy Cornette, William Keifer, and Dr. James M. Rose, looked for an individual to fill Morehead State's presidency. William Jesse Baird, a native Kentuckian, a faculty member and administrator at Berea College for many years, was named as Morehead State's fifth president on August 6, 1946. In accepting the position, Baird stated his intention to build a strong educational institution. Somehow, he managed to exude confidence while accepting the presidency of an institution which had fired every previous president. In turn, the board unanimously pledged support to their new leader. They also

*William Jesse Baird, Morehead State's fifth president, 1946-51. He is the only president to have died in office.*

admitted for the first time that their decisions about the previous administration had perhaps alienated almost everyone but asked for continued support from "the citizens and the press in the institution's area and in the state in their hopes for an ever stronger educational institution."

A native of Knox County, Baird looked upon the Morehead position as an opportunity to return home. He received his bachelor's degree from Berea College in 1915. After teaching in Kentucky's public school system a few years, he joined the Berea faculty; in 1925, he became dean of Berea's Foundation School and director of teacher training. Two years later, he received his master's degree from Cornell and subsequently received an honorary doctorate from the University of Kentucky. While on a leave of absence from Berea in 1940, he visited fifty-six college campuses doing advisory work as a representative of the Danforth Foundation. Baird left Berea in 1943 for Rome, Georgia, to accept the leadership of the Berry Schools—a private institution similar in many ways to Berea. Morehead State hired him from this position in 1946.

President Baird was in poor health when he arrived at

Morehead State and further "ruined his health in getting us reaccredited," stated John Collis, a student from 1946 to 1949. The president had "white hair which flowed rather freely and was a very good orator as well as a man of vision and a very knowledgeable person," Collis continued. Wilhelm Exelbirt, a history professor who joined the Morehead State faculty in 1948, always characterized the president as "the sainted Dr. Baird." He also "had this wonderful way with children," says Nolan Fowler, another professor of history. "He came to our home for dinner one evening. Our little daughter went up to him, and he immediately had her on his lap." He was known for his ability to mix toughness with a good sense of humor. The president had signs erected at various points on campus which read, "Stay Off the Grass! Ouch!" Alumnus Jeanne Dotson, remembers that Baird stopped her brother as he marched across the stage at graduation and told him, "This is the only way we can keep you from cutting across the grass—graduate you."

## Loss and Regaining of Accreditation

Before leaving Kentucky, Vaughan announced his decision to request both the Southern Association and the American Association of Teachers Colleges to determine whether his dismissal had been for real cause or for politics. Aware of Morehead State's previous involvement in politics, the Southern Association lost no time in beginning its investigation. In June 1946 Chairman Rufus C. Harris directed Mike Huntley, executive-secretary of the Southern Association, to investigate Vaughan's formal complaint that political influence brought about his dismissal without preferment of charges. Between June 25 and 29, 1946, Huntley conferred with Governor Willis, Superintendent Williams, President Vaughan, all members of the Morehead State Board of Regents, faculty and staff members, and various educational leaders in Kentucky.

As might be expected, Huntley was told during his two-hour session with the governor that there was no basis for the *Courier-*

*Journal's* article claiming that Morehead and Eastern's presidents would be replaced with Republican leaders. Asserting he had nothing to do with the dismissal of Vaughan, whom he knew only slightly, Willis stated that he afterwards instructed the Board of Regents to find the strongest available replacement. The only reason Putnam, a strong Vaughan supporter, had been removed from the board was that Willis needed a strong person he could appoint to the State Board of Education. The governor further stated that he selected Dr. Rose as a matter of vindication since Governor Chandler had previously removed him from the Morehead State Board for no reason.

Huntley concluded that had not Willis replaced Putnam with Dr. Rose in the spring of 1946 Vaughan would have continued as president. Williams told Huntley he would have joined Putnam and Keifer in voting for the renewal of Vaughan's contract. When asked why he failed to replace Mrs. Young whose term had also expired, Willis replied that he had not found a suitable successor. Vaughan told both Harris and Huntley that Mrs. Young had voted for him on his two previous contracts and had remained favorable to him until less than a week before his dismissal, at which time she had been called to Frankfort. Upon returning, she indicated to the president that since she desired to keep her place on the board, she could no longer support him for president. In his conversations with others, Huntley was told that Mrs. Young was willing to take whichever side was necessary for her continuance on the board.

Members of the Morehead State staff told Huntley that more had been accomplished in Vaughan's six years than under any previous administration. Members of the faculty were outspoken in their praise of Vaughan. Most of the faculty—89 in all—signed a statement requesting that Vaughan continue as president.

Huntley pinpointed the source of many of Vaughan's problems as being due to the quality of the Board of Regents. He described Keifer as "an able, alert man," who was also serving as a member of Kentucky Wesleyan's Board of Trustees. In his rather severe assessment of other board members, Huntley stated that Mrs. Young admitted that Vaughan had good qualities but was not strong enough to be president. Huntley concluded that Mrs. Young responded to political pressure in order to continue on the Board of Regents. Huntley sized up Cornette, an alumnus of Morehead State, as "a limited man of background and perception" who was convinced he knew exactly how the institution should be operated. Perhaps Huntley's sharpest assessment was reserved for Dr. Rose. Describing his visit to the doctor's office, located over a drug store in Olive Hill, twenty miles from Morehead, Huntley asserted that Rose sat, "hat on the back of his head, feet on table, and made no effort as I entered or as I left to move a foot, a hand, or a hat." He considered Rose as well as Young and Cornette unqualified for their positions. Huntley stated that the board brought "no charges of inefficiency, dishonesty, or even autocratic leadership against the president. All they say is that he is not strong enough for the position. Apparently, it took them some time to realize this, since Dr. Vaughan had been a member of the administrative staff for eighteen years."

Huntley concluded that Vaughan's troubles could be traced to his predecessor, Harvey A. Babb, who had suspected Vaughan, his academic dean, of undermining him in such a manner as to bring about his dismissal in 1940. Several Kentucky educators informed Huntley that Babb, executive director of the Unemployment Commission in Willis' administration, was influential in bringing about Vaughan's downfall. Believing that Vaughan's dismissal was primarily political, Huntley favored drastic action. Members of the Executive Council agreed, in most respects, with Huntley's report. Rufus C. Harris concurred with the recommendation for drastic action.

While the Huntley Report was being circulated, the American Association of Colleges for Teacher Education was conducting its own investigation. Vaughan had been vice president of this organization and chairman of its committee on standards. This second accrediting association sent W. P. Morgan, president emeritus of Western Illinois State Teachers College to Kentucky, where he conducted interviews with Willis, Williams, and former President Babb, among others. The American Association's conclusions were the same as those of the Huntley Report, and drastic action was likewise its recommendation.

The Southern Association announced on Friday, December 13, 1946, that Morehead State had lost its accreditation. The Executive Council of the Southern Association chose not to submit a judgment on possible administrative blunders by the outgoing president or to rule on his effectiveness since the agency endeavored not to get involved in evaluating outgoing or incoming presidents. Noting that

*The Maypole Dance was a major social highlight in the spring. Here students are waiting in front of Allie Young Hall for the dance to begin.*

Vaughan reportedly had a vacillating nature without sufficient aggressiveness to serve as an effective president, the Executive Council concluded that all persons who testified, either orally or in writing, presented evidence that "political influence or interference has been recurrent throughout the history of the institution," including Vaughan's administration.

In reaching its decision, the Executive Council rejected Baird's contention that Morehead State was no longer subject to interference and therefore should receive less drastic punishment, perhaps only a two-year probationary status. Ignoring pledges by the board that Baird's administration would be free to conduct the institution on a professional basis, the Executive Council held that the structure of the board was not in compliance with governance requirements and thus recommended that changes be made. Morehead State should be dropped from membership, effective on September 1, 1947. Appearing "stunned and surprised," Governor Willis and State Superintendent Williams, when asked for their responses, replied, "No comment."

Ironically, external politics had brought punishment upon an institution saturated with internal politics since its inception, though it had managed hitherto to escape the anathema of accrediting agencies. Through his unwise use of power, the governor not only contributed to Morehead State's loss of accreditation but also called attention to a system that, if not corrected, could well have jeopardized the standing of all other public institutions of higher education in Kentucky. The American Association of Colleges for Teacher Education likewise decided in February 1947 to dismiss Morehead State from membership in its organization.

The loss of accreditation was Morehead State's darkest hour. Since no previous Kentucky institution of higher learning had experienced this grave situation, the college was in uncharted waters. Although no measure of academic damage was available, the school's loss of prestige which accompanies dismissal by an accrediting agency was significant. Faculty members did not wish to teach in, and students were fearful of graduating from, an institution that had lost its academic standing. The Southern Association anticipated students facing difficulty in transferring their credits to accredited institutions. The University of Louisville Medical School informed Morehead State that it could no longer accept the school's pre-med students, and graduates sometimes encountered trouble in obtaining teaching positions in schools that were fully accredited. Veterans were in danger of losing financial support under the GI Bill of Rights, which contributed to a decline in enrollment from 614 in the fall semester of 1946 to 435 a year later.

Baird spent the first half of his tenure trying to restore Morehead State's accreditation. He notified the Southern Association, on November 20, 1947, of his intention to present Morehead State's proposal for readmission at the annual meeting in Louisville the following month. His request having been granted, he appeared before the Association along with Governor-elect Earle C. Clements and State Superintendent of Public Instruction-elect B. B. Hodgkin. Clements assured the gathering that the January 1948 legislature would repeal the 1934 law, thereby removing the power of the governor to replace college board members at will and without cause. Clements began his gubernatorial campaign of 1947 in Morehead's Jayne Memorial Stadium with the promise that Morehead State would no longer be under political control.

The Southern Association responded that once these changes became reality, another study would be made of the institution and its status would be reconsidered at the December 1948 meeting. On January 8, 1948, H. L. Hubbard, Chairman of the Commission on Institutions of Higher Education, wrote to Baird, expressing satisfaction that the governor planned to ask the legislature to grant tenure to members of boards of regents in all state colleges. Baird was instructed to notify the Executive Secretary as soon as the legislature passed the proposed bill. On June 18, 1948, Baird sent the Southern

*W. H. (Honie) Rice served for decades as superintendent of buildings and grounds during the era of Morehead State's most dramatic growth.*

Association a copy of House Bill No. 84 that denied the Governor the right to remove board members without cause. Signed by Governor Clements on March 25, 1948, the new law was to become effective on June 17, 1948. The Southern Association was perplexed as to why Baird waited so long to notify it of the major change.

On June 10, 1948, a week before the new law went into effect, Clements installed a completely new board at Morehead State. In a letter to the Southern Association, he explained that the terms of two regents had expired and that a third board member resigned at the governor's request; he then removed the fourth member who had refused to resign. He justified his action by saying it would speed the reaccreditation of Morehead State. Clements was proud of the qualifications of his new appointees — James T. Norris, associate editor of the *Ashland Daily Independent* and president of Centre College Alumni Association; W. W. Ball, president of State National Bank and State Trust Company in Maysville; Emory R. Price, superintendent of Inland Steel Company at Wheelwright; and M. K. Eblen, a Hazard attorney who had graduated from the University of Kentucky Law School.

When an institution had been dropped from membership, the Southern Association customarily reviewed it again to judge whether it should be readmitted. Therefore, on June 21, 1948, Hubbard named a special committee to conduct a study of Morehead State. The committee, consisting of Huntley and three college presidents, spent three days, July 19-21, 1948, interviewing Morehead State's new Board of Regents, Governor Clements, Superintendent Hodgkins, and Morehead State faculty and administrators. Baird called the committee's attention to four significant improvements: First, Governor Clements had successfully pushed Kentucky's General Assembly to change the "ouster law," thereby clearing up one of the major problems detected in Kentucky's higher education system. Second, the new board was well qualified. Third, the board had adopted regulations of tenure providing security to faculty and staff. Finally, faculty and staff had confidence in the board, which, in turn, expressed confidence in the president and faculty.

The committee presented the results of its study to the Executive Council in Birmingham, Alabama, on July 26, 1948. W. P. Morgan, who had previously conducted an investigation for the American Association of Colleges for Teacher Education, was present. The Southern Association was satisfied that remedies had been applied to the deficiencies that had led to the institution's loss of accreditation. In a July 1948 follow-up examination, the committee, however, uncovered persistent inadequacies: the discovery that Morehead alumni entering graduate and professional schools within the immediate past five years had fared poorly; the failure of the registrar's office to develop an adequate record system; the need for greater discrimination in the admission and retention of weak students; the existence of excessive vacancies in departmental headships and professorships; an urgency for substantial increase in faculty members with doctoral degrees; the necessity for the appointment of a dean of students; and the imperative to add hundreds of volumes in library holdings, especially in professional education, since Morehead State was primarily a teacher-training institution and had been offering a master's degree in education since the early 1940s. In spite of these citations, the committee stated its belief that Morehead State College had a real future in serving the Commonwealth of Kentucky. The committee gave the Morehead State administration until the Southern Association's annual meeting in December 1948 to comply with its recommendations, pending a decision on the college's readmission.

Correcting all of the weaknesses outlined previously in less than six months was next to impossible. Baird had to submit a detailed, workable plan to achieve all of the objectives, and he had to show that the college was making genuine progress towards meeting them. A considerable influx of state money was needed, and the governor and legislature came up with this extra money. Baird's quick and thorough response met the December deadline, thereby prompting the Southern Association to restore Morehead State to membership, retroactive to September 1947. The use of this date insured that the credit hours earned by students would not be in jeopardy. The news of Morehead State's regaining reaccreditation on December 2, 1948, set off a tremendous emotional explosion on the campus and in the town of Morehead. The American Association of Colleges for Teacher Education took the same action at its next annual meeting in February 1949.

While Morehead State suffered temporarily from losing accreditation, the institution ultimately benefited. The resulting changes made for long-term improvements, both in governance and in internal operations. Although Morehead State was the only state college in Kentucky to lose its accreditation, every college and university reaped the benefits of the new state law which forbade a gov-

ernor to remove board members and presidents for personal or political reasons.

As significant as the change was, Governor Clements and the
press through editorials exaggerated the magnitude of the new tenure act when they assured the accrediting associations that politics
had been removed from Kentucky's higher education system. During the succeeding decade two of the most powerful political figures
in the history of Kentucky higher education appeared on the scene—
Adron Doran at Morehead and Robert Richard Martin at Eastern.

## Campus Personalities

The Morehead State Teachers College faculty included a combination of outstanding talents and interesting personalities. When
Ralph Hudson arrived at Morehead State in 1931, the art department
was located on the first floor of Johnson Camden Library. As is often true in small colleges, Hudson wound up teaching a wide variety of classes, including art, creative writing, English composition,
and journalism during his five years at Morehead State. Among his
favorite memories was the female student in his art appreciation
class who informed him that "her father would kill her if he saw
these pictures of Roman and Greek nude men." Another student,
James Stuart, told Hudson after class one day that he had a brother
Jesse who was doing some writing, so they invited him to come to
campus and talk to their class. Hudson remembers teaching an off-
campus journalism class at Salyersville. "When the weather was
good, it was only 50 miles; when it was bad, the fields along the road
were sometimes better than the road itself, so we occasionally would
get over in the fields and drive along."

Hudson also served as advisor for the *Raconteur.* During the
"Mayday celebration" in 1932, a "barnstorming plane" came through
the region offering rides for a fee. At the edge of town, a fence had
been taken down "between two cow pastures" so the plane could
land. Hudson and A. Y. Lloyd, history and political science profes-

sor and later father-in-law of Governor Brereton C. Jones, shared a ride. "While A. Y. held on to my belt, I leaned over the cockpit and made a picture of our campus. The pilot, who was familiar with photography, would bank the plane whenever I was ready to take the picture." Hudson's aerial view of the campus was used for several years both in the *Raconteur* as well as in college catalogues as a frontispiece. He left Morehead State in 1936 to become chairman of the art department at the University of Arkansas.

When George T. Young began a 40-year tenure as a history and social science teacher on April 7, 1932, he was impressed with the new Johnson-Camden Library as "the loveliest of all of our campus buildings." Next door, the faculty had a private dining room at the east end of Allie Young Hall. Faculty meetings were held in the Administration Building with teachers attending from the training school as well as the college.

Ophelia O. Wilkes, a geography professor from Tennessee, was described by one of her colleagues as "a daughter of the Old South, very correct, young and impressionable, and a most excellent instructor." Faculty and students looked upon "gentle Henry A. Carey" as so humble that he "couldn't even look at people" but instead stared out the window or at the ceiling while teaching sociology and anthropology. However, his masterful handling of such difficult topics as hieroglyphics or cuneiform commanded student respect.

Rex L. Hoke, psychology professor, was inclined to be eccentric and forgetful. He is remembered for both his brilliance and his absent-mindedness. Among other incidents, the story is often related about the day he reported to City Hall that his car was missing. Immediately, the police located his automobile in front of the post office on Main Street. He had driven down town from his home on Wilson Avenue and then walked the two blocks back home without remembering his automobile.

An air of informality prevailed on the Morehead campus. A few minutes before the beginning of class, Neville Fincel would surround himself in the hallway on the second floor of the Administration Building with those students who wished to have "a last-minute smoke" with their professor. One young lady was habitually late for her 7:30 summer class; when Fincel came to her name in calling the roll, he made it a practice to walk over to the open window, and shout her name across the valley below. Jeanne Dotson, an art major in the mid-Forties, enjoyed being in a department where, "if you were 'in,' you could call Naomi Claypool, the chairperson, 'Puddle.' There was this closeness or family. You could call Miss Juanita Minnish, foreign language teacher, 'Minnie.' We had 'Minnie and the Tadpoles'—students were the Tadpoles."

Lucien H. Rice, an alumnus who became a Boy Scout executive on the national level, remembers Linus A. Fair as a "stern and good teacher who required a great deal" in his mathematics classes. According to Dr. Harold and Jane Young Holbrook, "People like Mr. Fair hung in there during the rough times. Everybody called him 'Fair.' He was such a strong proponent of Morehead State."

W. H. (Honie) Rice, superintendent of buildings and grounds was also a colorful figure. After obtaining a degree in engineering at the University of Kentucky, he accepted the Morehead position in early 1931 and remained long enough to see his staff of seven expand to more than 200. The nature of his work perhaps made him more fully aware of what happened on campus than anyone else with the exception of the president. Once a distraught coed ran away from her dormitory after threatening to kill herself over an unhappy romance. Her roommates and the dorm director finally located the student on a hill overlooking the campus. Since Honie was familiar with the terrain, he was called for assistance and arrived at the dorm just as the search party was returning with the weeping coed. When he proffered his assistance, the dorm director asked, "Can you mend a broken heart?" Honie's sage reply was, "Why not? I've fixed everything else around here." On another occasion, several football players decided they needed a day off from classes. They fastened the front door of the old Administration Building (where most classes were held) with a log chain and announced a strike. Having been called to campus to reopen the building, Honie marched up to the front door with a pair of bolt cutters in his hand, and while some of the players protested, "Cave Man" (a nickname Honie picked up while playing football at UK) muscled his 240-pound frame up to the door and snapped the chain with the classic pronouncement, "Strike's over!" You can be sure, it was!

## Student Life

In spite of national depression, world war, and political intrigue, Morehead State students created pleasurable diversions, as young people have always managed to do. The *Raconteur,* the institution's yearbook, suggested that it was the duty of every student to be an active member of some organization. Thus, campus organizations became a vital feature of college life as well as an expression of student initiative. Students, however, had to create their own campus organizations since national fraternities and sororities were forbidden. President Payne stated that a student's financial status was so inconsequential that "you can dishwash your way through and still go with the best looking girl on the campus." The faculty and administration held that for the student body of Morehead the fraternity idea had no place on the campus. Since Morehead State was primarily interested in the training of teachers, the faculty recommended that immediate steps be taken to secure a chapter of a national educational fraternity, preferably Kappa Delta Pi. They further suggested that departmental clubs be established and that existing debating and library clubs look toward affiliation with appropriate national groups. In the opinion of the faculty, the popular county clubs, started in the Twenties, should be discouraged since they led students to spend time with friends from home exclusively rather than associating with other students.

Another issue which surfaced frequently on the Morehead

State campus concerned the development of a suitable school policy on dancing. In the spring of 1934, the faculty voted 33 to 4 to accept the dancing mandate which was presented by a committee composed of Dean William H. Vaughan and Professors E. V. Hollis and Warren C. Lappin. Again, policy on dancing came up in 1937 when the Social Committee presented new regulations for dances. All of these rulings were concerned with the number of dances that were to be held, hours, chaperons, sponsors, and overall behavior. For example, five chaperons were required for each dance, and a "floor committee," consisting of eight students, would report any misconduct to the chairman of the Social Committee.

Another governing body, the Discipline Committee, remained active throughout the eighteen-year era of Morehead State Teachers College. In the early 1930s its membership consisted of President Payne, Dean Vaughan, Professor Lappin, and two others. Standards remained strict. In 1930 a student who was found guilty of changing the price on meal tickets was sentenced to four hours of shoveling coal. Three other students could

*Tears glistened in the eyes of Ellis T. Johnson when MSU's new basketball arena was named in his honor in 1987. A native of Rowan County, he served as the institution's athletics director and head coach in all sports from 1936 to 1953. One of the founders of the Ohio Valley Conference, he also led Morehead State into the NCAA.*

not eat in the cafeteria the rest of the semester for breaking line and laughing at the teacher in charge. A student was placed on probation in 1931 for using profane language around Fields Hall. As late as 1947 the committee considered the case of a woman who had spent the night away from the dormitory without permission. She was placed on probation for the rest of the quarter and was told to observe the following regulations: She could have no dates; she had to be in her room each evening by 7:30; she could have no weekend permits; she could not visit anywhere in either the town or the county, including restaurants and theaters; and she must get permission from the dean before leaving campus at any time. Even then, she must be accompanied by another student. If she violated any of these regulations, she would experience immediate dismissal.

Faculty members were often reluctant to trust students with making decisions. At a meeting in April 1934 the faculty decided that they, rather than the students, should select the college representative to the Mountain Laurel Festival in Pineville. A faculty committee of four men was appointed to select ten candidates who would subsequently appear before a faculty meeting where one would be chosen to represent Morehead State. Katherine Daniels was chosen in 1935 to be Morehead State's first entry in the Mountain Laurel Festival. The utter lack of student involvement in the process was evident in the *Raconteur's* sarcastic statement that Evelyn Harpham, the second year's candidate, was "chosen for her poise and charm by a representative committee of the faculty, and we, the students, feel that she is representative of all the qualities demanded."

Since few national organizations were on campus, students developed special interest groups. Those who enjoyed music, drama, language, literature, or art formed relevant clubs. The Revellers, organized by drama students in 1930 to develop student dramatic talent, soon became one of the most active organizations on campus. Under the direction of Lucille Caudill, in 1934 and 1935, the Revellers produced Sutton Vane's *Outward Bound* and Philip Barry's highly sophisticated comedy *Holiday* among others.

Music students organized the Foster Choral Club in 1930. Named for the famed Stephen Collins Foster, the group was composed of twenty-four voices, chosen through competitive tryouts. Under the direction of Lewis Henry Horton, the singers added to their repertory several choral arrangements of Kentucky mountain music. Horton felt driven by a mission to perpetuate this truly American music. During the 1930s and 1940s, the Foster Choral Club made many regional and national appearances, including radio station WHAS in Louisville, the 1934 Chicago World's Fair, and the New York World's Fair in 1940. Except for a one-year absence from campus, Horton directed the group during its first eleven years.

Emma Shader, Morehead State's first music instructor, organized the initial college band in 1923 which provided both campus and community with musical programs. Music professor Marvin E. George's marching band started performing at athletic events in 1931; the band was composed of students from the training school and the college. Frequent band clinics on campus not only benefited Morehead State students but also helped recruit new students for the college. The King's Jesters Orchestra, a dance band, was organized by Professor Earl K. Senff, history professor, in 1936-37, by blending talents on campus with those from the town. The name of the group was changed in 1937-38 to the Blue and Gold.

The Lloyd Debating Club, named for faculty sponsor A.Y. Lloyd, was started in 1932 to promote interest in the art of public speaking as well as to increase opportunities in intramural and intercollegiate debating. The club also taught parliamentary procedure and stage presence. In its first two years, it experienced only two defeats in twenty debates; a separate girls debating team went undefeated for three years. During its first five years, the club participated in 107 intercollegiate contests, losing only six debates with universities from twenty-five states. In 1934-35 the team partici-

*The Morehead State football team of 1937 had the most successful record, 7-1, in the history of the institution. From left are Wyant, Marzetti, Mosley, Ishmael, Anderson, Fair, Hammonds, Radjunas, Fitch, Robertson, Greenholz, Horton, Stanley, Edwards, Rose, Bailey, Triplett, Reynolds, Carter, Vinson, Adams, Kiser, Houston and Lowman.*

pated in the Mid-South Debate Tournament in Conway, Arkansas, against the best competition from nine southern states; Elijah Hogge and Melvin Huden reached the quarterfinals. Competing against outstanding schools in Pennsylvania, West Virginia, Vermont, and ten southern states, Morehead State did not lose a single decision in twenty-five debates.

The sciences also organized special clubs. The Caduceus Club was founded in 1933 to foster interest and advise students in the pre-medical field. The group's first sponsor was Katherine Carr. Carr and W. A. Welter started Beta Zeta in 1933 to focus on biology. Beta represented the botanical sciences, and Zeta, the zoological sciences. The club's first two projects were building and stocking an aquarium and classifying all birds and wild flowers in Rowan County. A later project involved planting a wild flower garden in the woods behind Allie Young Hall. In 1948 the club became Beta Chi Zeta and included those majoring in chemistry as well as botany or zoology.

Peri-Estotes, meaning "standing around" or "being on the spot," was Morehead State's first press club, organized and directed by Mrs. Rex L. Hoke. Members of the organization came from her journalism class or the staff of the *Trail Blazer*, which she advised. Full-time membership was open to those who either published as many as five articles in the campus newspaper or rendered "some distinct service" to the paper for a year. The organization changed its name to the Press Club in 1934.

Language-oriented organizations were also organized. Flola Shepherd, foreign languages instructor, and Emma Bach, head of the foreign language department, started Le Club Francais in 1931. Plays, games, and lectures in French enriched club meetings. The cultural background of club members was broadened through the study of outstanding French artists, writers, and composers. Der Deutsche Verein, a similar organization for students studying German, made its appearance in 1933. The Quill and Quair Club, composed of English majors, was started in 1935, with Paul Holman as editor of its publication. Inez Faith Humphrey, chairperson of the English department, served as sponsor and Ralph Hudson, art instructor, was faculty advisor. The club's publication was issued each semester with the objective of stimulating interest in creative writing. Its first issue received special attention since the renowned Jesse Stuart was invited to submit some of his poetry.

The Beaux Arts Club, organized in 1935, furthered interest in the fine arts and furnished students an opportunity to take part in art activities. "Art appreciation, like love, cannot be done by proxy," its motto stated. Naomi Claypool and Ralph Hudson served as the club's original sponsors. Beaux Arts sponsored excursions to the Cincinnati Art Museum as well as art entertainments such as puppet shows, lectures, art contests, exhibits, and the annual Beaux Arts Ball, a costume affair. Art professor Thomas D. Young succeeded Ralph Hudson as co-sponsor in 1937.

The Agriculture Club, founded by Henry C. Haggan in 1938,

planted shrubbery behind Fields Hall, made Christmas wreaths, and established an outdoor campsite in Rowan County. Along with the Industrial Arts Club, it landscaped the grounds of Science Hall. In 1941-42, the group also assisted in landscaping and making Christmas wreaths for the home management house and some private homes in Morehead. From 1945 to 1947, students transplanted several native shrubs from the hills of Rowan County to the campus of Morehead State. The club planted over 5,000 flowering bulbs and plants and furnished the community with a collection of hybrid rhododendrons.

By 1938, chapters of national organizations began to appear on campus. Among these was the Kappa Mu Society for students majoring in commerce. Its sponsors were Rienzi W. Jennings and Ross C. Anderson. Another national organization was Phi Mu Society, started in 1939, for those interested in mathematics and physics. Its sponsors were James G. Black and Linus A. Fair. At the request of President Vaughan, Frank B. Miller organized a chapter of the Future Teachers of America early in the fall semester of 1940; a national charter was granted before the end of the term. Morehead State's chapter was the largest of six chapters in Kentucky during that school year. Kappa Delta Pi (Epsilon Theta Chapter) was installed at Morehead State in the spring of 1942. This organization was primarily interested in promoting fidelity to humanity, service, and scholarship. Membership served as a mark of distinction in the teaching profession.

Student government at Morehead State evolved from student efforts to assist the directors of the residence halls in which they lived. In the fall of 1931, a Student Council was organized to assist Martha Blessing, dean of men, to deal with problems arising in Thompson Hall. Likewise, women in Fields Hall organized a council in 1933 under the initiative of Curraleen C. Smith, dean of women. The Fields Hall council placed a silver cup in the dormitory and inscribed on it each year the name of the girl achieving the highest scholastic standing.

The Niwatori Club, composed of students in Allie Young Hall, began in the fall of 1931 under the leadership of Exer Robinson. Besides concerns with Allie Young Hall, Niwatori involved itself in several projects to improve the appearance of the campus. Each year, the club sponsored the Winter Carnival, with proceeds going to the *Raconteur.* In the mid-Thirties, the club sponsored a trip to Pike's Peak as well as efforts to broadcast Morehead State's first radio program over WCMI, Ashland.

The first Winter Carnival was conducted in 1934, crowning Claude Clayton as king and Marianna Thomas as queen. The event was originated by the *Raconteur* staff and sponsored by the Niwatori and Campus Clubs. By 1937 the Winter Carnival had taken its place as one of the highlights of the year, along with Homecoming, Junior Prom, and Campus Club Ball. Since the *Raconteur* had become self-supporting by this time, proceeds were turned over to the Social Committee to pay for social events.

Intramural sports were enthusiastically supported on campus. Beginning in 1929, Allie Young Hall, Fields Hall, and the Town Team competed in women's basketball. The county clubs also organized a basketball tournament; seventeen teams, for instance, entered the intramural county basketball tournament in 1934. The Women's Athletic Association was started during the 1933-34 school year in response to student demand, with Ernestine Troemel, a graduate of Columbia University, who had been hired as director of physical education for women, serving as its first advisor. She also supervised the women's intramural basketball tournament. The WAA offered a class in ballroom dancing and staged intramural tournaments in girls' basketball, tennis, volleyball, mixed volleyball, and tennis. Louise Caudill, physical education instructor, served as the WAA faculty sponsor in 1938-39.

Seventeen charter members started the Campus Club in 1933 "to promote school spirit and good fellowship within the student body and to recognize and honor men of good scholarship and outstanding merit within the college." T. Henry Coates was its first faculty advisor and Harold Holliday its first president. Club membership was open to male upperclassmen who had shown leadership, promoted school spirit, and excelled in extra-curricular activity with a desire to build a better Morehead. Members were quite proud that State Senator Allie Young accepted honorary membership in the club. The Campus Club took on new life in 1936 by making an appeal on behalf of the athletic program at the college, and the organization gave President Babb strong support in his efforts to create a successful football program. The Campus Club Spring Dance, known to students as the "Dance of the Year," brought a different, outstanding band to campus annually.

Religious organizations also flourished, including the YWCA and YMCA. With Curraleen C. Smith serving as YWCA sponsor for many years, the group worked to make the vesper services on Sunday evening interesting and inspirational. A second accomplishment was the development of a student loan fund for females, resulting in over twenty girls being able to stay in school in the late 1930s who probably could not have done so without such assistance. The organiza-

*Earl Duncan was selected as Morehead State's first basketball All-American in 1943.*

124

tion also conducted vespers on Monday evenings, as well as special services at Christmas, Lent, and Easter. The YWCA furnished a recreational room in the basement of Fields Hall for women students and operated a secondhand bookstore in the basement of Fields Hall, with profits going to the Student Loan Fund. The YWCA had 114 student members by 1938, a large number for a small college. The YMCA, which came to the campus in 1930, never drew a large membership. It did, however, maintain a student loan fund and develop a "Student Handbook" for campus newcomers.

## Athletics

### Baseball:

Although Morehead State fielded baseball teams throughout most of the Roaring Twenties, no documentation is available until the 1927 season. After posting respectable records of 6-4 in 1927 and 7-3 in 1928, Morehead State claimed to be "state champions" in 1930 with a 9-1 record, with its only defeat at the hands of Centre, whom they had defeated earlier. Edgar McNabb pitched eight of the team's nine victories, including two shutouts, and veteran shortstop Lawrence Fraley led the team with a .500 batting average. Raymond Carroll and Captain Hubert Counts pounded out the most extra base hits.

Yet, the baseball program began to encounter significant problems at the time when it appeared Morehead State might excel in this sport. The baseball team had to practice indoors until spring football practice ended late in March; however, the most vexing problem was that by 1932, most Kentucky colleges were discontinuing baseball as an intercollegiate sport. Playing schools like Morris Harvey in West Virginia and Marietta College in Ohio, Morehead State posted a 6-3 record in 1931 and a 4-1 mark the following year. Few baseball games were played the rest of the decade because of difficulty in scheduling enough teams to have a meaningful program. Finally, the Babb administration cancelled baseball from 1937 to 1940 in order to emphasize football.

After Coach Ellis Johnson's respectable 5-2 season in 1941, Morehead State did not compete in baseball from 1942 to 1945 due to World War II. The baseball Eagles reached their pinnacle of success in 1947 when they captured the KIAC championship with a 10-4 record. By the time Morehead became a charter member of the Ohio Valley Conference in 1948, the scanty records indicate that the school had won 69 games in baseball while losing 36.

### Football:

Intercollegiate football made its appearance on campus in 1927 under Coach George D. Downing. From 1927 through 1935, his teams won 28 games, lost 32, and tied 3, as he led the Eagles to four winning seasons. Downing, who produced a fair gridiron record until 1931, won only 20 percent of his games for the next four seasons. In its maiden season, Morehead State went from one extreme to the other. The Eagles' first football game ever played resulted in a 77-0 shellacking by Morris Harvey. Then Morehead ended its season by shelling Anderson-Broaddus, 83-0. Morehead State's 7-2 mark in 1928 was the best football record of any Kentucky college that year and still ranks as the college's third greatest season. Morehead won its first game ever against Eastern, 18-0, in a sea of mud. With a squad of fifteen and using only one substitution, Morehead again defeated Eastern, 13-6, in a mediocre 4-4 season in 1929. With starters playing the entire game, the Blue and Gold delighted alumni with a 20-0 Homecoming trouncing of Morris Harvey, its other major rival in those days.

Morehead State's first recorded athletic policy, framed in 1930, included lofty standards. Athletics should be engaged in as a means of "physical development," an instrument for "engendering college spirit," and for "publicity values" that grow out of it. In spite of a desire for victory, "we believe that it is more important to play the game squarely than to win." Preferring that all athletes be students with the primary purpose of obtaining an education, Morehead State believed that its football team should not be judged solely by its won-lost record but by athletes' efforts to give their best to the institution.

After suffering through a 2-6 record in 1930, Downing's team posted a 4-2-1 mark the following year, highlighted by a scoreless tie with Eastern in a Homecoming game before a Jayne Memorial Stadium crowd of 3,000. The season's opener against Concord College featured a Morehead interception by Parney Martindale, giant tackle from Mississippi, which resulted in a 6-0 Eagle squeaker. Halfback Claude Clayton sparked a 12-6 win over Union by returning a pass interception for a ninety-eight yard touchdown, to this day Morehead's record for the longest pass interception return. Downing's 1932 team wound up with an identical 4-2-1 season. Highlights included a 20-0 victory over Louisville, with Eagle quarterback, Pearl (Mouse) Combs, hurling three touchdown passes, to establish himself as the most outstanding passer in the conference.

In the fall of 1935, Morehead State settled on the name "Eagles" for its athletic teams. "Bald Eagles," selected in a public contest in 1926, evolved into "Golden Eagles," to conform with school colors. "Golden Eagles" was dropped when Morehead remembered that the name conflicted with that of Morris Harvey, a bitter rival. "Eagles" seemed a fitting name since most of their football victories for three seasons had come by the aerial route.

Pent up frustration due to recent failures to win games burst into the open in two widely publicized developments shortly before the 1935 Christmas break. On December 15 the Campus Club, composed partly of athletes, called a meeting at a time when faculty advisor Neville Fincel could not be present and passed a resolution urging the Board of Regents to investigate Morehead's athletic situation, charging that the athletic department had taken no steps to remedy the school's poor record. Bill Thompson, club president and a football player, ordered that copies of the resolution be mailed to board members, President Babb, Dean Vaughan, Coach Downing, and Professor Romie D. Judd, chairman of the athletic council. Two days later Fincel arranged a second meeting of the Campus Club and requested members to reconsider their resolution. Their second vote, like the first, was unanimous. Three weeks later Fincel resigned as faculty advisor and was succeeded by A. Y. Lloyd, who shared the views expressed in the resolution. At the annual football banquet on December 16, President Babb promised that changes would be made in the athletic program.

Influenced by public opinion stirred up by the Campus Club, Morehead State let it be known that a coaching change was about to occur. In June 1936 the Board of Regents named Downing the director of the physical education department and hired Ellis T. Johnson to head basketball and football with Len Miller as his assistant. Johnson, a native of Morehead, had moved to Ashland while still in elementary school and had been captain of the Ashland Tomcats who captured the national championship in 1928 in Chicago. Johnson graduated in 1932 from the University of Kentucky, where he was an All-American in football and basketball. He afterwards coached high school football and basketball in Williamson, West Virginia, and was an assistant coach in Ashland, his hometown. After playing football and basketball at UK, Miller was employed as an assistant coach there for five years under football coach Harry Gamage and basketball coach Adolph Rupp; he then served as head coach at Coal Grove High School in Ohio.

President Babb was credited with bringing Johnson to Morehead. In 1909 and 1910 Babb had starred at end for the University of Kentucky and later coached football two years at Springdale, Arkansas, and three seasons at Henderson, where he won a conference championship. He deeply believed the way to put Morehead State on the map was through developing a strong football program. The president frequently conferred special benefits on football, such

*Warren Cooper was chosen as Morehead State's second All-American in 1945. Here, he is shown being honored in 1972 with his wife Lake, mathematics instructor.*

as installing a new electric scoreboard in Jayne Memorial Stadium, showing not only the minutes remaining in a quarter but also the additional seconds.

The four seasons of the Babb administration stand out as Morehead State's golden age in football. Babb prided himself in the fact that the Eagles won twenty-two games, while losing only five and tying three during his tenure. Coach Johnson's very first game, against Murray State, created great expectations on the Morehead campus. Murray, a five touchdown favorite, barely escaped with a 14-7 victory. Coach Johnson hungered for a real win in Morehead's outing against Transylvania. On a freakish play, Morehead State's John (Buck) Horton crashed through the middle of the line and jumped high in the air to block a pass; sophomore guard Jody Adams caught the ball as it came down and wormed his way across the Transy goal line for a 7-0 victory.

Eagles of that era still regard their 1936 contest with Eastern as the most spectacular sporting event in the school's history. The game inaugurated the colorful pageantry associated with the "Old Hawg Rifle" tradition. The Campus Club initiated this tradition after purchasing the pre-Revolutionary War muzzle loader from a mountaineer who claimed it had been used in the Rowan County War in the mid-1880s. Fred Caudill, basketball player and president of the club, took the rifle to Eastern where it was introduced to the student body in chapel exercises on the day of the game. Later, Caudill presented the "Hawg Rifle" to Presidents Harvey A. Babb of Morehead and Herman L. Donovan of Eastern. The plan called for the president of the losing team to present the relic to the president of the winning team each year at the end of the contest. The "Hawg Rifle" would then be retained by the winning institution for a year.

Excitement reigned in anticipation of this first "Hawg Rifle" contest. Unbeaten Eastern enjoyed the only spotless record in Kentucky, but Morehead diehard enthusiasts felt their Eagles had an outside chance of knocking off the Maroons in spite of having dropped their last six contests with Eastern. Arrangements were made for a special train to carry Morehead State's 50-piece band and approximately 300 fans to Richmond; the band was led by Linda Lee Eaton, the first female drum major at Morehead. Those unable to make the journey were overjoyed to learn that a play-by-play broadcast would be heard in Morehead.

As enthusiasm mounted, Coach Johnson asked Earl K. Senff, history professor from 1933 to 1942 and leader of a band called the King's Jesters, to write a "fight song" for the initial "Hawg Rifle" game. The saxophonist and pianist sat down one night and composed the words and music to "Fight, Fight, Fight for Morehead."

Fight, fight, fight for Morehead.
Fight on, varsity.
Ever onward marching to our victory—
We're gonna fight, fight, fight for Morehead,
Colors gold and blue,
Our hopes on you we're pinning
Whether losing or winning,
Go, you Eagles and fight, fight, fight.

Senff led his musical group in the first public performance of this composition at a student assembly on Thursday morning. Students received the song enthusiastically and then sang it with zest the following Saturday afternoon during the first "Hawg Rifle" contest. The fight song has remained a tradition at Morehead State for 61 years. Senff, who had also served as tennis and swimming coach, received no compensation for the song and gave all rights to the school. Senff was a nephew of the late Earl W. Senff, member of the commission which had selected Morehead as the site for the college.

After Eastern dominated the first quarter of the initial "Hawg Rifle" game, Eagle captain and star center Robert (Bushog) Brashear intercepted a pass and dashed sixty yards to paydirt. Later in the second quarter, Yonnie Reynolds broke through tackle and galloped sixty-five yards for a 13-0 halftime lead for the Eagles. Eastern finally scored its single touchdown in the fourth quarter. But with two minutes remaining, Eastern punted, and Eagle quarterback (Tiny Tim) Wyant took the ball on his one-yard line and raced 99 yards for the final touchdown—the longest punt return in Morehead's history—making the winning score 19-7. Thus, Morehead State proudly carried the "Hawg Rifle" back to campus, where it was kept a year in a special case in the library.

Coach Johnson's 7-1 record in 1937 stands out as Morehead State's greatest season in football history. After shutting out Cincinnati, East Tennessee, Georgetown, and Alfred Holbrook College, the Eagles escaped with a scant 7-6 defeat of the hard-fighting Transylvania Pioneers. With six minutes remaining, Custer Reynolds, the "Bull of the Buckhorn," gave Morehead its fifth consecutive victory by slashing through the line 63 yards to score.

The *Courier-Journal* headlined Morehead State's Homecoming game with Eastern, "Morehead Snipes Eastern 26-0 in Mountain Feud for Hog Rifle." The game was witnessed by 3,500, the largest crowd at Jayne Stadium to that day. Holding the "Hawg Rifle" before his team, Johnson fired them up with an enthusiastic pep talk:

> Boys, I want you to click with all the precision and power with which this old rifle used to click when it was in its prime. You are in your prime, and you are primed and cocked for the task ahead this afternoon, the task of dropping, honorably, our Eastern foes. I want you to perform like our forefathers who used to shoot such a gun. I want you to advance with a steady nerve, draw a fine and chilling bead on the targets, and then blaze away with all you have. I want you to conduct yourselves just as the bullets used to conduct themselves that sped from this old rifle.

The following weekend, Morehead State eked out a 9-6 victory over Tennessee Tech in Cookeville, Tennessee. Going into the Murray State contest at the end of the season, the undefeated Eagles had been scored upon by only two teams. But with Murray's 85-piece band playing "The Old Gray Mare Ain't What She Used to Be," the Thoroughbreds scored on their opening drive. After Morehead State tied the score in the second quarter, Murray retaliated to lead at halftime. The Eagles were in scoring territory five times in the third quarter without registering any points. Murray added two touchdowns in the final period to clobber the proud Eagles, 32-7. This defeat brought Morehead State's longest winning streak to an end—

eleven games in 1936-37.

With seventeen lettermen returning in 1938, the Eagles posted a 5-1-1 record, marred only by a 14-0 loss to Murray and a scoreless tie with Eastern. In his past two seasons, Johnson's teams dropped only two games—both to Murray State. Although unaccustomed to winning prior to Johnson, Eagle fans were now shocked if they lost! On Armistice Day, in Ashland, 4,000 fans turned out to support their own Ellis Johnson as his Eagles wiped out a decidedly inferior foe—Central Indiana College. Buck Horton, one of the Eagles' greatest centers, ended four seasons without missing a minute of playing time. Although injured in the fourth quarter at Ashland, he remained in the game. Coaches Johnson and Miller had already decided that if Horton could not stand on his feet, they would play only ten men and thereby allow him to lie on the sidelines so he could complete his unusual record.

Four of the Eagles' five victories in 1938 stand out among the ten largest margins ever registered by Morehead State football teams: a 76-0 rout of Lawrence Tech and identical 58-0 victories over Alfred Holbrook College, Central Indiana College, and Homecoming foe Georgetown College. Beverly (Jug) Varney's 30 points against Holbrook represent the most points ever scored by a Morehead player in a single game; his 252 yards in that game was also the most yardage ever gained by an Eagle. And Varney's 90 points during the 1938 season were the most points ever scored by a Morehead player in one season and made him the nation's highest scorer. The 1938 team gave up only 14 points during the season.

Morehead won six games while losing two in 1939. The two losses were to Murray and Western. Morehead State defeated Transylvania by 20-0, when James (Unc) Gant intercepted a pass and returned it 85 yards for a touchdown shortly after suffering a serious knee injury. The Homecoming game against Eastern featured Benny Vaznellis who scampered 38 yards for an Eagle touchdown and then scored the extra point. Trailing the Eagles by 7-0, the Maroons retaliated on a scoring pass in the closing moments of the game. However, Paul Adams, Eagle center, blocked the extra point attempt for a 7-6 victory, thereby keeping the "Hawg Rifle" in Morehead another year.

In 1939, Vaznellis, a "high stepping importation from Connecticut," was Morehead State's offensive star. He was rewarded by being chosen to a backfield position on the All-KIAC football team although just a sophomore. Stanley (Rajah) Radjunas, also from New Britain, Connecticut, made the All-KIAC football team as a guard in 1937-39 and was selected on the All-SIAA team the latter year. Sophomore Paul Adams, who had played for Coach Miller at Coal

*The 1946 Breckinridge Training high school basketball team won the state championship and Coach Bobby Laughlin was named Kentucky Coach of the Year. Don Battson and Sonny Allen made the All-State team. Shown with the "Sweet 16" trophy are the cheerleaders, from left, including Barbara Tolliver, Betty Jane Wolfford, Janet Patrick, Ann Nickerson and Mary Jo Mobley. The second row, from left, consists of Jim Leach, Bill Fraley, Don Battson, Dicky Scroggins, Fred Bays and Clayton Skaggs. The third row, from left, includes Coach Bob Laughlin, Bill Litton, Sonny Allen, Marvin Mayhall, Frank Fraley and Bill Vaughan.*

Grove, Ohio, was chosen as the center on the All-KIAC team. Beverly (Jug) Varney, a junior who had formerly played football under Coach Johnson at Williamson, West Virginia, made All-SIAA in 1938 and All-KIAC on both the 1938 and 1939 teams. The Eagles produced two All-Americans during the latter 1930s: John (Buck) Horton, Mount Sterling center, in 1938 and Stanley Radjunas the following season.

Four players made the All-KIAC team in 1940: (Jumping Joe) Lustic, regarded as one of the Eagles' all time best fullbacks; Paul Adams, perhaps the most versatile man on the team, switching from center to end and then the backfield because of injuries to others; Joe Ruchinskas, who played sixty minutes per game; and Varney, among Morehead State's most productive scorers in history. Adams was also named to the All-American team.

The Eagles made a bid at becoming a football power again in 1942, when its great defense held the opposition to a total of 21 points during a 4-1-2 season. The Eagles' only loss came at the hands of the Western Hilltoppers, 9-0. The Eagles finally broke the Murray jinx by defeating the Thoroughbreds 13-0, their first win ever over the institution which shared birthdays with Morehead State. Morehead also reclaimed the "Hawg Rifle" in a 20-0 victory over Eastern at Richmond. Vincent (Moose) Zachem, Ashland center, was named as an All-American. The Eagles' football program was discontinued from 1943 to 1945 because of the war. How could they do otherwise when Morehead's enrollment included only nine young men—not enough to field even one team!

After the 1942 season ended, Coach Johnson was drafted into the military service and played quarterback for the Iowa Pre-Flight Seahawks for two seasons against the likes of Notre Dame, Ohio State, and Illinois. Johnson returned in 1946 to direct the Eagles to a 6-1 season, their second best record in history. Their old nemesis, Murray State, was the only team to defeat them—and that by a crushing 38-19 margin. Morehead State posted impressive victories, however, over Morris Harvey, West Liberty, Eastern, Western, Marshall, and Union. This was the first time the Eagles had ever defeated either Western or Marshall in football. Joe Lustic, Maysville running back, returned after the war and was named an All-American. Morehead State then managed only one victory and two ties in nine games in 1947—its last in the KIAC.

By the time Morehead State entered the Ohio Valley Conference in 1948, its football fortunes had been directed by only two football coaches—Downing and Johnson. The latter was well on his way to becoming the Eagles' most successful football coach in history with a 54-44-10 mark from 1936 to 1952. Under him, the school enjoyed eight winning seasons out of thirteen. Five of Morehead State's ten All-Americans played under Johnson from 1938 to 1946, and several on the 1938 and 1946 teams made All-American Honorable Mention.

### Basketball:

The college gymnasium and intercollegiate basketball made a joint debut at Morehead State in 1929. Downing enjoyed greater success in basketball than football; his 51-45 record included three winning seasons during seven years of coaching. Downing's inaugural season was by far his most successful with an impressive 9-3 record, including two victories over Pikeville. Morehead State entered the Kentucky Intercollegiate Athletic Conference in 1933-34, but then experienced three successive losing seasons under Downing.

His successor, Ellis Johnson, put together a 196-158 record during his fifteen seasons, making him the most successful basketball coach in Morehead history. His 14-3 initial season can only be described with superlatives—his most successful season, the best record of any team in Kentucky, and one of the Eagles' greatest records in history. Johnson and his assistant, Len Miller, took mostly sophomores and molded them into an outstanding team. The Eagles won their first eight games before dropping a 46-44 tilt to the Louisville

Cardinals. The only other regular season loss was to Eastern 40-38. After defeating Union twice in the regular season, Morehead lost a 29-26 KIAC tournament game to the Bulldogs. The scoring and quickness of Stanley Arnzen of Newport "thrilled crowds and chilled opponents" that year.

Johnson's third season proved successful as the Eagles won 16 and lost 8 in 1938-39. After losing four games near the end of the season, Morehead State played one of its most successful KIAC Tournaments, advancing to the finals by defeating Centre, 42-21, Union, 36-23, and Murray, 44-37, before missed free throws cost them the championship game against Western, 37-33. James (Unc) Gant, a Cumberland Junior College transfer, was an all-KIAC guard and a unanimous selection for the All-Tournament team, while being awarded the "Sweetheart of the Tourney" honor.

Handicapped by injuries, Morehead State finished the 1939-40 season with a 7-14 record. The Eagles, however, emerged as the surprise team of the KIAC tournament, defeating Murray and regular-season champion Eastern before falling to Western as the Hilltoppers captured their ninth consecutive championship. Morehead State bounced back to take the KIAC seasonal crown in 1940-41 with an 11-7 record. Earl Duncan, sophomore forward, was the team's high scorer and one of the leading scorers in the state. In the KIAC Tournament, the Eagles defeated Louisville, 60-44, before losing to Union, 50-40.

Johnson's 1942-43 team won 12, including beating Marshall twice, while losing 7. In the KIAC Tournament, the Eagles were victorious over Kentucky Wesleyan and Eastern, but as usual in those days, were eliminated by Western. Forward Earl Duncan of Georgetown was named as Morehead State's first All-American after scoring 1430 points in his 74-game collegiate career for an average of 19.3 points per game.

Before the start of the next season, Johnson was in the armed forces, and Assistant Coach Len Miller stepped up to guide the

Eagles' basketball fortunes effectively during his absence. In 1943-44, Miller won the KIAC title with a 12-3 record. The KIAC tournament was not held from 1943 to 1945 because of the war. In 1944-45, Miller's Eagles posted an impressive 16-6 mark. Center Warren Cooper of Brooksville became Morehead State's second All-American, finishing his career with 1,011 points in 54 games for an 18.5 average.

Johnson returned after the war to guide the Eagles to a 13-8 record in 1945-46. Marshall, Murray, and Western fell to Morehead State. The Eagles lost seventeen while winning only ten in the 1947-48 season. Johnson served as head coach and Bob Laughlin as assistant during this last season that Morehead was a member of the KIAC.

Before entering the Ohio Valley Conference in 1948, the Morehead State Eagles were led by three basketball coaches—Downing, Johnson, and Miller. Downing had three winning seasons in Morehead State's first seven years of basketball. In ten seasons before 1948, Johnson had six winning years with a record of 112-101. Miller posted a phenomenal 28-9 record during his two seasons as head coach. Johnson won one KIAC title and Miller another. In 1948, Morehead State, along with four other KIAC members, Louisville, Eastern, Western, and Murray, withdrew from the Kentucky Intercollegiate Athletic Conference and joined with Evansville to become charter members of the Ohio Valley Conference.

After regaining its accreditation and with its athletic teams competing in a new conference, the school boasted a clean bill of health with a new name—Morehead State College.

# Chapter 4

# Morehead State College:
# Years of Growth, 1948-1966

In 1948 Morehead State received a clean bill of health, a fourth
name, a new athletic conference, a revitalized Board of Regents, and
a restoration of membership in the Southern Association of Colleges
and Secondary Schools. From 1948 to 1966, the institution faced no
problems of the magnitude it had borne the previous eighteen years.
In fact, the college reaped numerous benefits from previous adversities: Alumni rallied to the defense of their institution which they
felt had suffered unduly from outside forces; other supporters were
inclined to give Morehead State a second chance; and the youth of
Eastern Kentucky knew they could obtain college credits that would
transfer anywhere without venturing far from home.

Morehead State was poised for growth. The GI Bill attracted a
group of students around whom increased enrollments could be
built. The new Minimum Foundation Program added an incentive
for public school teachers to pursue college credits and degrees,
thereby prompting them to return to college in large numbers to
obtain the additional education necessary for salary increases.
Emergency teaching certificates were on the way out in Kentucky.
Throughout the nation, a steady growth occurred in the number of
college age youth, along with a greater percentage of high school
graduates going on to college. The civil rights movement enabled a
whole new segment of society to attend colleges like Morehead State
for the first time. Sputnik led to the creation of the National Defense
Education Act, thereby providing funds to students and colleges in
selected disciplines. Federal aid to education made it easier for stu-

dents in every field to obtain a college education and for colleges to construct additional buildings to handle dramatic increases in enrollment. The Great Society began to improve life in myriad ways for the counties served by Morehead State.

Fewer institutions of higher learning were vying for limited state funding than would compete later. The community college system had not been put into place, Northern Kentucky University had not been founded, and the Commonwealth of Kentucky had not incorporated the University of Louisville into its system of higher education. The Council on Higher Education was unable to prevent college presidents with political savvy from obtaining a larger slice of the budget for their schools by exerting pressure on the governor and state legislators.

From 1948 to 1966, Morehead State was led by three individuals: William Jesse Baird, who died in office in February 1951; Charles R. Spain, with the briefest tenure of any Morehead president to that time; and Adron Doran, whose longevity of leadership surpassed any other individual in Morehead State history. Only Frank C. Button, who served both the private and public institutions, had longer service as a leader on the Morehead campus.

## Baird Finishes His Term

In 1948 Morehead State received its fourth name in twenty-six years. As early as July 20, 1943, a lengthy faculty meeting addressed the possibility of dropping "Teachers" from the name of the college. Although all the faculty preferred the adoption of the new name, "Morehead State College," no recommendation was made to the president or the Board of Regents. Five years later, the 1948 Kentucky General Assembly voted to eliminate the word "Teachers" from the name of all four state colleges which had once been normal schools. Thus, Morehead State College became the new name in time for the celebration of regaining accreditation in the Southern Association of Colleges and Secondary Schools.

*Charles R. Spain, sixth president of Morehead State, 1951-54. Installed at age 38, he was the youngest leader in the school's history.*

News that the Southern Association had reinstated the college arrived shortly before students left for Christmas vacation in 1948 and set off the greatest impromptu celebration on campus since the end of World War II. Immediately after Baird's telegram arrived from the Southern Association's convention in Memphis, approximately 550 students and half the town's 4,000 residents gathered on campus to give vent to their long pent-up feelings. Classes were either dismissed or unattended. There was a noisy parade downtown led by the college band. The *Rowan County News* published its premiere "extra" edition and its first front-page banner headline since W. E. (Snooks) Crutcher assumed his duties as the paper's publisher/editor.

An official celebration occurred the following week, the day after President Baird and Dean Lappin returned from Memphis. "A stranger entering Rowan County today would have been hopelessly confused," the *Lexington Herald* stated. "For about one hour this morning, things were as still as a ghost town and all the rest of the day, the parading, singing, band playing, dancing, and just general celebrating would have startled anyone not familiar with the circumstances." The festivities included a special convocation in the college auditorium at 11 a.m., after which classes were canceled for the day. School was also dismissed at Morehead Consolidated School, Morehead High School, and Breckinridge Training School, allowing students to join their parents for this formal history-making ceremony. Mayor William H. Layne issued a proclamation, requesting Morehead businesses to close from 11 a.m. to noon and urging citizens to attend the ceremonies in the College Auditorium, which seated 1,300.

It was altogether fitting for Baird, who had led the institution back from the brink of disaster, to serve as master of ceremonies. The president described the day's activities as a "victory celebration for Morehead and all of Kentucky's higher educational institutions." A. Y. Lloyd, director of the Legislative Research Commission and former head of Morehead State's history and political science department, represented Governor Earle C. Clements, who had been ordered by his doctor not to attend the historic occasion because of a leg injury. Gene Lutes, manager of Morehead's two motion-picture theaters, announced a special free movie at 2 p.m. to honor the "finest piece of news we've heard since the war ended." Postmaster Claude Clayton, former Eagle football star, closed the local post office from 11 a.m. till noon, the first weekday it had ever closed except on national holidays. Baird read to the audience the report that the college was reinstated retroactive to September 1, 1947, the date it was dropped officially. Wiping out the entire fifteen-month suspension meant that none of the students' credits during the interval would be in question. Although these credits generally had remained acceptable in Kentucky, they risked being challenged elsewhere.

Each participant's remarks that day were carefully noted. In his presentation of Dean Lappin, Baird proudly stated, "I never saw a dean in the whole Southern Association for whom I would trade Dean Lappin." The president then presented Crutcher who referred to the occasion when Governor Clements appointed the new Board of Regents as the "day on which political entanglements at Morehead were removed." Lloyd pointed out that Morehead State College was never intended exclusively to benefit Morehead or the citizens of Rowan County.

After convocation, the college cafeteria was thrown open to the student body with food "on the house." Faculty, students, alumni, and townspeople continued to celebrate the college's hard-fought "victory" by enthusiastically singing the school's fight song as the Morehead State College band led them in a triumphant parade around campus and downtown. Several-spur-of-the moment dances took place later in the day.

During the fall semester of 1948, Morehead State and local townspeople experienced another major event. The MSC band serenaded President Harry S Truman during his famous Whistlestop Campaign through Morehead. Also responding to a request from the local Democratic committee, Ted Crosthwait arranged to have the high school band at the depot to "play a piece or two." Truman was characteristically feisty that day. As he appeared on the caboose, with bees swarming all around him, he quipped, "There must be something sweet around Morehead." "I'd like to introduce my two bosses" was the signal for his wife Bess and his daughter Margaret to appear, which brought a rousing ovation. President Truman then went through his usual tirade against that "do-nothing 80th Republican Congress." Dorothy Holbrook and John Will, her husband, had just completed "the building on Railroad Street where we moved our business, and many people came and climbed on the roof so they could see the President."

It was appropriate that Governor Clements should deliver the commencement address for the first graduating class after Morehead State regained accreditation. During his presentation, on May 19,

1949, the governor assured the graduates that "politics no longer hampers Kentucky's college officials and teachers," and "the officers and teachers in Kentucky's institutions of higher learning are now secure in the thought that they are judged solely by their own competence."

A state institution of higher education, however, is never completely divorced from politics. As soon as the new academic year opened in September 1949, Baird became heavily involved in making speeches on behalf of the passage of two amendments to the state constitution. One amendment permitted the state to distribute not more than 25 percent of the common school funds on the basis of need. The other allowed Kentucky to raise the salary limit for

*The Morehead Normal School Club erected a marker in 1955 in honor of the "Courting Spot." Located in front of Allie Young Hall, this old pump once furnished water for the entire school and had served as a convenient meeting place for young couples. Shown at the dedication are MNS Club members Otto Razor, Claude Tussey and Harlan Powers.*

state officials to above $5,000, where it had been kept for six decades. After the passage of the latter amendment, Baird became the first Morehead State president whose annual salary exceeded $5,000.

Morehead State's enrollment figures were watched carefully to detect effects of reaccreditation on institutional growth. Its enrollment, though, experienced only a slight increase from 1948 to 1954. The fall enrollment of 1948 included 519 students on campus during the semester when accreditation was restored. In the fall of 1952 Morehead State's on-campus enrollment reached 702, with 460 registered in off-campus classes. Sixteen of the seventy-four veterans had served during the Korean War. The student body represented forty-six Kentucky counties, fourteen states, and one foreign country, Korea. Enrollment jumped to 910 in the fall of 1954, with 375 enrolled in off-campus classes. Those counties sending the most students to Morehead State were Rowan, Carter, Lewis, Floyd, and Elliott, in that order. Ohio led out-of-state enrollment with twenty-six students, followed by Indiana with nineteen and West Virginia with eighteen.

Exciting positive developments occurred after accreditation was restored. In February 1949 Morehead State College invited Jesse H. Stuart, well-known Eastern Kentucky author of *Taps for Private Tussie*, which had sold more than a million copies, to speak in chapel. The dynamic educator had recently published an autobiographical work, *The Thread That Runs So True*. After the English department hosted an afternoon tea for Stuart in the library lounge, a faculty dinner was given in his honor on Wednesday evening.

Morehead State College opened its first art gallery on April 14, 1949, in Johnson Camden Library, with Justus Bier, head of the Art Department at the University of Louisville, as the featured guest. Fifteen paintings by famous Kentucky artists were displayed. Bier's infectious enthusiasm for art inspired the large crowd as he presented brief sketches of the artists along with explanations of the background of each masterpiece on display.

Problems or no problems, Baird always managed to keep a good sense of humor, especially when dealing with the faculty. Shortly before the 1949 Christmas break the President informed the faculty that a "student" had written the following to Santa Claus:

> Please send me for Christmas an instructor: Who knows his subject—who likes to teach—who makes me interested in his subject, no matter what I thought about it before I got in his class—who sets higher standards of preparation for the day's lesson for himself than he expects from the students —who sees to it that light, heat, ventilation, and seating arrangements are comfortably made to affect the least possible interference for the students—who lets me know what he expects me to learn in the form of assignments that are not so easy that they are trivial, yet not so hard that they discourage me—who lets me know how I am getting along, and what I can do to improve my learning—who has a sense of humor— who speaks distinctly without shouting—whose tests are hard enough to make me review everything significant in the course, but which never contain catch questions or quibbling over words—who presents clear objectives for every problem— whom I can respect.

The Morehead State faculty presented the highly-venerated Baird a wrist watch for Christmas in 1949. On January 4, 1950, the president wrote the faculty, "There will be no good reason why I should be late to any appointments this New Year—1950. If you will stop me on the street, in the hall, on the campus or drop in at the office and ask me, 'What time is it?' I can certainly and gladly tell you accurately. It is a nineteen jewel, fourteen karat, solid gold, Hamilton wrist watch. Am I proud!" In closing, he wished the faculty a New Year "full of rich living." Regrettably he would be dead within a year.

In January, 1950, the U.S. Forest Service granted approximately fiftly acres of the Cumberland National Forest (later renamed for Daniel Boone), including Lockegee Rock, to Morehead State for the purpose of making educational and recreational improvements. The land, located approximately six miles south of Clearfield and two miles southwest of Clack Mountain, was known far and wide as a superior site for the scientific study of rocks and plant life. A research team from the University of Illinois had recently been making a study of the area.

From the beginning of his administration, Baird had sought funding for a student union/music building combination. Music rooms were crowded into the basement of Fields Hall while extracurricular student activities centered mainly in the basement of Allie Young Hall. Baird also sought improved housing as an enticement for recruiting prospective faculty. In an October 4, 1950, appearance at the Rowan County Courthouse, Governor Clements announced that more than $1.5 million would be given to Morehead State during the next year for construction of both the student union/music building and a faculty-staff apartment complex. The Board of Regents, however, was disinclined to take on the heavy bonded indebtedness which would accompany the construction of a student union/music building since the college would have no forthcoming income to pay off interest on revenue bonds and because the college's budget could stand no additional financial strains. At its January 1951 meeting, the Board of Regents lowered its sights and decided to proceed with plans for a new music building to be located on the playground of Breckinridge Training School. The Board also requested funding for the construction of a separate student union building across the street from the President's Home on the site of the original Morehead Normal School.

Failing health made it increasingly difficult for Baird to maintain the activity level necessary for a college president. Many Moreheadians pointed out later that Baird was not physically well when he became president in 1946 and that he over extended himself to meet deadlines leading to Morehead State's reaccreditation. Baird became gravely ill with a heart ailment in September 1950. Upon returning to Morehead from a Cincinnati hospital in November, he wrote the faculty, "I cannot tell you how good it is to be home. . . . I have never felt your deep friendship, and the meaning of it to me, so much as I have within the last few weeks while flat on my back."

Because of the seriousness of his health problems, the Board of Regents granted Baird an eight-month leave of absence, beginning January 9, 1951. Dean Warren C. Lappin was named acting president for the second time in his distinguished career; he was serving in that capacity before Baird arrived in 1946. However, on February 19, 1951, the 60-year-old Baird died in a Cincinnati hospital, where he had been a heart patient since December 12. Following funeral services conducted in the College Auditorium by English professor Gabriel C. Banks, Baird was buried in Berea, where he had served as dean of the Foundation School for more than twenty years. Baird, who had guided Morehead State through the most tumultuous period of its history, was the institution's only president to die in office. The previous four leaders had either failed to get their contracts renewed or had been fired. For this reason one of the steps required before Morehead State could be reaccredited was a tenure regulation prohibiting the firing of a college administrator or member of the faculty without cause and guaranteeing them the right of appeal.

Lappin worked through his college roommate and longtime friend, A. B. (Happy) Chandler, to arrange for Branch Rickey, one of the nation's most colorful sports figures as general manager of the Pittsburgh Pirates, to deliver the commencement address on May 30, 1951. The acting president then invited baseball commissioner Chandler, an equally colorful figure, to introduce Rickey.

## Charles R. Spain: The First "Outsider," 1951-1954

At its meeting on April 17, 1951, the Morehead State Board of Regents discussed the selection of Baird's successor but deferred a decision until the next regular meeting on May 10. One regent explained, "This is such an important matter that all the board felt we should take our time and look over every possibility." Boswell B. Hodgkin, state Superintendent of Public Instruction and chairman of the Board of Regents, announced that two applications had been received. One was from R. E. Jaggers of Alabama State Teachers College, Florence, who had served as an official with the Kentucky Department of Education, and the other from Ellis Hartford of the College of Education at the University of Kentucky. Although they had not submitted their names for consideration, two other individuals were also mentioned: John W. Manning, on leave from his state government position as Commissioner of Finance, while serving as director of the Office of Price Stabilization in the Commonwealth; and Adron Doran, speaker of the Kentucky House of Representatives.

Doran, who had served four terms in

*Adron Doran, seventh president of Morehead State, 1954-77, served longer than any other leader of Morehead State as a public institution.*

149

the House, was Speaker of the House during the 1950 legislative session when public school teachers failed to gain an appropriation of $34,500,000 for education. Many teachers were unable to understand why Doran, a former president of the Kentucky Education Association, did not support their cause. In 1951, therefore, Doran had two strikes against his appointment as Morehead State's president: He was a politician at the time when MSC was endeavoring to break away from its political image, and he was a controversial figure among teachers.

The press was serving as an unofficial watchdog to prevent the selection of a political figure for president. Editorials decried the baleful influence of politics on the state's institutions; however, according to the *Rowan County News,* pressure was being brought to bear on the Morehead Regents to appoint a Democrat to succeed Baird. The names most frequently mentioned in that connection were Manning and Doran. A *Courier-Journal* editorial on May 8, 1951, regretted that these two were being touted for the position and went on to suggest Dean Lappin as a candidate. While Lappin was not an applicant, the Morehead State Alumni Association had recommended him for the position. The editorial concluded by stressing the necessity for a free process of selection.

Two days later at its quarterly meeting, the Board of Regents, in addition to routine matters, also considered candidates for the Morehead State presidency. Although no major disparity arose over the approximately fifteen candidates who had either made application or had been suggested for consideration by alumni and other friends of the college, the board felt it needed more time to ensure naming the best person to head the institution. The session succeeded in reducing the number of candidates to four; their identities, however, were not revealed.

Board Chairman Hodgkin then called a special meeting in Lexington for May 28. Every member was present, including Hodgkin, Emory R. Price, Wheelwright; M. K. Eblen, Hazard; W. W.

Ball, Maysville; and J. T. Norris, Ashland, all of whom had been appointees of Governor Clements. Major discussion centered around two individuals—reportedly Warren C. Lappin and Charles R. Spain, whose name, it was learned, had been under consideration from the beginning. Spain was selected but requested a week to consider the offer. On June 5, 1951, he accepted the presidency. Spain assumed his duties as the institution's sixth president on August 20, 1951, at a salary of $7,500 annually, plus residence in the President's Home.

As the school's youngest president ever, the thirty-eight-year-old Spain and his wife, Virginia, moved to Morehead with their two children. After graduating from Bethel College, the Huntingdon, Tennessee, native received a master's degree from George Peabody College and a doctorate in education from Columbia University. His career was punctuated by service as a lieutenant in the United States Naval Reserves during World War II. Spain's educational career had taken him to Alabama, Arkansas, Kansas, Kentucky, New York, Tennessee, and Washington, D.C. He had been dean of instruction at George Peabody since 1949. When asked, "Is he a Democrat or a Republican?" Hodgkin replied, "I don't know. The board didn't ask him, and he didn't tell us. We don't know, and don't want to know." How the board had changed! The board invited President-elect Spain, widely known in educational circles as a public speaker, to present the summer commencement address in 1951. Graduation exercises were held in Jayne Memorial Stadium on July 26, the first outdoor commencement in the history of the college.

Morehead State was one of three Kentucky colleges, along with Transylvania and the University of Louisville, to inaugurate a president in 1951. In accordance with Spain's wishes, no procession was held before the ceremony on December 14, 1951, although the participants wore academic robes. Attendance was hampered by dismal weather, with a cold rain providing one of the year's worst days in Eastern Kentucky. Road conditions thwarted travel plans of visitors from other counties, including Regent W. W. Ball, of

*Science Hall, built in 1937, was renamed in 1958 in honor of Dean Lappin's lifetime of service to the institution.*

Maysville. Boswell B. Hodgkin, state Superintendent of Public Instruction, presided, while Superintendent-elect Wendell Butler was a guest.

In his charge to the new president, keynote speaker Harold Benjamin, professor of education at George Peabody College and author of several books including *Saber-Tooth Curriculum,* referred to the burden of responsibility laid on a college president. In his inaugural address, the tall, scholarly Spain predicted a brilliant future for Morehead State and pledged himself to work to produce a greater institution. At the close of the long day, the consensus was "This fellow Spain seems to have what it takes!"

One of the first problems facing the new president was the need to decide on the role of football at Morehead State College. The president, who was an avid sports enthusiast, asked the Board of Regents in January 1952 for its prudent consideration of the following staggering facts: The college was losing approximately $25,000 annually on its football program; declining gate receipts were insufficient to defray the cost of football as played in the Ohio Valley Conference; and expenses of travel, equipment, and scholarships were escalating. In June 1952 the board accepted Spain's recommendation for a "drastic" reduction in athletic scholarships. Beginning with the 1952-53 academic year, the football program would have only twenty-seven complete scholarships and basketball, fourteen, with the total of both not to exceed forty-one. Coach Ellis Johnson complained that since some OVC institutions were granting as many as seventy-five scholarships for the two major sports, "It'll be tough competing against them."

Having given "serious attention" to the financial strains which athletics imposed upon Morehead State's "already inadequate budget," the board then requested each of the other OVC schools—Eastern, Evansville, Marshall, Murray, Tennessee Tech, and Western—to make "a thorough review" of their own athletic policies to find ways of controlling the number of athletic scholarships. Otherwise, Spain said, Morehead might drop out of the conference. The same board meeting also approved the establishment of fifty $100 academic scholarships.

During its March 1952 meeting in Lexington, the Ohio Valley Conference set the maximum number of scholarships at thirty-three to thirty-five for football and fifteen to seventeen for basketball; the number could not exceed fifty for both sports. Evansville withdrew from the OVC during the Lexington meeting and Middle Tennessee was added. On December 20, 1951, charter member Marshall had chosen not to remain in the Conference at the end of the academic year. Neither Marshall nor Evansville had been able to compete in OVC basketball—each institution had lost more conference games than it had won.

Speaking in 1952 at the spring basketball banquet, sponsored by the local Kiwanis Club, Spain spiked rumors that Morehead

State might discontinue football as an economy measure. He went on to say that Morehead would allocate fifty athletic scholarships in 1952-53—the same as all other OVC schools. The president also announced that Morehead State had made application to the state for a new gymnasium to be constructed near Jayne Memorial Stadium within two or three years. Not to be outdone by the president's optimistic predictions, Coach Johnson avowed Morehead's lean days in football were over.

Morehead State had thus initiated a statewide discussion of college sports. In February 1952 a panel of Kentucky college presidents debated the value of athletics during University of Kentucky halftime basketball broadcasts over the Reynolds Aluminum Network, with former Governor Keen Johnson, vice president of Reynolds Metals Company, serving as the moderator. Opinions ranged from University of Kentucky President H. L. Donovan's staunch defense of post-season tournaments and special contests like bowl games to Western Kentucky President Paul L. Garrett's concerns that, in spite of valuable experiences players gained from travel, such activities increased the amount of time lost from classes, as well as the possibility that "a college might be tempted to buy a winning team, if monetary returns were sufficiently large. The major evil is the unholy recruiting that goes on all over the nation" in college sports, not these "extra" activities, Donovan added. Eastern Kentucky President W. F. O'Donnell and Morehead State President Spain agreed that post-season events should be considered part of the regular schedule and therefore placed under the control of the participating colleges. While Donovan and Garrett explained that the major sports funded minor sports and intramural programs at their institutions, Spain indicated that gate receipts at Morehead State "do not contribute to the support of minor sports or other activities."

Athletics played a role in Morehead State's decision to apply for a Reserve Officers Training Corps unit in February 1952. During the

Korean War, draft deferment was permitted for ROTC students, who upon graduation would then be commissioned in the Reserve program. Morehead State remained the only OVC institution having no ROTC program. Coach Johnson felt that obtaining an ROTC unit would place Morehead in a more favorable position with other conference institutions to recruit student athletes. When MSC discussed the establishment of a unit during the Korean War, the Army informed officials that any training offered would have to be compulsory for all physically capable freshmen and sophomore men. The Board of Regents then authorized the polling of students with the understanding that an application would be forthcoming if a majority favored compulsory training. Nearly 75 percent of the male student body and even a higher percentage of the faculty approved mandatory training along with bringing an ROTC unit to the campus. However, Morehead State's application to the Army was ultimately rejected, primarily because the institution had waited until late in the Korean War to apply.

In the summer of 1952 Morehead State College held a writers' workshop, becoming the first institution in Kentucky to sponsor such a program. Amateur writers converged on the campus from all over Kentucky and nearby states. James R. McConkey, founder of the workshop, brought in well-known poets and authors, including Jesse Stuart and Hollis Summers, who along with members of the college's English department, conducted discussions on the craft of writing. These visiting writers offered evening lectures where classrooms were filled with informality and an "atmosphere of freedom in thought and speech." Class members were given an opportunity to schedule an interview with guest writers and present their manuscripts for constructive criticism.

Spain placed major emphasis on hiring an outstanding faculty. On January 27, 1953, he requested the Board of Regents to increase salaries for capable faculty members. Substantial increases should go to those of "most value" to the institution. The board approved a salary schedule that ranged from a top of $7,000 for professors and administrative personnel to a low of $2,800 for instructors. In a memo of May 22, 1954, Spain noted that the average instructional salaries at the college and the training school had increased from $3,779 in 1951 to $4,546 in 1954. While proud of increasing faculty salaries, Spain believed that still greater progress in this area would be necessary in order for Morehead State to keep its high quality faculty.

Morehead State had a remarkable faculty on the occasion of its 30th anniversary in 1952. James McConkey, English professor from 1950 to 1956 and author of ten books including *Rowan's Progress,* described this era as "a little golden period" in the history of Morehead State. John H. Long, an authority "on Renaissance drama and a very, very good violinist," was "the best scholar of us all." Gabriel Banks, who had taught at Morehead State since the early 1930s, possessed a "strong insight and knowledge of Eastern religions" and was "of considerable help as I was writing my dissertation on the novels of E. M. Forster," McConkey asserted.

McConkey thought the faculty as a whole had "one name after another of people who had a strong academic record and credentials." Dr. Wilhelm Exelbirt, "a man of infinite cultural attainments," excelled as the "true scholar of the whole college." In *Rowan's Progress,* McConkey referred to Wilhelm and Gisa Exelbirt as "noble presences" in the town of Morehead. Born in Austria-Hungary in 1901, Exelbirt later taught at the University of Vienna until he left in 1938 after witnessing the Nazi takeover and agonizing over the threats of the Holocaust. After nearly starving in Paris, he arrived in America in 1940. Unable to obtain a teaching position while living in New York from 1940-48, Exelbirt was unhappy because "once a teacher, always a teacher," he stated. Learning of a teaching position in European history at Morehead State for $3,600, he "looked up Morehead on the map." Exelbirt stated that when he got off the train on Railroad Street on January 8, 1948, at 6 a.m., "I had a terrible

*The Doran Student House, above, was the first building completed in the Doran administration. Later, it was renovated and expanded and renamed the Adron Doran University Center, below.*

scare; it looked like a setting for a Western movie." Although Main Street seemed "a little depressing, I was reassured when I turned the corner and started toward Lappin Hall." A few minutes later, he met President Baird, "a very cordial, genial man." Exelbirt's first class that morning had only five students at a time when the total student body consisted of only 600. But "I've never seen a group of five such bright boys," one of whom was "a gangly, young man with a mop of hair on his head—Charles Pelfrey, who later taught in the English department." Immediately, Exelbirt had to adjust to changing from academic customs at the University of Vienna to those of a small college in Eastern Kentucky. Three differences stood out: A professor never checked the roll in Europe; European students rose and remained standing until the teacher reached his desk; and he was amazed at being expected to chaperone a dance at Morehead State because on European campuses, "no one was concerned about your private life."

Among other memorable faculty personalities was Nolan Fowler, another history professor, who possessed "Lil' Abner's physique and an ability to work in the outside world as well as in the world of the mind." Art teachers Thomas E. Young and Naomi Claypool towered as examples of "opposition and competition because they were in a kind of tension with each other, professionally, and in every other way—in what they did as artists and the way they taught students," McConkey stated. "But together I think they made a marvelous art department." McConkey stated that he "had never seen a department that worked so well." McConkey looked upon Ione Chapman as "a very efficient and good librarian" who always managed "to get what he needed." Sociologist Henry Carey was a "rather mystical" personality who "sat outside my window when I was working on my Forster book and talked to me about Hinduism."

J. E. Duncan, who served as head of the music department, chairman of the Division of Humanities, and dean of the School of Humanities from 1958 to 1982, manifested great pride in the faculty he hired. In his initial interview with Duncan, President Adron Doran assured him, "I can finance anything you can justify in building an excellent music department." Duncan added Robert Hawkins as the director of symphony and marching bands. The band director frequently said, "Don't call me Dr. Hawkins; call me Hawk." That name stuck—especially with students. Hawkins proceeded to put such quality into Morehead State bands that students with great ability were attracted from all over the eastern half of the nation, especially Pennsylvania, New York, and New England. Since theater, under W. P. Covington III, was "so far ahead of speech that I wanted to beef that up a little bit," Duncan hired Julia Webb, who had "consistently taken high school debate teams to statewide competition, and she always won." After joining the Morehead State faculty, she "proceeded to take first place in the nation with her debate teams on three different occasions." Duncan cited Lewis and Ruth Barnes as the only faculty members in the humanities at that time who had been hired by someone other than himself. President Doran was credited with these two major additions. "What a catch! Lewis had five earned doctorates, including literature, psychology, and linguistics; Ruth had three."

Allen Lake, biology professor, characterized the early death of Fenton West, chairman of the Division of Sciences and Mathematics, in 1958 as "a tragedy because he exemplified most of the things I believed in." West was "articulate, a keen thinker and yet he was a kind and a sincere Christian." William B. Owsley, his successor, thought everyone should start out the day by being at Lappin Hall; the "best way to make sure of that was to assign them to an 8 a.m. class." When Owsley left Morehead State to become academic vice president of Kentucky Wesleyan, Matt Pryor, one of his former Morehead State students, succeeded him as chairman of the biology department. Pryor, former MSU football standout, had spent 18 months in Antarctica while doing research for his dissertation. As Lake thought back to his arrival at Morehead State in the late Fifties, he recalled that attending college at that time demanded "a good deal of sacrifice," and the "typical student looked at that sacrifice as sort of a holy responsibility."

Clifford Rader served as chairman of the Division of Social Sciences until his death in 1963. Roscoe Playforth, who succeeded Rader and later was the first dean of the School of Social Sciences, remembers that Rader and his wife, Addie, "probably had more people into their home for dinners than anyone else ever at the university." Allen Lake recalls a scholarship fund raiser once in which Rader, a "former vaudeville actor," was the "star of the show" as a master of the art of "soft shoe dancing."

Building on Rader's previous efforts, Playforth assembled a faculty which by the time its last member retired in the late 1990s, had made one of the

*Morehead State featured a Writers' Workshop during the Fifties and Sixties. Shown from left are President Doran, Albert Stewart, director; Ione Chapman, head of Johnson Camden Library; and James Still, workshop participant and famed Appalachian author.*

most distinguished records in the history of the institution, including providing leadership on campus. John R. Duncan, who first taught sociology, later served as graduate dean, academic vice president, and two terms on the Board of Regents. Alban Wheeler was head of the department of sociology and social work before succeeding Playforth as dean of the School of Social Sciences and being elected twice as faculty regent. And Charles Holt, along with Kent Freeland of the School of Education, intitiated the International Studies program at MSU. Dean Playforth was also chairman of the athletics committee for seventeen years; his responsibilities included making sure that Morehead State "did not get into trouble with the NCAA and approving grants-in-aid." Playforth Place, connecting Breathitt Sports Center with US 60, was named for him. He has since been recipient of the University's Founders Day Award for University Service.

In keeping with academic practice, Morehead State refrained from naming campus buildings after its own personnel while they were still living. This principle had been adhered to with Frank Button, founder of the institution which he led for nearly three decades. After his death in 1933, each Morehead State president intended to name a building after Button, but every effort faced obstacles. In successive board meetings in 1935, motions to name the College Auditorium in his honor were tabled for lack of support. Later attempts to name Science Hall or East Men's Hall after Button failed because Morehead State's loan contract agreement with the federal government prohibited naming any structure built with federal money after an individual.

In the summer of 1953 alumni wished to place Button's name on the Fine Arts Building then being completed. Eighty-two white-haired graduates of the old Morehead Normal School used their reunion to renew attempts to perpetuate the memory of their beloved president. George Johnson, one of the first students to enroll and father of Coach Ellis Johnson, served as spokesman for this group which extolled Button's gentle character. Holding the American flag and pointing toward the skies as tears trickled down his cheeks, Johnson told everyone, "Up there in heaven is Brother Button looking down on us, with a smile on his face." The alumni invoked the assistance of newspaper editor W. E. (Snooks) Crutcher in their campaign. The following week Crutcher penned an editorial in the *Rowan County News* to the effect that the requested action was long overdue.

President Spain renewed the effort to name a building after Button. A week after the reunion, the Board of Regents voted unanimously to name the College Auditorium the "Frank C. Button Memorial Auditorium." Board members concluded that the most fitting commemoration for this soft-spoken gentleman was linking him with the building where, in convocations, he had carried his philosophy and Christian teachings to the hearts of his students.

When the Morehead Normal School Club met in the summer of 1954, the members prided themselves on finally reaching their goal of honoring President Button. The "Old Grads" also used their meeting to commemorate a "courting" spot from the olden days—the site of a pump which once furnished water for the entire school. Located just outside Hodson Hall, the girls' dormitory in the Normal School, the pump served as a convenient meeting spot for couples in the evening. The alumni club placed two stone benches on the site, installed a plaque reading, "Donated by MNS, 1955," and replaced the pump with a drinking fountain.

In the summer of 1953 the board completed the reorganization of Morehead State's athletic department and provided for a balanced intramural program for men and women. Ellis Johnson requested relief from his heavy duties as basketball coach, football coach, and athletic director. The decision was made to retain Johnson as basketball coach and hire Wilbur (Shorty) Jamerson, former University of Kentucky football player, to coach football. Robert Laughlin was elevated from basketball coach at Breckinridge Training School to athletic director and head of the department of physical education at the college. The following month, however, Johnson abruptly resigned, ending his seventeen-year association with Morehead State. Making this move primarily for financial reasons, he continued to live in Morehead and work in the insurance business. In September 1953 Morehead State gave Johnson an appreciation dinner with Earl Ruby, sports editor of the *Courier-Journal,* as the keynote speaker. Adolph Rupp joined the crowd of 200 admirers.

Morehead State's search for Johnson's replacement resurrected an issue which has often plagued this Eastern Kentucky institution. Spain offered the position to Lou Watson, one of Indiana University's most outstanding All-Americans and later head coach of that institution, but Watson's Board of Education in Huntington, Indiana, refused to release him from the last year of a three-year contract. Most people believed that MSC then decided not to fill the position with a permanent replacement and thereby keep it open for Watson a year later. In the meantime, Spain made newly-appointed Athletic Director Laughlin acting head coach of the Eagles' basketball team. No sooner had word gotten out that Morehead State was holding the coaching position open for Watson, a Hoosier, than a storm erupted over bringing in an "outsider."

On October 8, 1953, Gordon (Red) Moore, past president of the Morehead State Alumni Association, dashed off a letter to the editor of the *Rowan County News* expressing alarm that his alma mater was so determined to go out of state to locate a basketball coach that it would wait a year to obtain his services. Moore posed the question, "Are there not plenty of capable coaches in the state of Kentucky who could fill the Morehead basketball position?" A week later, Nolan Fowler, newly-appointed track and field, and cross country coach, wrote a tongue-in-cheek letter of resignation to President Spain declaring himself a "foreigner." In his letter Fowler pointed up the absurdity of the controversy, concluding by citing Kentucky's greatest heroes—Daniel Boone and Henry Clay—both foreigners.

This controversy reached an anticlimactic resolution when Spain refused to accept Fowler's resignation.

During his final year at the Morehead helm, Spain employed two individuals who stayed long enough to leave a lasting mark on the institution. Roger L. Wilson, principal of Jenkins High School, succeeded Marjorie J. Palmquist as Morehead State's dean of students on September 1, 1953. (Palmquist resigned to join the College of Education faculty at the University of California at Berkeley.) A native of Madison County, Wilson received a B.A. degree from Eastern Kentucky State College and a M.A. degree from the University of Kentucky. He had served as teacher, elementary principal, and high school principal in the Jenkins City Schools for twenty-eight years before accepting the Morehead deanship.

Robert G. (Bob) Laughlin, who had been serving as acting basketball coach after the resignation of Ellis Johnson in July 1953 was named head basketball coach. The Morehead opening occurred when Lou Watson announced his decision to remain in his Indiana high school coaching position. Laughlin had coached the Breckinridge Eaglets from 1935 to 1953; his record included a state championship in 1946. A native of Montgomery County, Laughlin received his M.A. degree from the University of Kentucky in 1941 and was working on a Ph.D. degree at Indiana University at the time he was hired.

Spain, who had a reputation for not remaining long at one place, decided to leave in 1954. After informing each board member by telephone, Spain called a faculty meeting on March 3, 1954, in the Art Gallery, where he announced he would leave Morehead State at the end of the academic year to become dean of the College of Education at the University of New Mexico on July 1, 1954. Spain, whose frequent career moves had always represented promotions, received $5,000 more as dean of education at the University of New Mexico than he had been making as president of Morehead State. Spain arrived at his decision not only because of receiving a better professional opportunity but also because of his wife's health. Suffering from a severe sinus condition throughout their stay at Morehead, she had recently been released from a Lexington hospital, where physicians advised that her physical condition was not likely to improve in the climate of the Ohio Valley. In June 1955 Spain was named Superintendent of Schools in Albuquerque; two years later he died of a heart attack at 51.

*The old Administration Building, below, the oldest building on campus, was later renovated and renamed Rader Hall, above, in honor of Clifford Rader.*

## Adron Doran: The Administrator/Builder, 1954-1977

As soon as Spain submitted his resignation, excitement mounted over the choice of his successor. In the March 11, 1954 issue of the *Rowan County News,* Crutcher took great pride in his certainty that there would be no coercion from Frankfort over this appointment, not realizing that this Board of Regents would not be permitted to choose the next president. Instead, Governor Lawrence H. Wetherby orchestrated the selection from Frankfort. Three weeks after Crutcher's column appeared, two former Morehead State students, Dr. Elwood Esham, Vanceburg, and Dr. Lowell Gearheart, Grayson, replaced E. R. Price and W. W. Ball, whose terms had recently expired. Superintendent of Public Instruction Wendell P. Butler, chairman of the Board of Regents, then called a special meeting in Spain's office for April 6, 1954. All board members attended, including Esham; Gearheart; M. K. Eblen, Hazard attorney; and J. T. Norris, Ashland newspaper publisher. Esham and Gearheart were duly installed as new members by Judge W. T. McClain, Rowan County. Spain's resignation was formally accepted, effective on July 1, 1954; he was then granted a two-weeks vacation, beginning June 15.

Having disposed of routine business, Butler introduced the question of Spain's successor by reading the names of a number of educators who had either applied or been recommended for the opening. Before holdover board members Eblen and Norris realized what was happening, newly-sworn-in Regent Gearheart presented the name and qualifications of Adron Doran and moved for a four-year contract, effective on June 15, 1954, at $8,500. The other new Regent, Dr. Esham, seconded the nomination. Eblen and Norris protested that the Board of Regents had been given insufficient time to study the applications and move on such an important decision. When the vote was called, Eblen and Norris opposed the appointment while Esham and Gearhart voted for Doran. Butler, who had missed several recent board meetings, made sure he was present to cast the deciding ballot. Thus, Frankfort's plans were followed to the letter again at Morehead State, as Adron Doran became the school's seventh president by a 3-2 margin. Unlike Lyndon B. Johnson, who bristled when journalists nicknamed him "Landslide Lyndon" after winning his Texas Senate seat in 1948 by a tiny 87-vote margin, Doran's sense of humor made it possible for him to relate the 3-2 story throughout his career. Later, Eblen and Norris were favorably impressed with Doran's leadership.

Few aspirants had major interest in the Morehead presidency when Doran was chosen on April 6, 1954. The institution, which had been back in the good graces of the Southern Association for only six years, continued to struggle for respectability and was poised for growth if it could attract a larger percentage of graduating seniors from Eastern Kentucky's high schools. The small college was hardly known outside Kentucky. Only one building had been erected on campus since 1937. The institution had barely survived World War II. Salaries were not attractive since only recently had the state been allowed to pay any official, including a college president, more than $5,000 annually. Candidates for the Morehead presidency may have questioned Spain's leaving after less than three years. But Doran's enthusiasm over the appointment energized both himself and those working with him.

A native of Graves County in Western Kentucky, Doran graduated from Freed-Hardeman Junior College, in Henderson, Tennessee, and held bachelor's and master's degrees from Murray State. Shortly after enrolling at Freed-Hardeman in 1928, he became so captivated with President N. B. Hardeman, perhaps the most widely-known preacher in Churches of Christ in that era, that he too started delivering sermons. While a junior at Murray State, Doran married Mignon McClain, also a student, whom he thereafter affectionately referred to as his "roommate." Coming from a large family with limited means, Doran was forced to work his way through college by pursuing a wide variety of jobs—on the farm, in a clothing store, selling newspapers on trains out of St. Louis, as a singer in a college quartet, and as a minister.

Doran's educational career included seventeen years as teacher, basketball coach, and high school principal in Kentucky's public school system. At twenty-two, he became one of Kentucky's youngest principals at Boaz High School in rural Graves County, near Mayfield. His next assignment was principal and basketball coach at Sylvan Shade High School, in Fulton County, in the southwestern corner of the commonwealth. In 1938 Doran began a ten-year stint as principal of Wingo High School near his birthplace in Western Kentucky. During this period, he completed his master's degree at nearby Murray State and began receiving statewide recognition in education and politics as well. In 1943 Doran was first elected to the Kentucky General Assembly. In his fourth term as a state legislator, he was selected Speaker of the House in 1950.

In 1946 Doran became more involved in statewide activities, including election to the presidency of the Kentucky Education Association. In 1947 he was tempted to parlay his various statewide contacts through KEA into a statewide race for the position of state Superintendent of Public Instruction. Convinced, however, that he could accomplish more for education by assisting in the election of his close friend, Harry Lee Waterfield, as governor, he shelved a campaign for the superintendency in order to work tirelessly for Waterfield. After Waterfield lost to Earle C. Clements in the Democratic primary, Doran informed the winner of his willingness to work for his election in November. Doran's ability to adjust quickly to political reality proved to be an enormous asset throughout most of his career.

Beginning their "footsteps across the Commonwealth" in 1948, the Dorans left Wingo in Western Kentucky for Central Kentucky, where he pursued a doctorate at the University of Kentucky. Living in Lexington, he continued serving his constituents in Western Kentucky as state legislator and preaching on weekends for the

Nicholasville Church of Christ. Receiving his doctorate in 1951, Doran spent the following summer as a visiting professor of education at the University of Georgia before returning to his native state to serve three years as director of the Division of Teacher Education and Certification in the State Department of Education.

Doran found it necessary in the early 1950s to choose between the ministry, education, and politics, as his major career pursuit, after experiencing outstanding success in all three. Always too much of a maverick for either a full-time position as a minister or as an administrator in a church-related college, he turned down attractive offers to serve in such capacities. A combination of circumstances and opportunities then nudged him into an educational rather than a political career.

Doran, at 44, was the youngest college president in Kentucky at the time. Prominently identified with educational, religious, and governmental circles, he used his position and contacts to push the interests of the institution with which he became identified. From the very beginning, his speaking ability was especially helpful on behalf of Morehead State. In fact, his first Thursday and Friday in office were spent at Georgetown College in addressing Girls' State.

Crutcher, local newspaper editor, was Doran's ally and avid supporter. He predicted the new president would receive wonderful cooperation from Morehead people. In addition to having Crutcher in his corner, Doran had the cooperation of William Whitaker, general manager of the town's new radio station. WMOR took the airwaves on Friday, February 19, 1955, as a 1,000-watt station. Its early announcers included Don Holloway, Bill Pierce, and Don Young, all of whom later joined the Morehead State faculty, and John R. Duncan, who later served as academic vice president of MSU, and Tom T. Hall, who subsequently achieved fame as a country musician and songwriter.

Mayor William H. Layne proclaimed October 22, 1954 as "Dr. Adron Doran Day" in Morehead. All businesses were asked to close from 2 to 3 p.m. during Doran's inauguration. Governor Wetherby presided at the inauguration and introduced over fifty special guests, including practically all state officials. Doran was sworn in by John A. Keck, judge of the 37th district. Chester Travelstead, dean of the College of Education at the University of South Carolina, was the principal speaker. The invocation and benediction were given by Gabriel Banks. Wetherby introduced Doran with the affirmation that "he is the man that I feel Morehead State College needs." Blessed with an audience including Governor Wetherby, Lieutenant Governor Emerson Beauchamp, and leaders of both the state Senate and the House, Doran waxed eloquent in sharing his vision of the establishment of a Foundation Program for Public Higher Education in Kentucky. Several governors and members of the General Assembly had publicly complained over the years about how pressure was put on them for available funds every time the legislature met. Doran was the first Kentucky educator to appear on the side of a flat formula as the basis for distributing funds to the state's institutions of higher learning. Yet, when Kentucky failed to act upon his inaugural proposal for higher education, Doran reaped the benefits since no one could play the game of politics better than he. He would find ways of getting more than Morehead State's slice from governors and legislators even when the money seemed unavailable or when other institutions claimed to be more deserving.

Doran had the distinct advantage at Morehead State of working with Dean Warren C. Lappin, who had by this time become an institution unto himself. Born in Illinois in 1900, Lappin had never heard of Morehead until his father, Warren O. Lappin, a Christian Church minister, moved to Morehead as principal of the old Normal School from 1919 until its closing in 1922. The son obtained a position as mathematics and history teacher in his father's school in 1920. Completing a degree at Transylvania, Warren C. Lappin won athletic letters in baseball and basketball while developing a lifelong relationship with teammate Albert B. (Happy) Chandler, later

*Norman Tant, professor of library science, taught at MSU from 1952 to 1977 and left a lasting memorial with his $200,000 bequest to create a scholarship fund.*

Kentucky's governor and U.S. senator, as well as commissioner of professional baseball. While the Normal School was closed in 1922-23, Warren C. served as principal of Morehead High School. Once Morehead State opened, he managed to find time to coach the college baseball team while continuing as principal. In 1924, he joined Morehead State for a year as a mathematics teacher while debating whether to settle down as a teacher or become a lawyer. His one year at Morehead State turned into a half century of serving the school in virtually every capacity!

Placing Lappin's name on a campus building in 1958 was a popular move on Doran's part. Before the Doran era, when a building was named after an administrator or professor, the action took place after the individual's death. Still very much alive, Lappin had already dedicated more than three and a half decades to the institution—as teacher, coach, director of the training school, academic dean of the faculty, and acting president upon two occasions. At Morehead State's Homecoming in 1958, when Science Hall was named after Lappin, Doran referred to him as "the best college dean in Kentucky."

From the beginning of the Doran administration, certain departments attracted positive attention from the press. The Morehead Players, under the direction of Walter P. Covington III, took the Children's Theater on the road, playing before as many as 6,000 youngsters during a tour of such places as Olive Hill, Maysville, Beattyville, Danville, and Morehead in the 1954-55 academic year. Packed auditoriums included school children, some of them seeing their first play. One young actor stated, "You really know where you stand with an audience of kids. If they like you, there's no mistaking it—but heaven help us if we don't keep up the kids' interest!"

The players' opening on the Morehead campus was typical, with busloads of school children from all over Rowan County arriving before noon and 1,500 chattering fans packing Button Auditorium by curtain time. Covington, a soft-spoken drama professor, explained, "We are trying to give these youngsters an opportunity to see, at least once a year, a production that is designed for their age group but which is also an example of good, professional theater. . . .Our hope is that this will help to cultivate within them an appreciation of the theater that will extend into their adult lives."

In the Division of Languages and Literature, James R. McConkey directed Morehead State's fourth consecutive Writers' Workshop in July 1955. Harriette L. Arnow, Hollis P. Summers, Jesse H. Stuart, and James Still lingered on the steps outside Button Auditorium on the final evening of the two-week program to make themselves available to some forty men and women of all ages and occupations who were students at the workshop. Student writers included housewives, teachers, college students, a maintenance worker, a secretary, and an army major—people from six states. Summers, a novelist, short story writer, poet, and member of the University of Kentucky's Department of English, and Still, Knott County novelist, short-story writer, and poet, had served at every workshop since its inception. New to the staff was Leonard Press, radio and television script writer and member of the University of Kentucky Broadcasting Service, and Arnow, who had written *Hunter's Horn* and *The Dollmaker.*

Beginning in 1955, John H. Long, member of the English department, published *Shakespeare's Use of Music* with the University of Florida Press. It was the first extensive study in which music was considered as an essential dramatic element in the plays. He had served as concertmaster for the University of Florida Symphony Orchestra while working on his B.A., M.A., and Ph.D. degrees. Long himself played a lute built for him by Thomas D. Young, professor in Morehead State's art department. In fact, Long's enthusiasm for medieval instruments proved contagious. Shortly after arriving in Morehead in 1950, he organized an Elizabethan Consort, consisting of seven faculty members and their wives, who played for their own pleasure. Long's book and his interest in early music were featured in the *Courier-Journal* on May 29, 1955.

Town and gown relationships were never better than in 1956 when Rowan County celebrated its centennial. Local people pointed out to visitors that the town really started to grow with the advent of the state college. During the week's celebration, more than 20,000 people crowded into Morehead, which had a population of only a little over 3,000. Males sported luxuriant growths of beard, while women walked around town dressed in old-fashioned costumes complete with sunbonnets. On opening day, some 12,000 people thronged into town. With Governor Chandler's arrival in a motorcade, a parade, including nine bands, got underway stretching from one end of the county to the other. Natives and visitors alike gathered at Morehead State's Jayne Memorial Stadium that evening to witness the premiere performance of the centennial's historical pageant, "Within This Valley."

Healthy local relationships were nourished by civic organizations, such as the Lions Club, the Optimist Club, and the Kiwanis

Club. Perhaps no group played this role better than the Morehead Mens Club, composed of nearly equal numbers of college personnel and townspeople. It supported no causes and stood for nothing except good fellowship and mental stimulation.

A heated argument developed one night at the Mens Club over the question of who or what was the most important element on a college campus. One group said it was the faculty who in this way or that inspired the young people under their tutelage. Others argued for the primacy of the administrative staff which supplied direction, planning, cohesion, and finances. A few championed the cause of the student body. All of a sudden, from the back of the room, came this roar: "You ignorant so-and-sos! The most important element is physical operations. How long are you people—students, faculty, administrators—going to operate without heat, light, water, plumbing facilities, and someone to keep all your filth cleaned up and disposed of, unless you are willing to teach as Jesus Christ and Socrates did—using streets, mountain sides, and seashores as your classrooms? You would last less than a week without your pampered existence!" A longtime member of the club stated, "I never saw a discussion ended as quickly in all of my eighty plus years!" And the man who cut short the discussion was W.H. (Honie) Rice, superintendent of buildings and grounds at the school for four decades, whose righteous indignation was stirred.

Both the college and the town took great pride in the school's dramatic growth. National enrollment escalated by nearly 50 percent throughout the Fifties. The Commonwealth of Kentucky witnessed a 62 percent increase in college enrollment in its six institutions of higher learning, from 12,296 to 19,928. Kentucky's four regional colleges alone vaulted from 5,829 in 1950 to 13,461 in 1960, an increase of 132 percent. Morehead State's growth was even more astounding, from 783 students in 1950 to 2,890 in 1960, a 266 percent increase during the decade. By 1964 Morehead State had 3,694 students, a phenomenal 359 percent increase since 1950.

Several factors explained the skyrocketing of Morehead State's enrollment. First, there was a steady increase in the number of college-age youth in Eastern Kentucky. Second, a higher percentage of these were continuing their educational training beyond high school. Third, Kentucky's Minimum Foundation Program, enacted in 1954, placed a financial premium upon public school teachers returning to college for additional educational training. Fourth, federal aid to education made huge amounts of money available to students and colleges through the National Defense Education Act. From 1958 to 1962, the federal government contributed $262,216 to this fund, which provided 750 students with part or all of the money needed for their college education. In the latter part of this era, Great Society programs made it easier for American institutions of higher learning to expand in order to take care of their growth.

Fifth, striking down color barriers in the 1950s gave black students new opportunities. Early in 1950, Kentucky's General Assembly modified the Day Law to permit integration in institutions of higher learning. On May 17, 1954, the Supreme Court decision, *Brown v. Board of Education,* Topeka, Kansas, necessitated opening public schools to black students. The meeting of Morehead State's Board of Regents on September 17, 1956, in the high-ceilinged conference room of the old Administration Building turned out to be a historic one. Eight people sat around a large rectangular table, with chairman Robert Martin, superintendent of public instruction, in charge. Doran requested the board to address the question of enrolling black students at Morehead State. "It may be questionable for the college to admit Negroes unless action has been taken by the Board of Regents authorizing acceptance," he said. "I should like for the board to consider what action should be taken in this matter." A motion was then made by new board member Dr. W. H. Cartmell and seconded by Dr. Esham that the college be directed to enroll students without regard to race, color, or creed. The motion was adopted without dissent. Segregation ended at Morehead State in June 1956

*Two record-breaking MSU athletes are shown reminiscing. Marshall Banks, left, was guest speaker at a Martin Luther King Day event on campus. Banks, a professor at Howard University, was the first African-American athlete in the Ohio Valley Conference. His former teammate, Steve Hamilton, right, was the second person in history to play both major league baseball and professional basketball.*

with the summer enrollment of two Mason County black women, Anna Luise Randolph, who enrolled in a master's program, and Ida Mae Ross, who signed up for courses in commerce and library science. Randolph and Ross were roommates in Fields Hall.

Morehead State was the first state-supported institution in Kentucky to integrate dormitories and athletic teams and the first Ohio Valley Conference school to allow blacks to participate in athletics. Morehead State student Marshall Banks was the first black to participate on a varsity athletic team in the Ohio Valley Conference. In 1959 this Ashland freshmen entered Morehead State and competed in the broad jump, the 880, the mile and 440-yard relays, and set a Kentucky record in the 100-yard dash. He remained unbeaten in dual meets in the 220-yard dash during his career; his time of 21.7 seconds for the event persisted as the conference record for a long time. Banks, a 1962 graduate, was hired as the institution's first black faculty member in September 1965 when he became an instructor in physical education and assistant track coach. He had earned an M.S. degree and was then working on a doctorate at the University of Illinois. Another black, Howard Murphy, who enrolled at Morehead in 1960, became the first of that race to play football on a varsity team in the Ohio Valley Conference. Thus, Morehead State was one of the first public state colleges in the South to integrate.

Sixth, Morehead State enhanced its appeal by adding various scholarships and student workships. By the 1963-64 academic year, the institution was providing nine types of scholarships and one loan fund in addition to NDEA. Opportunities were also provided for students to earn part of their expenses by working in the dormitories, bookstore, offices, cafeteria, or college post office.

Seventh, the blending of Morehead State's needs and President Doran's leadership traits equalled a nearly perfect mix. His arrival coincided with the beginning of the institution's most dramatic growth in history. He knew both how to influence parents to send their young people to Morehead and how to obtain Morehead's ample share of finances from Frankfort and Washington. Doran was a builder second to none. In addition to enhancing the physical facilities, he interpreted the college to the region in such a manner as to entice its high school graduates to come to Morehead. Doran was heavily involved in making commencement addresses, speaking to civic organizations, and networking with high school superintendents and principals, always "preaching the good news" that high school graduates could obtain an excellent education at Morehead State.

From the very beginning, Doran placed emphasis upon maintaining good public relations. Thus, his selection of a replacement for N. B. McMillian, public relations director and assistant to President Spain, was one of his most important early decisions. Within a short time Doran named Raymond R. Hornback, a recent graduate of the School of Journalism at the University of Kentucky, to that position. The wisdom of this selection was soon apparent as Hornback excelled in two of the foremost things expected of him—maintaining good relations with the press as well as the public in general and demonstrating loyalty to the president at all times.

Morehead State's president and Board of Regents felt the school had not been funded in proportion to the other three regional colleges. Hence, Doran invited Eastern Kentucky representatives to a dinner meeting in the college cafeteria on December 20, 1955, after which they were granted a reserved section in Button Gymnasium where the Eagles defeated Marshall, 102-89. Doran told them that all Morehead State wanted was fair treatment. In a Frankfort meeting that same week, Doran and Dean Lappin informed Governor Chandler and certain members of the General Assembly that Morehead State must have additional funds because its faculty was not being paid on the same scale as the University of Kentucky and other state colleges. Doran's firsthand knowledge of the operation of state government, along with his acquaintance with most of Kentucky's political and educational leaders, benefited Morehead State immensely during this era of growth..

Sensational growth triggered a phenomenal building program at Morehead State. Shortly after moving to Morehead, Doran engaged Governor Wetherby and Senator Clements in a conversation about the school's most urgent needs. The three agreed that the two priorities were building a basketball gymnasium and a student union. The art department was housed in the Johnson Camden Library, the music department in a girls' dormitory basement, and the agriculture department had only one teacher and no farm to serve as a laboratory for class! Initial plans were drawn up to deal with these problems, but the Chandler administration, because of lack of funds, canceled some of the building projects approved in the waning hours of the Wetherby administration. Plans for a long-awaited $725,000 student center at Morehead State were, however, left intact. Work was also immediately begun on the construction of a $625,000 gymnasium to seat 5,000.

Accompanying the growth of MSC's physical plant, academic programs were supplemented. The curriculum witnessed the addition of the departments of philosophy and Spanish. Morehead State also became affiliated with the nursing and medical technology programs of the United Mine Workers' hospitals. Added services included a science institute, aided by the federal government's annual $60,000 appropriation; conservation, mental health, and art workshops; a human relations conference; and a beginning teachers conference.

During a campaign speech at Bowling Green in the summer of 1955, Chandler proposed to increase the number of regents for each of the four state colleges to nine. The existing system allowed four appointive members, including two Democrats and two Republicans, plus the Superintendent of Public Instruction, who served as chairman of each of the boards. Under this arrangement, governors could appoint two new members and then control the internal operations of a college by having those two join the state superintendent to make up a majority vote on close issues. After his election, Chandler sponsored an administration bill to increase the membership of boards from five to nine. The bill stated that new board members would assume their duties on April 1, with staggered terms, that no more than five of the nine board members could be members of the same political party, and that the Superintendent of Public Instruction would continue as the chairman. Even with a larger board, Doran fared well because most governors heeded his preferences as to the composition of the board.

As a result of the exciting developments taking place at Morehead, the institution was finally receiving favorable attention in

newspapers. The December 6, 1959 issue of the *Courier-Journal* ran
the headline, "Booming Morehead College Brings Prosperity, Culture
to Community." In 1959 the Ashland *Daily Independent* headlined
one story, "Progress at Morehead Takes Big Strides in Past 5 Years,"
and another story, "Affable Educator Sparks MSC Growth and Development." David S. McGuire described how President Doran
greeted each student by his or her first name in walking across campus. The Lexington *Herald-Leader* and the Huntington *Herald-Ad-
vertiser* also devoted full pages to Morehead State in the 1959-60
academic year.

Insufficient housing for married students was one of
Morehead State's most pressing problems. In April 1959 the Federal
Housing and Home Financing Agency approved the full amount of
$800,000 requested by the college to construct 100 units of married
student housing. The married housing units were constructed on
what had been a picnic ground at the base of the college reservoir to
the rear of Breckinridge Training School. Lakewood Terrace was occupied in September, 1960, thereby replacing barracks-type frame
apartment buildings, Quonset huts, and small cottages which had
been used temporarily as expediencies. A stone bridge was built
across Evans Branch to reach the area. Eight units in the center were
named for the eight original teachers in the state college: Charles D.
Lewis, Henry C. Haggan, Charles O. Peratt, Dan Holbrook, Inez Faith
Humphrey, Evelyn Royalty, Emma Shader, and Ruby Vansant.

Doran was the recipient of frequent honors during these years.
A long-time advocate of equal opportunities, the president was
awarded the 1959 Lincoln Key by the Kentucky Education Association for integration of Morehead State College "without fanfare or
incident." This annual award to a Kentuckian was given by KEA in
conjunction with the Lincoln Foundation in Louisville for outstanding service in the education of blacks. In the same year, the Kentucky Press Association selected Doran as Kentuckian of the Year.
The coveted honor had previously been bestowed on Alben W.

Barkley, John Sherman Cooper, Paul W. (Bear) Bryant, A. B. (Happy) Chandler, Jesse H. Stuart, and Edgar A. (Ed) Diddle. Doran was cited "for superior service to education in Kentucky and other Southern states as a member of the Southern Regional Education Board, and for his acknowledged leadership in dealing with racial problems." The Morehead Chamber of Commerce also named Doran its Outstanding Citizen of the Year in 1959.

During this era, one could listen to former Morehead State students as they returned to campus and excitedly commented on the many changes. J. W. Owen of Salyersville enrolled in summer school in 1960, his first time on campus since 1940. Staring in astonishment at the Doran Student House, he recalled that when he had attended, "we had a path across there to town." Upon going to the basement of the old Administration Building to check his mail box, he learned that the college post office had been moved to the Doran Student House. "I was even more surprised," he continued, "when I went to the basement of Allie Young Hall to eat and found the cafeteria, too, had been moved to the new Student House." Walt Tooley, music teacher from Greenup County, was startled when he returned to summer school in 1960 and looked from Baird Music Hall toward the dam. "There is a small community up in that hollow alone!"

While serving as Morehead State's president, Doran was also considered as a possibility for the Democratic candidacy for governor upon two occasions. In March 1958 the local paper reported a move underway to have Doran enter the gubernatorial race. The president, however, publicly indicated his satisfaction with his present position and expressed no interest in political office. The Democratic nomination went to Eastern Kentuckian Bert Combs instead. Essentially the same story unfolded in the Sixties. On December 14, 1961, veteran Frankfort reporter Kyle Vance came out with a front page story in the *Courier-Journal* that political maneuvering was centering around Doran as a frontrunner and the Democrat most likely to be nominated for governor two years later. The

Morehead president was regarded as strong in all sections of the state—in Western Kentucky because of being a native son; in Central Kentucky because of politics and church work; and in Eastern Kentucky because of his position at Morehead State. The highly personable Mignon was considered by many as a political asset to Doran. Most people believed that Doran would run well among black voters after he received the Lincoln Key. His association with such Democratic leaders as Harry Lee Waterfield and Earle C. Clements was looked upon as significant. The *Rowan County News* ran a headline, "Possibilities grow that Dr. Adron Doran may be drafted for Governorship in 1963" and speculated that Wendell Butler would become president of MSC after Doran moved into the Governor's Mansion! Despite the swell of opinion urging him to run, Doran again made it clear that he had no desire to enter politics.

Personal misfortune struck the Dorans on June 22, 1959, when Mignon was critically injured in a three-car collision during a heavy rainstorm near Zanesville, Ohio. Doran was driving but experienced only minor injuries. However, Mrs. Doran suffered a double fracture of the pelvis and four fractured ribs, as well as a broken collarbone. In September 1959 when she had almost recovered, Mrs. Doran fell while vacationing and refractured her collarbone.

Early during convalescence, Mignon bought a hat. From the time she became Morehead State's First Lady, Mrs. Doran's wide selection of hats for all occasions produced a hat craze among many of the women of Morehead. Mrs. Deane Tant, wife of Dr. Norman Tant, director of audio-visual aids at Morehead State, shared Mignon's millinery interests and created original designs for the First Lady. In addition to her activities on campus, Mrs. Doran served as president of the Kentucky Federation of Woman's Clubs. Struggling to keep up with duties at home while serving as KFWC president, she credited her "marvelous housekeeper," Nellie Carr. "The day Nellie leaves, I get a slow boat to China!"

Graduate education became increasingly important at re-

*The 1955-56 basketball team was Morehead State's first squad to play in the NCAA Tournament. From left in the front row are Kenny Thompson, Howard Shumate, Donnie Gaunce, Jess Mayabb, and co-captain "Fats" Tolle. The second row includes Jim Jewell, Dan Swartz, Bob Richards, Omar Fannin, Gene Carroll and Coach Bobby Laughlin. In the third row are co-captain Steve Hamilton, Bernie Shimfissel, Dave Keleher and Thornton Hill.*

gional colleges in Kentucky. Morehead State, which had granted its first M.A. degree in 1942, awarded sixty-nine M.A. degrees in 1960. On July 1, 1961, the four regional colleges were permitted to offer twenty-four hours of graduate work beyond the master's level instead of twelve as had been allowed previously. The objective was to qualify teachers for Rank I, the highest salary rank in the Minimum Foundation Program. The twenty-four hours were offered for the sole purpose of upgrading Kentucky's teachers to Rank I, not as part of a doctoral program. At least twelve of the twenty-four hours had to be taken in an academic field outside professional education.

In 1962 Robert Douglas Fraley was the first undergraduate student to graduate with a perfect (4.0) average with all work done at Morehead State. Fraley, who received a B.S. degree in business administration, became a certified public accountant. Fraley now is executive vice president and chief financial officer of Baldwin Development Company in Chicago. In 1968 Ronald L. Richardson, who earned a B.S. in biology with emphasis in pre-medicine, was the second Morehead State student with a perfect standing. Richardson is a gastroenterologist in Louisville. Two years earlier his brother, James David Richardson, had graduated from MSU. Presently vice chair of the American Board of Surgery, David will become chairman of the Board in 1998. Both are members of the teaching faculty at the University of Louisville School of Medicine.

During the Fifties and Sixties, the English department produced an outstanding record in promoting literary work. Morehead State became the first state college or university in Kentucky to publish a book of poetry—Robert Hazel's *Poems: 1951-1961*, the first Eagle Edition of the Morehead State College Press. In its introduction, Allen Tate described Hazel in glowing terms: "He ought to be one of the best of the second half of the century." Hazel had served on the staff of the Morehead State College Writers' Workshop for four years while teaching at the University of Kentucky. Albert F. Stewart, associate professor of English and director of the Writers' Workshop, published the second Eagle Edition, *The Untoward Hills,* in 1962. This native of Knott County had been a member of Morehead State's English department for six years and was sponsor of the Literary Arts Club. Stewart felt there was much to write about in the "dark, unsleeping land" of Kentucky and that many Kentuckians could do it well.

Academic affairs did not always go smoothly in the Doran era. There were dissidents among students and faculty. According to Harry E. Rose's doctoral dissertation, the English and music departments were the most restive in the early years of the Doran administration; yet, their contributions were frequently cited by the press. Doran encouraged some faculty members in both departments to adjust or to resign. By 1956 members of the music department had become quiescent. But trouble in the English department persisted until 1960 when Morehead State finally settled on a department head who, it was hoped, would keep his staff in line. George Boswell assumed the chairmanship of the English department in the fall of 1960; a few years later Boswell resigned to become a faculty member at the University of Mississippi.

Some of Morehead State's faculty members were perturbed over the choice of keeping quiet when their views deviated from those of the administration or moving elsewhere. Associate Professor James McConkey resigned to become a member of the English department at Cornell University. Other faculty members, such as John Long, Leonard Roberts, and Nolan Fowler, left Morehead State to make outstanding scholarly contributions elsewhere.

No sooner had the music and English departments been brought into line than dissension broke out in the social sciences. Roscoe Baker, professor of political science, charged that he was forced to resign by threat of unfavorable comments in his record. Theron Montgomery, of Jacksonville State College in Alabama, was appointed by the Southern Association to investigate Baker's allegations. After spending two days in conferring with Baker, Doran, and other college personnel, Montgomery concluded that Doran had made two mistakes with respect to Baker. "One was hiring him and the second was not firing him sooner than he had."

Doran summarized his faculty personnel problems since 1954 in a presentation to a meeting of the Board of Regents on June 22, 1960. "Some of the people on the faculty," the president stated, "did not agree with our philosophy that we ought to increase our enrollment, provide an educational opportunity to every youth in Kentucky, and to endeavor to help this youth." They found it necessary to seek "employment elsewhere in a situation more comfortable and less demanding." A second group "disagreed with the objectives and direction of the college and endeavored to hinder our progress or change our direction. Some of these were advised that they should allow us to proceed as we were going." But Doran was pleased that others "were converted to the new responsibilities and challenges," and hence, remained. Still, other faculty members, Doran suggested, "left the college because of opportunities for promotion, increased salaries, or a desire to advance their studies."

Through a combination of charisma and his frequent references to "a bus going east and a bus going west," (shape up or ship out), Doran kept students under control. Organizations like the Open Forum provided students with opportunities to voice protests and complaints. During the summer of 1964, however, a student protested to the Southern Association, alleging that he was kept under surveillance, his mail opened, and his phone tapped. The Southern Association, however, did not respond to the student's charges.

In 1960, in another case involving students, professors in the Administration Building (now Rader Hall) were convinced that their examinations were being stolen. After receiving a tip that someone had taken a copy of his final exam, Zell Walter, professor of education, walked to the front of his classroom the next day, tore up the prepared exam in front of everyone, wrote on the blackboard a brand new exam consisting of five essay questions and settled back to observe the squirming of class members. Based upon their behavior, Walter always felt he knew the identity of the culprit. On another occasion, a student was standing guard for two others as they pilfered the top floor of the Administration Building in search of tests. While the two lingered above, the student on the ground, hearing someone approaching, fled the scene. Finally, the students on the third floor called out below, "Everything clear?" Henry Carey, sociology and anthropology professor who was now standing at the foot of the ladder, called back, "Everything, come on down!" Somehow, they still managed to escape. But campus and city policemen finally managed to break up the test theft ring when a student was spotted one morning as he lowered himself from a window on the top floor of the Administration Building at 12:55 a.m. As he tried to run away, he was cornered at a bridge near the Baird Music Hall by the security officer and two city policemen who happened to be cruising in the vicinity. The student not only admitted his guilt but implicated three others who had been stealing and selling examinations for some time. Five to ten dollars was regarded as a "fair price" for a set of examination papers, their value depending on whether it was a "routine or a final test." The four students, one of whom had almost completed his work for a master's degree, immediately dropped out of school.

Doran's success in leading a small campus was forever arousing speculation that he was ready to leave for greener pastures. The *Rowan County News* ran a front-page headline in September 1962 that "Dr. Adron Doran May Become President of University of Kentucky." "High sources" both in Lexington and the State Capitol identified Doran as "the number one possibility" to succeed President Frank Dickey who had just resigned. However, nothing ever came of these rumors.

Moreheadians felt a need for Doran's leadership in executing the college's "Master Campus Building Plan," a blueprint for the institution in its expansion from a dormant little college of 700 to a proposed enrollment of 6,000 students by 1970. The early 1960s witnessed a land boom in the vicinity of the college because of the institution's remarkable growth and expectations of additional development. Because of land shortage, the Master Plan included construction of high-rise buildings of up to ten or twelve stories to make the best use of available land and to keep the campus compact. Most of the money necessary for campus expansion would come from long-term revenue bonds.

Morehead State completed a new administration building in

1962 diagonally across the Boulevard from the old Administration Building. A landmark yielded to progress as the new building was located on a site that had been occupied by a rain gauge since 1941. Agriculture professor Henry C. Haggan had initiated this service for the U.S. Weather Bureau when the state college opened its doors in 1923. He had recorded the rainfall at first with a "pail and a ruler."

A six-story semicircular structure to house 300 women was also completed in 1962 and was named Mignon Hall in honor of the president's wife. The Board of Regents made this decision after receiving petitions from the Alumni Association and the Student Council. Shortly afterwards, the college named a men's dormitory after Dean Roger Wilson, dean of students since 1953. Wilson was also a director of student housing and an associate professor of education.

The editor of the *Rowan County News* wrote of the "dazzling skyline" formed by college residence halls and classroom buildings. Forced to go skyward, the college had recently built a four-story classroom building and a four-story men's dormitory, both of which would soon be overshadowed with the completion of the six-story Mignon Hall, a women's residence hall. Doran explained, "We are rapidly running out of land and the extremely high prices being placed on property adjoining the campus is forcing us to go to multistory residence halls and classroom buildings." Another six-story women's residence hall similar to Mignon Hall was expected to be under construction by the end of the year.

Morehead State was really dreaming in the spring of 1965 when the administration unveiled a proposal for a five-acre lakeside campus to supplement the college's existing facilities. The proposal was drawn up by J. E. Duncan, chairman of the Division of Fine Arts, and C. Nelson Grote, chairman of the Division of Applied Arts. The lakeside campus would be located about ten miles from town along a section of Cave Run Lake, a flood control project planned by the U.S. Army Corps of Engineers. The proposed campus would include an administration-hotel building with a cafeteria for 500 and housing in double rooms, a 450-seat assembly hall, two cottages each to house twenty-four students, two outdoor theaters, five classroom buildings, and extensive recreational facilities. However, nothing ever came of this project!

The growth of the campus continued unabated. At its September 1, 1965, meeting the Board of Regents approved plans for seven buildings on the existing campus at a total cost of $8,187,000. Construction would begin within six weeks on a $750,000 addition to Breckinridge Training School; a sixteen-story circular dormitory for 300 women, to be known as Mignon Tower, would then complete the Mignon Hall complex, housing 1,800 coeds in four residence halls. Alumni Tower, a sixteen-story twin-tower residence hall housing 400 men and a third-story addition to the new administration building would round out the first stage. By January 1, 1966, the college hoped to begin construction of an addition to Lappin Hall, an addition to the fieldhouse, and a four-unit apartment project for married students. Cooper Hall, a 220-bed men's dormitory, and East Mignon Hall, a 240-bed women's residence hall, would be opened by the spring semester of 1966.

In June 1965 Morehead State became the first regional college in Kentucky to own and operate a radio station. The original staff consisted of one full-time faculty member and seven students. WMKY was established as a 10-watt station. In April 1971 WMKY began a new era as the station expanded to 50,000 watts with coverage extending into 15 of the university's 22 service region counties. Less that one year later, WMKY joined the National Public Radio Network as one of 143 charter member stations serving 38 states. Donald F. Holloway was the station's general manager from 1965 to 1975; then Larry Netherton served until his retirement in 1996.

Morehead State College continued to expand its academic offerings. On March 31, 1965, the board voted to include non-degree terminal programs of study. Beginning in the fall semester of that

*Top: Dan Swartz (1953-56) has the highest scoring average per game (27.5) in the history of Morehead State basketball. Left: His son, Chris, quarterback (1987-90) holds the career passing yardage record (9,028 yards) in Morehead State football.*

same year, Morehead State offered one- and two-year programs for clerks and secretaries in office management, secretarial science, agricultural business and farm production, as well as pre-professional study in agriculture and food management. Students completing one-year programs were awarded certificates of achievement; those finishing two-year programs received associate of applied arts degrees. At the same meeting, the Board of Regents authorized M.A. degrees in history, English, and biology. Previously, the institution offered M.A. degrees only in professional education.

Presidents had come and gone since the birth of Morehead State. But the institution lost its last direct connection with Opening Day when Anna Carter retired in 1963. "Miss Anna" had served as secretary to Morehead State's first seven presidents, from Frank C. Button to Adron Doran. She attended Morehead Normal School as a high school student and then taught three years in Rowan County rural schools. However, her ambition had always been to be a secretary. "My father thought it was unladylike for girls to work in offices," she stated, "but I finally told him that I was quitting teaching and he would just have to let me take secretarial training." Her starting salary was $1,400 plus room and board in a dormitory. At one time, she was secretary to the president, book store manager, postmistress, business agent, and "problem solver" to students and faculty. Miss Anna claimed responsibility for decreasing working hours from the original six-day week to a five-and-a-half-day week. "I started closing the office at noon on Saturday instead of 5 p.m. and others followed suit." After her retirement as secretary to President Doran, she worked in the Alumni Office for a few years and was secretary to the Board of Regents until 1968. Shortly before her death, Miss Anna was secretary to Morris Norfleet for one day in order for the record to show she had served under the first eight Presidents.

Since 1963, four persons have worked as secretary to presidents including Troy Burgess, who served in that capacity under Doran and Norfleet; Joyce Hart, who worked for Doran; Betty Philley, who served under Grote; Carol Barker, who now works there; and Carol Johnson, who has been on the Morehead staff since 1968 and has been executive secretary to the president and secretary to the Board of Regents since the 1980s.

## Student Life

The editors of the 1960 *Raconteur* summed it up, "There is an essence on every college campus that separates it from all other campuses. It is not just the buildings, nor the staff, nor the academic standing of the school. It is all of these and hundreds of other factors as well...It is our hope that in the following pages you will find something to remind you of that thrilling intangible that we have chosen to call COLLEGE LIFE."

Morehead State College organized its first Student Council

during the fall semester of 1948. Students elected as their officers: John Malone, president; Earle Seedhouse, vice-president; Pauline MacKenzie, secretary; Mary Lou Elam, treasurer; and William Clarkson, reporter. The council, composed of members of every class, worked for better student-faculty relationships. Limited in authority, the council could only make suggestions to the administration. Two projects sponsored by the council in the early Fifties were a song contest to replace the existing Alma Mater and a contest to design signs for all roads leading to Morehead, designating the city as the home of Morehead State College.

Morehead State's present Alma Mater was written in 1952 when Elwood Kozee won the song contest and Betty Jo Whitt composed music to accompany his lyrics. Kozee's winning entry was:

> Far above the rolling campus
> Resting in the dale,
> Stands our dear Ole Alma Mater,
> Her name we'll always hail.
> Shout in chorus, lift our voices,
> Blue and gold praise thee,
> Winning through to fame and glory,
> Dear Old MSC.

After the institution attained university status in 1966, "thee" was changed to "you" and "MSC" became "MSU." The Alma Mater written by Kozee, who later became a psychiatrist in Ashland, replaced the original one—"A Song to Morehead"—of which both the words and music had been written in 1930 by Lewis Henry Horton, head of Morehead State's music department from 1930 through 1942.

Faculty members often found their greatest opportunities for identifying with students while working together in campus organizations. Many student clubs were formed during this period.

The "M" Club, launched in December 1949, was composed of students who had earned a letter in any varsity sport or activity.

The organization championed the wearing of school letters by those who had earned them at Morehead State and discouraged wearing unearned letters as well as emblems acquired elsewhere. The club brought famous sports figures to campus as speakers each year. Endeavoring to create interest in varsity sports and to promote social activities, the "M" Club soon became one of the largest and most active groups on campus.

The Open Forum Club, with Charles E. Apel as sponsor, enabled students to engage in public discussions in which they could express their opinions on campus matters as well as other current topics. In 1954, for example, students covered such subjects as Communism, the Kinsey Report, segregation, and racial differences. The club sponsored the first Citizenship Day for Morehead State in 1956, during which John Sherman Cooper, Republican senator, and Lawrence W. Wetherby, Democratic governor, addressed over 2,000 newly registered voters on the philosophies of the two major parties. The following year, the club initiated presentation of the Citizenship Award to the most outstanding senior. A plaque, with the names engraved, was placed in the lobby of the Doran Student House. During the 1963 governor's race, the Open Forum Club invited Republican candidate Louie B. Nunn and his Democratic opponent, Edward T. (Ned) Breathitt, Jr., to campus convocations in the fieldhouse as part of the Charles Apel Citizenship Days.

Americans' interest in organized religion during this era was manifested by efforts of denominations to establish student organizations on or near the campus. The Newman Club was started in 1947 by twelve Catholic students. The Wesley Club, for Methodist students, was the oldest church-related organization on campus. Other local churches became increasingly interested in forming clubs with which their students could identify. The Disciples Student Fellowship was sponsored by the Morehead Christian Church to promote fellowship, Christian character, and understanding. The Baptist Student Union, organized on campus in the spring of 1954, served as a connecting link between students and the local Baptist Church. The Warner Fellowship, started in 1956, was affiliated with the First Church of God. Its Morehead chapter was only the third in the nation.

The Morehead Players whetted the appetites of those interested in drama by presenting diversified theatre. Examples of their productions in the Fifties included *The Glass Menagerie, Oedipus, Murder in the Cathedral, The Heiress,* and *Lady in the Dark.* In the first half of the Sixties, their presentations included *Harvey, See How They Run, Brigadoon,* and *The Rainmaker.* The Players had memberships in the Southeastern Theatre Conference and the American Educational Theatre Conference.

The Vets Club was founded during the fall semester of 1954 with Lester Breeding as its first president. In addition to disseminating relevant information to veterans on campus, it sponsored various social activities for the entire student body to answer those who claimed "there was nothing to do in Morehead on the weekends." During its very first week, the club won first place for its float in the Homecoming parade. The club also provided an impressive color guard for home football games in the days before Army ROTC.

The Cosmopolitan Club was founded in 1956 by Mignon Doran and Sun Ling Hong, a student from Korea, to foster human relations on campus. All foreign students and members of minority groups were automatically members; others were members by invitation only. The Cosmopolitan Club cooperated with the National Conference of Christians and Jews to sponsor a high school session at Morehead State on human relations, attended annually by fifteen students each from Kentucky, Ohio, and West Virginia.

Morehead State established such an outstanding record for contributions to human relations that, in 1963, the Louisville chapter of the National Conference of Christians and Jews, awarded Morehead and its Cosmopolitan Club its first annual distinguished merit plaque for their work in human relations. While accepting the award on behalf of Mignon, the club sponsor who was unable to attend because of illness, President Doran credited the club with helping to solve Morehead's integration problem.

President Doran inaugurated the Council of Presidents in 1957 to promote a closer relationship between students and the office of president. Meeting once each month, the council selected a president to serve as chairperson during each meeting; the only permanent officer was the secretary. The group included presidents of classes and all campus organizations. The Council of Presidents was expected to develop a spirit of institutional unity, provide cooperative planning, and schedule social and recreational activities. In 1958 Doran used the Council of Presidents to initiate efforts to improve relations with Eastern Kentucky State College.

Morehead State's Marching Band, under the leadership of Fred Marzan, expanded from eighteen members in 1956 to more than 130 by 1960. The group was known for its formation of a massive eagle on the football field at halftime of home games.

In January 1958 Morehead State inaugurated a "Better Dressed Week," which was highlighted by a style show and dance. Mrs. Doran coordinated the style show with campus leaders. Students modeled their wardrobes during lunch hours in the cafeteria. The week reached its climax at Thursday's convocation, imitating Dave Garroway's *Today Show* on NBC and including student models, commercials, and news flashes. The style show featured twenty-four male and female students, modeling both formal and casual wear from their own wardrobes. A committee from the Council of Presidents chose the models. The week concluded with a candlelight dinner and a formal all-campus dance on Friday evening in the Doran Student House. "Better Dressed Week" immediately became one of the major events at Morehead State.

The Fifties also saw more students with disabilities on the campus. Elwood Miracle, an English and history major from Middlesboro and blind for eighteen of his twenty years, was accepted as a student by President Doran after he had been refused admittance to several other institutions of higher learning. Tempted to quit during the first three weeks of his freshman year, Miracle stayed because he felt that his example would encourage other students who were blind. Extremely popular and with a fine sense of humor and an ever-present smile, Elwood received a standing ovation when he walked across the stage unassisted to receive his diploma during summer commencement exercises in August 1961.

## Athletics: Charter Member of the Ohio Valley Conference

### Football:

A charter member of the newly-formed Ohio Valley Conference, Morehead State College had difficulty competing in football from 1948 to 1965. The team managed only a 31-82-1 conference record by the end of this era.

With a respectable 6-3 season in 1949 and victories over four OVC opponents in 1950, the Eagles managed to win only one conference game, along with a tie, in 1951 and 1952. Morehead then dropped every conference game from the beginning of the 1953 season until midway in the 1959 schedule, when the team eked out a victory over Murray. The school's greatest success came in 1962 when the Eagles reigned as tri-champions with East Tennessee, Eastern Kentucky, and Middle Tennessee. With a tie sandwiched in, Morehead State endured thirty-three OVC games without a victory from 1952 to 1959, setting a national record of twenty-seven consecutive losses. The Eagles agonized through eight winless seasons in the conference between 1948 and 1966. However, individual talent stood out in this time period. With sixteen All-OVC players from 1948 to 1966, Morehead State averaged almost one conference star a year.

Four coaches directed the Eagles during their first eighteen years in the OVC: Ellis T. Johnson, with a record of 15-25-1 from

1948 through 1952; Wilbur (Shorty) Jamerson, who lost all 26 games from 1953 through 1955; Paul Adams, who improved only slightly to 4-21-1 from 1956 through 1958 but with no conference victories; and Guy D. Penny, with a 28-32-1 record from 1959 through 1966. Overall, Johnson's 54-44-10 record for a .551 winning percentage from 1936 through 1952 established him as Morehead's most successful coach ever. Guy Penny's overall 39-39-2 mark for a .500 winning percentage placed him third.

Led by co-captains Manuel Lyons and Tom Queen, tackles from Louisa, Morehead State defeated Tennessee Tech 19-7 in its maiden OVC game in 1948. The school put together a successful season in 1949 with a 6-3 mark, as the Eagles brought home the "Hawg Rifle" in a storybook finish over rival Eastern 27-26. Charles (Izzy) Porter scored early from the one yard line; touchdowns by Jim Siple and Jerry Wing ensured a 20-6 lead at the intermission. Trailing 26-20 with five seconds left in the game, Wing passed to Siple to tie the game; tackle Harold Mullins, who had been injured, was helped on the field and managed to boot an extra point for the victory. Homecoming featured a 21-0 victory over Murray with the spectators including Governor and Mrs. Earle Clements. Matt Pryor, who had missed four games because of a broken foot, scored twice and set up a third touchdown with his outstanding running. At the end of the season Mullins was selected for the All-OVC team.

The 1950 Eagles recorded wins over OVC opponents Evansville 53-0, Marshall, 51-6, Tennessee Tech 20-16, and Middle Tennessee 31-7. In spite of a 4-4 record, Morehead placed four on the All-OVC team: Corky Kirtley, Paintsville end, a unanimous choice and captain; Clyde MacLaughlin, center from Russell; Porter, Prestonsburg quarterback; and Jerry Wing, halfback from Dayton. Porter completed 145 out of 219 passes while piling up over 2,500 yards through the air; eight of his twenty touchdown passes went to Kirtley. The Eagles managed to win only six additional conference games throughout the decade of the Fifties.

*Harold Sergent holds the record of 52 points in a single game in Morehead State basketball history.*

In 1953, Johnson was succeeded by Wilbur Jamerson as head coach, with Si Prewitt, 1935 captain of Western and 1947 Kentucky high school coach of the year, as his assistant. The Eagles scored a mere twenty points during the entire season. Unable to win in three seasons, Jamerson was replaced as head coach in 1956 by former Eagle great, Paul Adams, who was then head coach at Raceland High School. News of Morehead's 18-13 victory over Maryville touched off a celebration on campus and downtown, which lasted well after midnight. As the team returned home on Sunday evening, fire trucks and a caravan of cars, cheerleaders, and supporters met Adams and the team at the city limits and escorted them to Jayne Stadium.

Guy D. Penny, considered by some as the savior of Morehead football, succeeded Adams as head coach in 1959 and led the Eagles out of the wilderness to their only two OVC championships. Selected from a pool of twenty-five applicants, Penny had achieved great success as a high school coach in Alabama and as an assistant coach at Tennessee-Martin. With only one assistant, Earl Bentley, the new Morehead coach guided the Eagles to their first conference victory since defeating Evansville 14-0 in the opening game of 1952. In the middle of the 1959 season, Murray was leading Morehead going into the final quarter, when halfback Buford Crager scored a touchdown, thereby giving the Eagles their first conference win, 9-8, in forty OVC games. In another contest, Crager, who later served as Morehead State's vice president for student affairs for fifteen years, ran an East Tennessee kickoff 100 yards for a touchdown although the Eagles lost 27-21. Despite MSC's lack of team success throughout the Fifties, the Eagles still boasted nine All-OVC selections!

Morehead State started the Sixties with a 5-4 record, the first time the Eagles had won more than half their games since 1949. The institution began using the expression "Penny's from Heaven" to give credit to its new leadership in football. Trailing previously unbeaten West Virginia Tech 7-6 at intermission, the Eagles thrilled Homecoming fans by storming back to trounce Tech, 49-13. Freshman halfback Howard Murphy, from Springfield, Ohio—the first black to play football in the OVC—gained 136 yards in eleven carries and scored a touchdown as well as a conversion, and halfback Bud Ogden scored two touchdowns. For the first time since joining the OVC, Morehead defeated Western, 12-6. Crager scored Morehead's opening touchdown; Mike Brown's booming punts kept Western in the hole most of the game, while Howard Murphy picked up 72 yards on fourteen carries and scored the winning touchdown. The Eagles closed out their season by defeating Eastern 21-9, thereby reclaiming the prized "Hawg Rifle" for the first time since 1949. With Morehead trailing 9-7, Tony Gast recovered an Eastern fumble on the Maroons' 37-yard line; Crager carried five of seven plays on the subsequent scoring drive. Murphy stiff-armed three would-be tacklers to add another touchdown in the final quarter.

Having won only one game in 1961 and a pre-season pick to finish in the cellar in 1962, the Eagles finished in a four-way tie for the conference championship with East Tennessee, Eastern Kentucky, and Middle Tennessee, all at 4-2. A Kentucky team had not won the OVC championship since Eastern Kentucky took the trophy in 1954. With Paul West, versatile 155-pound quarterback/halfback, gaining 132 yards in 13 carries, MSC squeezed out a 14-10 win over East Tennessee, even without the services of All-OVC performer Murphy who was out with injuries. In Morehead's final game of the season, the Eagles gained the "Hawg Rifle" and a share of the conference championship with a 20-12 victory over Eastern after trailing by two touchdowns earlier in the game. Freshman quarterback Mike Gottfried broke the game wide open with bullet passes for two touchdowns. Morehead's Ernie DeCourley, from Savannah, Tennessee, repeated as an All-OVC selection at tackle. Roy Kidd and Carl Oakley had joined Earl Bentley as Morehead State assistant coaches at the beginning of the season; after one season, Kidd moved to Eastern Kentucky as an assistant and then was picked as head coach the following year and proceeded to build a football dynasty.

Morehead State opened the 1963 season with a 31-13 defeat of Butler in the annual Shrine Bowl game in Ashland and followed with a 19-6 defeat of Marshall. Before the largest Homecoming crowd ever, Mike Gottfried hurled two touchdown passes, and Tally Johnson booted three conversions along with a 28-yard field goal for a 24-10 victory over Murray State. A first-quarter touchdown pass from Gottfried to end Jack Smith was enough to defeat Austin Peay, 7-0. Morehead retained the "Hawg Rifle" by prevailing over Eastern 6-0. Afterwards, Eastern decided that 1963 would be the final year for this colorful tradition.

The year 1964 had two distinct seasons, as Morehead opened with five victories only to lose its final four games. After defeating Butler 26-7, the Eagles whipped Marshall 6-0 in the Shrine Bowl game before an overflow crowd of 8,500 at Ashland and followed with a 35-0 shellacking of Tennessee Tech in the first game played in the new 10,000-seat Breathitt Sports Center. Tally Johnson kicked a 35-yard field goal for the winning margin as the Eagles defeated Murray 17-14. Behind Austin Peay 13-0 going into the final stanza, Morehead stormed back. Johnson scored a touchdown and Gottfried teamed up with end Jack Smith for the pass play of the season, as Smith made an almost unbelievable catch for a 14-13 victory. Morehead State placed three on the All-OVC team including Jack Smith, tight end from Decatur, Georgia; Richard Pare, defensive end from New Britain, Connecticut; and James Osborne, defensive tackle from Hindman. An inexperienced Morehead team dropped to 3-6 in 1965, the school's final season under the name of Morehead State College. Although Morehead lost its final game to arch rival Eastern 38-20, quarterback Mike Gottfried and end Rico King continued to assault the record books as Gottfried passed seventeen times for 187 yards; King caught seven of these aerials for 55 yards, one touchdown, and a two-point conversion. By the end of the season, King had set a Morehead record for pass receivers with 40 receptions for 624 yards, six touchdowns, and three two-point conversions.

Gottfried ended a brilliant career, rewriting all Eagle passing and total offense records until then and setting an OVC passing record by completing 114 passes in 251 attempts. He also set three school season records with 1,634 yards in total offense, 1,585 yards in passing, and thirteen touchdowns. During his 1962-65 career, the Crestline, Ohio, native completed 262 passes out of 576 attempts for

3,544 yards and 31 touchdowns, the latter tying an OVC record. Gottfried's distinguished college coaching career included head positions at Murray State, Cincinnati, Kansas, and Pittsburgh. After leaving coaching, he became a football analyst with ESPN.

### Basketball:

Morehead State enjoyed a great deal more success in basketball from 1948 to 1966 than in football. The Eagles won the conference championship four times: They finished in a three-way tie in 1955-56 and 1960-61 and were co-champions in 1956-57 and 1962-63. MSC made three appearances in the NCAA: in 1956, 1957, and 1961, winning three games and losing four.

Three coaches directed the Eagles during this period. A fourth-place finish was the highest reached by Coach Ellis T. Johnson during his five seasons, as his teams won 64 and lost 57. Bobby Laughlin achieved the most success, with four OVC championships and three second-place finishes in twelve years, while his teams were winning 166 and losing 120. Bob Wright's one team in this era went 12-12, finishing fourth in the OVC.

The Eagles were loaded with individual talent, including four All-Americans: guard John (Sonny) Allen, of Morehead in 1950; center Dan Swartz, of Owingsville both in 1955 and 1956; forward Steve Hamilton, of Charlestown, Indiana, in 1957; and guard Harold Sergent of Ashland in 1963. Seventeen Eagles made the All-OVC first team. Sergent was selected as OVC Player of the Year the first season this award was given, and Bobby Laughlin won the first OVC Coach of the Year award.

Morehead State's initial OVC team, with three freshmen as starters, compiled a 14-9 record. With the exception of one Buckeye, all fourteen players hailed from Kentucky high schools. In the first OVC tournament, Morehead defeated Evansville, 57-54, then was soundly beaten by Louisville, 77-54. Sonny Allen was All-KIAC his freshman and sophomore years and All-OVC during his junior and senior years. Allen finished his career as the Eagles' third highest scorer in history with 1,923 points. He became only the third Morehead player ever to be named an All-American. When Allen played his final home game on February 18, 1950, Mayor William H. Layne officially designated the occasion as "Sonny Allen Day."

Morehead State's 14-12 record in 1950-51 was highlighted by a loss of 90-88 to Tennessee Tech at Cookeville, Tennessee, on "the night the clock stood still." The Morehead Eagles finished with only four men on the floor after the other eight fouled out. With 1:40 remaining, the Morehead coach jerked off his coat and tie and ran to the scorer's table in jest where he pounded his fist on the table while bellowing, "Coach Johnson in for Morehead!" After the game it was discovered that the clock was slow so that the game actually lasted sixty minutes instead of the regulation forty! Near the end of the game, players on both sides were staggering from exhaustion. Although the game was not exceptionally rough, 77 personal fouls were called, 41 against Morehead and 37 against Tech. Ellis Johnson's final season at Morehead State was 1952-53, when the Eagles posted a 13-12 record. His 196-158 record made him the most successful coach in Morehead State's history.

Assistant Bob Laughlin succeeded Johnson as head coach. His 16-8 mark in 1953-54 was Morehead's greatest season since joining the OVC, with the Eagles finishing as high as second in the conference for the first time. In Laughlin's first five seasons, the Eagles lost only three times on their home floor. Center (Dangerous) Dan Swartz of Owingsville was named to the All-OVC team; his 44 points against Eastern Kentucky represented the highest score for any Eagle in a single game during that season.

Morehead State had a respectable 14-10 record in 1954-55, as Sonny Allen joined Laughlin as an assistant. Highlights of the season included a 93-73 victory over Colorado State and a 111-90 defeat of Memphis State. Perhaps Morehead State's most exciting game in history was its 130-117 victory over Furman University. The game established several NCAA records, including the most total points ever scored in one game—247. Furman's 117 points represented the most points ever scored by a losing team in NCAA play. Furman's Darrell Floyd netted 67 points, on twenty-seven field goals and thirteen free throws, the most points ever scored in a Morehead game by an opposing player. The Eagles made 50 out of 63 free throws and shot over 60 percent from the floor while Furman shot 57. Coach Laughlin told Billy Thompson of the *Lexington Herald,* "You'd have to see it to believe it!" When asked about his defensive strategy, Laughlin replied, "The only defense a team needs is to score one more goal than its opponent!" During the season, this exciting Eagle team went over the century mark in eight victories. Dan Swartz was named to the All-OVC Team for the second year in a row; forward Steve Hamilton joined him on the first team.

The *Raconteur* referred to the 1955-56 Eagles as "the greatest team in the history of Morehead State College." The NCAA Tournament had just granted an automatic bid to the Ohio Valley Conference. At that time the NCAA field was composed of only twenty-four teams in contrast with today's sixty-four. Morehead State forged an impressive 19-10 record in spite of playing 21 of 29 games away from home because of a delay in completing its new fieldhouse. The Eagles' 2,782 points remains the school record for the highest number of points scored in one season. In the opening round of the NCAA tournament at Fort Wayne, Indiana, Morehead State defeated Mid-American Conference champion Marshall, 107-92, as the two teams set the tournament record of 199 total points in one game. Swartz garnered 39 points and Hamilton, 27. Big Ten champion Iowa then ousted the Eagles 97-83 in the Midwestern Regionals on the former's home court at Iowa City; the Hawkeyes subsequently defeated Adolph Rupp's Kentucky Wildcats 84-72 to advance to the NCAA finals. Governor Chandler issued a proclamation stating that Morehead State "as a David among the Goliaths of basketball, has by its superlative skill, commanded the respect and admiration of vast audiences throughout the nation."

Senior center Swartz, who netted 97 points in Morehead State's three NCAA Tournament games, was a unanimous choice for the All-Tournament teams at both Fort Wayne and Iowa City. He was also named Most Valuable Player at Fort Wayne. His 828 points during the 1955-56 season represent the most points ever scored by a Morehead player in one season. Breaking every Morehead State scoring record, Swartz stood out as the third highest scorer in the nation with a 28.6 average. After transferring from the University of Kentucky, Swartz was the most prolific scorer in the history of Kentucky college basketball to that point, with 1,925 points in his three seasons for a career average of 27.5 points per game. Swartz made All-American in his two final seasons. Captain Donnie Gaunce was second in

*Coach Nolan Fowler and Carl Deaton survey the trophies, medals, and ribbons which Deaton earned as a member of Morehead State's dominant track squad in the 1950s.*

scoring in 1955-56 and has often been spoken of as one of the finest playmakers to perform at Morehead State.

For the 1956-57 season the Eagles moved into their new 5,000-seat fieldhouse, inaugurating it by defeating Villa Madonna 107-49. Morehead State then defeated Florida State, 97-75; Cincinnati, 78-70; and Louisville, 85-74, when the Cardinals were ranked No. 6 in the nation. The Eagles whipped Eastern 92-75 to become co-champions as Morehead and Western finished the season with identical 9-1 conference records. But Western conceded to Morehead without a play-off since two Hilltopper starters were ineligible for NCAA tournament competition because they had played varsity ball as freshmen. In their second NCAA tournament, the Eagles, with a 19-8 record, were nosed out by the Pittsburgh Panthers, 86-85, in St. John's Arena at Ohio State. The fast-breaking Eagles had one of the tallest front lines in the nation, with Steve Hamilton and Dave Keleher, both 6-7, and Bernie Shimfessel at 6-9. Morehead State led the nation with 64.8 rebounds a game. Co-captain Hamilton, who led the Eagles with a 24.5 scoring average and also in rebounding with 543 for a 20.1 average per game, was named the most outstanding player on the team. His 51 points against Ohio University established a new single game scoring record. His 38 rebounds against Florida State comprised a Morehead record which has never been broken. Hamilton's efforts were rewarded by his being named an All-American and a member of the All-OVC team. His 1,829 career points made him the fourth highest scorer in Morehead annals. Co-captain Harlan (Fats) Tolle was an excellent playmaker while managing a 12.1 point average with his long set shot.

Pre-season favorite to win the conference in 1957-58 and ranked in the nation's top 20 in pre-season polls, Morehead State dropped its last four games, thereby throwing away any chance at a third straight NCAA appearance. Laughlin had suffered through his worst season ever, with a 13-10 record. Season highlights included a 98-91 victory over Alabama and a 103-59 drubbing of Washington and Lee. In spite of having All-American Bailey Howell on its team, Mississippi State felt the need to throw a "deep freeze" at Morehead State in winning, 46-41. Tennessee Tech handed the Eagles their first home loss in Wetherby Gymnasium in 35 games, thereby making Tech the OVC champion. In spite of Morehead State's losing record from 1958-60, guard Herbie Triplett made the All-OVC team both years.

Although picked to finish in a tie for fourth place, the Eagles bounced back to take the OVC crown again in 1960-61. In the OVC playoff, they nosed out Eastern, 55-54, after trailing at halftime and then also came from behind to defeat the Western Hilltoppers, 80-72, in overtime. Morehead broke open a 33-33 game at intermission to defeat Xavier of Cincinnati, 71-66, in its first NCAA tournament outing as guard Granville (Granny) Williams and center Ed Noe hit 21 points each, followed by guard Hecky Thompson's 16. Although four-point underdogs to the University of Kentucky, Morehead led the Wildcats until 2:37 to play in spite of center Ed Noe's fouling out with 14:30 remaining. The Kentucky Wildcats went on to defeat the Eagles, 71-64. Center Noe and both Morehead guards—Granny Williams and Hecky Thompson—made the All-OVC team. Williams also led the nation in free throw accuracy with 89 percent. Laughlin's teams had won three out of seven NCAA tournament games in 1956, 1957, and 1961.

A national magazine ranked the Eagles twelfth in the nation in its 1961-62 pre-season poll and designated senior Ed Noe as one of the best cagers in the South. For the first time in history, radio stations outside Morehead carried Eagle basketball games. Some of their most exciting games included two victories over arch-rival Marshall and a 107-81 win over Miami-Florida, a game in which Granny Williams tallied 48 points on 22 of 33 field goals and four free throws and the team hit a sizzling 51.6 average; forward Norm Pokley, Morehead's leading rebounder for two consecutive years, snared 26 rebounds and scored 22 points. The Eagles, however, failed to live up to expectations as they finished in second place in the OVC, with a 14-8 overall record but only 7-5 in the conference. Williams and center Ed Noe repeated as members of the All-OVC team. Playing only three seasons, Williams, who had transferred from Lees College, finished with 1,637 points, making him the seventh highest Eagle scorer in history.

Morehead State tied with Tennessee Tech as co-champs in 1962-63, with a 13-7 overall record and a 9-4 conference mark. The Eagles, however, lost to Tech in a playoff to determine which team would play in the NCAA tournament. Norm Pokley, at 6-9, one of the biggest men in the OVC, was the leading team rebounder for the third straight year and had a fourteen point scoring average. Pokley switched from forward to the pivot his senior year. Sophomore guard Harold Sergent, with a 20.4 point average, was a unanimous selection for the All-OVC team. Guard Roy Ware of Camargo finished as the team's second highest scorer, with a 15.9 average, and joined Sergent and teammate Norm Pokley on the All-OVC team. A member of Ashland's state championship team which included such other greats as Larry Conley, who later starred for the University of Kentucky, Sergent was a tremendous floor leader. With a deadly jump shot, he could also move with blinding speed. *Basketball News* named him OVC Player of the Year and listed him as one of the top ten sophomores in the nation.

The Eagles fell all the way to a sixth-place finish in the OVC in 1963-64, with a 6-8 conference record and 10-11 overall. Center Henry Akin averaged 20 points per game and was selected on the All-OVC team. Sergent's 26-point average led the conference in scoring. Not only did he make the All-OVC team for the second consecutive year, but he also became Morehead's sixth All-American. Morehead State finished 13-10 in Laughlin's final season as head coach in 1964-65. Akin averaged 18.6 points per game and 12.5 rebounds, repeating as a member of the All-OVC team. Sergent broke Steve Hamilton's record of 51 points in a single game by scoring 52 against Middle Tennessee. He also set a new OVC record of 42 consecutive free throws, only eight short of the national record. Sergent was named to the All-OVC team for the third straight year; his 1,469 career points made him the eighth highest scorer in the annals of Morehead basketball. Because of the long-range accuracy of such Laughlin guards as Sergent, Herbie Triplett, and Granny Williams, Eagle fans have always wondered how many points these players would have scored if the three-point rule had been in effect then.

Bob Laughlin then became the full-time athletic director after his twelve years at the basketball helm had produced a 166-120 record. The new physical education building was named after him. Bob Wright, with a successful seven-year coaching career at Paul Blazer High in Ashland, was named head coach after Laughlin. In his first season, Wright and assistant Lake Kelly led Morehead State to third place in the OVC with an 8-6 record and 12-12 overall.

### Baseball:

Morehead State's baseball program continued to be successful from 1948 to 1966. Coach Sonny Allen guided the Eagles to an OVC championship in 1957. MSC also captured six eastern division championships, with Coach Rex Chaney's teams taking four of these. There were four baseball coaches during this time. Stan Radjunas won 42 games while losing 35 during the Eagles' first five seasons in the OVC. Chaney's five seasons resulted in a 89-45 record. George Cooke coached one year with a 6-13 mark, and during Sonny Allen's seven seasons in this era, Morehead won 78 while losing 55.

Having captured a KIAC title in 1947, Radjunas's greatest success in OVC baseball came in 1952 with a 12-3 record, including winning the OVC eastern division championship. Radjunas accumulated a 68-49 overall record during eight years ending in 1953. Under Coach Sonny Allen in 1957, the Eagles won twelve and lost five, winning the eastern division of the Ohio Valley Conference on their way to becoming conference champions.

In Rex Chaney's first season as Eagle coach, Morehead captured the OVC eastern championship with a 12-9 record in 1961, and Stan Morgan was chosen to the NCAA Helms All-American team. Chaney's team repeated as eastern division champions in 1962 with an 11-9 record. Morehead State enjoyed its first twenty-game winning season in the 1963 season while again reigning as conference champions. At this time, former Eagle Steve Hamilton, called "The Young Professor" by his New York Yankee teammates, returned to campus as an instructor of physical education and assistant basketball coach during the off season; he also worked with Eagle pitchers.

Morehead State featured a 22-8 season in 1964, while repeating as the OVC's eastern division champions. In 1965 rain forced Morehead State to reschedule more than twenty of its games and to cancel four games with Tennessee Tech. Eastern Kentucky, with the same number of conference losses as Morehead State but more wins, was awarded the division championship in spite of the Eagles' 24-9 season. Freshman Greg Paulin led in hitting with .462, while Mike Collins was home run king with six. Jim Martin stood out as the ace of the pitching staff, with a 4-0 record and a 1.45 earned run average.

### Track:

Under Coach Nolan Fowler, who had taught at the college since 1943, Morehead State participated in its first full track season in 1953. The cross country harriers captured first spot in the OVC meet and placed second in the famed Shamrock Run in Louisville, where they defeated, among others, the University of Kentucky. During its second full season in 1954, Morehead State won the Gazette Relays in Charleston, West Virginia, and placed fourth in the OVC meet. In the latter, Carl Deaton won both the mile and two-mile, which no athlete had done previously. The *Courier-Journal* called Deaton "the track man of the year in Kentucky." Champions of the OVC for the second year in a row, the cross country team won four of six meets and came in second in the other two.

Fowler's "Dauntless Dozen" journeyed to Bowling Green and returned home with the 1955 OVC track and field championship. This was the first OVC championship Morehead State had ever gained in any sport except in the minor sport of cross country. The Eagles captured half of the fourteen titles. Morehead's six highest scorers were Carl Deaton, undefeated in distance runs; Ed Wells, sprints; Kenny Thompson, jumps; Kenny Daugherty, distance runs; Joe Wheeler, 440 and mile relay, and Steve Hamilton, hurdles and jumps. Deaton did the impossible by smashing two conference records on a track which was made heavy by two downpours less than twenty-four hours before the meet.

Daugherty was also captain of the cross country teams as the harriers went undefeated in nine meets. The greatest feat was winning the Shamrock 5,000 meter run on Thanksgiving Day in Louisville, as perennial Southeastern Conference power, Tennessee was defeated. The team's "Big Five" included Deaton, Daugherty, Wheeler, Paul Whiteley, and Richard Wilson, who later became an authority on higher education in Kentucky while serving as a *Courier-Journal* reporter. Wilson later singled out Fowler and Ray Hornback, in journalism, as the two individuals who had exerted the most influence on his life.

Track reached an all-time high at Morehead State in 1956 as the Eagles took seven of ten meets, leading to their second consecutive OVC victory. Two of the wins were over SEC opponents, Kentucky and Tennessee. Carl Deaton established new OVC marks in both the mile and the half mile. Kenny Thompson was unbeaten in the high jump, completing the season with a record of 6'3" in the OVC meet. Joe Wheeler set a new school mark in the half mile. Kenny Daugherty lost only two races in the two-mile during the season. The cross country team won both the Shamrock Run, soundly defeating SEC champ Tennessee in the process, and the William Jennings Bryan Invitational.

After seventeen years at Morehead State, Fowler left in 1960 to become track coach and history professor at Tennessee Tech. Looking back over his coaching experience, Fowler was proud of the fact that "four of my boys got the doctorate." Those four were: Kenny Daugherty (distance thrower) at the University of Upsala (Sweden) in geodicy; Harold Falls at Purdue in physiology, "especially as it applied to athletics;" Bernie Fieler (shot putter) at the University of Florida; and Rex Chaney (discus thrower) at Indiana University, in recreation.

### Other Sports:

Morehead State participated in other sports during these eighteen years. The tennis, golf, swimming, and soccer teams compiled respectable records against a variety of opponents.

The 1960s were difficult times for Southern teams in the process of integrating while other Southern teams were dragging their feet. In 1963 Morehead received an invitation from the Southeastern Intercollegiate Wrestling Association to its tournament in Atlanta only to have it rescinded because of Morehead's unwillingness to leave one of its better athletes, Allie Leftenant, a black freshman from Amityville, New York, at home. Athletic Director Laughlin stated, "We wouldn't feel so bad if we hadn't received a bid at all, but to receive it, and then have it pulled back simply because we have a fine black athlete on our squad, is upsetting to the whole team. We have set the pace in integration in athletics in Kentucky," he concluded, "and we are proud of it."

The 1965-66 Morehead State wrestling team took first place in the OVC. The Eagles fell short of an undefeated season by one point when Milligan College played the spoiler role by defeating Morehead 20-19. Leftenant, 160 pound tri-captain, won ten times and completed four years of competition without a single loss. Leftenant was voted the outstanding wrestler in the Miami Invitational Tournament. The two other tri-captains, Dick Roche and Roger Colvin, along with Bob Whitaker, reached the quarterfinals of the Wilkes College Christmas Tournament, sometimes looked upon as the "Rose Bowl" of wrestling.

---

From 1948 to 1966, Morehead State experienced its greatest years of growth—in student enrollment, expansion of buildings, and size of faculty. The institution had also enjoyed significant athletic triumphs. Was it better to continue as a good college or to experiment with becoming a university? In 1966 Morehead State concluded it was ready to discover the answer!

*(Above) In 1966 Governor Edward T. Breathitt signed the bill making
Morehead State a university. From left are State Rep. Sherman Arnett,
Morehead publisher W. E. Crutcher, Gov. Breathitt, President Doran and State
Sen. Ed Kelly. (Below) The bill signing was reenacted in 1996. Looking on from
left are Arnett; Pat Skaggs and Marilynn Johnson, daughters of the late Mr.
Crutcher; former President Doran, and Lake Kelly, son of the late Senator Kelly.*

# Chapter 5

# Morehead State University:
# Years of Transition, 1966-1986

Morehead State had worn four different names during its first forty-four years as a state institution of higher learning. By 1966 the college looked toward status as a university. Was it ready for the major transition? Could the same factors that had pushed the small mountain school into a state college be effective in transforming it into a regional university? How would Morehead State, along with its administration, manage such a metamorphosis?

While searching for answers to these significant questions, Morehead State was led from 1966 to 1986 by three different administrations. Adron Doran succeeded in bringing the name of "University" to Morehead State as well as in overseeing construction of the last major expansion of the campus. Then, faced with difficulties in contending with new social and political conditions, he grappled with the timing of his retirement. Stepping down from the presidency on January 1, 1977, he watched two successive presidents come and go during the next decade. Morris L. Norfleet experienced only limited success as he introduced a vastly different style of leadership while retaining most of the Doran people in key positions. A combination of unwise decisions and questionable practices led to his demise as Doran's successor seven years later. At a most difficult time, Morehead State then brought in Herb. F. Reinhard as its second "outsider" president. After the Board of Regents had authorized the new leader to generate changes, its own composition shifted even before Reinhard arrived on campus to carry out the mandate he had been given. The new president's style of leadership, along with major changes he introduced, forced him out with seemingly little to show for his two-year stint except bad feelings and controversy. The passage of more than a decade has subsequently made it easier to place his troubled presidency within an historical perspective.

## Morehead State Becomes a University

Shortly after becoming governor in December, 1963, Edward T. (Ned) Breathitt created the Commission on Higher Education, composed of eleven college presidents and seven laymen. The Commission's duty was to recommend a distribution of the federal funds available to Kentucky public and private colleges under the Higher Education Facilities Act of 1963. Later, Breathitt authorized the Commission to assume the difficult chore of analyzing the long-range needs of the state colleges and universities and of making recommendations on how to fulfill these. To assist, the Commission hired three experts on higher education: M. M. Chambers, Raymond C. Gibson, both of Indiana University, and Truman Pierce, of Auburn University. With Chambers serving as chairman, this panel spent six months in interviewing presidents and faculty members, collecting financial and enrollment data, and preparing a report for the Commission.

In accordance with the Chambers Report, the Commission on Higher Education presented several recommendations to the governor for changes in Kentucky's system of colleges and universities. Most controversial were those recommendations involving membership on the Council of Public Higher Education and granting university status to the four regional colleges. The latter proposal received the most attention since it was opposed by three of the Commission's eighteen members: John Oswald, president of the University of Kentucky; Irvin Lunger, president of Transylvania College; and John Murphy, president of Villa Madonna College. In general, the presidents opposed any suggestion that would make them non-voting members of the Council, thus giving effective power to the nine lay members appointed by the governor. President Doran argued that laymen should not determine policies and procedures without executive officers of the institutions having a voice.

On February 16, 1966, the Kentucky House of Representatives passed House Bill 238, by a resounding vote of 83-0. House Bill 238 provided for a nine-member Council on Public Higher Education, appointed by the governor for staggered terms and "composed entirely of lay persons," with college presidents serving as non-voting members. The power of the new council was strengthened as it became the agency for overall research, planning, budget review, and all other statewide aspects of higher education not otherwise delegated to one or more institutions of higher learning. House Bill 238 also provided for new community colleges to be located in Jefferson and Mason counties and granted university status to the four state colleges. Only Kentucky State College, a land grant institution founded in 1886 for blacks but now racially integrated, was not designated a university.

House Bill 238, in addition, outlined the functions of each echelon of higher education in the Commonwealth: the University of Kentucky, its community college system, Kentucky State College, and the new regional universities. In the sensitive area of graduate education, the bill turned over to the University of Kentucky programs at the master's, doctoral, and post-doctoral levels, including joint programs beyond the master's level in cooperation with other institutions of higher education in the state. The University of Kentucky also retained professional doctoral instruction including law, medicine, education, engineering, and dentistry. The four new regional universities and Kentucky State College could offer graduate programs at the master's level in education, business, and the arts and sciences in addition to programs beyond the master's degree to satisfy requirements for teachers, school leaders, and other certified personnel. The University of Kentucky was also permitted to continue as the principal state institution to conduct statewide research

and service programs. The other five schools were granted authority to offer only such programs as were related to the needs of their
geographical areas and to provide programs in their own area comparable to the University of Kentucky community college system.

Two-year community colleges administered by the University
of Kentucky were already located at Ashland, Covington,
Cumberland, Fort Knox, Elizabethtown, Henderson, Hopkinsville,
Lexington, Louisville, Maysville, Prestonsburg, and Somerset; addi-
tional community colleges were later added at Hazard, Madisonville,
Owensboro, and Paducah. In a most uncommon organizational pat-
tern, all the community colleges would be administered by the
Board of Trustees of the University of Kentucky. By the end of the
1980s, the community college system enrolled over a quarter of all
Kentucky students who were then taking college-level courses.

On February 25, 1966, the Senate killed an amendment to au-
thorize a four-year college at Paducah before passing original House
Bill 238 by a vote of 29-6. Senator Richard L. Frymire, Democrat
from Madisonville, deplored what he regarded as "the mad rush to
enact a bill without a scintilla of an idea as to how many millions
of added money it will cost." Although his words came back to
haunt higher education, Frymire's motion to recommit House Bill
238 to committee until added costs could be approximated was defeated 25-5.

When Governor Breathitt signed the bill into law on Saturday
morning, February 26, 1966, there was exuberance over the new
prestige now conveyed upon the four regional institutions and how
this image would enable them to recruit better faculty and students.
But perhaps the three most significant aspects of the bill for
Kentucky's system of higher education were the composition of the
Council on Public Higher Education, the ruling that placed community colleges under the University of Kentucky, and the failure to
provide financing for these major developments.

House Bill 238 was important not only for its provisions but

*The original vice presidents after Morehead State became a university were, clockwise from top right, Warren C. Lappin, academic affairs; Roger L. Wilson, student affairs; Morris L. Norfleet, research and development; Raymond R. Hornback, university affairs; Russell R. McClure, fiscal affairs.*

*President Doran visited in 1965 with President Lyndon B. Johnson at the White House. Also present was U. S. Rep. Carl D. Perkins (D-Ky.).*

also for its omissions. First, the Commission had recommended that the Council on Public Higher Education prepare a long-range financial plan. This was ignored in the bill. Second, a proposal that the University of Louisville be invited to become a state university also failed to make it into House Bill 238. The General Assembly in 1966 did create a committee to suggest means by which the University of Louisville might enter the state system, as it finally did in 1970, but without any provision for financial support. Consequently, the allocation of Kentucky's limited resources for higher education became an even greater source of contention. Third, the Commission suggested that as need for additional community colleges arose, some of the existing community colleges might become four-year institutions. By 1968 Northern Kentucky State College (University in 1976) evolved from Northern Community College, but again little attention was given to the question of its financing.

The passage of House Bill 238 was so certain that most of the regional colleges had already reorganized in order to be ready for university status when it officially arrived. Thus, on January 31, 1966, the Morehead State Board of Regents unanimously approved the school's looming legal designation as a university and the creation of four vice presidencies—over student, academic, public, and business affairs. It also authorized formation of five schools in a major reorganization of the administration, based on a study which had been underway on campus since 1960.

Governor Breathitt and President Doran addressed an overflow crowd in a campus fieldhouse convocation on Tuesday, March 22, 1966, during "University Appreciation Day" at Morehead State. Breathitt conferred upon Doran the "Distinguished Kentuckian" award and presented to him an engraved silver bowl. B. F. Reed and Lloyd Cassity, two members of the Board of Regents, were present on this historic occasion, as were individuals from an estimated fifty counties. Doran singled out Sherman Arnett, representative from Morehead, and Ed Kelly, senator from Flemingsburg, for their contributions to the passage of House Bill 238 and for their dedication to and support of Morehead State University.

Participating in the program were also representatives of various segments of the college, past and present. Gary Cox, a Louisville senior who later became executive director of the Council on Public Higher Education, spoke for Morehead State University students, and Dean Warren C. Lappin, for its faculty. Jim Mastrodicasa, president of the senior class, addressed the audience on behalf of the first graduating class of Morehead State University. Harry Weber of Louisville represented the Morehead Alumni Association, of which he was vice-president. Harry Sparks, state Superintendent of Public Instruction, was there for the Board of Regents. Grace Crosthwaite, a Rowan County teacher, represented Morehead Normal School, and Lottie Powers, Morehead secretary, Morehead State Normal School. Russ Williamson, principal at Inez High School and president of the Inez Deposit Bank, was present on behalf of Morehead State Normal School and Teachers College; in 1927 he had been the first graduate of the state institution. Edgar McNabb, assistant principal at Beechwood High School, represented Morehead State Teachers College, and J. Phil Smith, president of the First National Bank of Jackson, for Morehead State College.

Following convocation, the Morehead Senior and Junior Chambers of Commerce jointly sponsored a banquet. The throng of 1,000 people overtaxed the seating and dining facilities of the Doran Student House, which were located on the very spot where Phebe and Frank Button had founded the old Morehead Normal School in 1887. In his welcoming address, Michael Keller, president of the Morehead Chamber of Commerce, praised the University and cited its importance to the community and to Eastern Kentucky. English professor Gabriel Banks gave the invocation and benediction. In his remarks, Doran referred to the selfless work of the Button family and to the leadership of Allie Young.

Optimism was the order of the day. The University's enrollment, which had risen 737 percent during the previous twelve years, reached 4,669 in the fall semester of 1965; its faculty numbered 208.

Having spent $17,437,299 on capital improvements from 1954 to 1966, Morehead State was planning to spend $13,500,000 in just the 1966-68 biennium. The school's operating budget was more than eight times greater than it had been when Doran became president in 1954.

Morehead State was busy during the spring semester of 1966 in making further preparation for its switch to university status in June. Effective July 1, new administrative appointments implemented a reorganization approved by the board as early as January 1966. Morehead State University formed a graduate division, with master's degree programs in biology, education, English, and history. Dean Warren C. Lappin, member of the faculty since 1919 and its academic dean since 1940, became vice president for academic affairs. Paul Ford Davis was brought in as dean of undergraduate programs, Jarvis Hill, as dean of graduate programs, and Marvin Cole as dean of institutional programs. The University was divided into five schools—with the head of each titled as "Dean"—Applied Sciences and Technology under C. Nelson Grote; Humanities under J. E. Duncan; Sciences and Mathematics under William C. Simpson; Social Sciences under Roscoe Playforth; and Education under Kenneth Dawson. Breckinridge Training School was renamed University Breckinridge School. In 1968, three additional vice-presidencies were created. Roger L. Wilson was elevated from dean of students to vice president for student affairs; Morris Norfleet became vice president for research and development; and Raymond E. Hornback was named vice president for university affairs. Russell R. McClure would be named later as MSU's vice president for fiscal affairs.

Morehead State resumed an extensive building program after attaining university status in 1966. Five major buildings were completed the following year: Mignon Tower, a 16-story women's residence hall; Alumni Tower, a ten-story men's residence hall; Normal Hall, a four-story 41-unit married housing apartment building; Downing Hall, a two-story residence hall for athletes and named for the first football and basketball coach at Morehead State; and Laughlin Health Building, named for Bob Laughlin, athletic director and former basketball coach. Located on the old football field, the Laughlin Building contained classrooms and offices for the department of physical education, dance studios, gymnastics rooms, handball courts, a wrestling room, bowling lanes, and a large all-purpose room the size of four basketball floors to be used for intramural activities. The year also saw the finishing of two major renovations: Three stories were added to University Breckinridge School and included a cafeteria, library, band room, choral room, art department, general classrooms, and extensive television facilities; a third-story was added to the administration building to provide offices for the dean of students, the director of admissions, the director of graduate study, and data processing.

In 1968 Morehead State University opened two new buildings: the Claypool-Young Art Building, named for Naomi Claypool and Thomas Young, former art teachers; and the Lyman V. Ginger Hall (education building), named for the state superintendent of public instruction. The remodeling of Button Gymnasium to house the new Army ROTC unit was finished the same year. A four-story addition to Lappin Hall was opened, thereby doubling the original building which housed the departments of sciences and mathematics. The University also acquired a 212-acre farm in Rowan County and developed it into a place for agricultural students to gain practical experience.

Morehead State University added two buildings to its skyline in 1969: W. H. Cartmell Hall, a 17-story residence hall which housed 512 men and was named for a long-time member and first citizen chairman of the Board of Regents; and Nunn Hall, a residence hall for sorority women in particular and named for Beula Nunn, wife of the governor. Nunn Hall represented an unusual design, built across a hollow and over the road leading to it. After the Doran Student House was enlarged in 1969, it was renamed the Adron Doran University Center. Campus construction continued in the 1970s with the completion of B. F. Reed Hall, a classroom and office building for applied sciences and technology, which was named for another long-term member of the board, and major renovations of Rader Hall, the oldest campus facility. The latter was transformed into an ultra-modern classroom and office building, and its architectural style was drastically modified. By mid-1972, Morehead State's building program had produced more than $50 million worth of new facilities and had won four awards for architectural excellence since 1954.

These were exciting times on the campus of More-head State University. Having connections with a multitude of public figures enabled Doran to bring many celebrities to campus throughout his administration. These included Senator Edward (Ted) Kennedy, who spoke at a Homecoming convocation in 1968. Fog had so engulfed the

*Victor B. Howard, professor of history, received the Distinguished Faculty and Researcher awards and was the first MSU faculty member to be published by the University Press of Kentucky.*

225

Huntington, West Virginia, airport that Kennedy was three hours late; a crowd even larger than the original one greeted him when he finally arrived. In spite of being late for his speaking engagement, Kennedy asked his driver from the airport to stop at a country store along US 60 between Ashland and Morehead. Upon seeing the stranger, the store owner mused, "That man looked just like Ted Kennedy."

Other celebrities appearing on the campus included Arthur J. Goldberg, former U.S. Secretary of Labor and associate justice of the United States Supreme Court; Harrison E. Salisbury, author and distinguished editor of the *New York Times*; Senator Wayne L. Morse, maverick political leader from Oregon; Dr. Benjamin M. Spock, authority on child rearing and an outspoken critic of the Vietnam War; novelist Vance Packard; television personality Bill Cosby; popular singer Pat Boone; Art Buchwald, syndicated columnist and political satirist; and T. Harry Williams, Pulitzer Prize winner for his biography of Senator Huey Long.

Morehead's lack of easy access by air, however, sometimes prevented important figures from coming to campus. Senator John F. Kennedy canceled an October 6, 1960 campaign speech at Morehead State because the local airport was too small to handle a trio of four-engine DC-6's used by his entourage, including more than 75 reporters. Absence of a paved runway negated plans by former President Harry S Truman to speak at Morehead State in September 1962.

The Morehead State faculty during this era included several members who had followed unusual routes in becoming professors. In addition to Wilhelm Exelbirt, Jewish professor from Austria who had left Europe just in time to escape the Holocaust, there was Norman Tant, professor of education from 1954 until his retirement in 1979. After surviving the "Bataan Death March," he spent the duration of World War II as a prisoner of war operating a water pump in a coal mine on Kyushu Island in Japan.

John Gartin, professor of geography from 1959 to 1973 including five years as departmental chairman, had been a member of "Task Force Smith," the first American unit sent to Korea in 1950. Since the group was there chiefly as a delaying tactic of "sacrifice force" until larger numbers of American troops could be sent in, most of the 443 members were either killed or captured. One of his fellow POWs for three years was Ernest J. Charles from Pike County. Having met Ernest's sister, Norma Jean, through her correspondence with her brother, Gartin obtained a weekend pass thirty days after the POWs had been freed and returned to America. He then used the pass to visit Norma Jean, whom he later married. In spite of getting down to 88 pounds while a prisoner, Gartin recovered sufficiently by 1954 to enroll as a student at Morehead State. After leaving Morehead in 1973, Gartin taught for 20 years in Florida before retiring in Pike County.

Louis Magda also brought a wealth of experience and an unusual background when he arrived at MSU in 1966. Having been a university teacher, a stock broker, and a banker in Budapest, Hungary, he and his wife, Bobbie, found it necessary in 1956 to flee their homeland shortly before the Communist takeover during the Hungarian Revolution. They made their way to Cleveland, Ohio, where he worked seven years in a factory. After teaching two years in high schools in Ohio, he became a professor of economics at MSU, where he taught until his retirement in 1987.

Mohammed Sabie, member of the Palace Guard in Iraq, obtained a government scholarship in the Fifties to work on his doctorate at George Peabody College. There, he met former Morehead Dean and President William Vaughan, who put him in contact with Morehead State. From 1964 to 1997, Sabie served as a physical education professor and also achieved great success as a soccer coach. His wife, Layla, also joined the Morehead State faculty.

In 1964, the administration began placing more emphasis on rewarding the faculty for meritorious service. The MSU Alumni Association initiated the Distinguished Faculty Award; later, faculty were honored with the Distinguished Teacher, Distinguished Researcher, Creative Productions, and Service Awards. With Wilhelm Exelbirt (history) as the first honoree, the Department of Geography, Government, and History (three separate departments before 1984) garnered eleven of the 57 academic awards between 1964 and 1997. Other departmental recipients of the Distinguished Faculty Award included Victor Howard (history, 1973); Jack E. Bizzel (government, 1979); John E. Kleber (history, 1982); and Gary C. Cox (geography, 1985). Joining the MSU faculty in 1966, Bizzel served 16 years as chairman of the political science department. Later, he was one of 20 individuals nationwide invited to debate and discuss current Atlantic Alliance policy in Washington, Brussels, and Naples, under a

NATO-supported program. A native of Virginia and an alumnus of Morehead State, Cox joined the faculty in 1970 and later served ten years as chairman of the geography department. He received his doctorate from the University of Northern Colorado and did postgraduate study in an NDEA Advanced

*John Kleber, honors program advisor, Distinguished Teacher and Distinguished Researcher, interim dean of the Caudill College of Humanities, and editor of* The Kentucky Encyclopedia.

Institute of Urban Geography at Rutgers University. Victor Howard (history) also captured the first Distinguished Researcher Award in 1979 for his book, *Black Liberation in Kentucky*. Subsequently, he wrote four additional books, including *Conscience and Slavery*, and more than sixty articles, mainly dealing with the slavery controversy and reconstruction. The coveted award also went to four other members of the department. Stuart S. Sprague in 1985 was honored for articles on Kentucky and Appalachian history. Overall, his works included *Eastern Kentucky: A Pictorial History; His Promised Land;* and approximately fifty articles. William C. Green (government) was the recipient in 1991 for co-authoring *The Politics of Industrial Recruitment;* he has also written two other books: *The Unfulfilled Promise of Synthetic Fuels* and *North American Auto Unions in Crisis,* along with 21 articles, eight encyclopedic entries, and five book chapters. John E. Kleber was the honoree in 1993 for editing the *Encyclopedia of Kentucky*. He first gained recognition among the state's historical scholars for editing the papers of Governor Lawrence W. Wetherby. He also headed the University's Honors Program for 15 years and was acting dean of the Caudill College of Humanities from 1993 to 1995. Kleber was given the governor's Outstanding Kentuckian Award in 1993. In 1996, he began editing an encyclopedia of Louisville. Ron Mitchelson, departmental chair, earned the award in 1997. His 18-year career at the University of Georgia and Morehead State has included 21 funded projects of $525,000 from the U.S. Departments of State, Commerce, Transportation, and Forest Service. Most of his research dealt with movements of people, freight, and information. He has published 35 articles. In 1995, Mitchelson was appointed state geographer by Governor Brereton Jones. And shortly before his retirement in 1997, Don F. Flatt, whose career included eight years as department chair, was recipient of both the Distinguished Teacher Award and the first annual Greek Councils' Outstanding Professor Award, presented by the MSU fraternities and sororities.

## A Firm Hand on the Reins

Since an institution tends to reflect the personality of any leader with lengthy tenure, the personality and leadership style of Adron Doran were significant for Morehead State. Doran was a spellbinding orator. A magnetic evangelist both for the church and the school, he drew people to him. He convinced Eastern Kentuckians that their youth could come to Morehead State and leave with personal confidence that they would be successful. A visionary, Doran had ideas of what the school could be and never stopped until he realized his visions. While he reached decisions quickly, an amazing number of them, even those made under extreme pressure, turned out to be the right ones. As a pioneer in attempting many things, the president took a lot of criticism, much of it unjust since it resulted from his frequency in the spotlight. One administrator stated: "Working for him was challenging and exciting. With high expectations, he was demanding because he wanted everybody to work as hard as he did."

Doran had a special knack for dealing with controversy. A good example of this skill occurred the night following the shootings at Kent State in 1970 when hundreds of students, with a few faculty mixed in, marched to the ROTC building at Button Auditorium, where President Doran was waiting to receive them. There was the usual fear that the affair might get out of control. Amid strident outcries, Lt. Col. Art Kelly, professor of military science and head of the Army ROTC program at Morehead State, addressed the demonstrators. The students then wished to hear from President Doran, who addressed them in such a manner as to turn an angry protest into a prayer vigil. He explained that neither he nor anyone else in the crowd had any control over events at Kent State or in Southeast Asia, calmly answered questions, and then closed the session by leading the large gathering in a prayer for peace and brotherhood. Doran transformed the whole temperament and mood with his masterful prayer as demonstrators, administrators, and faculty linked hands in a prayer circle. Observers thought Doran earned his place in history that night! After the crowd dispersed, the demonstration continued; bomb threats were made and windows broken on the Morehead campus but no serious violence occurred. Doran was effective in handling such problems because he succeeded in keeping the lines of communication open.

In referring to those difficult days, Congressman Carl Perkins praised Doran's leadership: "You've got to let the students express themselves and try to iron out differences that may be legitimate. I certainly feel this is where Dr. Doran has demonstrated perhaps as great a leadership, as, if not greater than, any other university president in America." Governor Louie Nunn proclaimed an official "Adron Doran Day" throughout Kentucky, as he pointed out that he never feared what would happen at Morehead State University because he knew its president. Parents joined the governor in appreciation of Doran's method of handling these problems. Those very traits of President Doran which endeared him to parents and others in authority sometimes made him unpopular with some students.

Any assessment of such a complex personality as Adron Doran, however, must include another set of traits. Doran's powerful, controlling nature caused him to be dearly loved or intensely disliked. Biographer James Parton's assessment of Andrew Jackson, seventh President of the United States, is applicable to the seventh president of Morehead State University as well: "It can hardly be expected that the present generation will do justice to the character of Jackson because his opponents have ever been most bitter enemies, and his friends almost his worshippers."

Doran was given to taking strong stands when subordinates disagreed with him. He wanted other people's opinions but had difficulty making that desire known. With a low opinion of shared governance within an educational institution, Doran strongly believed that the president and the governing board were paramount.

The early period of Doran's leadership of Morehead State College had been characterized by such dramatic growth that good public relations at the time came naturally for both the institution and its leader. The administration always enjoyed support from the local newspaper and radio. State and regional newspapers during those years usually ran upbeat stories of Morehead's president and the construction that was taking place on the hillside overlooking the town and in the Evans Branch area.

But no sooner had Morehead State become a University than problems seemed to surface. As campus troubles became more frequent in the late Sixties, the president expressed his "bus going east, bus going west" philosophy more frequently. This expression was another way of saying, "If you don't like it here, you can go somewhere else." Such a philosophy could dominate a University for only so long, especially in the turbulent times it faced.

The Sixties produced many changes in the United States, and a different type student was entering American universities by the latter half of that decade. Furthermore, young people no longer were hesitant to speak out if they felt changes were in order. To be successful, administrative styles had to change. During his first 15 years from 1954 to 1969, Doran had guided a growth of student enrollment upward to more than 6,000 and oversaw the spending of over $55 million on new buildings. Although the campus had remained quiet during Morehead State's growth period, the late Sixties and early Seventies witnessed one of the most serious challenges to higher education in the nation's history. A combination of concerns over civil rights and the Vietnam War, along with the usual student grievances, resulted in an explosion of protests on campuses across America.

Morehead State University was not immune to such unrest. The Board of Regents' decision to establish a compulsory ROTC program on campus was made in 1967 in spite of a national trend toward voluntary programs. Small, persistent groups of Morehead students strongly opposed compulsory ROTC. But in 1967, without

*Alumnus Madison E. (Matt) Pryor, shown here during a research expedition to Antarctica, returned to MSU and served 30 years on the biology faculty. Soviet scientists in the project recognized his work by naming a glacier in his honor.*

consultation with students, the board rendered its decision that every able-bodied freshman male must have two years of ROTC. Coming at a time when national support was shifting away from President Lyndon B. Johnson's conduct of the Vietnam War, this decision disturbed students who felt the program should be optional. Other ROTC programs in the state were voluntary except for those at Eastern and Murray.

Student reaction was immediate and predictable. One student declared, "Our opposition to ROTC is based on both moral and educational grounds, and I don't think the administration here understands or wants to understand our arguments." Rhetoric escalated as petitions against compulsory ROTC circulated around the MSU campus; 300 to 400 signatures on the petitions included names of a small number of faculty. Linking his position on ROTC with his opposition to the Vietnam War, another student stated, "If you think the war is immoral, as many of us do, then forcing us to take ROTC is forcing us to do something immoral."

President Doran defended ROTC on two grounds. He thought the school had a responsibility to provide training for students in all areas, including the military, and he believed the training of military leaders was in the national interest. Admitting that the Army had not stipulated that Morehead must require ROTC of all able-bodied males in order to get the unit, Doran, explained, nevertheless, "We didn't believe a voluntary program would provide enough students for the advanced course to justify the program."

A second major controversy on the Morehead campus in the spring of 1968 related to non-renewal of three faculty contracts. Kenneth Vance, journalism instructor and part-time worker in the public relations office, Richard Norman, history instructor, and Robert Arends, associate professor of English, had been among those signing petitions opposing compulsory ROTC. The University was accused of retaliation when it refused to renew Vance's and Norman's contracts and asked Arends to resign. University officials, however, stated that Arends had earlier informed them of his intentions to resign. Charging their academic freedom had been violated, the three requested the American Association of University Professors to pursue an investigation of the Morehead State administration. Norman insisted that their troubles started when the administration learned of their membership in the Kentucky Peace Movement, which assisted in planning the anti-Vietnam War conference at the University of Kentucky in February 1968.

In July 1968 a nine-member committee, elected by the faculty, began studying these charges. James Latham, professor of education, chaired the committee, composed of Charles Payne, Mary Northcutt, Norman Roberts, Alex Conyers, Allen Lake, Maurice Strider, John Stanley, and Randall Miller. Latham announced that hearings would be closed to the public but would be witnessed by a representative from the AAUP, which had requested the investigation. Arends and Frederick Edling, former Russian teacher, had complained to the AAUP that they were late in receiving notifications that their contracts were not being renewed. The four brought charges that they had been dismissed because of their political activities both on and off campus and for voicing controversial opinions in class and elsewhere, especially on such subjects as compulsory ROTC at Morehead State University. Only Arends and Vance chose to appear before the committee to file charges and to call witnesses on their behalf; the administration also called witnesses. In the fall of 1968 the committee issued a report absolving Morehead State of charges that Arends and Vance's academic freedom had been violated. In fact, some faculty members were not aware of any threats to academic freedom at Morehead State. Wilhelm Exelbirt, who had been the recipient of the first Distinguished Faculty Award given by MSU in 1964, strongly commended Doran's support of academic freedom at the institution. Having taught at Morehead State since 1948, Exelbirt affirmed that he had never been aware of any administrative interference when controversial subjects formed part of classroom discussions.

A group of students who looked upon the atmosphere of Morehead State as not being congenial for "serious journalism" founded an off-campus newspaper, *Student Poll,* published in Lexington. Mike Embry, one of its editors, stated its purpose was to fill a gap because the *Morehead News* and the *Trail Blazer* consistently supported Doran and refused to criticize his administration. Another off-campus activity, the Free Forum, sprouted during the spring semester of 1968 to discuss national and international issues. Arends explained that its organizers did not petition for on-campus status because they did not expect it would be granted. A meeting in March 1968 scheduled in the Rowan County Courthouse, was canceled, according to Arends and Vance, because an article in the *Morehead News* contained hints of possible violence in an atmosphere of opposition from Morehead residents.

The numerous controversies in the late Sixties led the University to develop written policies governing some of its procedures. On March 26, 1969, the Board of Regents adopted a policy requiring that guest speakers be approved by the dean of students before they could address campus groups. The sponsoring group, which had to be an officially recognized campus organization, was required to provide a detailed explanation of the nature of the gathering and the reasons for inviting the speaker. Roger L. Wilson, vice president for student affairs, pointed out that the policy would not apply to individuals invited by professors to address their classes. The same board meeting also gave formal approval to reducing compulsory Army ROTC from two years to the freshman year only for male students. The Department of Military Science would continue offering elective courses for sophomores, juniors, and seniors. Gradually, the administration backed away from the compulsory feature of the original agreement. By April 1970 an entirely voluntary unit was able to maintain sufficient en-

*James E. Gotsick, professor of psychology, also received both the Distinguished Teacher and Distinguished Researcher awards.*

rollment to exist. Morehead State continued to recognize its responsibility to inform students of the need for military preparedness.
Hence, President Doran originated the National Security Class in the
spring of 1970. This voluntary class, balanced between military and
civilian topics and speakers, brought outstanding individuals to
campus to address the issues of national security. Doran then sold
the idea to the Army, and the concept was praised and imitated on
other college campuses throughout the nation. Because of his impressive backing of ROTC, the United States Army, in February 1971
presented Doran with the "Outstanding Civilian Service Medal," its
second highest civilian award.

Doran became involved in off-campus controversies as they
affected his school. In the fall of 1968, he began questioning whether
or not the community college system should be administered by the
University of Kentucky. Speaking at a luncheon held in conjunction
with Harry M. Sparks' inauguration as president of Murray State,
Doran, a Murray alumnus, recommended that the fourteen two-year
colleges be administered by the four regional universities and Kentucky State College. The Morehead president referred to the neighboring states of Indiana, Illinois, Ohio, and West Virginia as models
to demonstrate that regional institutions of higher learning should
be in charge of community colleges. Two weeks earlier, Robert R.
Martin, president of Eastern Kentucky University, had suggested
that the Council on Public Higher Education undertake a comprehensive review of the community college system. Unless such a
study were conducted, Martin contended, the Commonwealth
would eventually have a two-year college "in every county seat."

In a changing world filled with so much tension and strife, a
need developed for enhanced participatory campus democracy, allowing individuals at every level to speak their minds. Thus, in 1969
Morehead State created an innovative University Senate, composed
of twelve students, twelve administrators, and twenty-five faculty.
Doran said this represented the first time students at a state school

in Kentucky had been given so much voice in campus matters. When the University of Kentucky considered a similar plan a year later, the *Lexington Herald* suggested, "If UK adopts the plan, it will be doing what Morehead State University did more than a year ago" and then concluded, "We hope UK will follow Morehead's lead and adopt the plan." Morehead State also claims to be the first Kentucky institution of higher education to place students on all standing committees.

For three decades, Morehead State students had periodically expressed a desire for fraternities and sororities. Finally, the Greek system came to the Morehead State campus in the late Sixties. It was necessary for each sorority and fraternity to have a constitution approved by the Student Life Committee and filed with the vice president for student affairs. The Panhellenic Council became the coordinating body for sororities while the Interfraternity Council linked together activities of the fraternities. All "pledges" to fraternities and sororities were required to have completed twelve semester hours of college work with a 2.0 (C) grade point standing. Prior to fraternities and sororities, the first student social organization at Morehead State was the Campus Club, formed in 1933; today, the group is known as Sigma Alpha Epsilon. Tau Kappa Epsilon, recognized in 1969, was the first national fraternity on the Morehead State campus, and Delta Gamma was the first national social sorority.

A major change in leadership at Morehead State University started in 1971 with the retirement of Vice President Warren C. Lappin. Five years later, Vice President Roger Wilson died in office, and President Adron Doran announced his retirement. Lappin had served for half a century under all of Morehead State's seven presidents.

Dean Lappin had been connected with the University long enough to inspire endless "Lappin anecdotes." According to Mary Ella Wells, Lappin's daughter, he was "a handy man around the house, a gardener, a very loyal churchman, and a great lover of music." Among other things, he had been a violin teacher when he arrived in Morehead shortly after World War I; in fact, "that's how he and my mother met."

The first thing most people recall about Lappin was his stern countenance. While some have attributed his facial expression to various causes including a paralysis early in life and being hit "by a pitched baseball," Mary Ella rejected these assessments, while mentioning that "his father and brother looked exactly the same way; not smiling was simply a family trait." One of the few times Professor Allen Lake saw Lappin smile was when someone said, "If it hadn't been for his wife (Ruth), Warren Lappin would have been completely ruthless." But J. E. Duncan, former dean of the School of Humanities, remembers trips with Lappin, when "he kept me laughing for hours on end."

Typically, students and faculty alike were "scared to death" of Lappin. Allen Lake, biology professor from 1957 to 1983, remembered that "it was with some degree of apprehension" that you went to the dean's office. Most faculty members "would rather have taken a beating than to have been called on the carpet" by him, Lake added.

Mary Ella described her father as "a very logical man; if he knew what you wanted to do and he didn't want you to do it, you knew you were defeated before you even tried because he had every reason on his side." When a faculty member or an administrator requested a favor, J. E. Duncan recounted that the first thing Lappin usually did was say "No." Many failed to realize, however, that all the while Lappin "was sitting there waiting for you to change his mind. And if you changed his mind, you got what you went for. He made you sell whatever it was you wanted."

But Lappin's personality had another dimension. After Mary Ella began dating James (Toodles) Wells, whom she later married, the young man was once called before Dean Lappin over an incident in the dormitory. Wells began by sharing with Lappin that since he started dating his daughter, "Everybody's always watching me." Peering sternly over his glasses, Lappin countered, "Young man, you're a body that bears watching." When Lappin was director of Breck Training School, two students recalled watching him as he "iceskated" from his home on North Wilson Avenue all the way to his office. Some of the men in town once formed a "coffee club" which met at the Eagles' Nest at 4:30 each afternoon. They soon found out that Warren "didn't waste a lot of words." When he got ready to leave each day, he would "just get up and go." One day someone inquired, "Warren, why don't you make some comment like 'I guess I'll go now?'" only to receive a curt reply, "When I get up and go out the door, you will know I've left—I don't have to tell you."

Most people agreed on Lappin's role at Morehead State. His daughter looked upon her father's greatest acoomplishment as "keeping the faculty stabilized, regardless of what happened." She was not at all surprised that he never made it to the presidency because he was not "that kind of politician, and it took a politician at that time to get money out of the legislature." Nolan Fowler, historian in the Forties and Fifties, sized Lappin up as a man who had "a very logical mind and who could seize the essential things," traits which made him into a "Mr. Balance Wheel," especially during World War II and the loss of accreditation afterwards. Harold Holbrook, Morehead dentist and son-in-law of Allie Young, remembers Lappin as "the rock, the anchor, and the one that everybody went to" during turbulent times. Roscoe Playforth, former dean of the School of Social Sciences, regarded Lappin as "the heart and soul of the institution in all those early years."

Lappin's value to Morehead State is demonstrated by the difficulty the institution experienced in finding anyone to take his place. He was the leader of the faculty, whether called academic dean or vice president, from 1940 to 1971. In the twenty-six years since his retirement, eight individuals have held that position. Paul Ford Davis served from 1971 until Doran's retirement in 1976. Insta-

*The Greek system has added greatly to campus life since the latter 1960's.*

bility in this vice presidency was best illustrated in the Norfleet administration which had three different academic vice presidents in seven years. By way of contrast, Norfleet had only one individual, Buford Crager, as his vice president for student affairs.

A major controversy took place in 1972 over efforts to present President Doran with a luxury auto at Morehead State University's Golden Anniversary. Purchased by the MSU Alumni Association, the automobile was given as a tribute at a banquet by citizens of Morehead and Rowan County. Claims were made, however, that campus solicitations had been used to help raise the money. Anonymous because of "the repressive atmosphere at Morehead State University," a letter to the *Courier Journal* claimed faculty and staff members were "being forced this week to buy tickets to a dinner supposedly given by the city in tribute to the University's 50 years of existence." "This coercion," the letter continued, "follows arm-

241

twisting of faculty and staff members earlier this fall for donations to buy President Adron Doran an automobile." Several other professors, however, disputed these allegations. Raymond E. Hornback, vice president for university affairs, denied them emphatically. Reflecting on the 900 people in attendance, Hornback commented that it was obviously a popular event.

As this controversy died out, the University received positive publicity with the announcement that the MSU band had been invited to participate in President Richard Nixon's second Inaugural Parade on January 20, 1973. President Doran took great pride in the varied accomplishments of the music department, so in spite of his longtime association with the Democratic party, he was delighted when "The Big Band from Daniel Boone Land" was asked to appear in Washington, D.C. Tim Lee Carter, Republican representative from Kentucky's Fifth Congressional District, inserted in the Congressional Record: "I wish to commend Dr. Adron Doran, President of Morehead State University, and Dr. Robert Hawkins, director of the band, for their fine work toward making the band's participation in this great event a reality." After pointing out that 84 percent of Morehead State's dormitory facilities had been built since 1960, Carter said, "Nearly two decades of continuous dynamic leadership by President Adron Doran have transformed this half-century-old institution dedicated to training teachers into a broad-spectrum, multi-purpose regional university of superior merit."

## Adron Doran Steps Down

In the last few years of Doran's administration, speculations multiplied over when he would retire and who his successor would be. In spite of speculation, Doran, who had served more than three times longer than any other Morehead leader except Button, received a new four-year contract on July 1, 1974, when he was nearly 65 years old, thereby extending his contract until June 3, 1978. Amid speculation that he would announce his retirement on April 6, 1976, twenty-two years to the day after his selection as Morehead president, he ended the Founders' Day luncheon address by asking, "Whence cometh the end?" Keeping everyone guessing, the president relied on the words of Robert Frost for his reply, "I have promises to keep and miles to go before I sleep." And "away he rode, still in the saddle," George Wolfford wrote in the Ashland *Daily Independent;* "if and when Adron Doran ever does step down, Eastern Kentucky will lose its Camelot." Doran's "public parties, visiting grandees, performing troupers, and even his own smiling ride on the back of a MSU show horse are something out of King Arthur," Wolfford asserted. That same Founders Day included ground-breaking ceremonies for the renovation and expansion of Allie Young Hall and the construction of the Julian Carroll Library Tower.

A large contingent of the press who had journeyed to Morehead anticipating an announcement of Doran's retirement had to settle for a speech and ground-breaking. But the following month, with two years remaining on his contract, President Doran announced that he would take a sabbatical during the fall semester of 1976 and retire on January 1, 1977. Doran previously had pointed to his desire to support Julian Carroll's candidacy for governor as one reason for not retiring. Lt. Gov. Carroll had become governor when Wendell Ford moved to Washington as one of Kentucky's senators and then successfully campaigned for a full term. Perhaps thinking about how Morehead State had been overlooked by the Ford administration, Doran wanted to encourage the favorable financing that the Carroll administration had begun to provide. With the naming of the new library tower after Carroll, MSU now had at least one campus facility named for every living Kentucky governor except Ford. Doran's retirement plans included working as a minister of the Church of Christ and serving as vice president of Morehead's Citizens Bank as well as on the Board of Directors of Investors Heritage Life Insurance Company in Frankfort. He made his retirement announcement only a month after Robert R. Martin, his long-time

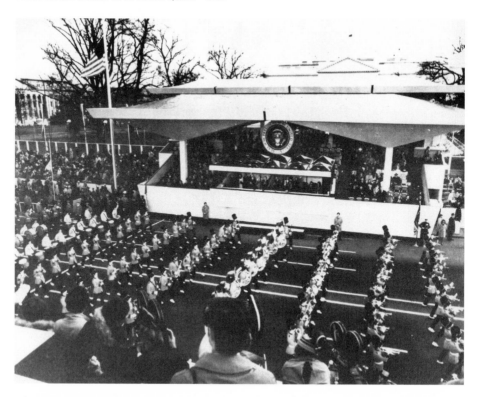

*The MSU band marched in President Richard Nixon's inaugural parade in 1973 under the direction of Robert Hawkins.*

friendly antagonist, stated he would step down as president of Eastern Kentucky University in September, 1976, after sixteen years at the helm.

The announcement of the president's retirement was appropriately made in the Adron Doran University Center, the first building constructed in the Fifties as he began putting his stamp upon the campus. Thus, his leaving the institution was handled with typical Doran flare beginning with a dinner party attended by more than 800 people on Friday, November 19, 1976. Some two dozen campus organizations presented gifts and awards to the Dorans. A copy of *Footsteps Across the Commonwealth,* a 50-page tribute to the

Dorans, written by Don F. Flatt, head of the MSU history department, was placed beside each plate. With twenty-three years to celebrate, the evening lasted nearly six hours.

In an interview with Richard Wilson of the Louisville *Courier-Journal*, Doran said, "When I came here, this was a provincial, parochial institution controlled by local people, local interests, and local competencies. To have provided the leadership to break it out of that shell and give it to the region of Northeastern Kentucky is the greatest contribution I've made." In commenting upon his style of leadership, Doran asserted, "I've always believed in a strong presidency....I'd rather have spent 22 years trying to make the presidency strong than 22 years as an indecisive, unassertive and milquetoast type of fellow."

Doran attributed much of his success as MSU's president to his friendly relations with political figures who helped him and the University. He believed it was "impossible to separate politics from higher education." But "to say that decisions were made on the basis of politics does not imply that they were bad decisions, wrong decisions or decisions arrived at in a clandestine way."

Some of Adron Doran's critics described him as an empire builder. During the interview with Richard Wilson, Doran responded to that charge: "If by empire-building, they mean comfortable facilities for a youngster to sleep in, a university center that provides recreation and an opportunity to eat good food, a classroom, a laboratory, or a good gymnasium—if that is an empire, then I rejoice in having that in my vision and I have no apologies for it." He went on to say, however, that he resented the imputation that he did such things for his personal aggrandizement. A less public side to Doran included the financial assistance he extended to students over the years. According to Russell McClure, a former vice president of the university, Doran had lent hundreds of dollars to needy students. He had known poverty in his own youth and remembered how his high school principal had given him money to attend college, asking only that he do the same for other deserving youth in the future.

It seemed fitting that Adron Doran and Robert Martin step down from the presidencies of their institutions at nearly the same time. If the two had been orchestrating a parade, Richard Wilson pictured Martin as "satisfied with planning it flawlessly" and Doran's insistence on being" the grand marshall." Unlike in manner and appearance—the one gruff and ponderous, the other slim and polished—the two men were alike in being consummate politicians who used their skills to further the fortunes of the schools they led. Moreover, they had played leading roles in the state, having helped to shape the decisions that affected the state's colleges and universities over the decades. In the words of John E. Kleber, MSU historian, "With the departure of Doran and Martin, we see a dying breed, perhaps never to be seen in Kentucky again." They left behind them two universities that had been built and molded by their energy and ambition.

One example of Doran's legacy was the unique horsemanship program at Morehead State. The University had purchased a farm in 1968 and had built a 42-stall stable, an indoor livestock pavilion, a lighted outdoor show ring, and a veterinary technology clinic. The 150 students in the horsemanship program were privileged to work with horses donated to Morehead State from all over the United States. The University owned 75 horses, including 25 Tennessee walkers, 25 show horses, and 25 others, worth almost $300,000. Three Tennessee walking horses worth an estimated $135,000 had been donated by H. Ross Perot, the Texas billionaire super-patriot who later would run for the American presidency. Since the horsemanship program began in 1973, MSU students have won over 100 ribbons in competition. "The beauty of the horsemanship program," Doran pointed out, "is that the University hasn't spent a dime of state tax money to buy the horses."

The Morehead president had a longtime interest in Tennessee walking horses. Not having ridden one in twenty-five years, Doran began riding again in the fall of 1973 and won a blue ribbon in the very first show he entered. His major achievement was winning a blue ribbon on "Pride of Merry Gold" at Shelbyville, Tennessee, the "Kentucky Derby" of walking horse competition, in the summer of 1975. Doran was perhaps inspired by the example of N. B. Hardeman, president and a founder of Freed-Hardeman College, who was widely known for his skills in riding Tennessee walking horses.

During his presidency of Morehead State, Doran had at his side a gracious and articulate First Lady. Mignon Doran assumed an obligation to be professional and active, while forming an effective team with her husband. In providing a role model for other women, she was sometimes unfairly criticized by those who could never see beyond the glamour of her high profile. She was, in truth, a sensitive, caring person who was committed to the institution.

Mignon Doran was one of the most active First Ladies in the history of Morehead State. She was well-known in Kentucky and beyond for the Personal Development Institute which she founded in 1969, for her rehabilitation work in two correctional facilities, and for her organ music at the Kentucky State Basketball tournament, the NCAA Finals in Louisville in 1958, and all MSU home basketball games. Having no children of their own, the Dorans devoted much personal time to students. Because of her belief that preparation for success in life must include more than academics and the development of professional skills, Mignon stressed the importance of lifelong total personal development with students. She helped others establish personal development programs around the country. Among those she assisted was MSU graduate Lyda Lewis, Miss Kentucky of 1973, who began her own personal development class for fifth and sixth graders.

The Personal Development Institute was established as a noncredit, five-week program to develop individual qualities ranging from manners to vocabulary expansion. The course consisted of ten classroom hours, with separate classes for men and women. Emphasis was placed on improving confidence, poise, personal appearance, and social graces. It was designed to augment the development of students in their preparation for professional life as well as citizenship in their communities. From a study, Morris K. Caudill of the Research and Development Center concluded, "If the worth of a program were measured totally by student response, the PDI program would be a great success." Edward E. Coates, director of special services, stated that the University had made "a concerted effort to recruit students for its program" since "PDI has been found to make a significant impact upon improving student retention and academic performance."

A favorite endeavor of Mrs. Doran was incorporating the teaching of PDI into Project Newgate, a 1969 experiment aimed at helping young prisoners prepare for post-high school education after being released. The work was conducted at the Federal Youth Center near Ashland where over 500 young men were confined for a variety of federal offenses, primarily auto theft. Mignon visited the center one day each week—along with other MSU professors—to teach the forty inmates involved in the project. Her attendance along with other women in the program was revolutionary as it marked the first time women had been involved in rehabilitation at the Ashland institution. Small groups of inmates were also transported to the Morehead State campus for tours and cultural and athletic events. Mrs. Doran also helped to provide rehabilitation programs for incarcerated youth at the Frenchburg Correctional Facility in Menifee County.

Carolyn Flatt served as a graduate assistant to Mrs. Doran in the Personal Development Institute in 1970 and assumed full-time teaching responsibilities the following year. After the Dorans' retirement in 1976, Mrs. Flatt became director and instructor of the Institute. Later, she began teaching men and women together, modified the focus of the course to meet current needs, and began offering one hour of credit along with a letter grade. The program evolved to ten nine-week sections per semester in addition to off-campus classes, and special sessions. Thus, thousands of students have taken the personal development course.

Having a president on sabbatical and an interim president both on campus provided a most trying time during the fall semester of 1976. Each experienced difficulty in accepting the role of the other. Although Doran moved out of the president's office, he still expected key decisions to pass through his hands.

For Doran to stay out of the process of naming his permanent successor was difficult. Many people thought that Doran encouraged the Board of Regents to make Morris L. Norfleet interim presi-

*Lyda Lewis, Miss Kentucky and former MSU Homecoming Queen; Carolyn Flatt, personal development director after the Dorans' retirement; Mignon Doran, founder of PDI; and Terry Meeuwsen, Miss America 1973.*

dent during his sabbatical as somewhat of a consolation prize for not getting the presidency. Doran was thought to favor John R. Duncan, vice president for academic affairs, over Norfleet.

After twenty-three years, Doran found it difficult to let go of the reins of power. He was painfully aware of what had recently happened at Murray State, his alma mater. After Murray brought in Constantine Curris to serve as president, he restructured the institution and demoted some members of the previous administration. Doran was concerned that people who had worked for him might suffer the same fate unless an "insider" succeeded him. So, he encouraged the Board of Regents to make its selection from individuals already on campus.

Concerned that infighting between the supporters of Norfleet and Duncan might divide the administration, Doran, on October 6, 1976, called a meeting of the Executive Council, which included the eighteen administrators who reported to the president. He told the Council that they must decide which of the two candidates they would support. If they divided their loyalties between these two, it would be easier for "outside forces" to bring in someone who was not familiar with the manner in which they had always done things, and some of the eighteen might indeed lose their positions. After reminding the group once more of the need to unite behind one of these internal candidates, Doran asked that a secret ballot be taken. When the ballots were counted, great excitement filled the room as Norfleet led Duncan, 8-7, with the final ballot still to be tabulated. When the sixteenth vote went to Norfleet, the die had been cast. (Only sixteen votes were cast since Duncan and Norfleet had left the meeting). Morehead State would likely have an "insider" but not the one who had been anticipated.

These explanations for Norfleet's victory are plausible. Doran had not made his preference clear that he seemed to favor Duncan. Some administrators were closer to Norfleet than had been realized. Norfleet had done more "campaigning" with members of the Executive Council than had Duncan. Some were concerned about losing Duncan as academic vice president. Duncan immediately withdrew his name from the search, and Interim President Norfleet was later hired as the eighth president of Morehead State.

## Morris L. Norfleet's Search for Direction, 1977-1984

Morris L. Norfleet had never looked upon the interim appointment as a political graveyard but had endeavored to use the position to solidify his hold on the presidency. The new president was granted a contract through June 30, 1979, at a salary of $40,000 annually. William Whitaker, Sr., Morehead businessman, referred to the selection of Norfleet as a popular choice in the local business community. Lloyd Cassity, chairman of the Board of Regents, claiming that both faculty and student sentiment were behind the new president, said Norfleet represented what the University needed.

After obtaining a bachelor's degree in agriculture at the University of Kentucky in 1952, Norfleet earned a master's degree in education at Purdue University in 1957 and a doctorate in education at the same institution in 1962. He had taught high school from 1952 to 1958 at Spiceland, Indiana. Norfleet then worked two years in public relations and marketing analysis for the Indiana Farm Bureau. After spending two years at Purdue as an education instructor, he came to Morehead State in 1962 as associate professor of education and director of student teaching. Norfleet then served as director of research and program development from 1965 to 1968, when he was elevated to vice president for research and development.

Loistene, his wife, was reserved yet gracious. Appearing not to relish a public role, she essentially did that which was necessary to meet her obligations as First Lady. In addition, she was an active member of the Morehead Woman's Club and the University Woman's Club. She was involved in church work, including teaching four- and five-year-olds for seven years at the First Baptist Church, where she also worked in Vacation Bible Schools and assisted with the church's social activities. Beyond that, she focused on being a supportive wife and mother while remaining in the background. The Norfleets had one son, Doug.

The new president endeavored to introduce a more open administrative style using the delegation of authority. But he retained most of the Doran people in key administrative positions—individuals who were versed in how things had been done during the past administration. Unfortunately, he never enjoyed the wholehearted support of some in key positions inside the administration. So, the Norfleet administration was marked by internal strife and competition, with the president apparently feeling he could not trust some of those close to him.

Norfleet was intelligent and hardworking, but his lack of charisma failed to inspire people or command their respect. He also experienced trouble in handling criticism. Norfleet wanted to be a builder; unfortunately, he came on the scene as the bottom fell out of the state's economy in the early days of Governor John Y. Brown's administration. Morehead State immediately suffered some Draconian budget cuts, and Norfleet had to downsize the administration. The eighth president was slow to accept the fact that the building era was largely a thing of the past, regardless of who happened to be president of the institution. A good "idea man," he often lacked the ability to execute those ideas. Since the president tended to keep a plethora of projects going at the same time, the institution seemingly lost its focus and direction at times.

Norfleet had been especially effective in state and federal grantsmanship—he blazed that trail and trained Carole Morella, who became an efficient leader and is still in charge of that area at MSU. Norfleet excelled in obtaining grants and understood how to persuade others to invest in new ideas. With the onslaught of budget cuts during the Brown administration, Norfleet was the first Morehead State leader to articulate the growing financial problem which became epidemic after his tenure. Ahead of the times, he saw the value of computer-assisted instruction and endeavored to get Morehead involved in this field. He also encouraged the athletic program to begin raising money to become more self-sufficient. Under Norfleet, the MSU Foundation, Inc., was created in 1979 as he was the first president to become involved in private giving. Although beset by managerial flaws in those hard fiscal times, Norfleet did his best and worked hard. At a time when Morehead State University could not have justified the construction of the Academic-Athletic Center and its 7,000-seat arena, he managed to seize upon an opportunity in Frankfort to get that project funded with the help of Russell McClure, former MSU administrator, who was secretary of finance in the Julian Carroll administration.

Indicative of the uncertainties in direction at the University was the succession of academic vice presidents. After a dispute over personnel matters, John R. Duncan resigned the position just two years into the Norfleet administration. A national search brought William F. White on board—but for less than three years; he was followed by Walter G. Emge who served during the last three years of the administration. The fac-

*Morris L. Norfleet, eighth president of Morehead State, 1977-84.*

253

ulty soon felt it was being short-changed by instability in this key position. Enrollment began to decline, and a malaise seemed to envelop the institution.

By August 1980 the Norfleet administration found itself in a situation which undermined confidence in its leadership. Less than a month after Norfleet had been granted a new four-year contract, a newspaper story broke concerning allegations about the use of "poor judgment"—a term used by the Board of Regents to characterize the whole incident. A state investigation discovered evidence of "alleged financial irregularities" by a number of MSU employees. A 396-page state report identified several areas of "questionable practices," including employees misusing the school's sales-tax exemption and discount-purchase privileges through a special "departmental purchasing fund," which the president had ordered discontinued in 1979. A state audit indicated that $1,141.75 in sales tax had been avoided in the purchase of 124 items costing $22,835.19 between July 1, 1976, and June 28, 1979. But the same report also included charges that MSU personnel, equipment, and materials had been used to improve private property owned by Norfleet. The state attorney general's office directed Morehead State's Board of Regents to determine whether university materials were misused and to seek restitution for any abuse. The report, including transcripts of Kentucky State Police interviews with current and former MSU officials and employees, was turned over to Governor John Y. Brown, Jr., and to Harry Snyder, executive director of the Council on Higher Education.

In reacting to recommendations from the attorney general's report, the board, on August 16, 1980, ordered several actions: Norfleet should submit new policies on disposal of university equipment and materials with marketable value and on the use of state equipment for any purpose not related to university activities; the president should present the board with new policies prohibiting University maintenance employees from performing non-university work during regular working hours; Morehead State attorney Buddy Salyer should correspond with the state Revenue Department to work out a procedure so unpaid sales tax on purchases through the special fund, plus any penalties, could be collected; Michael Walters, the University's comptroller, was directed to collect all money which employees owed the University for materials, property, or personnel they used for personal reasons; Norfleet should arrange for an independent audit, if necessary, to assure that the school was complying with state purchasing regulations; and John Graham, vice president for fiscal affairs, should pay for personal items, which he purchased through the special fund, if he had not already done so.

The Board of Regents met again on September 20, 1980, primarily for the purpose of receiving reports from the Norfleet administration on the previous allegations. While finding no instances of flagrant or intentional misuse of materials, property, or personnel, Walters stated that discrepancies between the attorney general's report and his own interviews made it difficult to separate fact from hearsay. Since "an uninformed, independent observer might reach conclusions that would question the propriety of how personnel, materials and equipment were used," Walters said that Norfleet and Graham had been billed for these goods and services in order "to eliminate the possibility of any misinterpretation." While denying any impropriety, Norfleet and Graham paid the University for alleged misuse of materials, equipment, and personnel to improve their personal property. Norfleet reimbursed the University $755.41, while Graham paid $37.14 to the University in addition to $166.24 to a MSU staff member for working in his private residence in 1976.

Norfleet assured the special Friday night board meeting, "I am innocent of any illegal or unethical act, and I did not intentionally sanction any activity which, unfortunately, may have resulted in the appearance of impropriety." While denying impropriety, Graham acknowledged he should have shown "better judgment in certain areas." While proposing no prosecution, a state attorney general's report had asked the board to seek restitution if University materials had been misused. Thus, the matter was settled.

The Norfleet administration received additional negative publicity in the spring of 1981. The admissions office had been under investigation by the Kentucky State Police and the FBI since mid-January, 1981. A grand jury investigated William A. (Bill) Bradford, former associate director of admissions, over accusations of taking bribes from foreign students, according to published reports from Commonwealth's Attorney Truman Dehner. The charge was made that five foreign students, failing to meet MSU's academic standards, were allowed to transfer from other colleges after paying money to Bradford. Morehead State regulations required that foreign students show proficiency in English and submit a financial statement. These students were granted "eligibility certification" after reportedly paying from $300 to $4,500 into the admissions office's account. Bradford subsequently pleaded guilty to diverting students' funds to his own use.

In the midst of these major problems, Norfleet angered some Morehead residents by pushing for the merger of University Breck-

*Herb. F. Reinhard, Jr.,*
*Morehead State's ninth*
*president, 1984-86.*

inridge School with the local school system. After a lengthy presentation by parents on April 22, 1981, the Board of Regents ordered that a study be made of the school, which was the teaching laboratory of MSU. University Breckinridge School's enrollment stood at 446 students from nursery level through high school, with 27 teachers. Only $31,000 of the school's budget of $497,322 came from tuition paid by its students. Michael Davis, dean of MSU's School of Education, had earlier recommended to the president that grades 6 through 12 be merged with Rowan County schools in the fall of 1981, while the other five grades would be phased into the county's schools within two years. Moreover, Harry Snyder, executive director of the Council on Higher Education, had said he would recommend that the state withdraw financial support for laboratory schools both at Morehead and Eastern, the only two state universities still supporting such schools.

Meeting on August 19, 1981, the board voted to merge University Breckinridge School with the Rowan County school system immediately. This move was expected to save MSU $325,000 its first year. With the closing of Breck, Morehead State lost a close link it had used for half a century to maintain town-gown relationships, although only a small percentage of town families had enjoyed this school arrangement over the years. The closing of University Breckinridge School was one of the most difficult and emotionally charged decisions a Morehead president ever had to make.

Meanwhile, Norfleet scored high with Morehead State faculty by hiring as Vice President for Academic Affairs Walter G. Emge, a Yale-educated philosophy professor who had served in the same position both at Bellarmine and Transylvania and was a champion of the liberal arts. Many looked upon the selection of Emge as the first effort to return to an academic leader similar to Warren C. Lappin. Emge voiced many concerns including his fear that Morehead State's vocational programs would duplicate the courses of a new technical school being built in Rowan County. While expanding job-oriented academic programs in 1981, Emge had to tackle the controversy over whether the University should retain its "open door" admissions policy or create "an on-campus, two-year community college for less-prepared students."

The American Association of University Professors censured MSU at its 69th annual meeting in Washington, D.C. in the summer of 1983. The action was taken against the University for violating academic freedom of faculty members. The censure resulted from MSU's failure in 1979 to renew contracts for two non-tenured art professors who became enmeshed in a dispute with the departmental chairman, Bill R. Booth. Among other charges, Morehead State University allegedly had not stated the reasons for failing to reappoint Franz Altschuler and Gerry Hoover and had not provided for due process. The AAUP further charged the administration with specific actions against other faculty members that disregarded academic freedom and tenure, academic due process, and a meaningful faculty role in academic government. With the climate being what it was at Morehead State, AAUP investigators regarded it as remarkable that a few faculty members had the courage to talk freely.

Norfleet's various problems led him in 1983 to commission A. D. Albright, former executive director of the Council on Higher Education and former president of Northern Kentucky University, to prepare a survey of the needs of Morehead State University with an eye on what could be eliminated in order to prevent unnecessary drains on the institution's budget. In October 1983, Albright offered the following key recommendations: Replace Morehead's six schools with two colleges, one to concentrate on the arts and sciences and the other on professional studies; downsize the athletic program; drop all but one-fourth of the twenty-two master's degree programs; cap enrollment at 5,500 including full- and part-time students; and streamline the administration by eliminating the jobs of some of the fifteen top administrators. Albright pointed out that setting an enrollment limit was one measure for maintaining an acceptable quality level. These changes were necessary in order for MSU to cope with a decrease in state money and a possible loss of program quality.

Norfleet, whose seven-year administration had been marred by frequent controversies, announced at the board meeting on November 12, 1983, that he would step down from the presidency by July 1, 1984, to accept the newly created position of chancellor of corporate relations. The ten members of the board unanimously accepted his appointment to the new position when his contract expired on June 30, 1984. Norfleet agreed to accept this post earlier if his successor as president were named before June 30. Board

*Some 500 students and faculty participated in a protest march to support an extension of President Reinhard's two-year contract. The extension was denied and Reinhard, shown at bottom right, left MSU for another presidency.*

Chairman Jerry Howell, Sr., expressed the Regents' appreciation for Norfleet's courage in making his decision and for his service to the University. Although Norfleet's decision came several months after a strong supporter, Lloyd Cassity, had been replaced as board chairman, Howell, Sr., made light of published stories about the Regents' disagreement over Norfleet's future.

Several board members, however, had privately questioned Norfleet's leadership after the eruption of numerous personnel conflicts which had to be brought before the board for final resolution. And, interestingly, shortly after Norfleet's announcement that he was stepping down from the presidency, an out-of-town reporter told an administrator at Morehead State that he felt Herb. F. Reinhard or someone like him would be the next president since different board members were impressed with his record at Slippery Rock University in Pennsylvania. At that same meeting on November 12, 1983, the Board of Regents voted against proposals from the Albright Report for reductions in the athletic program and attempting academic reorganization until after the selection of Norfleet's successor. By a vote of 9 to 1, the board approved a resolution to remain in the Ohio Valley Conference at the Divison I-AA level of competing in all sports. John R. Duncan, faculty regent, was the lone person voting against this resolution, stating that the issue needed further study.

As Norfleet was winding down his administration, he listed his major accomplishments as reducing faculty turnover, completing several campus buildings, and purchasing a computer system. He also mentioned new academic programs, improvements in student life, and private fund raising which had been necessitated by a loss of $2 million in annual state support. On the other hand, he presided over an institution which suffered a decline in enrollment from a record high of 7,758 in 1978 to 6,521 in 1983. Over the previous decade, the University's School of Education fell from preeminence as teaching majors plunged from 2,200 to approximately

1,000, thereby requiring a transfer of money and faculty members to other academic programs. The enrollment decrease had come at a time when the state budget was being deeply cut and the faculty was heavily tenured. Norfleet eliminated four academic departments while reshaping three schools—Sciences and Mathematics, Business and Economics, and Education. When funds were available, he put them into student-enticing programs such as robotics, veterinary technician training, mining technology, computer programming, engineering technology, and paralegal studies.

Norfleet thought the distinguishing contribution of his administration was expansion of public service programs. These programs included a $1.16 million joint effort with coal companies in reclaiming strip mined mountaintops for farm use; additional in-service training programs for teachers in Eastern Kentucky; off-campus graduate classes in business and education in six cities; and developments in regional research, water testing, arts instruction, and library service. However, expansion of the Derrickson Agricultural Complex and efforts to create the Appalachian Development Center nettled many faculty members, who felt the money could have been used more wisely to upgrade faculty salaries and instructional equipment.

Yet, an amazing aspect of the Norfleet presidency was that although he was a controversial president, he managed to gain for himself a generous settlement—called the "Golden Parachute" by the press—when he stepped down from the presidency. Faculty morale suffered and many of the faculty were upset at receiving a mere two percent increase in salary when money was available to pay such a handsome settlement to the departing president.

Taking advantage of the board's divisions, Norfleet negotiated a new contract that was the envy of other college presidents in Kentucky. During his first year as chancellor of corporate relations, a position created to recruit support from businesses and to promote the economic development of the region, Norfleet would receive his presidential salary of $72,000 while on sabbatical leave, which was more than the salaries of the presidents of Murray State, Northern Kentucky, and Kentucky State. Norfleet would be on paid leave, serving his first year as a consultant for the Washington-based American Association of State Colleges and Universities. He would receive no remuneration, however, for his work as a consultant. During the last three years of his contract, he was given $49,500 for being chancellor nine months each year. In addition to his salary, Norfleet as chancellor would receive university housing or a housing allowance, continued fringe benefits, including a retirement buy out of $33,000 for his previous service in Indiana, a leased car and expenses for his new post, a secretary and office space, equipment, supplies and expenses. He could terminate the contract at will, and the board could extend the arrangement beyond the original four years on an annual basis.

Before a search committee was named to choose a successor to Norfleet, a small group of Morehead State alumni, led by Russell McClure, former MSU vice president and former state finance secretary, started pushing for Bob M. Davis, chief administrative assistant for three years to Lt. Gov. Martha Layne Collins, who was about to become governor. Holding a master's degree in education from the University of Kentucky and a doctorate in education from George Peabody College, Davis had served as head basketball coach at Auburn University for several years. McClure felt that Davis's political connections could help Morehead State.

After a closed session on November 27, 1983, the Board of Regents created a nine-member committee to conduct a nationwide search for Norfleet's successor. The committee included five regents: Jerry F. Howell, Sr., board chairman; Robert M. (Mike) Duncan, vice chairman of the board and an Inez bank president; Ethel Foley, a Maysville public school librarian; John R. Duncan, faculty regent and education professor; and David L. Holton, student regent and president of the Morehead State Student Government Association.

To get more constituencies involved in the selection process, the board empowered Howell to select four outside members to represent faculty, students, alumni, and the general public. Thomas Spragens, retired president of Centre College, was hired as a consultant to the presidential search committee. Early in the search process, representatives from various campus groups met with the board to assist in the preparation of criteria for a new president. Howell insisted that the search committee use the criteria throughout its deliberations.

Although Morehead State was known for the fervent loyalty it generated from alumni and friends, some felt that this spirit of dedication to the school's historic mission had become a mixed blessing. Robert T. Garrett, writing for the *Courier-Journal,* claimed that the next Morehead president would face "a task so immense as to require Mosaic—if not Messianic—qualities." The feeling that helped recruit new students and produced an increasing number of private gifts also seemed to foster a suspicion of outsiders and a spirit of factionalism. Part of the dissension was undoubtedly produced by the fact that the faculty had grown in diversity while the administration was made up largely of a network of MSU alumni. Furthermore, academic deans and departmental chairmen were being constantly "recycled" into the teaching ranks, where they were often critical of their successors. The campus often joked about these so-called "FARTs"—"Former Administrators Reassigned to Teaching." Morever, the faculty now demanded a larger voice in governing the University. As a case in point, the University Senate and the Faculty Concerns Committee suggested that faculty members should be included on the presidential search committee. At the same time, Stuart Sprague, history professor and chairman of the senate, lashed out at purported attempts "to play politics" with the selection process. Sprague voiced faculty determination that MSU give more attention to academic programs and take itself off the AAUP censure list. Thus, a cry for change emerged on the campus of Morehead

State University—a demand that might well bring in a presidential
outsider for the first time since the early Fifties.

## Herb. F. Reinhard, Jr.: Second "Outsider," 1984-1986

On April 28, 1984, the Board of Regents appointed Herb. F.
Reinhard, Jr., who had been president of Slippery Rock University in
Pennsylvania for five years, the ninth president of Morehead State
University. He was given a two-year contract with an annual salary
of $73,500 in addition to fringe benefits. This same meeting saw an
unexpected development that, in retrospect, did not presage well for
Reinhard's future. Jerry Howell, Sr., a regent for sixteen years, announced his resignation after achieving two major goals: selecting
a new president and uniting the board. Several observers concluded
that Governor Martha Layne Collins had decided not to reappoint
Howell, whose term had expired on March 31, because he had supported her opponent, Grady Stumbo, in the Democratic primary.
Mike Duncan was elected chairman to succeed Howell.

Reinhard had earned a doctorate in higher education at Indiana University, a master's degree in counseling, and a bachelor's degree in psychology at Florida State. Prior to Slippery Rock, Reinhard
had served as assistant to the president at Florida A & M University,
assistant vice chancellor for academic affairs at the University of
Tennessee-Martin, vice president for student development at Western Carolina University, and dean of student services at Florida State
University.

His wife, Nancy, was a vivacious, energetic woman, who was a
gracious hostess with whom people were comfortable. The
Reinhards had four children, three of them in college. Nancy was
committed to her family, and much of her time and attention were
devoted to them during the Reinhards' two years in Morehead.

Members of the selection committee were highly impressed
with Reinhard. Howell, Sr., thought it significant that Reinhard, earlier in the week, had received a warm reception on campus. He

*Coach John "Jake" Hallum had the second best career football record at Morehead State.*

pointed out that one of the new president's priorities would be uniting the campus because of dissension left over Norfleet's tenure. Mike Duncan felt that Reinhard was strong in administrative ability and in public relations. John Baird, Pikeville attorney and one of the initial group to interview Reinhard, said the new Morehead State chief "has a personal touch that we feel we need on this campus."

A native of Covington, Reinhard indicated he was looking for another presidency because of an interest in returning to the South, a dislike for collective bargaining and a unionized faculty which he faced in Pennsylvania, a desire for a better financial contract, and his wish to live in a larger community. Richard Wilson, of the *Courier-Journal,* described Reinhard as Morehead State's first President "with no previous link" to Kentucky's public education system. President Spain, the school's first "outsider," had taught at the University of Kentucky. The new president's first priority was getting to know the school's students, faculty, and administrators, as well as learning the strengths and weaknesses of the institution. Reinhard stated that his

*Guy Penny was voted Coach of the Year and Tommie Gray Player of the Year in the OVC after the Eagles won the football championship in 1966.*

experience made him comfortable with schools the size of Morehead State and Slippery Rock because of the personal relationships presidents could have with students, faculty, and administrators.

New Board Chairman Mike Duncan said Regents would allow Reinhard to put together his own administrative team. "Knowing him," Duncan added, "he's not going to come in and clean house. But he's going to evaluate people." Reinhard told some Morehead State administrators he might eventually bring some members of his Slippery Rock administration to Kentucky. In retrospect, several of the early comments contrasted sharply with the way the brief Reinhard administration unfolded.

Reinhard's ideas were impressive. But the baffling part is that someone so well-educated and widely-travelled never seemed to attain a glimmer of understanding of—nor appreciation for—Eastern Kentucky culture or the institutional background. Inept at handling people, he soon turned the campus into a sharply divided war zone. Within his first seven weeks, the new president ordered a sweeping shakeup of the administrative and academic structures by removing four vice presidents, eliminating the positions of three deans, consolidating twenty-five academic departments into seventeen and reorganizing six schools into three colleges. With his blunt manner, Reinhard made these changes painfully and tactlessly in many cases. Many old timers on campus were disturbed not so much by what the new president did as by the way in which he carried it out. Some received word of their reassignment by the "grapevine," over the radio, or accidently seeing memos addressed to others. Reinhard was coldly clinical when it came to human beings. He apparently failed to understand why removing thirteen top administrators would cause upheaval in the school and its community. He never

Dave Haverdick
MSU's
All-American

seemed to grasp how personal and professional matters were interrelated and constantly implied that nothing of consequence had happened on campus during the twenty years prior to his arrival. Strong in his determination to produce change, he often failed to bring people along with him. The anguish resulting from his methods

*Dave Haverdick, one of Morehead State's ten All-Americans in football.*

helped to insure the president's demise within a short time. A script designed to alienate the most people possible could not have produced more havoc!

Yet, because of turmoil left by the outgoing administration and its Board of Regents, change was necessary. After carrying out the "executions," Reinhard could not persuade the board to support what he had done. Failing to receive a contract extension during his first year, he maintained a sort of holding pattern the remainder of his administration. Part of his problem derived from changes in the composition of the board. Four members had been replaced by the time Reinhard arrived to assume his duties on July 1, 1984. Enrollment, already in a tailspin, plunged dramatically during the Reinhard years. The last weeks of his administration represented one of the most trying eras in the history of the institution. In some ways, the situation was as bleak as during the loss of accreditation in the Forties. But campus life went on, teachers met their classes, and students continued to receive a first-rate education!

In the final analysis, when one gets through the "weeping, wailing, and gnashing of teeth," Reinhard was an effective administrator. The human element was so disruptive that for a long time it was nearly impossible to recognize any progress amid the chaos. And as Reinhard pointed out, "There is no painless way to carry out what people don't want done." At any rate, many positive things happened under the ninth president, several of which are still in place. Structurally, Reinhard can be credited with streamlining the institution through nearly two dozen organizational and procedural changes. Learning of numerous thefts from the bookstore, Reinhard made a dramatic improvement in physical security across campus by instituting a master key system. Morehead State University personnel was male-dominated in the early Eighties as was true at many other schools; Reinhard began to change this phenomenon by becoming the first Morehead president to take a serious look at affirmative action. Although he also pushed the racial side of affirmative action, he had less success in that area than in gender equity. But he succeeded in introducing the idea that the institution needed to be less provincial in terms of finding and hiring the best people available. Reinhard also stressed the idea that when people were not doing their jobs, the University had no choice but to remove them from their positions.

Initially, Reinhard had to spend a great deal of time and energy dealing with the controversial contract with former President Norfleet, which had been approved on June 27, 1984, only three days before Norfleet's contract as president ended. The Board of Regents, smarting from criticism for having approved the "Golden Parachute" in the first place, tried to schedule a meeting with Norfleet early in the Reinhard administration to reconsider the overly generous terms of his contract. Only Faculty Regent John R. Duncan and Student Regent David Holton had voted against Norfleet's original contract. On July 24, he made the board a counter offer that would have reduced the benefits somewhat. The board then voted to reopen negotiations with Norfleet, and Reinhard asked that Norfleet's title as well as his job description be revised since he apparently did not want Norfleet dealing with corporations. On August 31, Norfleet made a second proposal in which he expressed dissatisfaction at being made a special assistant to Reinhard. Finally, on September 25 Norfleet and the board came to terms. The renegotiated settlement provided the former president with an annual salary of $59,500 rather than the original $72,000 for the first year while he was on a sabbatical. He would then be paid $49,500 annually for the three remaining years, the same as in the original contract. Norfleet, however, would no longer receive a housing allowance while serving as special consultant to the president rather than chancellor for corporate relations. Although he would be reporting to Reinhard, neither Norfleet nor Board Chairman Mike Duncan could provide any specific examples of work he would be doing. The board agreed to pay Norfleet's expenses, including those for travel, office, and secretary.

In the posturing which followed, Board Chairman Duncan called the new contract a "great savings" to the state. Norfleet told reporters he harbored no bitter feelings against MSU and that he would use his future position to do "everything I can to help the University."

In the board meeting on September 25, 1984, the Regents also accepted the constitution of Morehead State's first Faculty Senate. President Reinhard supported this move and thought the senate would strengthen the faculty and its role in governing the University. Many members of the faculty needed reassurance after the charade in which the board had been engaged with Norfleet's contract. Cynicism about finances reigned supreme as the board sometimes had left the impression that there was plenty of money available.

Only two weeks after his inauguration on April 11, 1985, Reinhard's request for a one-year's extension of his two-year contract was tabled by a vote of 5-4, after a two-hour discussion in closed session. He and his supporters now realized that his two-year contract had been a mistake; some regents were already stating privately they did not regard Reinhard as the right person to lead the University. The president, who thought he had come to Morehead not for a year or two but for a career, began talking immediately about the possibility of looking for a job elsewhere.

Several Morehead State students, nevertheless, urged the Board of Regents to back Reinhard. Just ten days before spring commencement in 1985, the *Courier-Journal* reported that over 500 students joined a march on behalf of Reinhard; the following day, students and a few faculty members wore purple ribbons to indicate support for the president. The march was orchestrated in such a manner as to take advantage of a large awards program in Button Auditorium which had nothing to do with the controversy. Several parents who drove great distances to honor the accomplishments of their sons or daughters did not appreciate the impression being left that they were demonstrating on behalf of this controversial figure. Some students resented what they interpreted as his making fun of their

Eastern Kentucky cultural background, including the type of high schools they had attended. But more than 1,000 students, along with a few faculty and staff members, signed petitions urging an extension of Reinhard's contract; others were critical of his wholesale changes and the manner in which they had been carried out.

Reinhard's first year had provided the beginning of one of the most controversial eras in the history of Morehead State University. Richard Wilson stated in the Louisville *Courier-Journal* on July 7, 1985, that "the crux of the issue" was Reinhard's reorganization of the school's administrative and academic structure and his reassign-

*Phil Simms, one of the greatest athletes in the history of Morehead State, quarterbacked the New York Giants to a Super Bowl victory.*

271

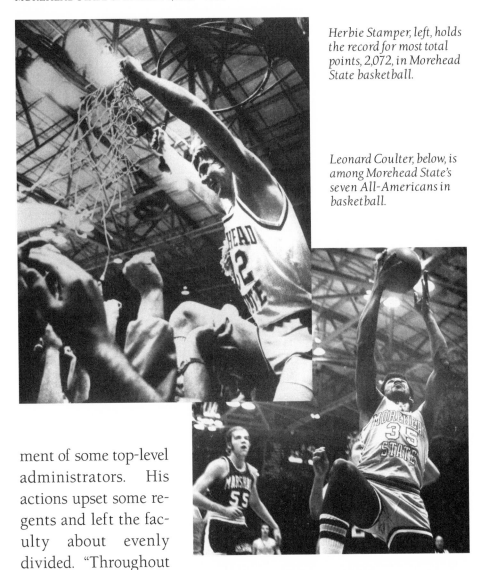

*Herbie Stamper, left, holds the record for most total points, 2,072, in Morehead State basketball.*

*Leonard Coulter, below, is among Morehead State's seven All-Americans in basketball.*

ment of some top-level administrators. His actions upset some regents and left the faculty about evenly divided. "Throughout the turmoil surrounding Reinhard's presidency," Wilson wrote, "his supporters have contended the school had become stagnant and was ripe for a shakeup. His critics countered that he moved too quickly and that many of his actions were either unnecessary or callous and counter-productive on a campus where 'the personal touch' has characterized previous administrations."

Reinhard's future at Morehead State University was shrouded

in uncertainty as he began his second year. When Athletic Director Sonny Moran introduced him at media day right before the beginning of the football season, he mentioned that a year ago he had presented Reinhard as the institution's new president. Before Reinhard welcomed the sportswriters, he turned to Moran and quipped: "Maybe next year at this time you'll have the same opportunity."

Interviewed by Richard Wilson a few days before the scheduled vote on a one-year extension of Reinhard's contract in August 1985, Mike Duncan said he was putting together a checklist of presidential responsibilities which he hoped the board would use in evaluating Reinhard. Conceding that some changes were necessary, Walter Carr, another regent, asserted, "It's the way he's done it. He just doesn't handle people well, and I'm afraid he's going to ruin the University if we don't do something about it." Faculty Regent John R. Duncan, a Morehead State alumnus, cited similar concerns. Reinhard seemed "to want to deny any kind of past contribution that anyone has made," Duncan added. "That really irritates some people."

On the other hand, David Brumagen, biology professor and chairman of the Faculty Senate, supported a contract extension. Impressed that Reinhard found money to finance full scholarships for outstanding students, Brumagen stated, "We haven't had anything before to give a full ride to these students." Harold Bellamy, a Reinhard supporter serving as vice president of the MSU Foundation, thought the president enjoyed substantial support in the community and region. "When massive changes occur, you're going to step on some toes," Bellamy said. David Bolt, president of the MSU Alumni Association, supported Reinhard and believed that "to a large extent, many of the alumni realize that the decisions that had to be made—and let me emphasize had to be made—were not particularly popular."

But when the Board of Regents met on August 23, 1985, they were silent on an extension of Reinhard's contract. Their silence was met with derision from an audience of about 275, mostly students. In voicing his displeasure, Reinhard received a standing ovation when he asked, "Am I to assume that members of the board will not even vote on this so the public can see how each member voted?" Near the end of Reinhard's first year, a faculty vote indicated that 123 members of the faculty (51 percent) disapproved a one-year extension whereas 118 (49 percent) favored it. About 59 percent of the staff, however, favored extension as compared with 41 percent who were opposed. Students voted 977-73 in favor of extending the president's contract. Taking into consideration the faculty vote as well as various other factors, the board voted 6-4 against the extension in September.

Governor Martha Layne Collins finally decided to take a hand in the situation and summoned the board to meet with her in Frankfort on November 16, 1985. After an hour's closed session with Governor Collins the eight board members requested that Reinhard resign before his contract expired. They hoped an interim president would be in place before the beginning of the 1986 General Assembly. Grady Stumbo, member of the Council on Higher Education, favored Reinhard's early resignation. The board met again, however, on December 4, 1985, and voted unanimously for the president to serve the remainder of his contract.

Meanwhile, unprecedented problems were facing the campus. The fall semester of 1984 witnessed another decline in enrollment, thereby forcing a $557,300 budget cut to make up for lost tuition and revenue from housing. The occupancy rate in the residence halls fell to 61.5 percent in the fall semester of 1985, its lowest rate in history. Two corporations temporarily shelved consideration to make contributions totaling over $200,000. Supporters withdrew some $400,000 in pledges of deferred gifts. While losing 26 percent in enrollment from 1978 to 1986, the University experienced a reduction of only ten full-time faculty members. Porter Dailey, vice president for administrative and fiscal services, estimated that MSU had

*Coach Wayne Martin's 1983-84 Eagles had the best record in Morehead State basketball history, 25-6. Two of his squads played in the NCAA tournament.*

40 more faculty than were needed by the end of 1985. By this time nearly three-quarters of the faculty were tenured. Retention of students had always been a major problem. Since Morehead's freshmen traditionally experienced the lowest entrance scores in the commonwealth, except for Kentucky State, a significant increase in the rate of retention was difficult to achieve.

Concluding that it would be wise to clean house with the board and start over, on January 10, 1986, Governor Collins called for the Morehead Regents to resign and for Reinhard to accept a sabbatical, since efforts to buy out the remainder of his contract had apparently stalled. Harry Snyder, executive director of the Council on Higher Education, threw his full support to Collins' requests. Governor Collins' first two appointments to Morehead's reconstituted board were former governors Edward T. Breathitt and Louie B. Nunn. Nunn told Collins he would accept the appointment if the governor would appoint other regents "who were interested in education and that the appointments not be political in nature."

By February 4, 1986, Collins' new appointees read like a Kentucky "Who's Who." In addition to former governors Breathitt and Nunn, the board included J. Calvin Aker, who had recently resigned from the state Supreme Court; William R. Seaton, vice chairman of Ashland Oil, Inc.; Dr. Allan M. Lansing, noted Louisville heart surgeon; Charles Wheeler, Ashland insurance dealer, and Barbara Curry, Lexington city official. Walter Carr, who had refused to resign, continued his service on the board.

Former Governor Nunn, selected on March 4, 1986 as chairman of the new Board of Regents, declared, "He's [Reinhard] the president of the University. I know not whether he's done good, bad or indifferent. That's something that, as far as I'm concerned, has yet to be determined." Nunn and Breathitt suggested that bringing Governor Collins to speak on campus would provide the kind of "pep rally" needed by everyone. The governor accepted an invitation to speak at MSU's graduation exercises in May 1986.

Shortly before Reinhard left Morehead State, he was predicting a nine percent decrease in enrollment for the fall semester in 1986. To assist with the financial plight which would undoubtedly accompany this distressing development, he recommended that the University drop from Divison I-AA to Division II in athletics. Approving a less drastic measure, the board voted to make up the difference by increasing student fees for activities, health, parking, and housing. After Reinhard left, he served as president of Frostburg State College in Maryland and led that institution to university status within a short time. After five years there, he became a consultant in Tallahassee, Florida, where he is presently retired.

## Athletics: Modest Successes

During this twenty-year transition period, Morehead State enjoyed its greatest success ever in athletics! The Eagles won their only football championship outright in 1966. Only five Morehead football teams have ever captured as many as seven games in a season;

two of these came in 1966 and 1971. The 1983-84 team was the only one ever to win an OVC basketball championship outright; the Eagles' 25-6 mark represented the school's greatest won-lost record in history! The 1978-79 Lady Eagles compiled their most impressive record, winning 28 and losing only 4, the second greatest OVC mark reached in the annals of women's basketball. The Eagles also won four OVC baseball championships during this era.

### Football:

From 1966 to 1985, Morehead State University won 74 games, lost 125, and tied 7. With a 6-1-0 conference record, the Eagles reigned as sole champions of the Ohio Valley Conference in 1966! The 1984 Eagles finished as the highest scoring team in the school's history, with 281 points, but they also gave up the most points—359. That team also produced the most total yardage of any Morehead team—3,706. The Eagles held Austin Peay to a minus 63 yards in 1971, the least rushing yardage ever permitted in a Morehead game; they relinquished only 641 yards for the season, which was also a record.

Morehead State produced a winning record in only five of their twenty seasons, with the last one in 1979. Only two of the Eagles' seven coaches won more games than they lost: Guy Penny's last two seasons included eleven victories, seven defeats, and one tie. With a total overall record of 39-39-2 from 1959-67, he was the school's third most successful coach in history and was voted the OVC Coach of the Year in 1966. John (Jake) Hallum's 22-17-1 tally placed him second to Ellis T. Johnson as the winningest football coach ever. The records of the other five coaches were as follows: Tom Lichtenberg, 9-11-1; Roy Terry, 15-25-1; Wayne Chapman, 6-21-3; Steve Loney, 9-24-0; and Bill Baldridge, 3-19-0, during his first two seasons.

In keeping with its tradition, MSU produced a large number of individual stars. Two players were voted OVC Offensive Player of the

Year: Tommie Gray in 1966 and Phil Simms in 1977. Gray holds Morehead's record for most points scored in a career—172—and for the most touchdowns—28. He enjoyed the greatest rushing career average—5.6 yards per carry. Simms accumulated the sixth highest number of career pass completions in OVC history with 409. Although becoming one of the most famous Eagle athletes ever as quarterback for the champion New York Giants and subsequently as a sports announcer for NBC, Simms starred as the quarterback of teams that never won more than three games per season.

During this period, the Eagles placed a total of 44 members on the All-Ohio Valley Conference team. In 1969, Dave Haverdick, defensive tackle from Canton, Ohio, became Morehead's sixth All-American. John Christopher, punter from Norwalk, Ohio, was the only Eagle ever to repeat as an All-American, in 1981 and 1982. Christopher holds the record for the most career yardage in punting—12,633 yards. He also earned the best career average with 42.4 yards per game. Don Russell, outstanding kicker from Louisville, was an Academic All-American in 1974.

Moreheadians will never forget the 1966 OVC championship season. In the Eagles' opener against Marshall, Tommie Gray tallied two touchdowns but the Thundering Herd won, 27-20. The Eagles then ruined Youngstown State's Homecoming with a 21-12 win. With Gray and Otto Gsell scoring touchdowns, Morehead held a 14-12 half time lead. When the Youngstown punter fumbled the ball into the end zone in the fourth quarter, guard Dave Moore recovered it with just 32 seconds remaining to clinch the victory.

In their first OVC game of the season, the Eagles downed Tennessee Tech, 14-7, in the Shrine Game at Ashland. With the score tied 7-7 early in the fourth period, Gray scooped up a Tech fumble and galloped 65 yards for the winning touchdown. Murray took an early 3-0 lead against Morehead, only to see the Eagles storm back with 30 points in the second half as Gray scored on two touchdown runs of 40 and 42 yards, while Leon Wesley ran 33 yards for another.

Homecoming morning dawned with a beautiful sunrise only to see the weather change and the football field become softened by rain. With Morehead State trailing Austin Peay 3-0 at halftime, Gray gathered in the second half kickoff and raced 97 yards for a touchdown. The fourth quarter was played in a sea of mud as the Governors regained the lead 10-7 with 6:08 remaining in the game. Halfback Leon Wesley then scored the Eagles' second touchdown after a 71-yard drive in five plays. Eagle end George Adams delivered such a crunching tackle on the ensuing kickoff that the ball was jarred loose from the Austin Peay receiver and recovered on the Governors' 13-yard line. Three plays later, Gray skipped into the end zone from eight yards out for another Eagle touchdown and a 21-10 victory.

Middle Tennessee then beat the previously undefeated Eagles, 20-7, in a game punctuated by a free-for-all during the third quarter. Just before the opening kickoff the following Saturday at Johnson City, Tennessee, the Eagles received word that Austin Peay had knocked off undefeated Middle Tennessee, 12-7, a stimulant which

*Mickey Wells was the Lady Eagles' most successful coach in history. His 1978-79 team had the best record in history.*

*Donna Murphy was twice voted as the OVC Player of the Year.*

fired up Morehead! Trailing 7-6 at intermission, Morehead took the lead in the third period, as Jim Ross, a middle guard, recovered an East Tennessee fumble at the Buccaneers' 28-yard line; shortly afterwards, Otto Gsell scored from the three. A strong Eagle defense preserved a 13-7 victory and a first place tie in the OVC. Even the elements reacted to these strange events in Morehead State football by delivering a snow storm on November 3 that threatened to close down the campus. The following Saturday's game with Western was played in a heavy downpour of rain. After Western went ahead 7-6 in the third period, Gray, who had been benched for two weeks, entered the game and scampered 66 yards for the winning touchdown in a 12-7 victory.

The weather was cloudless for the first time in weeks as fans traveled to Richmond for the closing game. The Eagles scored the first time they had possession of the ball, but Eastern stormed back to put two touchdowns on the scoreboard in just three minutes and then added a third touchdown with less than three minutes to go in the half. With Eastern ahead 19-7 at intermission and driving for another early second half touchdown, Scotty Reddick intercepted a Colonels' pass on his own 18-yard line. Later in the third quarter, defensive end George Adams "literally picked a pass off the fingers" of the Eastern quarterback and raced to the nine. Gray then added his second touchdown of the day. The fourth period was all Morehead as the Eagle defense allowed a mere three yards on the ground and nine in the air. Meanwhile, the Morehead offense controlled the ball for about 13 minutes. With time running out and trailing, 19-13, the Eagles gained possession on the midfield stripe. With only 22 seconds remaining, Morehead was still 16 yards away from pay dirt and needed a first down to retain possession. Gray dashed around left end to go out of bounds at the three-yard line and stop the clock. With ten seconds left in the game, Gray swept around right end for his third touchdown; the extra point gave the Eagles a 20-19 victory.

When the delirious fans returned with the victorious team, an impromptu celebration parade clogged the streets of Morehead and went down University Boulevard to the Doran Student House. Wildly cheering fans mobbed the players; classmates hoisted Tommie Gray to their shoulders and carried him above the crowd. Another cheer went up as President Doran announced that students would receive an extra day of Thanksgiving vacation. The evening was capped with the news that Middle Tennessee and Tennessee Tech had been upset by East Tennessee and Austin Peay, respectively. Immediately, a loud hooray erupted from the residence halls, and celebrations continued throughout the night. Unlike previous seasons, everything had gone right for the Eagles to make them sole OVC champions! MSU placed three players on the All-OVC team: Tommie Gray, Paul Conner, and Gary Virden.

In the opening game of the 1967 season Morehead State defeated Marshall, 30-6. The Eagles then achieved the near impossible with a 21-19 defeat of their old nemesis, Middle Tennessee, for the first time in sixteen years. After nine seasons, Coach Guy Penny could say he had defeated every team in the conference. The Eagles then dropped close contests to Murray and a Homecoming game to Austin Peay, after which they struggled in the last quarter to pull out a 20-16 victory over Kentucky State, a Division III team. Fans came back to earth to recognize "Morehead football" once again! The Eagles defeated Tennessee Tech, 21-16, before dropping three games in a row. Finally, Morehead State tied Eastern, 7-7, in what turned out to be Penny's swan song.

The 1968 season opened with new head coach John (Jake) Hallum directing one of the youngest and most inexperienced teams Morehead State had fielded in years. An otherwise lackluster season was marked by an exciting, come-from-behind victory over Young-stown State at Homecom-ing. Trailing 26-0 at intermission, the Eagles stormed back with three touchdowns in the third quarter and two in the final stanza for a 35-26 win. Sophomore tailback Louis Rogan set a Morehead State record of 1,125 rushing yards during a season.

Morehead downed Middle Tennessee 35-9 in 1969 for its third victory ever over the Blue Raiders.

*Donna Stephens made the All-OVC team three years.*

The season was highlighted by the closing match with Eastern. With bitter memories of Eastern's use of a lineman at quarterback after the game had already been decided the previous season, Hallum sent tackle Dave Haverdick in at quarterback, guard Bill Wamsley at tailback, and quarterback Bill Marston at guard near the end of the game. Morehead garnered a 23-11 victory as Marston broke Mike Gottfried's 1965 Eagle records in passing yardage and total offense. A strong defensive unit was led throughout the season by three-time All-OVC tackle Dave Haverdick. This senior defensive tackle who grew up within sight of the Professional Football Hall of Fame in Canton, Ohio, became the first Eagle to be named to the Associated Press's All-America team since Morehead entered the OVC in 1948. Haverdick then received a professional contract to play with the Detroit Lions.

After losing their first two games in 1970, the Eagles went on to register a winning season, with a 6-4 record overall and 4-3 in the OVC. In the closing game of the season, Morehead and Eastern were tied at 13-all when Kirk Andrews split the uprights for a field goal which gave the Eagles a 16-13 upset victory and thereby blocked Eastern's chances of capturing the OVC championship. Jake Hallum's most successful season was 1971, with a 7-3 mark, after which he resigned to join the staff of the University of Maryland. But the Eagles finished only fourth since all three losses were conference games. They had the best total offense—321 yards per game; the best passing offense—160 yards per game; and the finest rushing defense—allowing only 64 yards per game in the OVC. Three players led the conference in other departments: senior split end John High in pass receiving with 49 catches for 571 yards and four touchdowns; sophomore quarterback Dave Schaetzke in total offense, with 150 yards passing and rushing per game; and freshman tailback Jimmy Johnson in kickoff returns with 26 yards per return. Both High and senior defensive back Mike Rucker were named to the All-OVC team.

Wayne Chapman had a 3-8-0 record in his first season as head coach in 1976, including an opening 31-14 romp over Marshall, but the victory later had to be forfeited after the Eagles discovered they had used an ineligible player. The highlight of Morehead's season was sophomore quarterback Phil Simms' coming into his own as he led the conference in passing and placed third in total offense. Simms also established a new school record of 366 offensive plays in a season, including attempting 241 passes and rushing 125 times. Senior Don Rardin led the conference in punting and set a new season Morehead State record for best punting average with 42.8 yards per kick. Senior linebacker Jerry Spaeth also set a school mark for defensive plays in a season with 214 and established a career record with 382 total defensive plays.

Although a Morehead publication predicted that the 1977 season would be "a time when the past is forgotten and the team concentrates on the future with an optimistic attitude," the Eagles could do no better than finish with a 2-6-2 record. In spite of only two team wins, Phil Simms was voted the OVC's Offensive Player of the Year. In 1978, the *Raconteur* reported, "It appeared that Coach Wayne Chapman's three-year-old dream of rebuilding a winning football program at his alma mater was on the verge of becoming a reality." The Eagles, however, started out on a sour note by tying Kentucky State and then losing to Middle Tennessee. In the next game Morehead exploded for 49 points in the final three periods to defeat Murray, 49-32, as Simms completed 11 of 16 passes for 120 yards and three touchdowns while directing an offense which amassed 425 total yards. Later, playing before 7,000 fans in Jayne Stadium, Simms connected on 17 of 31 passes for 252 yards and two touchdowns, while Marcus Johnson posted a career-high 172 yards in 24 carries, but the team lost 21-20 to Tennessee Tech. In despair over losses Chapman resigned before Eastern blanked the Eagles in their finale, 30-0.

After the Eagles were picked as cellar dwellers in pre-season polls in 1979, Tom Lichtenberg, elevated from assistant to head coach, asserted, "They didn't hire me to lose." MSU opened with a 14-7 victory over Kentucky State in a lackluster contest but then held Middle Tennessee to only 73 yards rushing while defeating the Blue Raiders, 28-7, in their home opener.   Following a loss to Murray, the Eagles returned home to post a 7-0 victory over Austin Peay.   Before 8,500 Homecoming fans the following week, the Morehead offense scored on its first possession, while the defense gave a repeat performance, for a 7-0 first-ever win over Tennessee-Martin. Freshman Nick Rapier kicked a 34-yard field goal midway through the first half, and the Morehead defense made it stand up for a 3-0 victory over Western for only the sixth win ever over the Hilltoppers. At this point, Morehead stood at 5-1-1 and was ranked tenth in the nation in Division I-AA, as they had not given up a touchdown in four games and led the nation in scoring defense, permitting only 6.9 points per contest. But the Eagles dropped their three remaining games.

The highlight of the 1980 season was the first Eagle win at Murfreesboro, Tennessee, since 1950. But the 17-0 victory was marred by a brawl that erupted in the final quarter over what the Blue Raiders interpreted as a late tackle. Freshman kicker Len Duff drilled a record 51-yard field goal which fell through after bouncing on the crossbar. The ABC network chose to televise regionally, Western's game at Morehead, won by the Hilltoppers, 17-7. The defeat was allayed somewhat by the $70,000 MSU received from the network. Morehead State split its two final games with a win over Kentucky State and a loss to Eastern. Halfback Dorron Hunter picked up 1,001 yards for the season, while the Eagles went 4-7-0. Hunter, named as an All-OVC tailback, was selected as Morehead State's Most Valuable Player. At season's end Coach Lichtenberg announced his resignation to become an assistant coach at Notre Dame. Although Morehead State won only a total of eleven games from 1981 through 1985, Bill Baldridge, who had succeeded Steve

Loney as head coach, remained highly optimistic about the future of MSU football.

### Men's Basketball:

From 1966 to 1986, Morehead State had thirteen successful seasons while winning 261 games and losing 228. The Eagles played under four different head coaches during that era. Bob Wright won 46 games while losing 26 in three seasons; overall, Wright was 58-38 in his four years. Bill Harrell was victorious in 68 games while dropping 59. Jack Schalow won 45 while losing 56. In his eight seasons during this era, Wayne Martin's record stood at 116-106; overall, in nine years as an Eagle coach, his teams finished 130-120. Only two coaches in history have taken Morehead to the NCAA Tournament—Bobby Laughlin accomplished this remarkable feat three times and Wayne Martin, twice. During those five NCAA tournament appearances, the Eagles compiled a record of four wins and six losses. Although no Eagle was voted OVC Player of the Year during these twenty years, fifteen players made the All-Ohio Valley Conference team. In 1972, Leonard Coulter, Danville forward, became Morehead's seventh All-American.

During the 1966 OVC Holiday Tournament in Louisville, Morehead fans were looking ahead to the tourney's second game. After squeaking past Tech, 74-73, the Eagles engaged Western in an exciting contest. With only three seconds remaining and the ball out of bounds, Morehead's Jim Sandfoss threw the ball the length of the court to Larry Jordan, who dropped the ball through the nets as the buzzer sounded to send the game into overtime. The Eagles then dropped the contest, 80-77, to the eventual OVC champions. The Eagles entered regular conference play by soundly defeating Murray State, 108-93, as Willie (Hobo) Jackson scored 29 points and grabbed 23 rebounds. A highlight of the season was defeating Canisius, 63-62, in Buffalo, New York. Probably the most exciting game played at the Fieldhouse that year was a 112-98 double overtime victory over

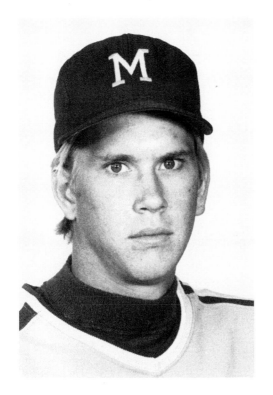

*Jody Hamilton was OVC Player of the Year in baseball in 1979.*

Marshall, the Eagles' 15th win in the previous 16 contests with the Thundering Herd! Sandfoss was the leading scorer with 39 points, including 17 of 17 free throws. With a 16-8 overall record and 8-6 in the conference, Morehead finished its first season as a University in a three-way tie for second place as Western captured the Ohio Valley Conference crown.

The 1968-69 season began with great expectations, since Morehead State had three seniors and two juniors comprising the starting five. The Eagles defeated Eastern Kentucky, Austin Peay, Tennessee Tech, and East Tennessee twice each. The Eagles and Western Hilltoppers played exciting ball with each taking a one point decision from the other at home. Lamar Green pitched in a free throw with three seconds remaining to give the Eagles a 78-77 victory over Western. As the Eagles were making a run for the championship, over 500 students made the long journey to Johnson City for the final game of the season where Morehead outlasted East Tennessee, 77-67, to tie Murray for the OVC championship. MSU classes were dismissed on Wednesday afternoon, March 5, 1969, for everyone to journey to Bowling Green to witness the playoff between the Eagles and Murray State to determine the OVC representative in the NCAA. The Racers ran off to a 94-76 victory before 12,500 fans in Diddle Arena. Morehead finished with an average of 88.6 points per game, which placed it in the top ten offensive teams in the nation.

Wright was replaced by Coach Bill Harrell for the 1969-70 season. The Eagles upset the University of Florida, 82-73, in the Sunshine Classic Tournament in Jacksonville, only to lose to Jacksonville, 117-63, in the title game. Don Byars notched 25 points to lead an 84-55 upset of Southern Mississippi in Morehead's home opener. The Eagles' 88-78 win over Marshall avenged an earlier defeat, as Jim Day pumped in 28 points.

But in 1970-71, the Eagles suffered through an 8-17 season, the most losses ever for Morehead in one year. Day, who averaged 24.3 points per game and 13.6 rebounds, was a unanimous choice for the second straight year on the All-OVC team and then signed a professional contract with the Portland Trail Blazers in the NBA. In spite of the devastating season, Harrell was optimistic because of his unbeaten freshman team. Those freshmen lost no time in making a name for themselves the following year. The 1971-72 Eagles topped Murray State, Middle Tennessee, and Tennessee Tech twice each in a schedule which had been upgraded to one of the strongest ever in non-conference foes. The season ended in a three-way tie between Morehead, Eastern, and Western. In the OVC playoff, the Eagles defeated Western, 82-79, before losing the next evening to Eastern, 98-86. Leonard Coulter was named to the All American Sophomore Team, selected by *Basketball Weekly*, along with such players as Bill Walton of UCLA and Tom McMillen of Maryland. Coulter also made the All-OVC team after finishing second in the league in scoring with a 24.1 average and leading the conference in rebounding with 14.2 per game. Howard Wallen made the All-OVC team as well. The sophomore-laden team averaged 91.4 points per game, placing it in the nation's top ten offensive teams.

Morehead experienced a disappointing 14-11 season in 1972-73, as the Eagles tied for second place in the OVC with a 9-5 record. The

288

Eagles inaugurated the regional OVC telecast with a thrilling 81-79 victory over Austin Peay, the eventual conference champion.  But the most thrilling aspect of the season consisted of sweeping the series with Western.  Coulter, Danville forward, who averaged 21.3 points, set a school record for field goal accuracy with 52.3 percent of his attempts.  Both Coulter and Eugene Lyons, forward from Johns Creek, were named to the All-OVC squad.

In 1973-74, the Eagles tied Austin Peay for the OVC championship.  Since Morehead had dropped both of its games to the Governors,  Austin Peay represented the OVC in the NCAA Tournament.  Morehead again took both games from Western.  The Eagles also defeated East Tennessee, Tennessee Tech, Eastern, Louisiana Tech, and Southern Mississippi twice each while posting a 17-9 mark overall.  Although his team had tied for the OVC championship, this was Bill Harrell's last season as head coach.

Beginning in 1974-75, the Ohio Valley Conference dropped its Christmas tournament in favor of a postseason tournament that would choose the OVC entry for the NCAA tournament.  Regular season champion, Middle Tennessee, disposed of the Eagles in the first game of the tournament, although the teams had split during the season.  Arch Johnson, senior forward known as the "Booneville Bomber," made the All-OVC team.  Although Coach Jack Schalow experienced a losing record of 13-14 in 1975-76, he tied for OVC's Coach of the Year after the Eagles knocked off Eastern and Austin Peay in the OVC Tournament.

Schalow's only winning record came in 1976-77, as the Eagles finished with a 15-10 mark but lost to Middle Tennessee in the OVC Tournament.  Herbie Stamper, whose 22-point average led the conference, and Ted Hundley, who averaged 17 points and also led the team in rebounding with 10.3 per game, were named to the All-OVC team.  Morehead State was the only conference team to defeat Austin Peay.

Wayne Martin took over as head coach in 1978-79 and led the

The Morehead State baseball park was named for John (Sonny) Allen, a standout in basketball and baseball who coached both sports very successfully. At the time of this honor, he had won more baseball games than any other coach in history. He is being congratulated by President Doran.

Eagles to a second-place tie in the OVC. In Morehead's 83-81 victory over the Western Hilltoppers, Herbie Stamper, from Knott County, broke Morehead's all-time career scoring record of 1,925, held by Dan Swartz. Later in the season Stamper became the first Eagle to top 2,000 points, a remarkable record for one who was once criticized by his coach for not taking enough shots in a game. The Eagles dropped their only OVC Tournament game to Western. Stamper was named to the All-OVC team for the third time.

After 25 years in Wetherby Gymnasium, Morehead State played its first game in the new 7,000-seat Academic-Athletic Center in the 1981-82 opener as the Eagles posted a victory over Western Illinois with Bobby Laughlin on the bench as honorary coach. The team's 17-10 record included double victories over Eastern, Tennessee Tech, Youngstown State, and Austin Peay. Morehead then dropped its OVC tourney game with Western. Norris Beckley, senior guard from Shelbyville, became the seventeenth Eagle to score 1,000 points in a career, Guy Minnifield, Lexington sophomore, was named to the All-OVC team, and Martin tied for Coach of the Year honors.

At the beginning of the 1982-83 season, Coach Martin suggested, "We're not pretenders; we're contenders." The Eagles responded with a 19-11 record. After finishing second in OVC regular play, Morehead defeated Tennessee Tech, 54-53, in tournament play, as Minnifield sacked a 20-foot jumper at the buzzer. The Eagles followed with their third win over Akron, 81-65, to capture the conference tourney and land a berth in the NCAA East Regional. Minnifield was named Most Valuable Player in the OVC tournament and was selected to the All-OVC team. Over 600 Morehead students and supporters journeyed to Hartford, Connecticut, where the Eagles were defeated in the first round by Syracuse, 74-59, in spite of making 48 percent of their field goal attempts.

The 1983-84 Eagles, under Wayne Martin, finished with the school's best mark in history at 25-6. The Eagles went 20-1 at home, losing only to Middle Tennessee, to become the only Morehead team in history to win the OVC seasonal championship outright. Morehead State established its longest winning streak ever—twelve games! Four of MSU's six defeats came at the hands of Kansas, Tennessee, and Louisville (twice). The Eagles won the OVC tournament, played in Morehead, by defeating Murray, 80-64, as Arthur (Peewee) Sullivan scored 20 points and Jeff Tipton had eighteen. Martin became the first Morehead State coach to win 100 games in only six seasons.

An estimated 1,500 fans accompanied the Eagles to Dayton, Ohio, to witness their first round NCAA game with North Carolina A & T. Minnifield delighted them by scoring his only points of the game with a field goal at the buzzer to give Morehead a 70-69 first round victory, Morehead State's first NCAA tournament win in 23 years. Shortly after the game, radio personality Paul Harvey noted on his program that for the first time in NCAA history, referees had consulted television monitors at one point to clarify which player had been fouled. Three buses of excited Eagle fans then made an exodus to Milwaukee for Morehead's second round contest with Louisville, which the Cardinals won, 72-59. Martin was again named OVC Coach of the Year. Earl Harrison, from Lindenwold, New Jersey, and Arthur (Pee Wee) Sullivan, of Shelbyville, were selected to the All-OVC team.

### Women's Basketball:

Morehead State began competing in women's intercollegiate basketball in 1970-71. By the mid-Eighties, the Lady Eagles had played under four coaches. Carol Stewart, the first coach, won five games and lost three. The records of the other three coaches were Sue Lucke, 20-19; Robert Michael (Mickey) Wells, 156-91; and Loretta Marlow, 110-116.

The Lady Eagles enjoyed twelve winning seasons out of sixteen during this era. Morehead State became the first college in the state to grant full scholarships to women—twelve—in 1975-76, and that was before the appearance of Title IX. The team won the Kentucky Women's Intercollegiate Conference in 1976-77, with a 16-9 record but then lost to Old Dominion and Clemson in the South Regional Tournament of the Association of Intercollegiate Athletics for Women. Their best season ever was in 1978-79 at 28-4, the OVC's second best record in history. After winning the KWIC for a second time, the Lady Eagles were defeated by South Carolina in the AIAW Regional.

Under the direction of Mickey Wells, the Lady Eagles became the team to beat in Kentucky during the Seventies. Wells began teaching at Morehead State in 1965. In addition to teaching a full load, he served as director of intramural sports and became director of Cooper Hall when it opened. He was voted KWIC Coach of the Year twice, in 1977 and 1979. Wells also was selected twice as OVC Coach of the year—1979 and 1982.

Donna Murphy was voted OVC Player of the Year twice, in

1978 and 1980; Priscilla Blackford was Player of the Year in 1983, as well as OVC Female Athlete of the Year. Donna Stephens made All-OVC three times, in 1979, 1981, and 1982; Donna Murphy belonged to this select group three times from 1977-80; and Priscilla Blackford was twice voted to the All-OVC team, in 1982 and 1983. Also placing on the team were Michelle Stowers in 1979 and Connie Appleman in 1985.

Murphy scored 600 points in 1977-78, all-time high for a Lady Eagle in a single season; others scoring above 500 were Donna Stephens, 594, and Priscilla Blackford, 560. Murphy also holds the rebounding record for a season with 437, in 1976-77. Murphy scored the most career points in history, with 2,059 in 1976-80, and Donna Stephens, 1978-82, placed second, with 1,710 points.

Other high scoring Lady Eagles during this period included Robin Harmon, 1,599; Priscilla Blackford, 1,481; and Michelle Stowers, 1,459. The rebounding career record was held by Murphy, with 1,442; Blackford was second, with 1,075, and Donna Stephens third, with 1,044. Former Lady Eagles who have been voted into MSU's Athletic Hall of Fame include Murphy, Stephens, and Debra Ames. The latter holds the OVC record for the most rebounds in a game— 30—against Georgetown College in 1975-76.

### Baseball:

During this twenty year era, Morehead State won 417 baseball games while losing 303. The Eagles turned in a winning season in eighteen of twenty seasons. The team played under four coaches: Rex Chaney went 22-11 his last season, which gave him an overall record of 111-56 for six years; during his eight seasons within this period, Sonny Allen posted a 148-81 mark, which gave him a 226-137 overall record for fourteen seasons; and Steve Hamilton, in his eleven seasons within this era, went 255-197; his overall record was 305-275 for fourteen years. Leston Stewart won 12 and lost 14 in his one season.

The Eagles captured four OVC championships along with six OVC East divisions and three OVC North divisions. Morehead State placed 39 on the All-OVC team in this era. Fifteen Eagles signed professional baseball contracts between 1980 and 1986.

Jody Hamilton (1977-80) holds various MSU records: the career highest batting average (.385); the most home runs in a career (49); the most home runs in a season (19); the most total bases in a career (376); and the career RBI record (155). Brian Stanley, 1986, has the season's record for most hits—70. Jamey Bennett hit four home runs against Tennessee Tech in 1979, an OVC record for a single game. Glenn Jones, 1979-81, holds the OVC record for the longest hitting streak, with 31 consecutive games.

Chet LaMay pitched seven victories in 1978, while losing none, for the best record ever among Morehead pitchers. Marc Griesenger holds the career winning percentage record—11-2— in 1976-78. The 1974 pitching staff posted the lowest earned run average—3.01—for a season, while the 1977 pitchers had the most strikeouts—398.

Morehead State captured the OVC championship in 1969 with a 22-6 record, the first of four under Coach Sonny Allen. By defeating Western, 7-6 and 6-3, on the Breathitt Sports Center diamond, the Eagles won their first conference championship since 1963. In the first game, Al Frazier's two-out single to left field in the seventh inning scored Eddie Wallingford from second to give Morehead the victory. Jim Martin pitched the entire game for his fifth win in seven games. The second game featured back-to-back home runs by Reese Stephenson and Mike Punko, the latter's seventh home run of the season, in the first inning. John Lysien went the distance for the Eagles in posting a 5-1 season's won-lost record. Allen was named OVC Coach of the Year.

The 1973 Eagles posted a 26-12 mark and became champions of the Ohio Valley Conference for the third time under Coach Sonny Allen. After winning the Eastern Division of the OVC, Morehead entered the championship series as an underdog to nationally

*Mike Gottfried, quarterback (1962-65), became head football coach at Murray, Cincinnati, Kansas and Pittsburgh. He is now a television analyst with the ESPN network.*

ranked Murray State, winner of the Western Division. The Eagles dropped a 1-0 opener but stormed back to take the nightcap 8-6. In the third and decisive battle, an almost flawless Morehead defense and the relief pitching of freshman Jim Duff held the Racers scoreless over the final five innings. The Eagles blasted three home runs to take the championship, 8-2. Allen credited improved pitching to Assistant Coach Steve Hamilton, who had retired the previous summer after eleven seasons as a major league hurler. On May 12, 1974, President Doran announced at the Alumni Awards Banquet that the baseball field had been named in honor of Coach Allen. John Allen Field boasted a new permanent grandstand with over 1,100 seats and an electric scoreboard, making it the pride of the Ohio Valley Conference. During Coach Allen's last season in 1975, the Eagles' record was 26-19.

Steve Hamilton took over as Morehead's coach the following season and guided the Eagles to a 28-11 record and the championship of the OVC East. His second year in 1977, Morehead went 27-

19, captured the OVC East, and reigned as champions of the OVC for the fifth time. The Eagles hosted the championship series and defeated Middle Tennessee, 8-5 and 14-1. Hamilton was voted OVC Coach of the Year. Eagles who made the All-OVC team were infielders Jim Brockman and Jeff Stamper, catcher Kirk Hudson, designated hitter Rick Gunterman, and outfielder Harry Hall. During his career, Stamper played all nine positions. In the eighth inning of a crucial conference game in which Morehead State was deadlocked 3-3 with Tennessee Tech, four consecutive Eagles swatted home runs.

Morehead won its sixth OVC championship in 1983 with a 28-17 record, in spite of what Coach Hamilton described as "the strongest schedule we've ever played." In the championship series, Morehead split a double header with Akron. In the first game, Rob Williams hurled a five-hitter to beat the Zips 8-1 and thereby pick up his fourth win in five tries. Senior Scott Haynes smacked a double to drive in junior Joe Mitchell, giving Morehead a one run lead in the second inning. Mitchell then slammed a three-run homer in the fourth to increase the lead to 4-0. With a single in the fifth inning, Mitchell knocked in two additional runs. The nightcap saw the Eagles lose, 3-1. The following day Morehead took the third game, 6-5, to win the conference title once more.

---

In the Seventies and Eighties, feuding on a more sophisticated level than a century earlier continued to dominate life in Morehead. After Morehead State had discovered respectability on the college level, the institution then struggled for two decades, with limited success, to find its identity as a regional University. The board failed to inspire even a modicum of confidence in setting up a munificent arrangement for outgoing president Morris L. Norfleet and then in squabbling with him over a contract they had already approved. Nor did the stormy relationship between the board and Herb. F. Reinhard during his two-year presidency inspire further confidence.

296

Reinhard left Morehead State in turmoil. Enrollment was dangerously low; relationships with the school's Eastern Kentucky constituency were in disarray, and the campus itself was seriously divided. The close of the institution's first century was bleak indeed. A new leader was needed to elevate Morehead State's image, bring peace to a troubled campus, and provide vision for a new century. And Morehead State University had to return to its mission of serving the economic, educational, social, and cultural needs of Eastern Kentucky!

*Mignon McClain Doran (inset), wife of the University's seventh president, set new standards of personal glamour and campus involvement for first ladies at Kentucky's universities. In recognition of her outstanding service, the Board of Regents named a residence hall complex in her honor. Nearly 900 students live today in the Mignon Complex.*

*A. D. Albright, Morehead State's tenth president, 1986-87.*

# Chapter 6

# Morehead State University: The Second Century, 1986-1997

The feuding between the Martins and the Tollivers on the streets of Morehead in the 1880s was transmuted a century later into a battle between Morehead State University's president and its Board of Regents. Throughout the history of the institution, power had shifted back and forth between the board and the chief executives. From 1922 to 1934, Judge Allie Young often dominated the school even while living in a Louisville hotel. Neither board nor president was dominant between the mid-Thirties and the mid-Fifties. The long tenure of Adron Doran featured a commanding president and a compliant board, with only one regent voting against a single Doran proposal over a span of more than two decades. Weakness in the Norfleet administration enticed the board to flex its muscles, while the power-wielding leadership style of Herb. F. Reinhard further aroused the board's determination to involve itself again even in the internal workings of the University.

The 1985-86 year emerged as one of the darkest in the history of Morehead State, rivaling 1946, when the institution had been stripped of its accreditation. Dismal clouds of hopelessness gathered after a troubled decade under Morris L. Norfleet and Herb. F. Reinhard. Enrollment declined; respect for the institution plummeted; bleakness was intensified by the desertion of the school's natural constituency in Eastern Kentucky.

As it had previously done in difficult times, Morehead State realized the leadership type needed for the decade beginning in 1986. A. D. Albright, "dean of higher education" in Kentucky, was enticed from retirement to play a crucial peacemaking role for the institution. What irony that such a gentle personality could quietly return the power that was necessary to drive the expression "troubled presidency" from the front pages of state and regional newspapers! After Albright's year of effective leadership as a reconciler, C. Nelson Grote, one of the most congenial MSU presidents, served the institution during a significant resurgence in enrollment.

From 1986 to 1996, state government once more invaded the Morehead campus; this time it benefited the institution. First, Governor Martha Layne Collins removed an embattled Board of Regents and replaced it with one that she thought could resolve the Reinhard controversy and subsequently provide strong oversight for an effective transition to better days. The General Assembly and Governor Brereton Jones changed the appointment process for all Boards of Regents, thereby creating boards which have sometimes been less subservient to the pressure of regional politics. By 1992 the Morehead State board felt comfortable enough with its own role to encourage the creation of another powerful presidency. William Seaton, board chairman, declared that the institution was

*Chando Mapoma, SGA president and the first international student to serve as a member of MSU's Board of Regents, hopes to become an ambassador.*

seeking a president with no political ties to Eastern Kentucky. The Eaglin administration has demonstrated that this regional University can have both a stalwart Board of Regents and a powerful president at the same time.

The success that has characterized the Grote and Eaglin administrations has demonstrated even to the staunchest supporters of Morehead State University that outstanding leadership can be rendered both by individuals with former Morehead ties and by those with none. Hence, future search committees can quit "beating this dead horse," examine the needs of MSU in a given time frame, and set about to find the most capable president for the job, regardless of geography.

## A. D. Albright: The Peacemaker, 1986-1987

The new Board of Regents, created through the intervention of Governor Collins, singled out one individual as uniquely qualified to tackle the pandemonium at Morehead. Hence, an invitation was issued to A. D. Albright to come out of retirement and lead the institution through a "cooling off" period. On May 16, 1986, the board appointed Albright to serve as president long enough to restore peace to a campus in turmoil until a permanent successor could be located. His appointment as the institution's tenth president lasted one year.

Albright, executive director of the Council on Public Higher Education from 1973 to 1976, had retired as president of Northern Kentucky University, having served from 1976 to 1983. During the 1960s, he had held various positions at the University of Kentucky, including dean, provost, executive vice president, vice president for institutional planning, and interim president in 1963, after the resignation of Frank G. Dickey. First Lady Grace Albright was totally committed to helping her husband be an effective leader. She had already successfully played a similar role in three other places. While well-educated and holding strong personal opinions, she accomplished her tasks away from the limelight; she once told a campus administrator that she thought a president's spouse had to be his refuge from the pressures and trials of his office.

Having made a thorough examination of Morehead State in the latter part of the Norfleet administration, Albright had the advantage of familiarity with the University. Moreover, he was rapidly gaining a reputation as a "miracle worker" in difficult situations. In the Louisville *Courier-Journal,* on August 3, 1986, Richard Wilson wrote, "At a time when most men his age have already slipped into retirement," Albright has been "thrust into another higher education hot-spot.... One of the state's most widely known educators for the past 2 1/2 decades," Albright had become known as "an educational Mr. Fix-It." In order to hire Albright, the board gladly waived MSU's policy of not employing individuals over 70. As the first executive director of a revamped Council on Public Higher Education, Albright had guided the Council through a transition from a weak agency to one capable of overseeing the state's universities. Northern Kentucky University's Regents then requested Governor Julian M. Carroll to persuade Albright to become its president to restore peace after President W. Frank Steely's controversial administration.

Problems facing Albright at MSU seemed almost insurmountable. Shrinking enrollment had precipitated overstaffing problems and with them a financial drain on an institution which had suffered a 26 percent decrease in enrollment over the past decade. Albright's primary mission was to restore confidence in the University's future. So, taking advantage of three decades of widespread contacts in Eastern Kentucky, he immediately set out on a tour of the twenty-two Eastern Kentucky counties in the MSU service region and met with superintendents and public officials to ascertain their feelings toward the University as well as their expectations of it. Albright quickly picked up insights on how to reverse Morehead State's sagging enrollment which had plummeted from a record high of 7,758 in 1978 to 5,695 in the fall of 1985. One

Eastern Kentucky principal, for example, informed him that his top graduate had already received a generous scholarship from another university in Kentucky, where her sister was a student. Although she preferred going to Morehead State, the high school senior had not been contacted by the school. Albright immediately offered her a scholarship, enticing both sisters to enroll as students at MSU. Revoking a Reinhard policy, Albright renewed merit scholarships to valedictorians and salutatorians in high schools in Eastern Kentucky.

Beginning with the fall semester of 1986, MSU guaranteed major academic scholarships to the two top graduates who enrolled from each of the 47 high schools and four junior colleges located in its 22-county area. Albright commented in the *Morehead News* of August 19, 1986, "We want everyone to know that we are renewing our historical commitment to the people of this region and that we intend to serve them first and foremost."

The new president received a warm welcome wherever he traveled in the MSU service region. One person he contacted summed up the feelings of many when he characterized Albright as "a quiet diplomat, with an unusual ability to listen." Albright asked Robert Goodpaster, one of his former doctoral students at the University of Kentucky and subsequently head of Ashland Community College, for additional cooperation from the community college system. Jack Webb, Greenup County school superintendent and Morehead alumnus, asserted, "Education people have a very positive feeling toward Dr. Albright and the University right now. If he continues on the path he's going, the University can make some great strides."

Albright assured the opening assembly of faculty and staff in the fall semester of 1986, "Some of our greatest days are ahead." Reflecting on his recent visits to the region's counties where MSU got eighty percent of its students, he reported, "It is the expectation of the people of Eastern Kentucky that Morehead State as a regional

University must dedicate itself to the people, problems, and prospects of this region." Comparing the University with the region, Albright described the faculty as representing 34 states with degrees from 154 American universities and two foreign countries. Referring to Morehead as the "University of the Mountains," he then challenged the faculty to increase their efforts to serve the region, including making visits to high schools. Albright expressed a "need to feel pride in our own accomplishments and pride in each other's achievements." Faculty members who had not heard such encouraging words in years were ready to follow the new leader.

The fall semester of 1986 witnessed a 3.5 percent increase in enrollment—from 5,695 to 5,894. Thus, Albright quickly began operating from strength since MSU's 1986-87 budget had been prepared based on a projected nine percent decline in students. In the *Morehead News*, of September 26, 1986, the president attributed the gain in enrollment to three primary factors: "a combination of an intensive recruitment drive, an image-building promotional campaign in the region's media, and the addition of a new program of upper division level course offerings at four two-year college sites." He also praised recruitment efforts of faculty members, singling out one department which had called 150 prospective students in a three-week period.

Albright was obviously providing the tonic needed for this strife-torn campus. He had started out by mending fences with regional school superintendents and politicians, thereby pointing Morehead State University toward the area where it had traditionally derived the most students. He then followed up by suggesting to the campus community that it was possible to disagree without being disagreeable. Albright's upbeat style restored confidence by leading everyone to work together for the good of the whole. By helping people believe in themselves, he succeeded in convincing almost everyone that MSU could return to those prosperous days of the past.

*Alumnus Dan Lacy, vice president for corporate communications at Ashland, Inc., presents President Grote with the first $75,000 of a $750,000 gift that represents MSU's largest corporate gift in history.*

Albright pursued avenues not only to increase enrollment but to decrease expenditures as well. To help solve budgetary problems, the Regents allowed the president broad authority to freeze hiring for vacant positions so as to trim a half million dollars from the budget. In another effort to improve the budget, the board approved an Albright proposal to provide faculty and staff with an optional early retirement system. Because of the institution's dramatic growth in the Fifties and Sixties, Morehead State had been forced to hire a large number of faculty members in a short time. As a result MSU was saddled with salaries for an extremely large number of full professors. At one time, for example, every member of the history department was a tenured full professor, drawing appropriately large salaries. The new policy made it possible for a faculty member to take early retirement, teach half time, and continue to draw half-salary for four years. The state's recent decision to lower from 30 to 27 the number of teaching years required before retirement without penalty further enticed a number of faculty to retire.

Any major scrutiny of Morehead State's budget during those years had to consider athletic costs. MSU had run up a $1.2 million deficit in its athletic program in 1985, including nearly $800,000 to support football. In the fiscal year 1986, athletic programs cost $1,630,222, while generating only $354,986. And $79,870 of this revenue had come from interaccounting within the University for complimentary tickets; another $119,775 of it came from a portion of the student activity fee. Income from non-university sources amounted to only $155,341. The Eagle Athletic Fund provided over one-third of that non-university income through fund raising.

In May 1987 the board approved an Albright proposal that the institution's general fund should not contribute more than one-half of the total athletic expenditures as of 1990-91. The board also approved Albright's further recommendations: that athletic revenues raised to support the athletic program and reduce the University subsidy must originate from outside sources; that the University encourage the OVC to permit the school "to seek its own level of competition in football" without forcing it out of conference competition in other sports; that any reduction in expenses should not affect MSU's commitment to women's athletics; that any future increases in the $40 student activity fee should not be designated for the athletics program; and that the MSU Foundation, Inc., founded in 1979 to receive and administer private gifts on behalf of the University, would establish a reserve fund by 1993 to replace the football field's artificial surface whenever such action should be warranted.

A major problem centered on complimentary tickets. Of the $127,208 generated from ticket sales in football and basketball (the only sports producing ticket revenue), $79,870 came from compli-

*Alumnus John Merchant was the first African American to become a partner in Peck, Shaffer and Williams, the most prestigious law firm in Cincinnati. He is in line to become president of the MSU Alumni Association.*

mentary tickets. G.E. (Sonny) Moran, athletic director, pointed out that the complimentary ticket system had been worse when he arrived at MSU in 1974. On the other hand, MSU's athletic picture might not be so out of line when considered with an NCAA report in 1989 indicating that only twenty-two colleges in the nation were making any profits on athletic programs.

In May 1987 the Board of Regents approved several proposals made by the president: implementing a staff congress, pending a review of its constitution and by-laws; establishing a School of Business and Economics as part of the College of Professional Studies; making West Mignon Hall a coeducational residence hall, and Regents Hall a residence for women; and establishing regional centers in West Liberty and Ashland.

Four days before he left the presidency, Albright received word from the American Association of University Professors (AAUP) that MSU had been removed from the group's censured list. Morehead

State had been placed on the list on June 17, 1983, because of a dispute between the Norfleet administration and two art department faculty members. For the censure to be lifted, it was necessary for MSU to offer some form of redress to the two former faculty members. So, both were offered reinstatement as members of the faculty but chose monetary settlements of an undisclosed amount instead. In the meantime, MSU enacted policies dealing with academic freedom, tenure, and due process in accordance with AAUP standards.

The president thus completed a successful year. In October 1986 the Morehead Optimist Club selected Albright as its Man of the Year. On June 18, 1987, over 325 friends and colleagues gathered on campus to express their appreciation for his service. Student Government President Steven Strathmann and Carlos Cassady, SGA's president the previous year, presented a silver tray to Albright in appreciation for his work with students. MSU Alumni Association President William L. (Bill) Phelps announced that Albright had been inducted into the Alumni Hall of Fame, the first person ever to be so honored without having an earned degree from the University.

*Janet Stumbo finished her pre-law studies at MSU and went on to become the first woman justice elected to the Kentucky Supreme Court.*

Louie Nunn, chairman of the board, presented Albright with an honorary doctorate of humane letters and declared that the 74-year-old educator had "provided leadership that leads." Albright then thanked the Regents for "the best professional year I've ever had." He turned out to be much more than a caretaker and healer who succeeded in getting people to work together again.

The renaissance of the institution began so quickly and the national search for a permanent successor moved so smoothly, however, that President Albright had no reason to remain beyond the year he had promised. He gave the institution new credibility. In fact, two major gifts—one for half a million dollars by Ashland Oil Company, Inc., and the other, a contribution by Terry S. Jacobs, Cincinnati businessman, of $681,878 for installment of an artificial playing surface on the football field and $79,000 for construction of a new athletic training facility—were probably more an act of faith in President Albright than in the institution.

## C. Nelson Grote: A Transition Leader, 1987-1992

Morehead State lost no time in beginning the process of locating its next president. By September 11, 1986, a national search committee had narrowed the field of candidates from eighty-six applicants to six in its effort to name the eleventh president of Morehead State University. These six were James Adams, a Morehead alumnus then serving as superintendent of schools in Indianapolis; C. Nelson Grote, chief executive officer of Spokane Community College in the state of Washington and a former Morehead dean; Olin B. Sansbury, chancellor of the University of South Carolina's Spartanburg campus; Gene W. Scholes, vice president for administration at Northern Kentucky University and another former Morehead dean; James W. Strobel, president of the Mississippi University for Women; and John Calhoun Wells, the only non-professional educator in the group. However, Wells withdrew from consideration before the final review of candidates.

In October 1986 the board met behind closed doors for three hours, making a thorough investigation of the five remaining candidates to examine their character and reputation in their communities as well as in the academic world. The committee had narrowed its consideration to Adams and Grote by November 10, 1986. These two candidates were then brought to campus for extensive interviews by each constituency within the University community. Grote held a trump card which Adams could not match. The *Morehead News* stated on November 14, 1986, "Dr. C. Nelson Grote's visit to Morehead State University Wednesday morning carried strong overtones of 'old home week' as the contender for MSU's 11th president addressed a public gathering in Breckinridge Auditorium." He pointed out how he had kept in touch during his fifteen years away by making several visits back to Morehead in addition to continuing his subscription to the local newspaper. Bringing up nostalgic episodes of his years in Morehead, he often referred to people by their first names. Grote said just the right things: "We would be part of the community but not try to run it."

On November 14, 1986, a two-hour closed session of the Board of Regents helped to reach a consensus for Grote, who had been an unsuccessful contender for the presidency when Norfleet was named in 1976 and Reinhard was selected in 1984. A native of Illinois and a former high school teacher, Grote obtained an undergraduate degree from Eastern Illinois University, a master's degree from the University of Missouri, and a doctorate in education at the University of Illinois. He had served as chairman of the applied arts division at Morehead State from 1960 to 1966 and as the first dean of the School of Applied Sciences and Technology from 1966 until 1971. Grote decided that his chances of leading Morehead State would be enhanced by leaving to become head of some institution elsewhere. Hence, he assumed the presidency of Schoolcraft College in Michigan, where he remained for ten years before moving to Washington State to serve as chief executive officer of the nearly 65,000-student

Community College system in Spokane until the time he was chosen to head MSU.

Wilma E. Grote, the new president's wife, was deeply committed to her responsibilities as First Lady. All her married life, she was mainly a wife and mother of four children—two sons and two daughters. As First Lady, she became immersed in community and church activities, including serving three years as treasurer of Habitat for Humanity and three years as a member of the board of directors of the Morehead Theatre Guild. She also contributed much time to the worship and human concerns committees of the First Christian Church, where the Grotes were members. Well informed on women's issues, she was a member of the advisory committee which led to the introduction of the Women's Studies curriculum at MSU. She also supported the MSU Women's Symposium, which was renamed the Wilma Grote Women's Symposuim in her honor. In the spring of 1991, she was the recipient of the Outstanding Community Service award given by the Morehead Lions Club. All the while, someone noted, "She never seeks the spotlight or expects more than friendship."

On July 1, 1987, his first day in office, Grote told a news conference, "I think it is very true, we have come home." When the 58-year-old educator assumed the MSU presidency, some claimed he had come back "home" to retire. But the following list of priorities indicates the new president did not appear to have retirement on his mind: Establish goals for MSU; meet area public school officials and politicians; explore methods of increasing private fund raising; and determine ways the University could stimulate economic development of the region. His other areas of improvement were upgrading MSU's teaching and learning environment through staff development activities, marketing the University to strengthen its credibility in the region, and working closely with public schools.

Although Grote had been part of a previous Morehead administration when public financing for education was plentiful, he knew the situation had changed drastically in just two decades. He was convinced that private fund raising would have to play a major role if his administration were to be successful. "State-supported institutions will continue to get bread and butter money" from state government, Grote stated. But "if we want to be better than good," he added, "we have to position ourselves in the marketplace, work with corporations, foundations and individuals, and bring private money into the University."

Grote's first major decision was one of the most popular ones ever made by a Morehead president. Shortly before leaving office, Albright had named Sonny Moran, who had been athletic director for thirteen years, as special presidential assistant for athletics. Moran would coordinate and supervise the University's pending self-study of athletics as recommended by the NCAA. He would also develop a plan for meeting the 1991 deadline to reduce Morehead State's athletic subsidy by 50 percent. Grote announced that Steve Hamilton, baseball coach for twelve years and one of the greatest athletes in Eagle history, would become athletic director on August 1, 1987. A more popular choice could not have been made.

The new president began his administration with a flurry of activities. He stated that Morehead State would fill a vacancy in the office of vice president for academic affairs, a familiar announcement to the faculty by this time. Also, a new School of Business and Economics was created on July 1, 1987, as part of the College of Professional Studies. With over 1,000 students, the new school included ten different four-year programs and five programs at the associate degree level. Classes were held both on campus and at Ashland, Maysville, Pikeville, and Prestonsburg. The School of Business and Economics operated an American Institute of Banking program and provided outreach services and technical assistance to the region through the East Kentucky Small Business Development Center.

On August 1, 1987, the University re-established the School of Education within the College of Professional Studies. Nearly 900 undergraduate and graduate students had been enrolled in teacher education courses on the main campus and at regional campuses in the fall semester of 1986. Reminding everyone that 1987 was "our year of record" with the National Council for the Accreditation of Teacher Education, Grote suggested that "the heightened visibility for teacher education will only enhance our NCATE report." Dan Thomas, professor of education, was selected to direct the NCATE study; associate professors of education Katherine Herzog and Jean Wilson were co-chairs of the study which would serve as the basis for NCATE's evaluation of Morehead State's teacher education program for continued accreditation.

Grote had a sense of knowing what was appropriate to say to a given audience. In his first speech to faculty and staff in August 1987, he listed an increase in salaries at the top of his goals. The new president also expressed concern over the small amounts regularly spent for classroom and institutional equipment. He further committed his administration to stimulate creativity and pro-

*As its second executive director, MSU alumnus Virginia (Ginni) Fox has led Kentucky Educational Television (KET) to national prominence in public television.*

*Nearly 50 years later, new officers in the U.S. Marine Corps are told to follow the leadership example of Capt. William Barber, MSU alumnus, who earned the Medal of Honor during the Korean War.*

ductivity among the faculty and staff. He then encouraged the audience to join his campaign for unity by wearing gold and blue buttons emblazoned with the slogan "Together We Can."

Grote had an imposing inauguration on October 30, 1987. As a former elder of the Christian Church, he was assuming the presidency of the institution which had been founded a century earlier by the same church. His first grade teacher, Leona Schafer, joined Governor Martha Layne Collins and two former governors, Louie B. Nunn, chairman of the Board, and Edward T. Breathitt, vice chairman, as they placed the presidential medallion, symbolic of authority, around Grote's neck. Tradition was the order of the day as former Morehead presidents A. D. Albright, Adron Doran, and Morris L. Norfleet were also seated on the stage. In his inaugural address, Grote said Morehead State "cannot let problems of the past serve as roadblocks, but as stepping stones to our future."

A week later, Richard Wilson reported in the *Courier-Journal* that former Governor Louie Nunn had signed notes for $25,000 in early 1986 to pave the way for President Reinhard's departure from Morehead State. Nunn was now endeavoring to raise $15,000 to close the books on "one of the most embittered periods" in the history of MSU. At a time when Reinhard had been threatening a lawsuit, Nunn and Breathitt had negotiated an unpublicized $50,000 settlement. Privately raised funds had been used. In July 1988 the MSU Foundation paid Nunn the remainder of the debt.

All in all, 1987 turned out to be a vintage year for MSU as the school entered its "Second Century of Service." An increase in enrollment prompted the administration to reopen three residence halls. Private gifts soared over $1 million for the first time in history. Morehead State received its largest corporate gift when Ashland Oil Foundation committed a half million dollars over a three-year period. In addition, the University's largest individual gift until then—$681,878—came from Terry and Susan Jacobs. Norman Tant, former Morehead State professor of education, had earmarked $100,000 to endow a scholarship fund and had designated the University to share in his residuary estate, the largest bequest MSU had ever received. A check for nearly $112,000 was presented to MSU in 1987.

The Grote administration basked in the sunlight of a period of growth once more. Just as there had been two primary eras of construction on campus—from the mid-Twenties to the mid-Thirties and throughout the first fifteen years of the Doran administration—MSU experienced two spurts of growth in enrollment. One occurred during those same fifteen years under Doran; the other came under the Albright-Grote regime. Morehead State's surge during both of these times was in keeping with what was happening on campuses throughout the commonwealth and the nation.

President Grote took the University to unprecedented heights in growth only to discover insufficient funds to take care of students' needs. He started out by continuing what Albright had instituted—namely, a very aggressive marketing strategy for admissions. Early in his administration, Grote told his vice presidents and deans that Morehead State could have 9,000 to 10,000 students "if we want that." Both Grote and his upper level administrators "wanted that" because such an enrollment would bring in more money, since Kentucky, through its formula funding system, was rewarding institutions based on "head count." After MSU hit 9,169 students in the fall of 1992, the state apparently had insufficient funds to meet the formula, thereby creating management problems.

Enrollment at Morehead State had dipped from an all-time high of 7,758 under Norfleet in 1978 to 5,695, a 19-year low in the fall semester of 1985. Albright's untiring efforts helped to insure a whopping 10.1 percent escalation in the fall semester of 1987, with the number of students jumping to 6,490. And most impressive of all, full-time enrollment shot up by 13.4 percent, from 4,147 to 4,703. One year into the Grote administration, the size of the student body jumped another 13.7 percent in the fall of 1988—all the way to 7,379. Full-time enrollment at Morehead State was up about 18 percent for a new school record. Mike Mincey, vice president for student development, stated in August 1988 that "those of us who are MSU alumni are particularly pleased with the extraordinary increase in the number of sons and daughters of alumni who have discovered the alma mater of their parents. MSU has a strong history of family loyalty and that tradition is reaching into a new generation."

Morehead State then witnessed a 7.3 percent boost in the fall semester of 1989, as 7,962 students matriculated. By the fall semester of 1990, enrollment had escalated more than 51 percent since 1985. Since Grote became president of MSU in 1987, enrollment had spiraled by 36 percent. And as the number of students on campus expanded, President Grote felt the need to promote such capital construction projects as the renovation of Thompson, Lappin, Mays, and Butler Halls. Some claimed that he went "a dorm too far" in terms of remodeling buildings, running up the institution's debt service. Supporters reminded critics that the president's action was necessary in order to restore pride in the appearance of the campus.

Apparently Morehead State University—in its selection of C. Nelson Grote as president—had gotten more than just a compassion-

*The Wilma E. Grote Symposium for the Advancement of Women was named in honor of MSU's eleventh First Lady, left. Presenting her recognition in 1991 was Judy R. Rogers, associate vice president for academic affairs and a 30-year member of the English faculty.*

ate, popular, fatherly type who had come back home to Morehead to retire. Having studied at the feet of Adron Doran, he had developed his own brand of "builder mentality." Grote was a rebuilder, restoring the physical beauty of the campus and improving its major facilities. He worked hard and left his mark by correcting what he regarded as deterioration of the physical plant. The campus was thus revitalized physically as Grote improved its utility system and remodeled its old buildings. By helping to reestablish a strong presence for Morehead State in the Kentucky legislature, he made his effectiveness obvious to anyone who examined the amount of capital investments that were made on the Morehead campus during the five years of his administration. One must go back more than two decades to the Doran tenure to see anything comparable to that kind of state money being spent on Morehead State University.

Accompanying MSU's dramatic increase in students was a tremendous growth in its number of alumni. Furthermore, the progress and good will created by the Albright-Grote era inspired more alumni to become active. Bill Redwine, executive director of the Morehead State Alumni Association, described the association as a mere caretaker group before President Doran's arrival in 1954. The first executive director, Billy Joe Hall, had been hired in 1959. Alumni Tower was dedicated to former students on October 7, 1967, and the present Alumni Association building was constructed in 1973 with contributions from former students. From 1985 to 1988, the number of active MSU alumni more than doubled, from 839 to 1,986. Although Homecoming and Founders Day were the main alumni events, activities increased enough throughout the years to keep Redwine, an assistant director, two secretaries, and two computer operators busy.

In February 1990 the Board of Regents approved another change in University organization. The College of Professional Studies was broken up into a College of Education and Behavioral Sciences and a College of Business. On June 22, 1990, the Board of Regents approved a 14 percent increase in faculty salaries for the 1990-91 academic year. Referring to the increase in salaries as "a giant step toward addressing a problem since I came here," Grote told the Regents that the new budget represented the highest percentage of the general budget which had been allocated for instruction at Morehead State—45.8 percent—in over ten years. That same board meeting also promoted Keith Kappes from executive assistant for university relations to vice president for university advancement. Having been at MSU since 1969, Kappes had become so familiar with the media, legislators, school superintendents, and corporate and business leaders that he often seemed like a "third arm" to presidents. Since the late Fifties, Morehead State has been fortunate to have the services of two of the state's most effective public relations professionals in this field—Ray Hornback and Keith Kappes.

In 1990 MSU received reaffirmation of its accreditation from the Southern Association of Colleges and Schools. John C. Philley, interim vice president for academic affairs and dean of faculties, served as chair of the SACS steering committee, while Judy Rogers, dean of undergraduate programs, and Marc Glasser, professor of English, were co-directors for the self-study which involved efforts of over 140 faculty, staff, and students. Among the recommendations made by SACS were changes in the policy for determining graduate faculty status, development of a faculty evaluation process, and adoption of a campus master plan.

On September 21, 1990, the Regents approved a campus master plan which was designed to guide MSU's development well into the next century and to provide for a planned growth of up to 10,000 students. They also ratified a proposal for higher undergraduate admission standards at Morehead State; under these new standards, students were required to score a minimum of 12 on the American College Test (ACT). Two years later a new admissions policy increased ACT scores for incoming freshmen from 12 to 14.

Grote informed the board as early as May 27, 1990, of his desire to retire on June 30, 1992. In that meeting, the members voted to give him a one-year extension on his four-year contract. Grote's final complete year—1991—turned out to be another banner year. Founders Day was celebrated with the announcement that Ashland Oil Foundation had pledged $750,000 to MSU over a five-year period, the largest corporate contribution in the history of the institution. Half of that commitment came in the form of a challenge grant which had to be matched by MSU each year and which could increase its value to more than a million dollars. The first year's match was raised by a campus-wide campaign, "Excellence in All We Do," which brought in more than $80,000 from faculty, staff, and retirees over a six-week period.

The year 1991 featured significant activities. Morehead received a major grant of $782,950 from the U.S. Department of Education to fund four Educational Opportunity Centers in Boyd, Floyd, Morgan, and Rowan counties, including staffing each site with a full-time counselor and a part-time tutor.

*C. Nelson Grote, Morehead State's eleventh president, 1987-92.*

Over a three-year period, the money helped disadvantaged adults identify and attain such educational goals as community college degrees, university degrees, and completion of specific college courses or vocational-technical training. A gift of 72 boxes of Jesse Stuart's papers, including both published and unpublished manuscripts, travel journals, working papers, notes, and other documents was received. Valued at nearly $56,000, the documents were turned over to the Jesse Stuart Foundation by the late author's wife, Naomi Deane Stuart; the JSF then transferred these to the MSU Foundation. In furthering Grote's goal of internationalizing the curriculum, MSU featured its third visiting international scholar in as many

*Ronald G. Eaglin became Morehead State's twelfth President in 1992.*

years—Victoria Carrasco, a Fulbright Scholar-in-Residence who was a fine arts professor from Central University of Ecuador. The University also sponsored a visit of the Chinese Youth Goodwill Mission from Taipei. Finally, the Big Sandy Extended Campus Center opened in the Highlands Plaza Shopping Center near Prestonsburg Community College.

In spite of progress on so many fronts, major problems were left for President Grote's successor, including refining the system of faculty evaluations and merit pay, getting actively involved in the state's education reform movement, and attacking the deficit in financing athletics, especially football. Both Reinhard and Albright had called for scaling back athletics at Morehead State even if it meant dropping from Division I-AA to Divisions II or III or losing membership in the Ohio Valley Conference of which Morehead State was a charter member. However, the problem of financing athletics was not limited to Morehead State. A Faculty Senate committee report at Western Kentucky University noted that its athletic budget had grown by 141 percent from 1978-79 to 1987-88, whereas the institutional budget had increased by only 92 percent during that time. The only two public universities in the state with self-supporting athletic programs were the University of Kentucky and the University of Louisville. At any rate, Grote contended that a competitive athletics program assisted the school in recruiting non-athletes and affected its overall image. "It's important to our overall fund raising, not just athletics," he stated.

In 1987-88, the MSU general fund subsidized nearly 73 percent of athletics cost. It pumped $1,269,700 in institutional funds, or state, private, and campus-generated money into athletics, which had a $1,745,400 budget. At other Kentucky schools, the subsidies ranged from a low of 46.8 percent at Eastern to over 96 percent at Northern, according to figures the institutions submitted to the state Council on Higher Education. In 1981, the Prichard Committee, a citizens' group that studied education, had recommended that institutional general funds for athletics be phased out over a period of four years. A rough draft of Morehead State's self-study for the Southern Association (SACS) said, "The large increases in athletic expenditures over the past decade, despite conclusions from two past MSU presidents, outside consultants, and the media that funding for athletics is excessive, does not suggest to this committee that intercollegiate athletic policies concerning funding are in harmony with and supportive of institutional purposes." Referring to the 1987 Regents' mandate that the athletic department must raise 50 percent of its funds by 1990-91 as "unrealistic," Grote said he would propose that the athletics department raise only one-third of its budget. He stated that private donations for athletics had increased from about $54,800 in 1985-86 to about $105,892 in 1988-89. Projections called for that figure to hit $152,000 by 1991-92.

On May 6, 1989, the Board of Regents rescinded a 1987 policy dealing with financing intercollegiate athletics and approved a new one that provided a larger subsidy for sports. The new policy, recommended by Grote, raised the allowable subsidy to two-thirds of the athletics budget by 1991-92. A recent internal report had criticized the Grote administration for failure to move toward compliance with the 1987 policy. The new policy required the athletics department to raise at least a third of its annual budget by 1991-92 and put a 3.6 percent cap on state appropriations and tuition revenues which could be allocated to athletics. The president told the Board of Regents that Morehead State could not unilaterally reduce athletic costs without accompanying action by the OVC. A report by the Athletics Committee concluded that complying with the 1987 policy would necessitate withdrawal from the OVC and produce problems in scheduling games as well as affect the athletics image of the institution. Thus, failure to resolve the long-standing problem of what to do with the athletics budget continued.

The faculty never seemed to grasp how to assess this president. On the one hand, Grote had responded to strong urging by the board that he greatly increase the salaries of teachers. On the other, he seemed to remain focused on the physical aspects of the campus, taking time and energy away from the academic operation. Hence, he left himself open to criticism from the faculty that he was not aggressive enough in strengthening the academic development of the University community. Failure to be ego-driven worked in two different directions for Grote. While many found this leadership style refreshing, some regarded his constant delegation of power as indicative of not being in charge. These individuals felt that the academic vice president had the least influence among vice presidents in the Grote years.

Overall, the Grote term was upbeat with one really tough budget year. When he neared the end of his presidency, MSU faced some management problems precipitated by having too many students and not enough money—coupled with a state budget reduction. Especially in that final year, the president had to make hard choices, including elimination of some positions. Many of these difficult decisions, however, were left to his successor. Overall, Grote's warmth and friendly nature helped to promote an era of good feeling on the campus; he loved the University and the people of the region. Even in retirement, the Grotes moved back to Morehead after living in Lexington three years.

## Ronald G. Eaglin: The "Janus" President

Rarely has a president given a Board of Regents a two years' notice of his retirement as did Grote. Both the board and the national search committee which it appointed made superb use of this time to conduct what some have regarded as the most professional search in the history of Morehead State University. Even when faced with the old ploy of using a national search as a cloak for appointing an "insider" who had been favored from the beginning, the committee asserted itself with such forcefulness that its operational method might well serve as a model for future searches. The committee was meticulous in trying to maintain the integrity of the process by remaining free of the influence of narrow interests.

At the board meeting in March 1991, William R. Seaton, chairman, appointed a search committee, with Regent Wayne Martin, Lexington television executive and former MSU basketball coach, as its chairman. Other members of the group were Regents William Cofield and Charles Wheeler; Faculty Regent Alban Wheeler; Student Regent Chris Hart; Faculty Senate Chairmen Robert Lindahl and Robert Wolfe; Staff Congress Chairwoman Teresia Parker; Alumni President Ted Coakley; and Madge Baird, wife of former Regent John Baird. Alban Wheeler served as vice chairman of the committee.

With plenty of time to accomplish its task, the Presidential Search Committee developed a thoughtful, well-conceived plan for locating the best individual available and taking steps to insure that he/she would be accepted by the various constituencies of the University. Taking their work seriously, committee members read widely, consulted specialists in the field, and attended workshops on how to conduct national searches. Holding six public forums throughout the region and one with the MSU academic community

*Brother Jed Smock, an itinerant evangelist who travels the college circuit, has been a yearly visitor to the campus for more than 20 years.*

on campus proved to be a helpful procedure. Research indicated that a large number of candidates would be unduly cumbersome to interview effectively and would increase the probability that the best candidates would withdraw from the search. Therefore, the committee proposed to recommend approximately six candidates to the board. Heidrick and Struggles, Inc., a Chicago-based national executive search firm, was hired to assist the committee in supplying candidates, the first time in MSU history that such action had been taken. The committee accepted a suggestion by Seaton that it meet with Morehead State alumni organizations for their input on the type person needed to lead the institution.

On January 25, 1992, the Board of Regents was surprisingly unanimous in narrowing the field of presidential possibilities to three out-of-state candidates. These were Joseph W. Alexander, dean of the College of Veterinary Medicine at Oklahoma State University; J. Ronnie Davis, dean of the College of Business Administration at the University of New Orleans; and Ronald G. Eaglin, chancellor of Coastal Carolina College, which was part of the University of South Carolina system. Several members of the board had earlier expressed displeasure that no Kentuckian had been considered; in response Wayne Martin pointed out that of the 177 possible candidates only eight had been Kentuckians. From the three candidates, the Board of Regents chose Ronald G. Eaglin to be Morehead State University's twelfth president. The board was reportedly seeking an aggressive president, and this desire may have inclined them toward Eaglin. Others cited Eaglin's experience at the presidential level as the main reason he was selected over the other two candidates.

During his visit to campus, Eaglin said he believed that Morehead State University, based on its heritage and mission, should emphasize teacher education. Like the Roman god, Janus, with two faces, Eaglin was already balancing Morehead State's past with its future, a paramount theme of his administration. He warned that expectations from the next president should take into consideration that MSU, along with other universities in Kentucky, was facing a "double whammy" in the form of a second five percent cut in Governor Brereton C. Jones' proposed 1992-94 budget. MSU's budget had already been cut by five percent in October 1991 because of the state's declining revenues. Eaglin indicated that the budget would be his most immediate concern.

Eaglin had been chancellor of the University of South Carolina's Coastal Carolina College at Conway since 1985. He had served as vice chancellor for academic affairs at USC's Spartanburg campus from 1974 to 1985, where he was also professor of psychology. Earlier, he worked as Southeast regional director for the American College Testing Program, where he was responsible for handling ACT scores for half of the United States. He had also served as assistant dean of students at the University of Nebraska and as assistant director of residence halls at the University of Utah. Eaglin received his doctorate in educational psychology at the University of

Utah, a master's degree in student personnel administration at Southern Illinois University, and a bachelor of science degree in biology and mathematics at Southeast Missouri State University.

Under Eaglin's administration, Coastal Carolina College had become the fastest growing public institution in the state. In the course of that growth he had overseen expenditures of nearly $40 million in construction and renovation projects. Many on that campus had given him good marks as an administrator who was strong willed, yet adaptable and open. These individuals noted three of Eaglin's strengths: raising funds, building community relations, and making difficult decisions when necessary.

The President's Home has been the center for both family-related activities and public functions since the Eaglins' arrival. For one of the first times in history, a president's son (Ron, Jr.) was married in an intimate ceremony at the President's Home in 1994. Although involved as a wife and mother with four grown children—Ron, Jr., Lori, Mike, and Jeff—and three granddaughters (including Lori's twins), Bonnie is energetic, creative, and well-informed about what is expected of presidents' wives in the 1990s. Like Mignon Doran before her, Bonnie Eaglin has a high profile in terms of public life and assumes active roles in University and community affairs.

One of the most dynamic first ladies in the history of MSU, Bonnie is a capable leader as well as a doer of the nitty-gritty tasks necessary in handling various details of public functions, especially festive occasions. In addition to continuing the annual Holiday Party initiated by the Dorans, the Eaglins started the Spring Gala as a fund raiser intended to involve every MSU department. With the department of music leading the way, Spring Galas netted over $150,000 in their initial four years. Bonnie spearheaded Partnership Against Violent Environments (PAVE) to provide an umbrella for anti-violence in the Morehead area and to encourage other communities in the region to attempt a similar activity. Commitment to this program led her to become chairperson of the Committee on Safety. The First Lady has taken an active role in the beautification of the Morehead State campus. She worked closely with the president in the renovation of the Gold Room into a showplace for emphasis on heritage. She then undertook improvement of the Patti Bolin room in the Department of Human Sciences located in the Lloyd Cassity Building. She was also instrumental in helping the president establish the Kentucky Folk Art Cen-

*First Lady Bonnie Eaglin assists her husband in spearheading numerous annual events and community activities.*

ter. Heavily involved in efforts toward long range planning for city and county, the First Lady served on the Board for the Sister Cities program to settle upon a location, possibly in England, Costa Rica, Lithuania, or the Netherlands, to be a sister city for Morehead.

On July 1, 1992, his first day at work, Eaglin said he wanted "to emphasize academics, look into athletics, and raise more money through alumni contributions," wrote Kim Hamilton in the *Morehead News.* "When people think of teacher education in the state, I hope they'll think of Morehead State," Eaglin said. When it comes to fund raising, Eaglin asserted, "We need to diversify our income. We're 93 percent dependent on state funds. I would like to see us get down to 75 percent." Although the institution faced a financial crisis, Eaglin took time to survey the entire situation before making any major changes—unlike Reinhard's approach in the mid-Eighties. From the beginning, however, Eaglin stressed that limited resources might force Morehead State to do only those things which were feasible, since it was obvious that the institution could not be all things to all people.

At his first convocation in the fall semester of 1992, Eaglin told faculty and staff, "It's hats off, shape up, and be involved. There's a new grade called N-Y; it means not yet. The most caring thing we can do for a student who is not ready is to say, 'Go home and come back when you're ready.' I'm tired of ignoring behavior in students that is self-destructive. We have a responsibility to say what is right or what is wrong. We have to share the wisdom of our lives," Eaglin advised. Sounding parental, the president stated, "A student can't be successful if he's burning it at both ends. You can't drink all night, burn yourself into oblivion, and try to make it in class." Eaglin told the faculty, "The continued success of this institution does not rest in the Howell-McDowell Building in administration; it resides in each and everyone of you." With an emphasis on Morehead State's heritage the new president considered it highly significant that three former presidents were able to attend the opening convocation: Adron Doran, Morris Norfleet, and A. D. Albright.

In August 1992 the Alumni Association reported that MSU had graduates living in every state. Over one-half of its graduates lived in Kentucky— 18,528—followed by neighboring Ohio, 4,170; Florida, 836; Indiana, 510; Virginia, 361; and New York, 312. Beyond the Mississippi River, Texas led with 255, followed by California with 205. Seventeen resided in Hawaii and thirteen in Alaska. Two-thirds of the alumni in Kentucky were in MSU's 22-county service region.

Fall enrollment topped 9,100 students in 1992, which represented a 2.2 percent increase. Morehead State officials were even more excited over the possibility that the entering freshman class might be one of the best prepared in recent history. The University's Admissions Index reflected an increase over that of the previous fall. Eaglin expressed more concern with quality than with quantity of students. In spite of an enrollment increase, an 8.4 percent reduction in the budget forced the University to operate with some $5.3 million less in funds than had been available the previous year.

Eaglin told the September 1992 board meeting that he wished to upgrade the division of academic affairs by adding the word "Executive" to the title. He named interim vice president John Philley as executive vice president for academic affairs. Indicating that such a change was not intended as window dressing, Eaglin explained, "We must focus our attention on academics; everything else is peripheral to that mission."

The year 1992 witnessed many changes. One of the most significant developments occurred when legislation was enacted to alter the selection process of board members by making it more difficult for presidents to control who was named. Also, the MSU board took on its first international flavor when SGA president Chando Mapoma, a senior from Zambia, was sworn in as student body representative. Mapoma was also the first international

*A gift of $1,000,000 from Lexington philanthropist Lucille Caudill Little is the largest in the school's history.*

student to head the student body. MSU established its Clearinghouse for School Services to assist in meeting challenges presented by the Kentucky Education Reform Act (KERA). Thanks to a matching grant from the National Science Foundation, students, under the direction of Ben Malphrus, associate professor of science, began construction of the Morehead Radio Telescope, allowing Morehead to have the state's only radio telescope used for research and educational purposes by science teachers and students throughout the commonwealth.

Faculty and administrative evaluations were incorporated by the Eaglin administration. Three percent across-the-board raises in 1993-94 were the last such increases handed out at MSU before a merit system came into being. A policy endorsing merit pay had been approved in 1991, to become effective only if the University had money for raises above three percent. Morehead State's new policy would go into effect, regardless. On June 23, 1994, the Board of Regents gave its approval to begin merit pay. The new contracts would allow for a two percent increase across the board, two percent merit pay, and one percent for promotions, change in rank, or other enhancements, including a confirmation of rank provision intended to bring all MSU ranks up to the level of other institutions in the state. On November 19, 1993, the Board of Regents also approved a form for assessing University administrators. The president henceforth would be evaluated by all faculty and staff biannually; other major administrators, annually.

In 1993 MSU completed its first new classroom construction in more than a decade—an addition to Lappin Hall. Governor Jones came to campus for its opening and to announce that the University would receive a $542,000 grant to purchase and renovate the old Union Grocery Building on Railroad Street to become the new home of the Kentucky Folk Art Center. The first schoolwide reunion of students and faculty from Breckinridge School took place in July, 1993. Nearly 700 alumni and 28 former faculty members were among the 1,100 on hand for the three-day event. The newly-established Breckinridge School Society raised over $65,000 to endow a scholarship fund for descendants of Breck alumni.

In January 1994 MSU received a $1 million gift from Lucille Caudill Little, Lexington philanthropist. Little had attended Morehead Normal School and taught at Morehead State in the 1930s. She was the daughter of Daniel Boone Caudill, a former Rowan Circuit judge, and the sister of Dr. Claire Louise Caudill, Morehead physician and one of the founders of St. Claire Medical Center. This largest single donation ever received from an individual will benefit the College of Humanities, especially MSU's fine arts programs. In recognition of the gift the board approved the renaming of the College of Humanities as the Caudill College of Humanities.

During spring commencement in 1994, President Eaglin introduced "a new sound from an ancient instrument—the bagpipe." He told the crowd of 7,000 at the Academic-Athletic Center that the bagpipe was symbolic of the heritage of Eastern Kentuckians who came from Scotland and Ireland. The 960 graduates joined more than 38,000 MSU alumni nationwide and abroad.

Fall semester 1994 enrollment dipped to 8,697. The number of full-time students also dropped from 6,947 to 6,675. John C. Philley, executive vice president for academic affairs, gave three reasons for the decrease: sluggishness of the regional economy, an increase in the minimum index for unconditional admission, and a smaller pool of high school students from which to draw. Eaglin identified the dormitory situation as potentially a major drain as only 3,000 students were living in residence halls, a decrease from 3,300 the previous fall, resulting in a $530,000 budget shortfall. Therefore, to insure that MSU would not henceforth overestimate income and then be forced to make cuts, the Eaglin administration proceeded to adopt conservative budget projections.

Morehead State University was fortunate in 1994 to have the only higher education capital construction project authorized and funded by the General Assembly—the second phase of Lappin Hall. Eaglin gave Vice President Kappes significant credit for this legislative accomplishment. This project included renovation of the original building. The first phase of renovation, completed in 1993, involved the construction of a 33,000-square-foot addition. In November 1994 the Morehead City Council gave approval for MSU to assume ownership of a portion of Third Street for the construction of a memorial plaza between Lappin Hall and the Combs Building to honor those who have enriched the school's heritage. This construction is part of the overall renovation project of Lappin Hall.

The year 1994 featured varied milestones at Morehead State University. Staff members elected Gene Caudill, administrative superintendent in the Office of Physical Plant, as their first member to the Board of Regents under legislation enacted by the 1994 General Assembly. The institution received a Special Award of Merit from the Council for Advancement and Support of Education (CASE) in honor of materials prepared for the University's first Spring Gala, "A Musical Fantasy Cruise." *Focus,* a first-time publication, also received a Special Award from CASE as a magazine devoted to faculty research and creative production. WMKY, the university's public radio station, and its staff members earned numerous awards throughout the year for excellence in news and sports reporting. For the fourth consecutive year, varsity cheerleaders, coached by Myron Doan, brought back the Division I title from the National College Cheerleading Championships held in San Diego, California. President Eaglin launched the Heritage Campaign, a multi-phased project aimed at honoring individuals who have served MSU for significant periods of time and made contributions to MSU's history. The first phase involved renovating the Gold Room, using native hardwoods, into a space where suitable recognition can be given those who have received awards for teaching, research, public service, creative expression, and leadership. The second phase will involve the development of an outdoor memorial plaza to honor those who have served the University since its beginning in 1887. The final phase will be an on-going expansion of the University Memorial Fund which underwrites scholarships in memory of deceased faculty and staff members. MSU recaptured the OVC's 1993-94 Academic Achievement Banner, having won in 1987, 1988, and 1993. Private giving reached an all-time high of nearly $1.8 million. Lucille Little gave her first $250,000 to establish the $1 million W. Paul and Lucille Little Endowment Fund, and $150,000 came from the Ashland Oil Foundation.

The MSU Foundation has enjoyed many highlights after its birth in 1979. As budget cuts surfaced in the administration of Governor John Y. Brown, President Norfleet and seven alumni (Lloyd

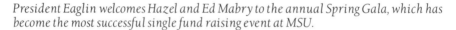

*President Eaglin welcomes Hazel and Ed Mabry to the annual Spring Gala, which has become the most successful single fund raising event at MSU.*

Cassity and Dolores Redwine, Ashland ; John Graham, Rondal Hart and Helen Northcutt, Morehead; Billy Joe Hall, Mount Sterling; and J. Phil Smith, Jackson) organized the MSU foundation to serve as the "umbrella" for all University fund raising activities and assets. In 1980 Mr. and Mrs. Alfred Hodgson of Lancaster, Virginia, established the first MSU endowment with a $10,000 scholarship gift for students from Stark in Elliott County. J. Dan Lacy of Russell became the first citizen to serve as board chair. In 1985 the Foundation relocated to the Palmer House. Foundation-managed endowments surpassed $1 million in assets in 1992. The following year, the MSU Foundation acquired the former Union Grocery property as future home of the Kentucky Folk Art Center. An artist was commissioned in 1993 to paint presidential portraits for display in the Heritage Room in the Adron Doran University Center. Endowment assets exceeded $2 million; B. Proctor Caudill of Morehead became board chair. In 1995 the Breckinridge School Scholarship Fund topped $100,000 as the largest group-funded endowment. Endowment assets exceeded $3 million the following year. In 1997 the Kentucky Folk Art Center was completed, and total endowment assets held by MSU and the Foundation topped $4 million.

As part of Morehead State University's celebration of its 75th birthday as a state institution, a 40-foot bell tower was constructed in the spring of 1997. Lucille Caudill Little, a native of Rowan County and a former teacher at Morehead State, "wanted a way to honor her husband and to instill in future generations what she describes as the essentials of life—justice, love, service, and wisdom," according to President Ronald Eaglin. Built of red brick and limestone like Morehead State's earliest buildings, the bell tower, located adjacent to University Boulevard and in front of Camden-Carroll Library, will become a landmark for generations to come.

In 1995 President Eaglin continued his efforts to maintain a student body of 8,600 since a drop significantly below this number would be "putting us on a path that is dangerous." The University, therefore, announced a plan providing a Tuition Assistance Grant (TAG), on February 10, 1995, to increase its recruitment of out-of-state students by using a scholarship program to counter an expected decline in the number of students from Eastern Kentucky, who in the past had made up about 80 percent of the enrollment.

A major highlight of 1995 occurred in March, when Morehead State's original campus was designated a Historic District and included in the National Register of Historic Places by the U.S. Department of the Interior and the Kentucky Heritage Council. Nine buildings, constructed from 1926 to 1932 at the center of the campus make up the 12-acre district: President's Home, Senff Natatorium, Button Auditorium, Fields Hall, Camden-Carroll Library, Allie Young Hall, Rader Hall, Thompson Hall, and Breckinridge Hall. President Eaglin stated, "We recognize the proud heritage symbolized by these majestic Collegiate Gothic architectural style buildings which were purposefully designed to illustrate and encourage academic pursuit."

In November, 1995, MSU's Percussion Ensemble captured top honors in the National Marching Forum at the Percussive Arts Society International Convention in Phoenix, Arizona. The 45-student Percussion Ensemble also won first place in "best bass drums" and "best pit." They were competing against all university marching percussion groups regardless of the size of the institution. Morehead State's ensemble, under the direction of Frank Oddis, associate professor of music, also won the national title in 1988 and 1992.

The beautiful MSU campus was hit by a tornado which swept through Rowan County on May 18, 1995. Although dozens of stately old trees, some of which dated to the beginning of the school, were uprooted by winds, buildings escaped serious damage. The worst structural havoc occurred when a 20-foot square section of the Academic-Athletic Center roof was ripped off by the storm. On a brighter side, the varsity cheerleaders claimed the national title in Division I for the fifth consecutive year. The squad won six of the last eight times it had competed. Myron Doan, cheerleader director, pointed out that Morehead State was the first institution ever to win five consecutive titles in any of the National College Cheerleading Championships divisions.

In spite of all these activities, the most attention was focused on deliberations over financial problems related to Morehead State's football program. President Eaglin tackled this situation head-on, something which had not been done since President Charles Spain introduced the topic six presidents earlier. On January 21, 1994, Eaglin told faculty and staff that football scholarships could be eliminated by 1998. He stated his intention to request permission from the Ohio Valley Conference to enter into another football league while remaining in the OVC for competition in other sports. Eaglin stated that gender equity as mandated by the NCAA was a major factor which influenced his decision. The University was spending about $400,000 on women's sports and $1.3 million on men's programs annually, according to Steve Hamilton, athletic director.

Morehead State's intercollegiate athletics budget reported deficit spending of $1.3 million during 1994-95. The football program had a $372,740 spending deficit. Men's and women's basketball programs showed deficit spending of $252,905. The largest expenditures were for salaries: $187,496 for football, $233,978 for both basketball teams, and $157,278 for other sports.

In January 1995 the OVC presidents, by a 7-2 vote, rejected MSU's request to remain in the conference while dropping out of football competition. Instead, they approved a motion requiring all member teams to fund a minimum 75 percent of the maximum number of scholarships permitted for I-AA football. This policy would require Morehead State to maintain 47 of the maximum of 63 scholarships in order to stay in the OVC.

In response to the presidents' vote, Board Chair Seaton established, at Eaglin's request, a 13-member committee on February 1,

1995, to chart the future direction of the athletics program. The board entrusted the committee with four tasks: to analyze the financial pressures facing the athletics program; to determine MSU's legal rights as a charter member of the OVC and other options regarding conference affiliation; to correlate strategic planning in athletics with institutional planning efforts; and to develop specific recommendations toward establishing at least a five-year course for athletics within the framework of NCAA Division I-AA.

The Board of Regents approved a special committee report on May 12, 1995, directing Eaglin to continue negotiations with the OVC concerning "need-based" scholarships for football. The report undergirded Eaglin's campaign to secure permission from the OVC to play football on a reduced scholarship basis outside the conference. Both Eaglin and Seaton stated that MSU was trying to save the football program rather than get rid of it. The committee called for Morehead State to affiliate with another conference if the OVC turned down Eaglin's proposal again.

On June 1, 1995, when the OVC presidents convened in Morehead, prospects for conference approval of Eaglin's plan seemed only slightly better than in January, when it was overwhelmingly rejected. In a surprise move, the presidents unanimously approved a resolution which permitted Morehead State to drop out of conference football, beginning in 1996-97, while continuing its participation in all other OVC sports. In return, Morehead State agreed to forfeit its share—some $40,000 annually at that time—of future NCAA basketball tournament revenue beginning with the NCAA Tournament in 1997. The University promised to honor all current football scholarships to their conclusion. By shifting to "need-based" scholarships, Eaglin expected an overall reduction of $450,000 in savings in four years. Both Eaglin and Dan Beebe, OVC Commissioner, said that Morehead State's contributions as a charter member of the 47-year-old organization was a major factor in explaining why the presidents agreed to this compromise proposal.

Although it is not possible to pass judgment on the current administration in its totality, some projections can be made on the basis of what it has accomplished thus far. Critics describe Eaglin as taking unilateral action on the football question without making significant efforts to bring the people along with him. Some faculty claim that Eaglin, backed by Seaton, greatly lowered morale at MSU with the introduction of faculty evaluation, which they view as a way to hasten oldtimers out of their positions. Others argue that he plays favorites by giving special support to select academic departments. Eaglin has been criticized for finding money for such things

*Alumnus Jerry Gore, minority student affairs director, is a national leader in preserving artifacts of the "Underground Railroad" anti-slavery movement in the area of his hometown of Maysville.*

*All official MSU photographs from the 60's into the early 90's were taken either by George Burgess, bottom, or Martin Huffman, top. Many appear in this book.*

as the Kentucky Folk Art Center and the Wellness Program while cutting back on other activities. The claim is made by critics that he is unduly concerned about the inadequacies of finances and thus has excessively pared down University offerings and discouraged development of new programs.

On the other hand, supporters credit Eaglin with turning around the academic side of the institution. From the beginning, he made it clear from the top down that quality teaching and learning would serve as the foundation of the institution. Improving the academic side of the University has come first even when it meant taking money from previously funded programs. Such an important thing as caring for the physical plant could not be allowed to create a shortage of funds for the academic community. In spite of his love for sports, Eaglin decided that academics could not be shortchanged by athletics at a time when finances would not permit the institution to do it all. He immediately created the position of executive vice president for academic affairs and filled this important post with the appointment of John Philley, who by the time of his retirement in 1997, had begun the stability the office had once known under Dean Lappin. Eaglin's style of leadership demanded that each departmental chairperson be strong enough to run his or her own department. Next, MSU "retooled" in terms of bringing in new deans. And it soon became evident that the president was more excited over quality of students than over quantity.

Eaglin appears comfortable with delegating authority as he operates on a somewhat corporate model. He has made the institution stronger by letting everyone do what he/she is paid to do, particularly on the administrative side.

Eaglin is committed to external relationships. He has a high profile in the region, probably second only to that of Adron Doran in terms of visibility, involvement at the state level, and contact with important people. This accomplishment is remarkable in view of the fact that Eaglin is a reserved person who at times does not seem to enjoy the political side of a university president's role. However, the president is the most productive private fund raiser in the history of Morehead State, forever challenging friends to help make this a first-class institution rather than one totally at the mercy of state dollars. In keeping with his own challenge, Eaglin negotiated the largest individual gift in the history of Morehead State University, the Little endowment. MSU is now considering embarking on a five-year major funds campaign.

In spite of being an "outsider," Eaglin recognizes and emphasizes the importance of the institution's heritage. He is working diligently and creatively on the preservation of Morehead State's legacy. The president sensed the need for people to know their own history—both the good and the bad—and more specifically how Morehead State got to where it is. Hence, part of the MSU legacy is being preserved through the writing of MSU's history and the expansion of its archives. Determined that the history of the institution should be written, Eaglin was satisfied to have his own administration omitted until he was convinced that MSU's heritage would be incomplete without inclusion of the twelfth president. No efforts were subsequently made to control what was written. Soon after he became president, Eaglin recognized the significance of 1887 as the birth date of the school rather than 1922 and changed the date on the obelisk at the entrance to the campus.

President Eaglin is boldly decisive when it means improving the health of the institution. In spite of criticism leveled at him, he made one of the most daring decisions ever in his commitment to slay the athletic dragon in order to get a handle on where dollars are being spent in the financing of college athletics. The institution is perhaps the strongest today that it has ever been—in terms of external support, internal commitment, and the professional quality of administration, faculty, staff, and students.

Eaglin stands out as one of the most professional among those who have served as president of Morehead State. In the same general time period when he was selected through a national search, a friend of the governor was being installed as president at the University of Kentucky—What a throwback to the past! Perhaps Morehead State was growing up!

## Faculty Recognition

Faculty from three areas received over half of the 57 academic awards from 1964 to 1997. These included geography, government, and history (11), covered in the last chapter; the sciences (10); and English (9). Jack Whidden (physics) was among those professors honored in the sciences, winning the Distinguished Faculty Award in 1978. For many years, Whidden was director of MSU's former planetarium which he constructed. Prior to becoming a faculty member in 1968, Whidden was an aerospace technologist with the National Aeronautics and Space Administration at Langley Research Center in Hampton, Virginia. In 1981, Ted Pass (biology) was named Distinguished Researcher. He established the MSU Water Testing

Laboratory in 1979 and continued to serve as its director. Pass also was coordinator of the University's Medical Technology program and was overseer of the Allied Health Education System program, providing clinical experiences for MSU's medical technology students and making them more competitive for advanced educational opportunities. Pass was also a recipient of the 1996 Distinguished Service Award.

David Hylbert (geology), Distinguished Researcher in 1982, was recognized as one of the top researchers in the field of coal mine safety. After conducting a detailed survey of the coal industry in Eastern Kentcuky for the Appalachian Coal Mining Institute, he served as Project Director for contracts between the U.S. Bureau of Mines and MSU from 1973-81. His research dealt with geologic aspects of coal mine roof control. Howard Setser (biology) won the Distinguished Faculty award in 1983. In addition to his personal research regarding plant life in Eastern Kentucky, he supervised numerous student research projects in the same subject area. Setser also served as a consultant to the U.S. Forest Service on the flora of the Daniel Boone National Forest. David J. Saxon (biology), was recipient of the Distinguished Teacher Award in 1994. A faculty member since 1967, he served as an adivsor for students in the pre-medical program which, over the years, experienced a higher than average student acceptance rate into medical school. His recent research was in platelets and factors associated with atherosclerosis.

A highly-visible couple served as professors of English. Judy Rogers, associate vice president for academic affairs and dean of undergraduate programs, was selected as an American Council on Education (ACE) Fellow for 1995-96. The program is designed to strengthen leadership in higher education by identifying and preparing promising faculty and staff members for major administrative roles in colleges and universities. Before retiring in 1997, to become vice president of Georgetown College, Rogers frequently chaired site visitation teams for the Southern Association of Colleges and Schools (SACS) and was MSU's liaison to that agency. She and her husband, Glenn C. Rogers, also an MSU professor of English, are co-authors of two textbooks dealing with developmental learning of English. A faculty member at MSU since 1967, Glenn Rogers was named the 1994-95 Distinguished Teacher Award honoree. He was one of seven leaders at a 1995 symposium on critical thinking conducted as part of national Collegiate Honors Conference. Committed to the art of teaching, he worked hard to make Shakespeare and other pre-18th century authors come alive for his students. Glenn also retired in 1997 after 30 years at MSU.

Mary Jo Netherton (French) received both the Distinguished Teacher Award (1993) and the Distinguished Service Award (1994). She is director of MSU's Eastern Kentucky Regional Foreign Language Festival. As advisor of the Chi Omega sorority, she was a two-time recipient of the University's Greek Advisor of the Year Award for her work with that sorority. She also received the sorority's national Award for Excellence. During its 25th anniversary celebration, the MSU chapter endowed a $15,000 scholarship in her name. She is active at the local, state and national levels with the national Association of Anorexia Nervosa and Associated Disorders.

Philosophy, one of the smallest departments, excels in quality. Frank Mangrum who taught at Morehead State from 1959 until his retirement in 1996, served as departmental chairman for 20 years until the department lost its separate identity in the University's reorganization in 1984. Mangrum received the Distinguished Faculty Award in 1968-69 and served as MSU's first faculty member of the Board of Regents. George M. Luckey Jr., professor of philosophy at Morehead State since 1961, received the Distinguished Teacher Award in 1990-91. He became director of the Academic Honors Program in 1989 and served as faculty coordinator for MSU's Faculty/Staff Professional Development Program in the 1990s. Luckey has also been active in the critical thinking movement at national, regional, and local levels. Since 1981, Luckey has presented papers or conducted

*John C. Philley retired in 1997 as executive vice president for academic affairs after 37 years of service to the institution which included vice president, college dean, department chair and professor of geoscience.*

workshop sessions at more than 38 meetings throughout the United States.

The music department traditionally has had great success in bringing students to Morehead State from distant places. Professor Larry Keenan has taught keyboards at MSU since 1967. He has won nineteen piano and organ competitions and was national champion in the Professional Organists Division of the Yamaha Electone Organ Festival and represented the United States at the international Festival in Japan with his original composition and improvisations. Keenan spent 30 seasons as the organist and associate music director for *The Stephen Foster Story* in historic Bardstown.

R. Jay Flippin Jr., associate professor of music, earned the 1995-96 Creative Productions Award, which was established in 1992 by the MSU Research and Creative Productions Committee. Flippin, who joined the music faculty in 1969, is a "musician's musician" as he excels in every area from jazz to classical and from arranging to composition. The keyboardist also writes advertising jingles and

*The W. Paul and Lucille Little Bell Tower, financed by a $175,000 gift from Mrs. Little, was dedicated in 1997 to the memory of Mr. Little.*

video post-scores. His most memorable jingles have been "We do chicken right" for Kentucky Fried Chicken and "We're American Airlines." Flippin has received several awards from the American Advertising Federation for his work. He has performed with numerous well-known recording artists from Wilson Pickett to Tom Jones and from Doc Severinson to Peggy Lee. Equally at home in the classroom or recording studio, Flippin is associate conductor, accompanist, and arranger for the Lexington Singers and keyboardist for the Lexington Philharmonic Orchestra.

For more than two decades, James Ross Beane, professor of voice and conducting at MSU, has served as director of the Lexington Singers, one of the oldest continuously operating choruses of its kind in the nation. A member of the MSU faculty since 1959, he also serves as conductor of the Concert Choir and Chamber Singers. Recipient of the 1976 Distinguished Faculty Award, Beane has served as festival conductor in seven states.

Earle L. Louder has been recognized for both his ability as a teacher and a musician. In 1987 Louder was named MSU's Distinguished Faculty Award recipient and was the Kentucky Music Education Association's Teacher of the Year in 1988. As a euphonium soloist with the U.S. Navy Band in Washington, D.C., for twelve years, he toured the nation 16 times and played at the inaugurations of presidents Dwight D. Eishenhower, John F. Kennedy, and Lyndon B. Johnson. In 1968 Louder left the Navy Band to begin his teaching career at Morehead State.

Christopher Gallaher, chair of the music department, was the 1996-97 recipient of the Distinguished Creative Productions Award. He has had over 40 pieces of music published, including both originals and arrangements. Gallaher has performed with major entertainment luminaries including 250 performances as trumpet player with Johnny Mathis and the late Henry Mancini combined. He once conducted for the *Bob Hope Show* and did an eight-day tour with Elvis Presley the year before the latter's death.

William J. Layne, associate professor of theater, whose creativity is on display constantly in his role as MSU Theater's scene designer and technical director, earned the 1994-95 Distinguished Creative Productions Award. The Morehead native became a member of the faculty in 1971. He has directed several plays and designed 18 university productions as well as shows for the Morehead Theatre

Guild and the Jenny Wiley Summer Theatre, Geogetown College, Ashland Community College, and Actors Guild of Lexington. Co-author and director of "First Shots of Rage," a play based on Rowan County's Martin-Tolliver feud, he helped establish a summer theater program on campus and later at Cave Run Lake during the 1970s and developed an MSU Theatre Ensemble which toured Eastern Kentucky elementary and high schools for ten years.

The department of communications has featured talented professors including Harlen L. Hamm, who personified service to MSU in various ways. In 1995, this professor of speech was chosen as a recipient of the Founders Day Award, the University's highest service award, which was established in 1978 by the Board of Regents. He began his career at MSU in 1965, teaching speech and theatre at University Breckinridge School. Over his three decades of classroom teaching, Hamm impacted the lives of thousands of students. Hamm coordinated MSU's forensics program, known as one of the best in the nation. He also founded and led the Kentucky Educational Speech and Drama Association for several years. He has done much to promote and enhance speech/theatre education and has been recognized for his efforts at the national and state levels. Additionally, he raised thousands of dollars for student scholarships while giving countless hours to assist the University with other special projects such as the annual Holiday Party and the Spring Gala.

Shirley Gish (speech), whose extraordinary talents enriched so many lives, was selected as the 1993-94 Distinguished Creative Productions Award honoree. A multi-talented artist who is recognized nationally and regionally for her creativity, she is a writer, performer, producer, and director as well as a teacher. Gish developed several original scripts, such as "Me 'n Susie," a full-length play based on the life and community of Dr. C. Louise Caudill, which premiered in 1993 as a benefit for MSU's theatre program. A finalist for the Kentucky Advocates for Higher Education's 1992 Acorn Award for outstanding teaching, she has been awarded three residency grants from the Helene Wurlitzer Foundation in Taos, N.M., for playwriting and two MSU Creative Arts Grants.

Some individuals at Morehead State have combined excellent teaching with administrative leadership. A native of Breathitt County, Charles M. Derrickson served as a professor at MSU since 1965 and dean of the College of Applied Sciences and Technology from 1975 until his retirement in 1992. As professor of agriculture, he was recipient of the Distinguished Faculty Award in 1975. He has been a leader in economic and industrial development efforts for Morehead and Rowan County. After retiring from MSU, Derrickson added a capstone to his administrator-educator career by accepting the presidency of Lees College in his native Jackson. During his four years as president of Lees, he successfully led the institution out of financial turmoil and helped restore academic freedom, allowing the institution to become part of the University of Kentucky Commu-

*Coach Bill Baldridge's 1986 football team was the highest ranked squad in the institution's history. The Eagles won their first six games of the season and were ranked in the Top 10 of NCAA Division I-AA.*

*Matt Ballard was appointed as Morehead State's first coach after the school began moving to non-scholarship football.*

nity College system by the end of his presidency.

The MSU family includes an efficient staff which has meant much to the institution's growth and stability. After receiving his bachelor's and two master's degrees from Morehead State, Jerry Gore of Maysville has worked at MSU in some capacity for 25 years, including ten years as dorm director. Presently director of minority student affairs, he is charged with increasing enrollment and improving retention and graduation rates of American minority students. Since 1985, enrollment rates of American minority students at Morehead State have increased over 100 percent while retention rates have become the best in Kentucky. Gore helped found and coordinate the opening of Maysville's Underground Railroad Museum, whose exhibits document how runaway slaves came through Maysville on their way to freedom. He conducts 150 skits a year at Kentucky schools, demonstrating African heritage and illustrating lessons to be learned from the struggles of blacks in America. Gore also serves as an advocate in investigations of complaints filed by minority students which contain racial overtones. Gore was the 1996 winner of the Chrisitan Appalachian Project's

Peace Award, created to honor Kentuckians who exemplify Martin Luther King's commitment to faith and non-violent change.

Several MSU retirees continue to make contributions to the institution's well being. Described as a pioneer in elementary school accreditation in the southeastern United States, Mary Northcutt Powell was honored as recipient of the Founders Day award on Morehead State's 70th birthday in 1992. Her career at Morehead State began in 1955 when she served as a supervising teacher at University Breckinridge School. Later, she spearheaded an effort that resulted in Breckinridge becoming the first elementary school in Kentucky to be accredited by the Southern Association of Colleges and Schools. Her classroom expertise had been recognized in 1967 when she became the fourth recipient of the Distinguished Faculty Award. She then served twelve years as chair of the department of elementary and early childhool education. After her retirement in 1982, she continued to teach when needed. She was honored by SACS in 1989 as recipient of its Distinguished Educational Achievement Award for her work with the Commission on Elementary Schools.

## Athletics:  A Time of Transition

### Football:

During its 66 football seasons, Morehead State has enjoyed 23 winning seasons while compiling a record of 229-357-22. Only three of its thirteen coaches won at least as many games as they lost: Ellis T. Johnson (54-44-10, with a winning percentage of .551 in 14 seasons); John (Jake) Hallum (22-17-1, and .546 in four seasons); and Guy Penny (with a 39-39-2 record and a .500 winning percentage in nine years). The Eagles put together a 154-304-10 mark during their 48 seasons in the Ohio Valley Conference. Since becoming a charter member of the conference in 1948, Morehead State has had only twelve winning seasons.

From 1986 through 1995 MSU posted a record of 32-76-0 under three coaches:  Bill Baldridge, in his four remaining seasons, shaped a 17-26-0 mark; his overall record in six seasons was 20-45-0; Cole Proctor, in four seasons, registered a 15-29-0 record; and Matt Ballard, who has headed the program during three transition seasons when Morehead has been moving away from scholarship football, compiled a record of 8-23-0.

Predicted to wind up in the OVC cellar, the 1986 Eagles enjoyed the best start since 1964 on their way to a winning season.  For the first time in eleven years, Morehead defeated Marshall, 19-10.  After trailing James Madison, 17-0, quarterback Adrian Breen put the Eagles on the scoreboard with a 5-yard touchdown run with only 1:16 remaining in the first half.  Trailing 24-7 in the third quarter, Breen took to the air to pull out a 27-24 victory.  At Wichita State, place kicker Charlie Stepp gave the Eagles the lead with a school record 54-yard field goal.  But the Shockers stormed back with 35 unanswered points to take a 35-3 lead into the locker room at half time.  Refusing to fold even against a Division I team, Morehead State opened the second half with a 12-yard touchdown pass from Breen to tight end Matt Jensen.  Stepp's 47-yard field goal made the score 35-14.  Before the third quarter ended, D. D. Harrison carried the ball into the end zone to bring the score to 35-21.  With less than two minutes to go in the game, Breen connected with wide receiver Metry McGaughy, senior from Youngstown, Ohio, for a 30-yard touchdown to narrow the gap to 35-28.  Morehead State then successfully pulled an on-side kickoff which permitted Stepp to recover the football only 12 yards downfield.  Nine plays later, Breen tossed a 4-yard scoring pass to tight end Steve Collins.  After Stepp missed the extra point to tie the game, an off-sides penalty gave the Eagles a second chance.  An excited Baldridge later explained, "Adrian [Breen] grabbed me and said, 'Let's go for two; we're going to win this game.' When your kids are that determined and worked so hard to come back, you have to believe in them." Faking a hand-off, Breen then ran the ball in for two points and an unbelievable 36-35 win for the Eagles. Their defeat of Wichita State catapulted Morehead State to a ninth-place ranking among the nation's I-AA teams. The Eagles' performance against Wichita set "a national record with the greatest comeback in NCAA Division I football history."

Morehead State returned home for a game on its new Omniturf field against Kentucky State. After a long delay because of heavy rain and lightning, the Eagles trounced the Thorobreds, 33-10. Their 4-0 record moved Morehead up to 5th place in Division I-AA rankings. Before a Homecoming crowd of 8,000, Morehead captured its first OVC game in two years by defeating Austin Peay, 27-10. The Eagles trailed 7-6 at intermission after Jonathon Cage scored a touchdown which had been set up by McGaughy's 42-yard punt return with only 47 seconds remaining in the first half. Morehead then took the lead, 14-10, as Breen engineered a 74-yard

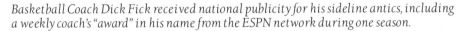

*Basketball Coach Dick Fick received national publicity for his sideline antics, including a weekly coach's "award" in his name from the ESPN network during one season.*

scoring drive. With a minute left in the game, Breen pitched the ball to Harrison on an apparent sweep to the right, then ran unnoticed toward the end zone where he received a perfect lob from Harrison for a touchdown.

Morehead's 28-20 defeat of Tennessee Tech was a costly one. Breen required ten stitches in his knee and had only one day of practice before the game with Akron, the top team in the OVC. Akron built up a 17-0 lead at intermission on its way to handing the Eagles their first loss, 30-7. Murray State then pounded the Eagles 45-11, and Middle Tennessee ran up a 24-7 score on a flooded field. But the "Comeback Kids" lived up to their name against Youngstown State. Trailing 24-20 with 29 seconds left in the game, Breen tossed a 7-

*Coach Larry Wilson directed his women's team to the National Collegiate Bowling Championship in 1989 in Las Vegas. Seated, from left, are Terri Kaeling and Lori Kizer. Standing are Lisa McGinnis, Sharon Owen, Coach Wilson and Kari Murph.*

*Coach George Sadler, whose name is synonymous with MSU tennis, retired in 1990. The tennis courts were named in his honor.*

yard touchdown pass to McGaughy to pull out a 27-24 win. After dropping a 23-6 final game to Eastern, the Eagles finished the season with a 7-4-0 record, while breaking five school records and one OVC mark.

During the remainder of the decade, Baldridge's best season—a 5-6-0 year which featured a 13-10 surprising victory over the University of Cincinnati Bearcats. Cole Procter, who had been Baldridge's teammate on Morehead's championship team in 1966, was selected as his Alma Mater's twelfth head football coach in 1990. A native of Meriden, Connecticut, Procter left the University of Utah, where he had been an assistant, to return to Morehead State and his first head coaching position on the college level. His first season reached its crescendo in the final two games, as the Eagles knocked off Murray, 69-6, and Eastern, 27-17. After eighteen years of frustration, the Eagles finally upset unbeaten Eastern in Hangar Stadium in Richmond, before 13,000 spectators at a time when the Colonels were ranked first in the nation! Chris Swartz hit 28 of 41 passes for 344 yards and two touchdowns. Jerome Williams, senior running back and MSU's all-time leading receiver, caught both touchdown passes and rushed for another touchdown to outscore Eastern, 18-17, singlehandedly. Trailing 17-7 going into the last quarter, the Eagles snatched victory from defeat by scoring 20 points in the final stanza. Morehead State won only a total of seven games during the next two seasons. The offensive star of the 1991 season was Darrin Harris, from Mount Sterling, who rushed for 964 yards and an average of 81.5 yards per game. Jim Appel, senior offensive tackle from Wilder, made the Academic All-American team. After dropping their first five games in 1992, the Eagles stunned Murray, 31-7, at Homecoming, with over 7,000 fans watching. Morehead State could do no better than 3-8-0 in 1993. The high point of the year was a 23-10 Homecoming victory over Austin Peay.

With plans underway to offer only need-based scholarships, Morehead State named Matt Ballard as interim head coach in 1994. Ballard had served as an assistant coach at Georgetown College, Gardner-Webb, and Morehead State and as head coach at Union College. The Eagles had posted only three winning seasons since 1970. Under no illusions, Ballard attempted to put sports into the proper perspective for a program like Morehead's, as he stated, "We want the football program to be a part of MSU and the players are no different than other students." As expected, the Eagles went 0-11-0; the UT-Martin game was the closest Morehead State came to victory as the Eagles lost 21-7. Before the beginning of the 1995 season, Morehead State had finalized its plans to compete on the level of non-scholarship football. The unexpected happened when the OVC presidents unanimously approved a plan for the school to remain in the Ohio Valley Conference to compete in all other conference sports except football.

### Men's Basketball:

Morehead State's basketball record has included 838 victories with 770 defeats. Since joining the Ohio Valley Conference in 1948, the Eagles have won 647 games while losing 615. Seven of

Morehead's ten coaches have had winning records; Len Miller had the best percentage record, with 28 victories and only 9 defeats during two years of the World War II era. Three coaches won over 100 games each: Ellis T. Johnson (196-158 in fifteen years; Bobby Laughlin (166-120 in twelve seasons); and Wayne Martin (130-120 in nine years). There were 39 winning seasons and five with an equal number of wins and losses.

Since 1986 MSU, with a record of 115-140, has been led by three head basketball coaches. In his one remaining season, Wayne Martin went 14-14; Tommy Gaither won 52 games while losing 64 in four seasons; and Dick Fick had 64 victories along with 101 losses in six seasons.

One of the most outstanding games of the 1986-87 season featured the Eagles' defeating Eastern, 87-82, before 6,500 fans, reportedly the largest crowd ever to attend a basketball game at Morehead. Other highlights of the 14-14 season included a 111-73 victory over Youngstown State, followed two nights later by a 62-52 win at Akron. Martin, dean of OVC coaches, resigned after the Eagles lost to Austin Peay, 78-76, in the OVC Tournament, to accept a position with the Bluegrass Broadcasting Company; eventually, he became president of WKYT-TV in Lexington. Bob McCann, a 6-9 senior from Morristown, New Jersey, was named OVC Player of the Year; he led the team in scoring and rebounding, averaging 18.6 points and 11.3 rebounds per game. McCann then made the first round NBA draft.

Tommy Gaither, head coach at Baptist College in Charleston, South Carolina, for the previous four years, was chosen over a field of 85 other applicants to succeed Wayne Martin. Gaither's 16-13 record in 1989-90 was Morehead State's first winning season in three years. Although Morehead posted an identical 16-13 record in 1990-91, the team finished in eighth place in the OVC, with a 4-8 record. The Eagles managed, however, to defeat Tennessee Tech, 88-83, in the OVC Tournament. Morehead's 89-61 loss to Murray in the tournament was Gaither's last game as coach.

Dick Fick coached the Eagles from 1991 to 1997. After serving as an assistant coach at Creighton University, Fick accepted the Morehead State head coaching position and posted a 14-15 mark in his first season. The year was highlighted by a strong showing against ninth-ranked University of Kentucky until the Wildcats pulled away 101-84 in a last minute scoring burst. Rick Pitino stated, "In my three years at Kentucky, I have not seen a tougher team than Morehead."

Fick's best season was in 1994-95 when Morehead finished 15-12 and was third in the OVC with a 10-7 record. He was named OVC Co-Coach of the Year, along with Frankie Allen, coach of Tennessee State. Tyrone Boardley, 6-7 senior forward averaging 16.1 points per game, was named to the All-OVC team. In the OVC Tournament, however, sixth-seeded Eastern Kentucky upset the third-seeded Eagles, 85-74, in Nashville.

### Women's Basketball:

The Lady Eagles are 333-321 in their 26-year history. Three of their five coaches have enjoyed winning records, led by Mickey Wells' 156-91 mark in nine years. There have been fourteen winning seasons and one with an equal number of wins and losses. Since 1986, Morehead State University has had a 98-146 record under its two coaches. Loretta Marlowe's six years within this era included 80 victories and 85 defeats; overall, she posted a 107-113 record in eight years. In five years, Janet Gabriel won 42 games while losing 92.

In 1986-87, the Lady Eagles finished 13-15 and tied for third place in the OVC. Kelly Stamper, who led the team in scoring, made the All-OVC team and set a school record with 27 consecutive free throws. A native of Wartburg, Tennessee, Loretta Marlowe played basketball at Tennessee Tech and then enrolled at Morehead State for her master's degree. Before becoming head coach, she served as an assistant basketball and softball coach at MSU. Morehead finished 15-13 in 1987-88 and placed fifth in OVC regular season play. The

*Through the 1996-97 season, Myron Doan, left, dean of students, had coached the MSU cheerleaders to eight national championships. He is shown here with 1992-93 team members Michael Cooper and Susan Lawson.*

Lady Eagles tied a school record for most points in a game—115—against West Virginia State. The three-point rule was added during the season. Kelly Downs, sophomore from Londonderry, Ohio, was the Lady Eagles' top scorer, averaging 15.3 points per game. Druecilla Connors, junior from Flemingsburg, scored 33 points in a 101-83 loss to Kentucky State. The following season, Morehead State improved to 18-10 and a third place finish in the conference, in spite of seven of its twelve players being freshmen. Connors was top scorer (14.0) and rebounder (8). Julie Magrane, freshman from Morehead, was the team's second highest scorer (13.5) and rebounder (7.8). Season highlights included victories over the University of Kentucky and the University of Louisville.

Morehead State dropped to 10-17 in 1989-90. The team finished with 13-14 and 11-16 marks in Marlowe's last two seasons. Janet Gabriel became the fifth head coach for the Lady Eagles in 1992-93. After playing three seasons at Penn State and one year at the University of Oklahoma, Gabriel coached Union College for two years. Morehead State won 10 and lost 16 during her first season, which included breaking a 21-game losing streak against Middle Tennessee with a 85-73 victory. The Lady Eagles dropped to 5-22 in 1993-94.

*Alumnus Ron Lewis (R-Ky.) is the first graduate to be elected to Congress. A native of Greenup County, he is chairman of the Republican Family Caucus in the U. S. House and represents the state's Second Congressional District.*

### Baseball:

Morehead State has posted a 908-688 record during the 59 years it has fielded a baseball team. There have been 41 winning seasons while six ended with the same number of wins as losses. Of its nine baseball coaches, seven posted winning records, led by Sonny Allen (226-137 in 14 years); Steve Hamilton (305-275 in 14 seasons); Rex Chaney (111-56 in 6 years); and Frank Spaniol (137-122 in 5 seasons). Since 1986, the Eagles have been led by two coaches, Steve Hamilton and Frank Spaniol.

Morehead State finished the 1989 season with an 18-26 record. A four-year starting pitcher, Scott Smallwood from Mount Sterling maintained a 3.72 grade point average and earned Academic All-American honors and was an OVC Scholar-Athlete. The Scholar-Athlete awards are given each year to male and female athletes who earn a letter in a varsity sport, maintain at least a 3.2 grade point average, and demonstrate leadership qualities in other campus activities. For the second year in a row, Morehead State won the Academic Achievement Banner, awarded to the conference team which scores the most points with its honor roll students and medal of honor winners.

Coach Frank Spaniol guided the Eagles to the OVC Championship in 1992. Picked by *Baseball America* as "Pre-Season Conference Player of the Year," Sean Hogan established several MSU records: complete games in a season (8), innings pitched in a season (98), strikeouts in a game (20), and strikeouts in a season (108). He tied the MSU record of appearances in a season (18). Mike Ferguson, another pitcher, posted a 7-3 record and a team high of four saves. Offensively, the Eagles were led by Butch Fulks, a junior, who hit .409, had 50 RBIs, and led the team with 10 home runs; Don Hackworth, sophomore first baseman, who hit .339 and had 40 RBIs along with nine home runs; and sophomore Devon Ratliff, who hit .339, had 23 RBIs, and led the team with four triples. In 1993 the Eagles jumped to 31-19, their most wins ever in one season, and won the OVC

Championship again. MSU went 29-25 in 1994 but lost the conference championship to Austin Peay.

### Non-Revenue Sports:

The Morehead State Lady Eagles volleyball team experienced tremendous success. They were regular season champions in the OVC in 1988 and 1989 and tied for the championship in 1987 and 1990. The Lady Eagles won two OVC Tournament Championships as well (1987, 1993). Jim McClellan was twice voted OVC Coach of the Year. In 1988 and 1989, Dayle Hammontree was honored as the OVC Player of the Year. Three Lady Eagles were selected as the OVC Tournament Most Valuable Player (Dayle Hammontree, 1988; Missy Blanford, 1989; and Shelly Rocke, 1993). Eighteen Lady Eagles were voted to the All-OVC team. The 1994 and 1995 Lady Eagles attained the highest team grade point average among all NCAA Division I schools in the nation, with a 3.52 mark.

In 1986-87, the Lady Eagles finished 28-14 against one of the toughest schedules ever, including Kentucky, Michigan, Georgia, Ohio State, and Eastern, all ranked in the top 20 in the nation. The Lady Eagles finished with a conference record of 8-2 and a second place trophy, losing to Eastern in the finals.

Coach Jim McClellan had his sixth winning season in a row in 1987, as the Lady Eagles captured the OVC championship from Eastern. Missy Blanford, who maintained a 3.9 grade point average in the nursing program, led the nation's collegiate volleyball players with the highest percentage of kills (.436) even though she was only 5'3" tall. She was named to the All-OVC tournament team .

In 1988 the talented Lady Eagles enjoyed a 34-8 season and went undefeated in the OVC, beating archrival Eastern to capture the OVC championship and landing three players on the OVC All-Tournament team. They ranked in the top ten of the South Region, in company with such teams as Texas, LSU, and Kentucky. In 1989 Morehead won its third OVC title in a row, and with a 25-9 record in

1990, repeated as OVC champions. MSU was again at the top in 1993. Shelly Rocke, junior from Elgin, Illinois, was named Most Valuable Player of the tournament.

Soccer proved to be a successful program from the time Mohammed Sabie introduced it as a varsity sport in 1964 until 1991 when it became a victim of the budget crunch. According to the 1988 *Raconteur,* Morehead was the first state school in Kentucky to field a varsity team. At that time, MSU had earned nineteen winning seasons and five state championships in the twenty-three years that soccer had been played as a varsity sport. Approximately 800 spectators turned out in Jayne Stadium for the first game in which the soccer team was permitted to use the new Omniturf football field. Coach Sabie asserted, "This sort of thing makes our team look good in the eyes of the visiting team." In 1988-89, playing schools like Ohio State, Miami University, Vanderbilt, Louisville, and Marshall, the Eagles finished 8-7-1. Coach Sabie was proudest of the game against Ohio State, which had a $40,000 budget and a full-time coach. The Eagles were tied at halftime, before losing, 2-0. MSU gave no scholarships but paid for the players' uniforms, equipment, medical insurance, and hotel and food expenses on trips for away games. Sabie explained that each player bought his own shoes since "there are so many kinds and each person should wear the ones he plays in best." In view of the success of soccer and the small cost to the University, the decision to drop the sport in the fall of 1991 because of budget cuts was puzzling!

The name of Coach George Sadler was synonymous with tennis from the time he arrived in 1966 until his retirement in 1990. He came to Morehead State from Campbellsville College, where he had served as basketball and tennis coach. During the time he coached men's tennis at MSU from 1968 to 1983, the Eagles compiled a record of 181-41 and captured the indoor OVC championship in 1972, which he regarded as the high point of his coaching career. His team was among the top three in the OVC during 11 of the 15 years he coached.  Although he retired from teaching in 1978, Sadler continued coaching for five more years.  After being involved in missionary work for his church, Sadler returned to Morehead, where he coached the women's tennis team on a part-time basis from 1986 to 1990.  His last team finished with a 16-4 record.  In 1991 MSU's tennis courts were named for Sadler.

"Club Sports," including such activities as  bowling, provided competition both at the regional and the national level.  With no MSU funding, the clubs must raise what money they need for competition.  The bowling team consists of fifteen members, male and female, who have made a name for Morehead State the past three decades.  Larry Wilson, a 1965 graduate of MSU who returned two years later to manage the bowling lanes, has served as the team's coach ever since.  The bowling club, partially funded by the Student Government Association, raises money by having steak dinners, working the concerts, and assisting with credit card registration.  Wilson explained that bowling started out in the Sixties with matches against Eastern.  "We would go there or they would come here when we had ball games.  We would give one another free tickets to the ball game, and the bowling was just a friendly game," he recalls.  But "we've gone hog wild ever since!"

Sharon Owen was selected as the Female Bowler of the Year by the Southern Intercollegiate Bowling Team Conference during two of the first three years the award was given.  Owen was also the first Eagle ever to be named an All-American Bowler.  Andy Parker, senior from Fairborn, Ohio, was also picked as the Male Bowler of the Year.  How incredible that both of the top honors were taken by Morehead, one of the smallest of the thirty schools from eleven states that were competing in the National Collegiate Championship games!

In 1988, the men's bowling team ranked third and the women's team fifth in the nation.  The teams had two All-Americans, Lisa McGinnis and Sharon Owen.  The following year the Morehead

*The 1997-98 basketball season will open with two new head coaches: Kyle Macy and Laura Litter.*

women became national champions as a result of winning over such teams as Penn State and West Texas. Sharon Todd, senior from Bowling Green, was named Most Valuable Player and first team All-American; she and Lori Kaiser made the All-Tournament Team.

The MSU women's team finished second in the nation in 1990. Kari Murph, junior from Dayton, was named Collegiate Bowler of the Year as a result of having the highest average (200). The coaches also voted her a member of the All-American team. In 1991, both the men's and women's bowlers earned a third place national collegiate ranking, while competing against Ohio State, Penn State, Michigan, USC, Nebraska, Indiana, Wichita State, and the University of Florida. In the National ACU-1 tournament in Chicago, the women's team was defeated in the finals by Indiana State, but Morehead's male bowlers defeated Idaho State for the national championship.

Just before Christmas 1992 the Bowling Writers Association of America voted the MSU women's bowling team first in the nation. Liz Johnson was named Intercollegiate Female Bowler of the Year and MSU's Most Valuable Player in 1993. Wilson has turned out three professional bowlers since 1967. Mike Fairchild was fourth in the Masters in 1984; Bill Watson was on tour in 1990; and Sharon Todd was ranked 13th among American bowlers in 1990.

### Cheerleading:

Morehead State University's cheerleaders have demonstrated excellence by winning eight national titles in ten years! In January 1988 they captured their first national championship in Division I of the Universal Cheerleading Association, commonly regarded as the Super Bowl of cheerleading competition. Under the direction of Myron Doan, squad advisor and dean of students, they competed with more than 200 squads and advanced to the nationals in San Diego along with Appalachian State, Furman, George Mason, and James Madison universities. Faced with preparation of a completely new routine for competion, they worked 25 hours per week during the Christmas break to perfect their two-minute, 20-second video, consisting of a floor cheer, sideline cheers, and a fight song.

Their victory in Orlando, Florida, in 1997, brought the cheering Eagles two national records. Morehead State is the first school in the nation in any division to win seven consecutive national cheerleading titles and to earn eight national championships overall. Competition incorporated stunts, gymnastics, pyramids, basket tosses, dancing, and cheering. The 1997 squad consisted of seven women and nine men, including seven former high school football players. Senior Erich Nelson, Huntsville, Alabama, stated, "This is a sport, and we work hard to be the best squad out there." "If one person loses his/her concentration," said Sharon Bolt, Morehead junior, "the routine falls apart, and the title goes to another squad." The Eagles are becoming increasingly aware of the fact that "other squads seem to arrive at the competition with only one goal, to beat the MSU squad because they want to be the ones who break our streak," according to Shay Whitehead, Lexington junior. Doan, who has coached the squad for 16 years, observed that each year the competition "becomes more intense as the level of talent of the teams continues to increase." In 1996, Doan prepared "The Collegiate Cheerleader," endorsed by the Universal Cheerleaders Association as the official college cheerleading coaches' manual.

The dedication of these athletes has been rewarded with standing ovations from the Kentucky General Assembly and their own Board of Regents as well as by national coverage on ESPN and in the *American Cheerleader.* The squad practices year round in addition to attending a camp each August at East Tennessee State University. While the group ordinarily spends seven to eight hours per week in practice, it pushes itself to the limit during the month before competition by increasing practice from three times per week to twice a day. Doan also attributed part of the team's success to recruiting from both junior colleges and high schools. The Eagles' phenomenal record brings hundreds of calls from high school cheerleaders asking about the program. With no recruiting budget, Doan gets videotapes from students and visits area high schools to check out top prospects.

## The Future

Morehead State's twelve presidents have been diverse individuals with varied backgrounds and distinctive traits, including strengths and idiosyncrasies. As a group, they have been remarkably free of personal scandal. Even during the darkest hours of the institution, the worst that could be said about anyone is that he used poor judgment.

As MSU faces a new millennium, a sense of excitement permeates the campus. In an effort to preserve the heritage of the school as it prepares for the challenges of the 21st century, the MSU Foundation is studying the feasibility of a major funds campaign. This effort had the twofold design of preserving traditions of great teaching, imaginative public service, practical research, and unbounded creative expression while preparing students to be well-rounded, productive citizens. President Button and his dedicated colleagues had longed for the day when public support in the form of state tax dollars would rescue the tiny school they had worked so hard to establish and to keep alive. That day arrived on March 8, 1922, after which "state supported" became the very foundation of the institution. Gone were the days when parents traded wagon loads of potatoes and cattle for tuition and room and board for their aspiring children. Institutional, federal, and state financial aid eased the money worries of sudents and their families, but realities of the 1980s and 1990s clouded that vision of financial stability so much that the University in 1997 is at risk if it relies solely on public funds.

Morehead State University's shared goals heading into the new millennium are excellence in academics, student services, delivery of educational and economic development services, and management of its capital, fiscal, and human resources. The institution has a good road map but likely cannot afford the trip without merging public and private support. However, MSU looks to the future with confidence as its leaders stand squarely behind Governor Paul E. Patton in his pioneer efforts to reform higher education in Kentucky's public colleges and universitites to better meet the needs of its youth in the 21st century!

An aura of school spirit also returned to campus with the hiring of two new basketball coaches in the spring of 1997. Morehead State has already experienced a significant increase in season ticket sales. Laura Litter, a two-time graduate of MSU and player under Coach Mickey Wells, was named head women's basketball coach. Litter's 16-year career record at Sullivan College in Lexington and Lees College in Jackson was 436-85. Her 1993-94 Sullivan squad established a National Junior College Athletic Association scoring record by averaging 107.6 points per game. Coach Litter promised, "We will recruit quality student-athletes who are willing to make sacrifices;" within six weeks, she had already signed five outstanding

## TEACHER'S
## COUNTY CERTIFICATE.

Class *First* : Expires *May 20*, *1905*.

[LEGAL PROVISIONS.—County certificates shall be first-class, second class, or third class, and shall apply only to the county in which they are issued, and shall be good for four years, two years and one year, respectively. Third class certificates shall not be issued more than once to the same person in any event. After July first, one thousand eight hundred and ninety-four, a certificate of the third class shall not entitle the holder to teach in any district reporting fifty-five or more pupil children, nor shall a certificate of the second class entitle the holder to teach in any district reporting seventy-five or more pupil children. A county certificate of the first class shall require an average grade of eighty-five per centum upon all the subjects of the common school course, and upon the science and art of teaching; and the lowest grade in any subject shall not be less than sixty-five per centum. A county certificate of the second class shall require an average grade of seventy-five per centum and the lowest grade on any subject shall not be less than fifty-five per centum. A county certificate of the third class shall require an average grade of sixty-five per centum, and the lowest grade on any subject shall not be less than fifty per centum. A person having taught for eight consecutive years in the same county under first class certificates, obtained as hereinbefore provided, may have the last one renewed annually for four years by the County Superintendent, who shall write upon it "Renewed," sign officially, and give date of such renewal.—School Law, Sec. 135.]

STATE OF KENTUCKY, *Rowan* COUNTY, SS.

*Rebie Vincent* having filed satisfactory evidence of **Unexceptionable** *moral character and of required age, and having passed an examination in Spelling, Reading, Writing, Arithmetic, Grammar, English Composition, Geography, History of the United States, History of Kentucky, Physiology and Hygiene, Elements of Civil Government; and Science and Art of Teaching, with the results indicated below, is hereby granted a Certificate of Qualification to teach in the Common Schools of said County, for the term of* *Four* *calendar years from date.*

| | | | |
|---|---|---|---|
| Spelling | 87 | Geography | 85 |
| Reading | 90 | History of the United States, } | 89 |
| Writing | 97 | History of Kentucky, } | |
| Written Arithmetic, } | 70 | Physiology and Hygiene | 94 |
| Mental Arithmetic, } | | Elements of Civil Government | 95 |
| Grammar | 92 | Science and Art of Teaching | 93 |
| English Composition | 92 | General Average | 89 7/11 |

*The holder is entitled to professional credit as indicated by answers of Examiners to these Questions:*

1. How many months has *she* taught? *15*
2. Does *she* read one or more Educational Journals? *1*
3. Is *she* a member of the State Reading Circle? *—*
4. Has *she* completed one course or more of the reading prescribed?

*Hiram Bradley*, County Superintendent.
*F. C. Button*, Examiner.
*H. H. Caudill*, Examiner.
*Rowan* County, *May 20th*, 1901.

*The twentieth century began with Rebeka "Reba" Elizabeth Vincent receiving her teaching certificate from Morehead Normal School in 1901 and ended with her grandson, Christopher Gallaher, professor of music, receiving the Distinguished Creative Productions Award in 1997.*

recruits. "We promise fans an entertaining and aggressive style of basketball," she concluded.

Kyle Macy, former two-time All-American and floor leader of the University of Kentucky's national championship team in 1978, signed a four-year contract as MSU head coach of men's basketball in April, 1997. He replaced Dick Fick, who was known for his flamboyant sideline antics while posting a 64-101 record in six seasons. Many believed that Macy could bring fans to campus once more and recruit outstanding talent for the program. President Eaglin expressed his conviction that Macy could "restore the proud basketball tradition" at MSU and "lead the Eagles back to the forefront of the Ohio Valley Conference." After playing seven years in the National Basketball Association and three years in the Italian League, Macy became a color analyst with the UK Wildcats' radio broadcasts. "Our team will play an exciting, up-tempo style that players like to be involved in and fans like to watch," the new Morehead State coach promised. In spite of getting a late start in recruiting, Macy had signed four Kentucky All-Staters by the end of his first month, including Brandon Davenport, Kentucky's "Mr. Basketball," the first time Morehead State had signed Kentucky's "best player" since Sonny Allen's decision in 1946!

In May 1997, President Eaglin made another of his most important decisions ever in choosing a new academic leader for the 21st century. Michael R. Moore became the new executive vice president for academic affairs and dean of the faculty. He had served as dean of the School of Liberal Arts and Sciences at Purdue University-Calumet since 1991. Moore, professor of communication, served as head of the department of communication and creative arts at the same institution from 1983 to 1991. With the appointment of Moore, MSU now has its president, executive vice president for academic affairs, and three of its four college deans with no previous connections with the institution, something which seemed impossible a few decades ago.

As 1997 drew to a close, Morehead State continued to serve as "a light to the mountains," forging tradition with optimism for the region's future. During spring commencement, attended by the largest crowd ever assembled in the Academic-Athletic Center, Eastern

Kentucky natives Tom T. Hall of Olive Hill and Ricky Skaggs of Louisa received honorary doctorates for their outstanding contributions to the world of country music. Perhaps that historic "light" was most prominent when President Eaglin posed the traditional request, "I will ask those of you in the class who are the first members of your family to graduate from college if you will please stand and be recognized." To a thunderous ovation, nearly 75 percent of the class stood!

*Michelle Johnson Roberts of Morehead joined more than 40,000 other MSU graduates when she received her bachelor's degree from President Eaglin during the spring commencement.*

## MSU History Advisory Board

John Kleber, chair
Robert S. (Bob) Bishop, community
William E. Clay, Breckinridge School Society
James Gifford, Jesse Stuart Foundation
Charles Hay, EKU Director of Archives
Jane Y. Holbrook, community
Carol Johnson, secretary, Board of Regents
Louis M. (Sonny) Jones, chair, Board of Regents
Keith Kappes, MSU Foundation, Inc.
Clara Keyes, MSU Archives
Gary Lewis, Rowan County Historical Society
Sue Luckey, faculty
Carole Morella, staff
Charles Pelfrey, retired faculty
Helen Pennington, member, Board of Regents
Bill Redwine, MSU Alumni Association, Inc.
James W. Wells, staff
Alban Wheeler, faculty
Judith Yancy, staff

## Principals of Morehead Normal School

| | |
|---|---|
| 1887-1892 | Frank C. Button |
| 1892-1896 | Ralph Julian |
| 1896-1911 | Frank C. Button |
| 1911-1913 | J. M. Robinson |
| 1913-1919 | J. Wesley Hatcher |
| 1919-1922 | Warren O. Lappin |

# Vice Presidents
# Morehead State University

### Vice President for Academic Affairs:

| | |
|---|---|
| 1966 | Warren C. Lappin |
| 1971 | Paul Ford Davis |
| 1975 | John R. Duncan |
| 1978 | William F. White |
| 1981 | Walter G. Emge |
| 1985 | Roberta T. Anderson |
| 1987 | Stephen Taylor |
| 1990 | John Philley |
| 1997 | Michael R. Moore |

### Vice President for Research and Development:

| | |
|---|---|
| 1968 | Morris L. Norfleet |
| 1977 | Phillip W. Conn |

### Vice President for Fiscal Affairs:

| | |
|---|---|
| 1970 | Russell McClure |
| 1979 | John Graham |
| 1984 | Wallace Porter Dailey |

### Vice President for Student Affairs:

| | |
|---|---|
| 1968 | Roger L. Wilson |
| 1976 | Buford Crager |
| 1985 | Gordon Gary Grace |
| 1987 | David Michael Mincey |

### Vice President for University Affairs:

| | |
|---|---|
| 1968 | Raymond R. Hornback |

### Vice President for University Advancement:

| | |
|---|---|
| 1990 | Keith R. Kappes |

# Deans

## School of Applied Sciences and Technology:

| | |
|---|---|
| 1966 | C. Nelson Grote |
| 1971 | Charles F. Ward |
| 1975 | Charles M. Derrickson |
| 1985 | Changed to College of Applied Sciences and Technology |
| 1993 | Gerald L. DeMoss |
| 1994 | Changed to College of Science and Technology |

## School of Education:

| | |
|---|---|
| 1967 | Kenneth D. Dawson |
| 1968 | James H. Powell |
| 1979 | John Michael Davis |

## School of Humanities:

| | |
|---|---|
| 1968 | J. E. Duncan |
| 1981 | Charles J. Pelfrey |
| 1983 | Robert L. Burns |
| 1985 | Changed to College of Arts and Sciences |
| 1985 | Robert L. Burns |
| 1986 | John C. Philley |
| 1990 | Gerald L. DeMoss |
| 1993 | Changed to Caudill College of Humanities |
| 1993 | John E. Kleber |
| 1995 | Lemuel Berry, Jr. |

## School of Sciences and Mathematics:

| | |
|---|---|
| 1967 | William C. Simpson |
| 1972 | Charles Payne |

**School of Social Sciences:**

1966        Roscoe H. Playforth, Sr.

1976        Alban L. Wheeler

**School of Business and Economics:**

1966        Thomas C. Morrison, Jr.

1973        Richard P. Baxter

1977        William M. Whitaker, III

**College of Professional Studies:**

1986        Larry W. Jones

**College of Business:**

1990        Bernard Davis

1994        Beverly J. McCormick

1995        Michael Carrell

**College of Educational and Behavioral Sciences:**

1991        Sylvester Kohut, Jr.

1994        Richard Daniel

1995        Harold Harty

## Distinguished Faculty Award Recipients

| | |
|---|---|
| 1964 | Wilhelm Exelbirt, history |
| 1965 | Margaret B. Heaslip, biology |
| 1966 | Johnson E. Duncan, music |
| 1967 | Mary Northcutt, education |
| 1968 | Madison Pryor, biology |
| 1969 | Franklin Mangrum, philosophy |
| 1970 | Allen Lake, biology |
| 1971 | Charles J. Pelfrey, English |
| 1972 | Julia C. Webb, speech |
| 1973 | Victor Howard, history |
| 1974 | Louise Quinn, business education |
| 1975 | Charles M. Derrickson, agriculture |
| 1976 | James Ross Beane, music |
| 1977 | Did not present award |
| 1978 | Charles J. Whidden, physics |
| 1979 | Jack Bizzell, government |
| 1980 | Ruth Barnes, English |
| 1981 | Lewis Barnes, English |
| 1982 | John Kleber, history |
| 1983 | Howard Setser, biology |
| 1984 | Lawrence Griesinger, education |
| 1985 | Gary C. Cox, geography |
| 1986 | Marc Glasser, English |
| 1987 | Earle L. Louder, music |
| 1988 | Dennis Karwatka, industrial education |

## Name of award was changed to Distinguished Teacher:

| | |
|---|---|
| 1989 | Diane Ris, education |
| 1990 | James Gotsick, psychology |
| 1991 | George Luckey, philosophy |
| 1992 | Rose Orlich, English |

| | |
|---|---|
| 1993 | Mary Jo Netherton, French |
| 1994 | David J. Saxon, biology |
| 1995 | Glenn C. Rogers, English |
| 1996 | Travis P. Lockhart, communications |
| 1997 | Don F. Flatt, history |

## Distinguished Researcher Award

| | |
|---|---|
| 1979 | Victor Howard, history |
| 1980 | Jules Dubar, geoscience |
| 1981 | Ted Pass, biology |
| 1982 | David Hylbert, geology |
| 1983 | Francis Osborne, psychology |
| 1984 | George Dickinson, sociology |
| 1985 | Stuart Sprague, history |
| 1986 | James Gotsick, psychology |
| 1987 | Bruce Mattingly, psychology |
| 1988 | David Rudy, sociology |
| 1989 | Lloyd R. Jaisingh, mathematics |
| 1990 | William Weikel, education |
| 1991 | William Green, government |
| 1992 | Thomas Stroik, English |
| 1993 | John E. Kleber, history |
| 1994 | Brian Reeder, biology |
| 1995 | Edward Reeves, sociology |
| 1996 | Did not present award |
| 1997 | Ron Mitchelson, geography |

# Distinguished Creative Productions Award

| 1992 | Robert J. Franzini, art |
| 1993 | Michelle Boisseau, English |
| 1994 | Shirley H. Gish, speech |
| 1995 | William J. Layne, theater |
| 1996 | Russell Jay Flippin, Jr., music |
| 1997 | Christopher Gallaher, music |

# Service Award

| 1992 | Joyce LeMaster |
| | Sue Woodrow |
| 1993 | John Michael Seelig |
| 1994 | Mary Jo Netherton |
| | Tim Rhodes |
| 1995 | Robert Meadows |
| | Betty S. Hurley |
| 1996 | Ted Pass |
| | Gene Caudill |
| 1997 | Frances Helphinstine |
| | Shirley Hamilton |

# Board of Regents Chairs

| | |
|---|---|
| 1924-28 | McHenry Rhoads |
| 1928-32 | W. C. Bell |
| 1932-36 | James H. Richmond |
| 1936-40 | Harry W. Peters |
| 1940-44 | John W. Brooker |
| 1944-48 | John Fred Williams |
| 1948-52 | Boswell Hodgkin |
| 1952-56 | Wendell P. Butler |
| 1956-60 | Robert R. Martin |
| 1960-64 | Wendell P. Butler |
| 1964-68 | Harry Sparks |
| 1968-72 | Wendell P. Butler |
| 1972 | Lyman Ginger |
| 1972-76 | W. H. Cartmell |
| 1976-83 | Lloyd Cassity |
| 1983-84 | Jerry Howell |
| 1984-86 | Robert M. Duncan |
| 1986-89 | Louie B. Nunn |
| 1989-96 | William R. Seaton |
| 1996- | Louis M. (Sonny) Jones |

# Faculty Regents

| | |
|---|---|
| 1968-71 | Frank Mangrum |
| 1971-74 | Madison Pryor |
| 1974-81 | Charles Pelfrey |
| 1981-87 | John R. Duncan |
| 1987-93 | Alban Wheeler |
| 1993- | Bruce Mattingly |

# Student Regents

| | |
|---|---|
| 1968 | Quentin Hatfield |
| 1968-70 | William Bradford |
| 1970-71 | Jack Hays Sims |
| 1971-72 | Mike Mayhew |
| 1972-73 | Peter Marcum |
| 1973-74 | Dennis Warford |
| 1974-75 | Robert E. Byrd |
| 1975-76 | Debbie Poore |
| 1976-77 | Gerald P. Mays |
| 1977-79 | Evan Perkins |
| 1979-80 | Karl Sclichter |
| 1980-82 | Steve O'Conner |
| 1982-83 | Donna Totich |
| 1983-84 | David Holton |
| 1984-85 | Michael Fox |
| 1985-86 | Margaret Holt |
| 1986-87 | Carlos Cassady |
| 1987-88 | Gregory Ramey |
| 1988-89 | Sheridan Martin |
| 1989-90 | H. B. Gilliam |
| 1990-91 | Chris Hart |
| 1991-92 | Tim Francis |
| 1992-93 | Chando Mapoma |
| 1993-94 | Brian Carlier |
| 1994-95 | Mark Anderson |
| 1995-96 | Brian Hutchinson |
| 1996-97 | Jason Newland |

## Staff Regent

1994-              Gene Caudill

## Board of Regents Citizen Members

| | |
|---|---|
| 1924-27 | Mrs. W. J. Fields |
| 1924-34 | Mr. Allie W. Young |
| 1924-26 | Mr. E. W. Pendleton |
| 1924-26 | Mr. J. B. Clark |
| 1926-30 | Mr. Glenn Perry |
| 1926-37 | Mr. Earl W. Senff |
| 1928-32 | Mrs. S. M. Bradley |
| 1930-38 and 1946-47 | Dr. J. M. Rose |
| 1930-34 | Mr. W. A. Stanfill |
| 1934-35 | Mr. D. B. Caudill |
| 1935-38 | Dr. A. O. Taylor |
| 1936-37 | Mr. C. B. Bennett |
| 1936-46 | Mrs. Allie W. Young |
| 1936-46 | Mr. Donald H. Putnam |
| 1937-40 | Mr. W. A. Caskey |
| 1938-44 | Mr. Ernest E. Shannon |
| 1940-42 | Mr. Harry H. Ramey |
| 1942-44 | Mr. Harry LaViers, Sr. |
| 1944-47 | Mr. Roy E. Cornette |
| 1944-47 | Mr. William H. Keffer |
| 1948-54 | Mr. W. W. Ball |
| 1948-56 | Mr. M. K. Eblen |
| 1948-55 | Mr. J. T. Norris |
| 1948-53 | Mr. E. R. Price |
| 1953-58 | Dr. Elwood Esham |

| | |
|---|---|
| 1954-58 | Dr. Lowell Gearheart |
| 1955-56 | Mr. John Keck |
| 1956 | Dr. Paul Hall |
| 1956-80 | Dr. W. H. Cartmell |
| 1957-58 | Dr. W. E. Day |
| 1957-69 | Mr. Charles Gilley |
| 1958-60 | Mrs. E. E. Shannon |
| 1958-66 | Mr. Alex Chamberlain |
| 1958-63 | Mr. Bruce Walters |
| 1960-62 | Dr. Joe Taylor Hyden |
| 1962-68 | Mr. David H. Dorton |
| 1963-86 | Mr. Lloyd Cassity |
| 1966-82 | Mr. Cloyd McDowell |
| 1968-84 and 1989-91 | Mr. Jerry Howell |
| 1969-73 and 1989-92 | Mr. Charles D. Wheeler |
| 1972-77 | Mr. William E. Justice |
| 1972-75 | Mr. Crayton (Bo) Queen |
| 1973-81 | Mr. Sam F. Kibbey |
| 1975-86 | Mr. James M. Richardson |
| 1977-80 | Dr. Daniel H. Stamper |
| 1979-82 | Mr. Billy Joe Hall |
| 1980-84 | Mr. John H. Baird |
| 1980-84 | Mrs. Ethel Foley |
| 1982-86 | Mr. Harry LaViers, Jr. |
| 1982-86 | Dr. Forest M. Skaggs |
| 1984-92 | Mr. Walter W. Carr |
| 1984-86 | Mrs. Eunice H. Caston |
| 1984-86 | Mrs. Patricia A. Burchett |
| 1986-89 | Mrs. Barbara Curry |
| 1986-91 | Mr. J. Calvin Aker |
| 1986-89 | Mr. Edward T. Breathitt |

| 1986-89 | Dr. Allan Lansing |
| 1986- | Mr. William R. Seaton |
| 1989-91 | Mr. Duane Hart |
| 1989-92 | Mr. Wayne M. Martin |
| 1989-92 | Mr. William E. Cofield |
| 1991-97 | Mrs. Lois Baker |
| 1991-92 | Mr. T. T. Colley |
| 1991- | Mrs. Helen Pennington |
| 1992- | Mr. Louis M. (Sonny) Jones |
| 1992- | Mr. Buckner Hinkle, Jr. |
| 1992- | Dr. Charles M. Rhodes |
| 1992- | Mr. John M. Rosenberg |
| 1992- | Mr. James A. Finch |

## University Senate Chairs

| 1969 | (no chair) |
| 1970 | John R. Duncan |
| 1971 | John R. Duncan |
| 1972 | Roger Jones |
| 1973 | Jack Bizzel |
| 1974 | James Quisenberry |
| 1975 | (no senate) |
| 1976 | James Smiley |
| 1977 | Charles Holt |
| 1978 | Paul Ford Davis |
| 1979 | Tom E. Scott |
| 1980 | Tom E. Scott |
| 1981 | Bill Pierce |
| 1982 | Patsy Whitson |
| 1983 | Stuart Sprague |

# Faculty Senate Chairs

| | |
|---|---|
| 1984 | Stephen Young |
| 1985 | David Brumagen |
| 1986 | Judy Rogers |
| 1987 | J. Michael Seelig |
| 1988 | James Quisenberry |
| 1989 | Janet Gross |
| 1990 | Robert Lindahl |
| 1991 | Robert Wolfe |
| 1992 | Beverly McCormick |
| 1993 | Rodney Stanley |
| 1994 | Larry Keenan |
| 1995 | Brian Reeder |
| 1996 | Charles Patrick |
| 1997 | Larry Keenan |

# Officers of the MSU Foundation

### Board Chair ("President" until 1996)

| | |
|---|---|
| 1979-84 | Morris L. Norfleet |
| 1984-86 | J. Dan Lacy |
| 1986-91 | Terry S. Jacobs |
| 1991-93 | Larry H. Fannin |
| 1993- | B. Proctor Caudill, Jr. |

### Vice Chair ("Vice President" until 1996)

| | |
|---|---|
| 1979-83 | Billy Joe Hall |
| 1983-84 | J. Dan Lacy |
| 1984-86 | Harold Bellamy |
| 1986-88 | W. David Bolt |
| 1988-91 | Larry H. Fannin |
| 1991-96 | Resvie Wheeler |
| 1996- | Wayne M. Martin |

### Secretary

| | |
|---|---|
| 1979-85 | Helen A. Northcutt |
| 1985- | Merl F. Allen |

### Treasurer

| | |
|---|---|
| 1979-81 | John Graham |
| 1981-86 | Phillip M. Tackett |
| 1986-88 | Gail B. Conley |
| 1988- | Lisa Browning |

**Chief Executive Officer ("Executive Director" until 1985; "Executive Vice President" until 1996)**

| | |
|---|---|
| 1979-81 | Rondal D. Hart |
| 1981-87 | Elmer D. Anderson |
| 1987-88 | W. David Bolt |
| 1988-93 | Robert F. Howerton |
| 1993- | Keith R. Kappes |

## Morehead State University Fellows

David F. & Rozella M. Abner
Hubert & Delia Allen
John E. (Sonny) & Merl F. Allen
Dr. James & Elizabeth T. Arient
Richard & Kathy A. Armstrong
Lexter Baldridge
Bernice Barbour & Dr. Roger W. Barbour
Harold & Alma Bellamy
Lemuel & Kayla Berry
Paul & Susanne Blair
Janet Blakeman
Bill R. & Louise Booth
Mr. & Mrs. James H. Booth
Mr. & Mrs. William E. Bradley
Lisa Browning
W. Thomas & Virginia Buckner
Homer G. III & Lucinda Cablish
Donnie & Wanda Canada
Michael & Colleen Carrell
John H. Cary
Hazel & Lloyd Cassity

B. Proctor & Bobbie Caudill
Dr. C. Louise Caudill
James R., Jr. & Candace Caudill
Jane Caudill
Ronald J. & Natalie Caudill
Lillie D. Chaffin
Harry Chakeres
Mr. & Mrs. Michael Chakeres
Philip & Melinda Chakeres
William W. & Linda Chapman
William E. Clay
Dr. Robert L. & Kim Coleman
Ted & Janet Coakley
Arthur Cole
James E. & Sandra S. Conley
Ted & Jean Crosthwait
Noveal Crosthwaite & Harold Crosthwaite
W. Porter & Pat A. Dailey
James S. & Phyllis Davis
Gerald & Diane DeMoss
Myron L. Doan
Adron & Mignon M. Doran
David H. & Nancy E. Dow
Margaret (Peggy) Dunlap
Ronald G. & Bonnie C. Eaglin
Sarah Emmons
Martha Enzmann
Family of the late Lindsay R. & Hazel R. Ellington
Larry F. & Barbara Fannin
Dr. Shirley L. Fannin
Dr. Thomas & Barbara Fossett
John R. Gaines
Bethel C. Gallaher & A. Frank Gallaher

Christopher & Linda Gallaher
Mary Gilmer
Lynn Glass & Jim Glass
Marc & Tamalyn Glasser
Dr. Randy H. & Judy M. Greene
C. Nelson & Wilma Grote
Don & Betty Hall
Billy D. & Laveta Hanlin
Dr. William S. Harris
Donna Hawkins
Alfred & Winifred Hodgson
Judge Elijah M. & Norma Hogge
Dr. Harold & Jane Y. Holbrook
D. H. & Irene Howard
Jerry F., Sr. & Buena Howell
Jerry F. & Lois Howell
Alpha & Mildred Hutchinson
Crayton & Bernice Jackson
Terry & Susan Jacobs
Mitch & Tami B. Jones
Louis M. (Sonny) & Joretta Jones
Waverly & Deloris Jones
Keith R. & Janet H. Kappes
Harold E. & Ruie Kelley
J. Dan & Nancy Lacy
Steven M. Lee
Steve & Janet Lewis
Lucille Caudill Little
Boone Logan
Irvin Lowe
George M. & Sue Luckey
E. Paul Lyon, Jr.
Dr. Paul & Patricia Maddox

Franklin & Nancy Mangrum
Pauline F. Marras
Wayne M. & Kathy G. Martin
John H. & Bobbie G. Mays
W. Terry McBrayer
Russell R. & Brucene McClure
Dr. Tom & Lois McHugh
D. Michael & Kathryn C. Mincey
Bill F. Moore
Frederick A. & Mary Mueller
Dr. Chester A. Nava
Robert & Susan H. Neff
Betty & C. E. Norris
Gary B. & Marti North
Denny & Helen Northcutt
B. Pat O'Rourke
Keith & Lynne Pack
Shirley M. Parker
Richard & Lucy Platek
Roscoe H. & Sibbie Playforth
John C. & Betty D. Philley
Charles (Izzy) & T. Starr Porter
Aubrey & Ruby Rather
Brett W. Redwine
William H. & Susette D. Redwine
Timothy P. & Cindy Rhodes
John M. & Anna Ridgway
Brownie & Claudine Rock
Raymond & Pauline Ross
Donald F. Russell
Monis Schuster
George D. & Alva Scott
William R. & Susie Seaton

Dr. Patrick J. & Jeannette Serey
E. L. Jr. & Ruth B. Shannon
Alfred A. & Marie Silano
Philip M. & Diana Simms
Robert A. & Mary Ellen Slone
Eugene Snowden
Stephen C. & Sharon Snowden
Thomas Sternal
Lawrence R. & Stellarose Stewart
Paul R. & Paula Y. Stokes
Philip M. & Lu Tackett
Norman & Deane Tant
Walt & Karen Terrell
Ronald & Kathy Timmons
Dale S. Turpin & James W. Turpin
H. Jack & Joie Webb
James C. & Brenda Wells
Dr. Byron & Helen T. Wentz
Mary Helen Westheimer
Alban L. & Sharon Wheeler
Hazel H. Whitaker
Harold & Barbara White
Alice Elaine Williams
Tim Wilson
E. Preston Young
George T. Young

## Most Valuable Giver

| | |
|---|---|
| 1985 | Boone Logan |
| 1986 | Terry S. & Susan Jacobs |
| 1987 | Ashland Oil Foundation |
| 1989 | Phil Simms |
| 1993 | Mt. Rural Telephone Cooperative |
| | Diederich Educational Trust |
| 1994 | Lucille Caudill Little |
| 1995 | Chakeres Theatres, Inc. |
| 1996 | Ted & Jean Crosthwait |
| 1997 | Lexmark International, Inc. |

## Volunteer Fund Raiser of the Year

| | |
|---|---|
| 1985 | Harold Bellamy |
| 1987 | J. Dan Lacy |
| 1988 | David Bolt |
| 1989 | Terry S. Jacobs |
| 1990 | John Baird |
| 1991 | Charles M. Derrickson |
| 1994 | W. Stu Taylor |
| 1995 | Resvie Wheeler |
| 1996 | Bronelle Skaggs |
| 1997 | Jack Ellis |
| | William E. Clay |

## Outstanding Faculty/Staff Fund Raiser

| | |
|---|---|
| 1985 | Charles M. Derrickson |
| 1988 | Chris Gallaher |
| 1989 | Jerry F. Howell, Jr. |
| 1990 | Harlen Hamm |
| | Larry Wilson |
| 1991 | Frank Spaniol |
| | Richard Hunt |
| 1992 | John R. Duncan |
| | Adrian Swain |
| 1994 | C. Lee Tyner |
| | Harlen Hamm |
| 1995 | James Smallwood |
| | Robert Hayes |
| | Jonell Tobin |
| 1996 | Janet Ratliff |
| | Clara Keyes |
| 1997 | Janet Kenney |
| | Michael Carrell |

# Presidents of the Alumni Association

| | |
|---|---|
| 1928-32 | Russell Williamson |
| 1933-34 | Bess A. Hurst |
| 1934-35 | Dennie Caudill |
| 1936-37 | Ova Haney |
| 1937-38 | Malcolm H. Holliday, Jr. |
| 1939-40 | Luster C. Oxley |
| 1940-41 | Robert F. Sanford |
| 1941-43 | Ashton Denton |
| 1943-44 | Grace Crosthwaite |
| 1944-45 | Heman H. McGuire |
| 1945-46 | Emory Gene Rogers |
| 1946-47 | Walter Roschi |
| 1947-48 | Gordon V. Moore |
| 1948-50 | Ted L. Crosthwait |
| 1950-51 | Clifford R. Cassady |
| 1952-53 | John E. Collis |
| 1954-58 | Fola N. Hayes |
| 1959-60 | Don Holloway |
| 1961-62 | George W. Jackson |
| 1963-64 | James G. Gibson |
| 1965-70 | Lucien H. Rice |
| 1971-73 | Larry W. Hillman |
| 1973-74 | W. Terry McBrayer |
| 1974-75 | Custer B. Reynolds |
| 1975-77 | Marvin G. Rammelsberg |
| 1977-78 | William D. Blair |
| 1979-80 | Harold L. Wilson |
| 1980-82 | James P. Pruitt |
| 1982-84 | Merl F. Allen |
| 1984-86 | W. David Bolt |
| 1986-88 | William L. Phelps |

| 1988-90 | Lisa Browning |
| 1990-92 | Ted E. Coakley |
| 1992-94 | L. M. (Sonny) Jones |
| 1994-96 | J. T. Holbrook |
| 1996-98 | H. Jack Webb |

## Executive Vice Presidents of the Alumni Association ("Executive Secretary" until 1988)

| 1959-63 | Billy Joe Hall |
| 1963-67 | Harry C. Mayhew |
| 1967-70 | Rondal D. Hart |
| 1970-72 | Harry C. Mayhew |
| 1972-87 | Don B. Young, Sr. |
| 1987- | William H. Redwine |

# Alumni Hall of Fame

Ron Abernathy, 1989
James A. Adams, 1982
Robert Addington, 1990
A. D. Albright, 1987
John E. (Sonny) Allen, 1980
Ray Allen, 1991
Robert R. Allen, 1975
Elmer D. Anderson, 1980
Sherman Arnett, 1966
Dr. Lena Bailey, 1979
Marshall Banks, 1981
Col. William Barber, 1990
Dr. Roger Barbour, 1984
Dr. Anna Barker, 1979
Harold L. Bellamy, 1980
Wanda D. Bigham, 1988
Marcheta Blackburn, 1982
David Bolt, 1987
James H. Booth, 1996
Dr. Peggy Burke, 1976
Dr. Lauretta Flynn Byars, 1994
Walter W. Carr, 1980
Anna Carter, 1966
Vic Carter, 1992
Lloyd Cassity, 1966
James C. Clay, 1976
Dr. Robert Coleman, 1987
Gary S. Cox, 1988
Ted L. Crosthwait, 1968
Arye Ellington Dethmers, 1995
Col. Mark Dille, 1997

Adron Doran, 1997
Dennis Doyle, 1976
Michael A. Dudley, 1978
Dale C. Emmons, 1977
Liz Everman, 1992
Dr. Shirley Fannin, 1989
Virginia G. Fox, 1993
Dr. Samuel Garten, 1978
Dr. John P. Gearhart, 1987
Michael Gottfried, 1980
Dale D. Greer, 1976
C. Nelson Grote, 1992
Billy Joe Hall, 1967
John R. Hall, 1981
Harlan Hatcher, 1966
Fola N. Hayes, 1969
Dr. William Higginbotham, 1982
Dr. William E. Jamison, 1982
Ann Karrick, 1994
J. Dan Lacy, 1988
Rev. Clyde Landrum, 1966
Glenn D. Leveridge, 1992
Sylvia L. Lovely, 1996
Irvin Lowe, 1981
Dr. Robert Lowe, 1973
Harry King Lowman, 1974
E. Paul Lyon, 1982
Dr. Paul Maddox, 1966
Wayne M. Martin, 1991
Lawrence A. Marzetti, 1976
W. Terry McBrayer, 1966

Russell R.. McClure, 1976
Cloyd McDowell, 1966
Frances S. Miller, 1983
Gary B. North, 1982
C. E. Norris, 1984
B. Pat O'Rourke, 1981
James P. Pruitt, Jr., 1981
Marvin G. Rammelsberg, 1981
Ruth Reeves, 1971
Custer B. Reynolds, 1972
Lucien Rice, 1970
Dr. J. David Richardson, 1995
Gary W. Riley, 1996
Dr. Carol S. Rivers, 1995

Dr. Richard L. Robinson, 1976
Dr. Harley J. Schneider, 1983
Dr. Walter Scott, 1978
J. Phil Smith, 1966
Dennis Speigel, 1994
Linda Steiner, 1997
Dr. Robert Stewart, 1966
Janet Stumbo, 1990
Marie R. Turner, 1979
Harry A. Walker, 1993
Nan K. Ward, 1993
Maj. Gen. Billy G. Wellman, 1979
Russell Williamson, 1966

## Founders Day Award for University Service

| 1978 | W. E. Crutcher |
| 1979 | Linus A. Fair |
| 1980 | Carl D. Perkins |
| 1981 | Warren C. Lappin |
| 1982 | Ted. L. Crosthwait |
| 1983 | Monroe Wicker |
| 1984 | Lloyd Cassity |
| 1985 | Grace Crosthwaite |
| 1986 | Boone Logan |
| 1987 | Rondal D. Hart |
| 1988 | George T. Young |

| 1989 | John E. Collis |
| 1990 | Wilhelm Exelbirt |
| 1991 | Roscoe H. Playforth |
| 1992 | Mary Northcutt Powell |
| 1993 | Sen. Woody May |
| 1994 | J. E. Duncan |
| 1995 | Sherman R. Arnett |
| | Harlen L. Hamm |
| 1996 | Adron Doran |
| 1997 | Robert S. (Bob) Bishop |
| | K. Martin Huffman |

# Men's Basketball

## All-Americans

| | |
|---|---|
| 1943 | Earl Duncan, Georgetown, forward |
| 1945 | Warren Cooper, Brooksville, center |
| 1950 | John E. (Sonny) Allen, Morehead, guard |
| 1955,56 | Dan Swartz, Owingsville, center |
| 1957 | Steve Hamilton, Charleston, Ind., forward |
| 1963 | Harold Sergent, Ashland, guard |
| 1972 | Leonard Coulter, Danville, forward |

## OVC Player of the Year
### (Began in 1963)

| | |
|---|---|
| 1962-63 | Harold Sergent |
| 1986-87 | Bob McCann |
| 1991-92 | Brett Roberts |

## OVC Coach of the Year
### (Began in 1961)

| | |
|---|---|
| 1960-61 | Bobby Laughlin |
| 1975-76 | Jack Schalow (Co) |
| 1981-82 | Wayne Martin (Co) |
| 1983-84 | Wayne Martin |
| 1994-95 | Dick Fick (Co) |

## Top Ten Scorers (Career)

| | Points | Player | Season | Yrs. | G | Avg. |
|---|---|---|---|---|---|---|
| 1. | 2,072 | Herbie Stamper | 1975-79 | 4 | 99 | 20.9 |
| 2. | 1,925 | Dan Swartz | 1953-56 | 3 | 69 | 27.5 |
| 3. | 1,923 | Sonny Allen | 1946-50 | 4 | 92 | 20.8 |
| 4. | 1,829 | Steve Hamilton | 1954-58 | 4 | 102 | 17.8 |
| 5. | 1,788 | Brett Roberts | 1988-92 | 4 | 107 | 16.7 |
| 6. | 1,781 | Leonard Coulter | 1971-74 | 3 | 77 | 23.1 |
| 7. | 1,637 | Granny Williams | 1959-62 | 3 | 76 | 21.5 |

| | | | | | | |
|---|---|---|---|---|---|---|
| 8. | 1,469 | Harold Sergent | 1962-65 | 3 | 63 | 23.2 |
| 9. | 1,450 | Ted Hundley | 1973-77 | 4 | 100 | 14.5 |
| 10. | 1,445 | Bob McCann | 1984-87 | 3 | 82 | 17.6 |

## Coaching Records

| Seasons | Head Coach | Years | W | L |
|---|---|---|---|---|
| 1929-36 | George D. Downing | 7 | 51 | 45 |
| 1936-43, 1945-53 | Ellis T. Johnson | 15 | 196 | 158 |
| 1943-45 | Len Miller | 2 | 28 | 9 |
| 1953-65 | Bobby Laughlin | 12 | 166 | 120 |
| 1965-69 | Bob Wright | 4 | 58 | 38 |
| 1969-74 | Bill Harrell | 5 | 68 | 59 |
| 1974-78 | Jack Schalow | 4 | 45 | 56 |
| 1978-87 | Wayne Martin | 9 | 130 | 120 |
| 1987-91 | Tommy Gaither | 4 | 52 | 64 |
| 1991-95 | Dick Fick | 4 | 49 | 62 |
| **Totals** | | **66** | **843** | **731** |

## All-Ohio Valley Conference (First Team)

| | |
|---|---|
| 1948-49 | Sonny Allen, G |
| 1949-50 | Sonny Allen, G; Bill Martin, C |
| 1950-51 | Jack Baker, F; Don Miller, G |
| 1951-52 | Elza Whalen, F |
| 1952-53 | Lindle Castle, G; Elza Whalen, F |
| 1953-54 | Dan Swartz, C |
| 1954-55 | Dan Swartz, C; Steve Hamilton, F |
| 1957-58 | Steve Hamilton, F |
| 1958-59 | Thornton Hill, C; Herbie Triplett, G |
| 1959-60 | Herbie Triplett, G |
| 1960-61 | Granny Williams, G; Hecky Thompson, G; Ed Noe, C |

| | |
|---|---|
| 1961-62 | Granny Williams, G; Ed Noe, C |
| 1962-63 | Harold Sergent, G; Norm Pokley, C; Roy Ware, G |
| 1963-64 | Harold Sergent, G; Henry Akin, C |
| 1964-65 | Harold Sergent, G; Henry Akin, C |
| 1966-67 | Jim Sandfoss, G |
| 1967-68 | Jerry Conley, G; Lamar Green, F |
| 1968-69 | Jerry Conley, G; Lamar Green, F |
| 1969-70 | Jim Day, F |
| 1970-71 | Jim Day, F |
| 1971-72 | Leonard Coulter, F; Howard Wallen, G |
| 1972-73 | Leonard Coulter, F; Eugene Lyons, F |
| 1973-74 | Leonard Coulter, F; Eugene Lyons, F |
| 1974-75 | Arch Johnson, F |
| 1975-76 | Ted Hundley, C |
| 1976-77 | Ted Hundley, C; Herbie Stamper, G |
| 1977-78 | Herbie Stamper, G |
| 1978-79 | Herbie Stamper, G; Charlie Clay, F |
| 1979-80 | Charlie Clay, F |
| 1981-82 | Guy Minnifield, G |
| 1982-83 | Guy Minnifield, G; Earl Harrison, F |
| 1983-84 | Earl Harrison, F; Jeff Tipton, C |
| 1984-85 | Bob McCann, C |
| 1985-86 | Bob McCann, C |
| 1986-87 | Bob McCann, C |
| 1989-90 | Elbert Boyd, F |
| 1990-91 | Rod Mitchell, C |
| 1991-92 | Brett Roberts, F |
| 1992-93 | Doug Bentz, C |
| 1993-94 | Tyrone Boardley, F |
| 1994-95 | Tyrone Boardley, F |

# Women's Basketball

### All-Americans
### OVC Player of the Year

| | |
|---|---|
| 1977-78 & 1979-80 | Donna Murphy |
| 1982-83 | Priscilla Blackford |

### OVC Coach of the Year

| | |
|---|---|
| 1978-79 & 1981-82 | Mickey Wells |
| 1988-89 | Loretta Marlow |

### OVC Female Athlete of the Year

| | |
|---|---|
| 1982-83 | Priscilla Blackford |

### Top Ten Scorers (Career)

| | Points | Player | Season | Yrs. | G | Avg. |
|---|---|---|---|---|---|---|
| 1. | 2,059 | Donna Murphy | 1976-80 | 4 | 105 | 19.6 |
| 2. | 1.710 | Donna Stephens | 1978-82 | 4 | 93 | 18.4 |
| 3. | 1,697 | Julie Magrane | 1988-92 | 4 | 107 | 15.9 |
| 4. | 1,599 | Robin Harmon | 1978-82 | 4 | 121 | 13.2 |
| 5. | 1,592 | Bev Smith | 1988-92 | 4 | 111 | 14.3 |
| 6. | 1,481 | Priscilla Blackford | 1980-83 | 3 | 94 | 15.8 |
| 7. | 1,459 | Michelle Stowers | 1976-80 | 4 | 109 | 13.4 |
| 8. | 1,392 | Sherita Joplin | 1991-95 | 4 | 106 | 13.1 |
| 9. | 1,313 | Kelly Downs | 1986-90 | 4 | 111 | 11.8 |
| 10. | 1,300 | Kelly Stamper | 1985-89 | 4 | 110 | 11.8 |

## Coaching Records

| Seasons | Head Coach | Years | W | L |
|---------|------------|-------|-----|-----|
| 1970-71 | Carol Stewart | 1 | 5 | 3 |
| 1971-75 | Sue Lucke | 4 | 20 | 19 |
| 1975-84 | Mickey Wells | 9 | 156 | 91 |
| 1984-92 | LorettaMarlow | 8 | 110 | 116 |
| 1992-97 | Janet Gabriel | 5 | 42 | 92 |
| Totals | | 27 | 333 | 321 |

## All-Ohio Valley Conference (First Team)

| | |
|---|---|
| 1977-80 | Donna Murphy |
| 1978-79 & | Donna Stephens |
| 1980-82 | |
| 1978-79 | Michelle Stowers |
| 1981-83 | Priscilla Blackford |
| 1984-85 | Connie Appleman |
| 1986-87 | Kelly Stamper |
| 1991-92 | Julie Magrane |
| 1992-93 | Bev Smith |

# Football

### All-Americans

| | |
|---|---|
| 1938 | John (Buck) Horton, Mount Sterling, center |
| 1939 | Stanley Radjunas, New Britain, Connecticut, guard |
| 1940 | Paul Adams, Coal Grove, Ohio, center |
| 1942 | Vincent (Moose) Zachem, Ashland, center |
| 1946 | Joe Lustic, Maysville, runningback |
| 1969 | Dave Haverdick, Canton, Ohio, defensive tackle |
| 1981 | John Christopher, Norwalk, Ohio, punter |
| 1982 | John Christopher, Norwalk, Ohio, punter |
| 1986 | Billy Poe, Ironton, Ohio, offensive guard |
| 1990 | Darrell Beavers, Louisville, defensive back |

### OVC Player of the Year

| | |
|---|---|
| 1966 | Tommie Gray, halfback |
| 1977 | Phil Simms, quarterback |

### OVC Coach of the Year

| | |
|---|---|
| 1966 | Guy Penny |
| 1986 | Bill Baldridge |
| 1990 | Cole Proctor (3-way tie) |

### Coaching Records

| Year | Head Coach | W | L | T |
|---|---|---|---|---|
| 1927-35 | George D. Downing | 28 | 32 | 3 |
| 1936-52 | Ellis T. Johnson | 54 | 44 | 10 |
| 1943-45 | (no football) | | | |
| 1953-55 | Wilbur (Shorty) Jamerson | 0 | 26 | 0 |
| 1956-58 | Paul Adams | 4 | 21 | 1 |
| 1959-67 | Guy Penny | 39 | 39 | 2 |
| 1968-71 | John (Jake) Hallum | 22 | 17 | 1 |
| 1972-75 | Roy M. Terry | 15 | 26 | 1 |

| 1976-78 | Wayne Chapman | 7 | 20 | 3 |
|---------|---------------|-----|-----|-----|
| 1979-80 | Tom Lichtenberg | 9 | 11 | 1 |
| 1981-83 | Steve Loney | 8 | 24 | 0 |
| 1984-89 | Bill Baldridge | 20 | 45 | 0 |
| 1990-93 | Cole Proctor | 15 | 29 | 0 |
| 1994- | Matt Ballard | 0 | 11 | 0 |
| **Totals** | | **221** | **345** | **22** |

## Athletic Hall of Fame

Paul Adams, 1985
John (Sonny) Allen, 1985
Roy Bailey, 1995
Marshall Banks, 1988
Charles Bowles, 1997
Robert Brashear, 1997
Jim Brockman, 1996
Lawrence Carter, 1994
Charles Dudley Carter, 1988
John Christopher, 1993
Warren Cooper, 1985
Debbie Ames Coppin, 1988
Leonard Coulter, 1985
Jim Day, 1996
Carl Deaton, 1994
Adron Doran, 1997
George D. Downing, 1987
Denny Doyle, 1989
Earl Duncan, 1985
Nolan Fowler, 1993
Lawrence Fraley, 1985

Ron Gathright, 1993
Tommie Gray, 1987
Jody Hamilton, 1991
Steve Hamilton, 1985
M. Frenchy Hammonds, 1990
Dave Haverdick, 1985
Donna Stephens Hedges, 1991
John (Buck) Horton, 1985
Carl Howerton, 1989
Ted Hundley, 1997
Bobby Jones, 1992
Ellis T. Johnson, 1985
Gordon (Corky) Kirtley, 1988
Bobby Laughlin, 1985
Mark Ledford, 1995
Joe Lustic, 1985
Wayne M. Martin, 1995
Lawrence Marzetti, 1993
Keith Mescher, 1997
Len Miller, 1985
Gordon (Red) Moore, 1992

Eddie Mudd, 1996

Donna Murphy, 1990

Lus Oxley, 1995

Guy Penny, 1989

Dr. Norm Pokley, 1993

Charles (Izzy) Porter, 1987

Stanley Radjunas, 1985

Custer Reynolds, 1988

Frank Robertson, 1994

Louis Rogan, 1994

Tebay Rose, 1991

Don Russell, 1996

William Scroggin, 1988

Harold Sergent, 1985

Sue Caulkins Sharp, 1996

Phil Simms, 1995

Martha Rust Sizemore, 1994

Bill Spannuth, 1992

Herbie Stamper, 1990

Glendon Stanley, 1996

Reese Stephenson, 1997

Leston Stewart, 1990

Dan Swartz, 1985

Walt Terrell, 1994

Henderson Thompson, 1991

Beverly (Jug) Varney, 1992

Mickey Wells, 1995

Myron (Granny) Williams, 1992

Larry Workman, 1991

Vincent (Moose) Zachem, 1985

# $\mathcal{B}ibliography$

## Primary Sources

### Collections in MSU Archives

Albright Report, 1983.

Alumni Series (3 boxes).

Alumni *Statement* Series, 1978-1997, (2 boxes).

Frank C. Button Collection (2 boxes).

Campus Telephone Directories, 1958-1997.

Adron and Mignon Doran Collection (75 linear feet).

Faculty Collection Series, 1904-1997, (6 boxes).

Faculty Senate (1 box).

Honors Program Series, 1959-1997, (2 boxes).

McVey Report (Report of the Committee on Inquiry), 1929.

Minutes of Morehead State Board Meetings, 1923-1997.

Minutes of Morehead Normal School Discipline Committee, 1904-1921.

Minutes of Morehead Normal School Faculty, 1904-1921.

Minutes of Morehead State Council, 1928-1947.

Minutes of Morehead State Discipline Committee, 1923-1935.

Minutes of Morehead State Faculty, 1923-1970s.

Minutes of the State Normal School Commssion, 1922.

Morehead Normal School Catalogs, 1901-1921.

Morehead Normal School History Series (2 boxes).

Morehead Normal School/Rowan County History Series (1 box).

Morehead State Catalogs, 1923-1997.

Morehead Teachers College History Series (1 box).

MSU Class Schedules, 1928-1997.

MSU Clip Sheet, 1986-1997.

MSU Commencement Series, 1931-1997.

MSU Eagle Baseball Press Guide.

MSU Eagle Basketball Press Guide.

MSU Eagle Football Press Guide.

MSU History Series (2 boxes).

MSU Lady Eagle Basketball Press Guide.

MSU Lady Eagle Softball Press Guide.

MSU *Newsletter,* 1969-1997.

MSU Student Handbooks, 1952-1997.

MSU Student Publications, 1935-1997 (4 boxes).

News and Photo Releases - Public Information Releases Collection, 1961-1997.

Office of the President (31 boxes).

Personnel Services Series (8 boxes).

Planning, Institutional Research, and Evaluation Series (2 boxes).

Presidential Papers (10 boxes).

Proceedings: Southern Association of Colleges and Schools, 1946-1948.

Publications Collection (5 boxes).

The *Raconteur,* 1927-1997.

Report by Mike C. Huntley, Executive Secretary of SACS, on Morehead State, 1946.

Report of the Executive Council to the Executive Committee of SACS on Morehead State. 1948.

Report of the Survey Committee of SACS on Morehead State, 1948.

Research Grants and Contracts, 1964-1997, (7 boxes).

University Senate Series (4 boxes).

Update, 1975-1997.

WMKY Series, 1966-1997, (2 boxes).

## Newspapers

Ashland *Daily Independent* (1922-1997)

Lexington *Herald-Leader* (1922-1997)

Louisville *Courier-Journal* (1922-1997)

*More-Head-Light* (1927-1929)

*Morehead News* (1963-1997)

*Morehead Independent* (1934-1945)

*Rowan County News* (1929-1962)

*Trail Blazer* (1929-1997)

*Mountain Scorcher* (1927)

## Interviews

### Conducted by Don F. Flatt (Adron Doran Project, 1976-1977):

Earle Clements, former governor and former U.S. senator

Carl Hill, former president of Kentucky State University

Robert (Bob) Martin, former president of Eastern Kentucky University

Carl C. Perkins, former U.S. congressman

**Conducted by John E. Kleber (Adron Doran Project, 1976-1977):**

Julian Carroll

W. H. Cartmell

Lloyd Cassity

Donald Cetrulo

A. B. (Happy) Chandler

Bert T. Combs

Adron Doran

Mignon Doran

Wilhelm Exelbirt

Octavia Graves

Holman Hamilton

Raymond R. Hornback

Earle Jones

Tilman Juett

Arthur Kelly

Terry McBrayer

Louie Nunn

Charles Roland

Otis Singletary

Harry Sparks

Richard VanHoose

Harry Lee Waterfield

Lawrence Wetherby

**Conducted by Don F. Flatt (Research for MSU History, 1990-97):**

A. D. Albright, former MSU president

John (Sonny) Allen, former MSU All-American (basketball) and instructor

Roberta Anderson, former vice president for academic affairs

Earl Bentley, former chair of HPER

LeMerle Bentley, former Camden-Carroll librarian

Robert S. (Bob) Bishop, member of Button family through marriage

Walter Carr, former member of MSU Board of Regents

Dr. Louise Caudill, Morehead physician and former MSU instructor

Ina B. Clark, widow of architect for MSU buildings in 1950s and 1960s

John Collis, former MSU student and former manager of MSU Book Store

Philip W. Conn, former MSU vice president for research and development

Lake Cooper, former MSU student and mathematics instructor

Warren Cooper, former MSU All-American (basketball)

Hubert Counts, student at Morehead State Normal School and Teachers College

Ted Crosthwait, student at Morehead State Teachers College

Edna Babb Darling, daughter of MSU President Harvey A. Babb

Calvin Dickinson & Harvey Neufeldt, authors of history of Tennessee Tech University

Adron Doran, former MSU president

Mignon Doran, former MSU first lady

Jean Dotson, former student at Breckinridge Training School and MSTC

J. E. (Gene) Duncan, former MSU dean of School of Humanities

John R. Duncan, former MSU vice president for academic affairs

Ronald G. Eaglin, current MSU president

Walter Emge, former MSU vice president for academic affairs

John Fitch, MSTC football player

Nolan Fowler, former MSU history professor and track coach

Lawrence Fraley, former Morehead State Normal School and Teachers College student

J. G. Gibson, former MSU assistant dean of men

Mike Gottfried, former MSU football star and current ESPN analyst

C. Nelson Grote, former MSU president

Lowell Harrison, author of history of Western Kentucky University

Harlan Hatcher, student at Morehead Normal School

Charles Hay, archivist at Eastern Kentucky University

Dorothy Holbrook, student at Morehead Normal School

Jane Y. Holbrook, daughter of Allie Young, and Dr. Harold Holbrook, her husband

Jerry Howell, Sr., longtime member of MSU Board of Regents

Ralph Hudson, art instructor at MSTC

Keith R. Kappes, current MSU vice president for university advancement

Arthur Kelly, former director of MSU ROTC

Allen Lake, former MSU biology professor

Lucille Caudill Little, MTSC drama instructor

James McConkey, former MSU English professor and author of *Rowan's Progress*

Robert Needham, former MSU professor of education

Morris L. Norfleet, former MSU president

Elaine Fowler Palencia, former Breckinridge School student

Roscoe Playforth, former MSU dean of social sciences

Jeanne Pritchard, former Breckinridge School and MSTC student

Bill Redwine, executive director of MSU Alumni Association

Herb. F. Reinhard, Jr., former MSU president

Lucian Rice, former Breckinridge Scool and MSC student

John M. Ridgway, student at Morehead State Normal School and
        Teachers College

Judy Rogers, former MSU dean of faculty

Harry E. Rose, Jr., author of unpublished dissertation on Morehead State

Mike Seelig, professor of sociology and former president of MSU AAUP

Al Silano, former "Blue Jacket" at Morehead State

Virginia Spain, widow of former MSU president

Stephen Taylor, former MSU vice president for academic affairs

Mary VanSant, daughter of first dean of Morehead State Normal School

William Vaughan, Jr., son of former MSU president

Mary Ella Wells, daughter of former Dean Warren C. Lappin

Jim Wells, grandson of former Dean Warren C. Lappin

Richard Wilson, former MSU student and reporter for the Louisville
        *Courier-Journal*

George Wolfford, former MSU student and reporter for the Ashland
        *Daily Independent*

George T. Young, former MSU history instructor

## Secondary Sources

### Books

Banks, Gabriel C. *Back to the Mountains.* Morehead: Bluestone Cottage, 1964.

Blair, Juanita and Fred Brown, Jr. *Days of Anger, Days of Tears: Rowan County,
Kentucky, 1884-1887.* Morehead: Pioneer Printing Service, 1984.

Cummins, D. Duane. *The Disciples Colleges: A History.* St. Louis: CBP Press, 1987.

Flatt, Don F. *Footsteps Across the Commonwealth: A Tribute to Adron and Mignon
Doran.* Morehead: The MSU Alumni Association, 1976.

Fortune, Alonzo Willard. *The Disciples in Kentucky.* Lexington: The Convention of
the Christian Churches, 1932.

Harrell, David Edwin, Jr. *Quest for a Christian America.* St. Louis: Bethany Press, 1966.

Harrison, Ida Withers. *Memoirs of William Temple Withers*. Boston: The Christopher Publishing House, 1924.

Harrison, Lowell H. *Western Kentucky University*. Lexington: The University Press of Kentucky, 1987.

Harrison, Richard L., Jr. *From Camp Meeting to Church: A History of Christian Church in Kentucky*. Lexington: Christian Board of Publication, 1992.

Harrison, Lowell H. and James C. Klotter. *A New History of Kentucky*. Lexington: The University Press of Kentucky, 1997.

Kleber, John E., editor in chief. *The Kentucky Encyclopedia*. Lexington: The University Press of Kentucky, 1992.

Klotter, James C. *Kentucky: Portrait in Paradox, 1900-1950*. Frankfort: The Kentucky Historical Society, 1996.

Klotter, James C. and Hambleton Tapp. *Kentucky: Decades of Discord, 1865-1900*. Frankfort: The Kentucky Historical Society, 1977.

Ligon, Moses Edward. *History of Public Education in Kentucky*. Lexington: The University of Kentucky Press, 1942.

McCarthey, Jeanette H. *Lest We Forget*. Morehead: The Keystone Printery, Inc., 1967.

McConkey, James. *Rowan's Progress*. New York: Pantheon Books, 1992.

Pearce, John Ed. *Days of Darkness: The Feuds of Eastern Kentucky*. Lexington: The University Press of Kentucky, 1994.

Sprague, Stuart S. *Eastern Kentucky: A Pictorial History*. Norfolk: The Donning Company, 1986.

Stroh, Margaret. *Pioneer Women Teachers in Kentucky*. Lexington: Delta Kappa Gamma Society, 1955.

Walker, Williston. *A History of the Christian Church*. New York: Charles Scribner's Sons, 3rd edition, 1970.

Williams, Cratis. *William H. Vaughan: A Better Man Than I Ever Wanted to Be*. Morehead: Appalachian Development Center, MSU, 1985.

## Theses, Dissertations, and Unpublished Manuscripts

Allen, George Jackson. "A History of the Commission on Colleges of the Southern Association of Colleges and Schools, 1949-1975" (Ph.D. diss., Georgia State, 1978).

Alston, Jerry Gordon. "The Role of State Legislature in Public Higher Education in Kentucky, 1950-1968" (Ph.D. diss. Southern Illinois University, 1970).

Button, Frank C. "The History of Morehead," unpublished paper, 1931.

Carr, John Wesley. "Recollections of Murray State College," unpublished manuscript, 1944.

Cole, Cathy Lynn. "A Historical Perspective of the Kentucky Council on Higher Education" (Ph.D. diss., Southern Illinois University, 1983).

Delgado, Rosa A. Cintron. "History of the Governing Board Concept As A Requisite for Accreditation" (Ph.D. diss., Florida State University, 1992).

Doran, Adron. "The Chronicles of Morehead," 1963.

Doran, Adron. "The Work of the Council on Public Higher Education in Kentucky" (Ed.D. diss., University of Kentucky, 1950).

Flatt, Don F. "A Light to the Mountains: Morehead State University's Formative Years, 1887-1922," paper delivered to Ohio Valley History Conference, 1994.

Flatt, Don F. "Morehead State University: Trouble in the Forties," paper delivered to Ohio Valley History conference, 1995.

Gifford, Jim. "A Proud Heritage: The People of Appalachian Kentucky." Funded by the Kentucky Humanities Council and sponsored by the Appalachian Development Center, MSU.

Hamm, Harlen L. "Forensic Program History, 1924-1994."

Higginbotham, William James, Jr. "Veteran Impact on the Four Regional State Universities of Kentucky" (Ed.D. diss., Indiana University, 1969).

Hudson, Ralph M. "Reminiscences of Morehead State Teachers College, 1931."

Hutchins, Robert M. "The Trend of Education," unpublished speech, 1930.

Morrison, Bessie W. "A History of Morehead State University Library, 1887-1974," graduate paper.

Rose, Harry Eugene. "The Historical Development of a State College: Morehead State College, 1887-1964" (Ed.D. diss., University of Cincinnati, 1965).

White, Charles H. "The Kentucky Council on Kentucky Public Higher Education: Analysis of a Change in Structure" (Ph.D. diss., Ohio State University, 1967).